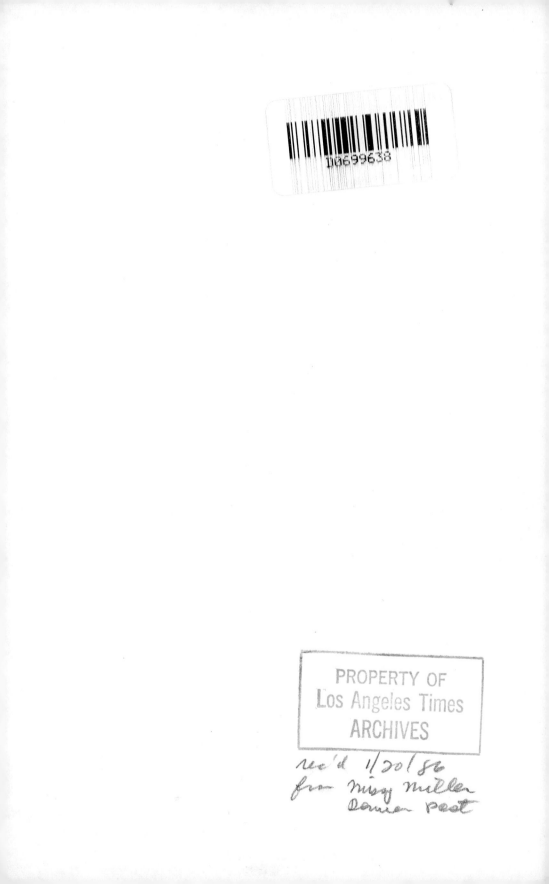

THUNDER IN THE ROCKIES
The Incredible *Denver Post*

Books by Bill Hosokawa

Thunder in the Rockies
The Two Worlds of Jim Yoshida
Nisei
The Uranium Age

THUNDER
IN THE
ROCKIES

THE INCREDIBLE *Denver Post*

BILL HOSOKAWA

WILLIAM MORROW & CO., INC. | NEW YORK | 1976

Printed in the United States of America.

3   4   5   80   79   78   77   76

Library of Congress Cataloging in Publication Data

Hosokawa, Bill.
  Thunder in the Rockies.

  Includes bibliographical references and index.
  1. The Denver Post. I. Title.
PN4899.D45P62   071'.88'83   75-23141
ISBN 0-688-02973-6

For Tam and Bon and all who came after them—
the respectable and the rascals,
the wise and the unwise, the leaders and the led;
sometimes it was difficult to tell them apart.

PREFACE

Each of this country's approximately 1,750 daily newspapers in the English language has a personality of its own. Like people, some newspapers are more interesting than others. They are dull or lively, aggressive, impudent, ponderous, abrasive, challenging, irresponsible, inspiring, useful, presumptuous, michievous, or, too often, just plain blah.

At one time or another since *The Denver Post* was founded in 1895 all the above adjectives have fitted it, but the blah periods have been infrequent. Rarely would it let its readers be neutral in their feelings about it.

The Denver Post was, and is, unusual because it was the product of two very unusual men, Frederick Gilmer Bonfils and Harry Heye Tammen. They in turn were the products of an unusual era in American and Western history. They responded and reacted to these times with a peculiar intensity.

Years after they were dead a new editor and publisher, Palmer Hoyt, would be confronted by loyalists who complained that he wasn't running the paper the way Mr. Bonfils and Mr. Tammen did. No, and neither would they, if they were still here, Hoyt would reply with undeniable logic. Bonfils and Tammen were shrewd businessmen who understood that newspapers must change, just as times and people change, if they are to remain vital.

When I came to work for *The Post* in July of 1946 the editorial staff was an interesting mix of old-timers and newcomers. Most of the latter had come aboard only weeks before I arrived, hired by Hoyt, who had joined *The Post* that February after a meteoric career at the Portland *Oregonian*.

We newcomers had been attracted by the implied promise of Hoyt's arrival—he would revitalize a newspaper that had become nearly moribund even though, strangely, its momentum enabled it to continue to dominate the Denver journalistic scene editorially and economically.

Few of us knew much about *The Post*'s colorful history aside from legend and common rumor. Oddly, newspapers whose function is to report history as it is being made rarely bother to record their own life stories.

But because *The Post* was more colorful than most newspapers, a few attempts had been made to tell its history. Perhaps the best-known is *Timber Line,* written by Gene Fowler in 1933. It is an amusing mélange of fact, legend, and rumor cooked up by a master storyteller. Fowler depicted Bonfils as a swaggering buccaneer of the Fourth Estate. Tammen was treated a little more kindly. In an un-inhibited time in a rough frontier city they had used their newspaper to assail their enemies and further their own not always modest ambitions. But enormous changes have come over our society, and *The Post,* since 1933.

The Denver Post today, aside from its name, bears scant resemblance to *The Post* of generations past. But in truth it has been sorely burdened in its years of responsible maturity by the disreputable image of its adolescence. Still, it remains a colorful newspaper, influenced in many subtle ways by its rip-roaring heritage. For better or worse, it has been a powerful factor in the day-to-day life of a vast section of the United States for more than three-quarters of a century.

Early in 1974 *The Post*'s present management, long removed philosophically from Bonfils and Tammen, considered it an appropriate time to tell the "full story" of the newspaper. William H. Hornby, the executive editor, asked if I would like to write it.

Thinking aloud, he said: "How much of the Fowler legends was true? How much was fable and how much was folklore that cannot now be pinned down? Perhaps recounting the story as it really was —warts, blemishes, scars, and all—would have a beneficial purging effect."

Equally to the point, what has happened to *The Post* since those rowdy days is sheer drama, and most of the details are unknown even to the employees.

Writing *The Post*'s story obviously would be a dream opportunity. In accepting it with delight I set down only one condition: It must not be a self-serving "official" history; it would be as frank and honest as I could make it, exposing the foibles and blunders of the people who ran *The Post* as well as their triumphs.

Hornby declared immediately that this was the only way the history should be written. His view was endorsed totally at another meeting with Donald R. Seawell, president and chairman of the board, and Charles R. Buxton, the editor and publisher. They agreed the story should be reported as I saw it, the facts interpreted as I understood them. And because there are many ramifications, particularly during the thirteen-year period when *The Post*'s leadership was deeply preoccupied with a series of debilitating lawsuits, I suggested they should see the manuscript prior to publication to ensure factual accuracy.

When the manuscript was about one-third completed, I asked Hornby whether he would like to see how it was progressing. He replied: "We promised to keep our mitts off and I want to be able to swear on a stack of Bibles that we exerted no pressure on you. I don't think I ought to read it at this time."

Then, when the manuscript was finally completed, I told Hornby it was ready for reading. His reply was both surprising and gratifying:

"Messrs. Seawell, Buxton, and myself have agreed to forgo reading any part of your story until the book is printed, handsomely bound, autographed, and delivered on our desks. This is the best way to pin down the truth that you were completely independent in preparation of the manuscript."

Indeed, they provided not only complete independence but every cooperation. The books and records of *The Post* were opened to me. I talked with whomever I pleased, including some with long and unremitting hostility toward *The Post* and its founders. Members of the management team were generous with their time for lengthy interviews about their experiences. For this—and especially for the freedom granted me—I am grateful. Out of it all has come this volume, which tells the story of *The Denver Post* through the stories of the people who created, shaped, and, in fact, preserved a thoroughly fascinating, rarely predictable, always vital newspaper.

BILL HOSOKAWA
Denver, Colorado

CONTENTS

Contents | 12

THUNDER IN THE ROCKIES
The Incredible *Denver Post*

1

"THE SINCEREST FRIEND
THE PEOPLE HAVE"

". . . that blackmailing, blackguarding, nauseous sheet which stinks to high heaven and which is the shame of newspapermen the world over. . . ."

". . . Denver long has been represented as living under the cloud of contemptible journalism. . . . These stories have been used to justify practically every assault that has been made upon the honor of the American press. The shame and humiliation of them has become a part of the consciousness of every sincere journalist. . . ."

". . . a corporation publishing a great newspaper such as *The Denver Post* is, in effect, a quasi-public institution. . . ."

Each of the three passages quoted above was written about the same newspaper, *The Denver Post.*

They were written at three widely spaced points in *The Post's* history and, allowing for hyperbole, each statement was reasonably accurate at the time. The important word to consider here is "time." Few institutions have changed with the years so drastically, or so dramatically, as *The Post.*

The first statement above was published in the rival *Rocky Mountain News* in the heat of a long-ago circulation war. *The Post* responded in kind as was the fashion of the day, and both survived the daily doses of vitriol. Their relations today, while not exactly warm, are somewhat more cordial.

The second comment was printed in *Editor & Publisher,* the weekly journal of the newspaper industry, as an aftermath of the 1922 Teapot Dome scandal, in which *The Post* played a prominent role. *Editor & Publisher* today would be unlikely to pass such strong moral judgment on any newspaper. But at the time it undoubtedly felt the criticism was necessary and justified.

The third is the opinion of a justice of the U. S. Court of Appeals, concurred in by two of his august colleagues. Their praise was an incidental but gratifying part of a 1972 decision that preserved the integrity of *The Post* as an independent newspaper.

To have deserved such immoderate brickbats and accolades, *The Post* has experienced many strange, wonderfully curious, and sometimes delightful things between its founding on October 28, 1895, and December 29, 1972, when the federal judge's opinion was made public. Equally fascinating are the people who parade through its history, revealing the baseness and nobility, the myopia and foresight that make them such interesting and sometimes tragic figures.

That *The Post* came into being at all was something of an accident. Called *The Evening Post,* it was created to fill a vacuum. Robert L. Perkin tells about it in his book *The First Hundred Years,* the history of the *Rocky Mountain News,* Denver's oldest newspaper and *The Post*'s staunchest opposition since the earliest days:

> The *News* had no one but itself to blame for *The Denver Post.* When it went soaring off on glorious crusades with the Populists and Bryan, the hard-shelled Democrats were left with no place to go. Their leader, Tom Patterson, had turned his back on them. So they started their own newspaper. Neither they nor anyone else in Denver anticipated that the sickly cub would be "weaned on tiger milk."
> The first *Post* appeared August 8, 1892. A group of die-hard Democrats got together $50,000 and rented dingy quarters at 1744 Curtis Street, just down the next block from the *News.* W. P. Caruthers was general manager. The new sheet held the banner high for Grover Cleveland and also declared itself for purity—political, municipal and female. It was promptly nicknamed "White Wings." But the events of 1892 made the name "Cleveland" a dirty word in Colorado, and . . . the first *Post,* blessed and sinless, died in its crib on August 29, 1893, shortly after its first birthday.

Less than a year later the newspaper was resurrected. A new corporation, The Publishing Company, was organized with $100,000 capital, and *The Evening Post* resumed daily publication on June 22, 1894, at 1734 Curtis Street. It was still a Democratic paper, and its backers couldn't have picked a worse time to go into the publishing business. The nation was in the throes of a financial panic and four other newspapers—the *News, Times, Express* and *Republican* —were vying for what little advertising Denver merchants could afford to utilize. Before long Stephen W. Keene, the president, and Charles J. Hughes, Jr., the principal owner, were looking for a buyer.

They found one in Harry Heye Tammen, operator of a curio-and-souvenir shop in the Windsor Hotel, then Denver's leading hostelry.

Tammen's only experience as a publisher was with a little monthly magazine called *The Great Divide*. It was being issued in conjunction with his curio shop in an effort to stir up interest in Western subjects. (Volume 1, Number 1 of *The Great Divide,* dated March, 1889, had eight pages and featured a story by Erminie A. Smith titled "Myths of the Iroquois." Stanley Wood was listed as editor.) Despite *The Post*'s troubles, Tammen astutely saw a great future for a newspaper in the then developing West. In 1880, when Tammen first arrived in Denver, the population was 35,629. In the next ten years Denver tripled in size to 106,713. "There is no city in the world increasing in population, wealth or substantial improvements more rapidly than the city of Denver at the present time," wrote George Crofutt in his *Grip-Sack Guide of Colorado*. Tammen's problem was that he didn't have the $12,500 cash necessary to buy *The Evening Post*. He found a man who did in Frederick Gilmer Bonfils.

The precise circumstances under which the two met and decided to pool their assets and talents have been obscured by time. One source suggests that they happened to meet in Chicago during the World's Columbian Exposition in 1893, and Tammen remembered Bonfils when the opportunity of buying the paper arose. Bonfils' secretary for the last dozen years of his life, Anne O'Neill Sullivan, recalls asking her boss about the meeting. He told her he won ten thousand dollars in the Louisiana State Lottery, that Tammen read about it in a newspaper and wrote to him, suggesting the prize be invested in a paper which was for sale. In view of Bonfils' experiences with lotteries, which will be detailed in a future chapter, this story does not appear probable. Perhaps Bonfils was trying to protect the young, impressionable Anne O'Neill from a more sordid version, which Gene Fowler tells in *Timber Line*. According to that story, Tammen went to Chicago in 1895 to sell tinted photographs of the World's Fair, which by then was only a memory. He found few buyers. Then he chanced on the idea of selling reproductions of the Declaration of Independence to the Chicago *Tribune* for free distribution to its subscribers. The paper agreed to buy one hundred thousand copies at $7.50 a thousand. Tammen then found a printer who would produce them for two dollars a thousand, bringing Tammen a tidy $550 profit for acting simply as a middleman. While at the shop Tammen happened to see some lottery tickets and learned they were being printed for a gambler in Kansas City named

This was page 1 of *The Evening Post* on October 28, 1895, the day H. H. Tammen and F. G. Bonfils bought it for $12,500. Sale was not announced in the paper until November 1.

Fred Bonfils. Bonfils seemed to have good credit and a willingness to take a chance. Tammen set out to meet him.

Two men could not have been less alike than Tammen and Bonfils, but some mysterious chemistry seemed to attract them. Legend has it that Tammen, after sparring briefly, told Bonfils: "You've got money. I've got brains, and there's the bargain of a lifetime waiting for us in Denver." Bonfils was intrigued by the little stranger who was "short on gold but had all the brass in the world." A short time later they met with Keene and his associates and consummated the sale of *The Evening Post*. The date was Monday, October 28, 1895. Tammen was then thirty-nine years old, Bonfils thirty-four.

It is a measure of the trust the two men had in each other that Bonfils, notoriously tightfisted and suspicious, supplied the money but the bill of sale was made out to Tammen alone. And although in later years they made and shared millions of dollars, no document was ever drawn up to attest to their partnership. There is no record that Tammen ever reimbursed Bonfils for his half of the purchase price.

Anne O'Neill Sullivan once asked Bonfils why he "gave" half the paper to Tammen. He replied, "Because if you're going to have a partner, you're going to need a whole partner, and we'll share in the profits as well as the losses." Each man owned half the stock less one share. That share was signed over to the other and filed away in a vault so that the surviving partner would be assured of owning control of the paper.

For the $12,500 price, the partners received a "Goss Perfecting Printing Press, all fixtures and appliances connected therewith and all furniture and machinery used in and about printing and publishing *The Evening Post* newspaper, including therein the stereotyping outfit and electric power motor and appliances now at 1734 Curtis Street, Denver, Colorado, also the right, title and interest . . . to the use of the name *The Evening Post* in printing said newspaper, also a contract with the Mergenthaler Typesetting Machine Company, rents under which are from this date hereof to be paid by the party of the second part, also the franchise in the United Press Association, also all contracts for advertising and the subscription lists."

It was hardly a bargain. *The Evening Post* was an eight-page paper which claimed a circulation of six thousand, probably a highly inflated figure. Subscription rates by carrier were three dollars per year or thirty cents per month. One day a short time after Bonfils and Tammen took over the paper, total receipts were only thirty-five dollars. The paper had to be built up and soon there were sixty-nine employees to be paid—twelve in advertising and general offices, twelve in the editorial department, eighteen in circulation, two in stereotype, and twenty-five in printing and typesetting. The average weekly payroll was more than a thousand dollars in addition to which $125 had to be paid each week for United Press news service.

The city *The Post* set out to serve in 1895 had only recently grown out of its frontier buckskin. Its location in 1858 at the eastern foot of the Rockies was an accident triggered by the discovery of insignificant amounts of gold near the confluence of the South Platte River and Cherry Creek. Even its name was something of a mistake. The governor of Kansas Territory, of which Colorado was a part, was Brig. Gen. James W. Denver, a Virginian who commanded Kansas troops in the Civil War. Hoping to win his favor, the earliest arrivals named their ramshackle settlement on Cherry Creek after him. But Governor Denver was replaced shortly before the honor was bestowed and he did not see the city until 1874.

A decade after the virulent California gold fever of '49 infected thousands of fortune seekers, a new wave of adventurers rushed to Denver. Stores, hotels, saloons, and gambling halls sprang up. The

Rocky Mountain News published its first issue April 23, 1859. The Cherry Creek sands never amounted to much, but rich gold and silver deposits were discovered in the mountains west of the city. Denver survived as a supply depot and jump-off point, the fleshpots to which successful prospectors repaired for booze, viands, a hot bath, and feminine companionship, not necessarily in that order of importance. In the long run commerce proved to be a firmer base for prosperity than mining. While scores of boom camps quickly withered into ghost towns when the ore was exhausted, Denver continued to grow.

In its first twenty years Denver's population leapt from zero to more than 35,000. During the next decade (1880 to 1890) the population tripled to 106,000. In the same period Colorado grew from 194,000 to 413,000. In 1867 Denver was chosen as the seat of government for the state, which would join the Union in 1876. These were the boom years of mining, when fortunes were made by the businessmen who had the courage and the capital to develop the lodes discovered by lonely prospectors. Bonanza kings moved into the city from their mountain cabins and ornate mansions lined the streets on the hill east of the original settlement. The free spenders who had amassed wealth in gold, silver, cattle, and land congregated at the Windsor Hotel. The world financial panic in the early 1890's spelled the doom of scores of silver camps, but Denver's rapidly diversifying economy survived. By 1895, just weeks before Bonfils and Tammen bought the faltering *Post,* Denver had enough confidence to celebrate "the end of the depression" with an elaborate Festival of Mountain and Plain. The event, which was not unlike the New Orleans Mardi Gras, was continued until 1911.

The Post's incorporation papers listed Tammen, Bonfils, and Carl Litzenberger as directors. (Litzenberger's father, a German gemstone craftsman, had for years cut and polished agates, topaz, and other semiprecious stones for Tammen. Carl was sent to the United States in 1890 to work for Tammen and in 1896 became a partner.) Tammen was president and secretary, Bonfils vice-president and treasurer. The two men listed themselves as copublishers. Before long Litzenberger's name disappeared from the corporate papers. He went back to running Tammen's curio-and-souvenir business and was replaced by Thomas L. Bonfils, Fred's older brother. But neither Litzenberger nor Tom Bonfils held more than a token share of stock to qualify them as directors, and Tom Bonfils served for many years as clerk of the Denver County Court.

The sale of the newspaper was not announced until Friday, November 1, when the following editorial appeared:

New management and ownership—new entirely and in every respect—now control and direct *The Post.* They have means, which they will not spare, to make it a newspaper in every sense of the term. They will seek first to make it complete in the strictest sense. They will have a telegraphic service that will bring every day the general happenings of the world complete and full. They will have a local force alert and capable. The news, the accurate news, will be printed without fear or favor.

The new owners of *The Post* will move the plant at once to the most central section of the city. They will occupy the Garson-Kerngood block opposite the Tabor opera house. There they will have ample room to make such mechanical additions as may be necessary to carry out their designs.

Owing to the arrangements made and obligations incurred before the change of ownership, *The Post* will for a few days continue the line of policy previously adopted, which, by the way, is not really inconsistent with its permanent purposes. The new managers propose to make *The Post* thoroughly and emphatically the people's paper—a paper that shall first and always work and fight for the promotion of the people's good and the advancement of their interests. It will be free from entanglements with political parties, corporations or special interests of any kind. Thus it will be free to do for the people and to be vigorously and unreservedly against whatever is against them. The new management ask the people to watch closely and see if the paper does not well demonstrate its loyalty to them.

The Post, in its renewal of life, will devote special and ceaseless attention to the material interests of the state and to the development of her vast and varied resources. It will seek to so direct its efforts that more acres of land shall be brought under cultivation; that more exchanges of trade shall be made; that more mines shall be opened and profitably worked; that more mills and factories shall be built and more foundries and smelters be put in blast; that capital shall command greater returns and labor secure larger rewards; that, in brief, the cheer of prosperity shall reach a larger share of the people.

With ample means for the making of a strong, untrammeled people's journal, *The Post* management tonight merely announces its control and prefers to illustrate its purpose by performance rather than mere promises.

The lead item in an adjacent column called "Afternoon Gossip" contained this additional intelligence: "Without any question the most central location in Denver, where the pulse of humanity beats the swiftest and the rush of trade has its liveliest hum, is Sixteenth Street, between Curtis and Arapahoe. At that point, in the very cen-

On November 5, 1895, the new owners added the word "Denver" and changed type style in the nameplate.

ter of the central section, the regenerated *Evening Post* will have its future and its permanent home. . . ."

The address was 1019 Sixteenth Street, a block and a half from the original site. The land is now part of the block occupied by the Prudential Plaza, and "permanent" meant twelve years. After that *The Post* moved once more. Nowhere in that edition did the names of the new owners appear, but few could quarrel with their broad statement of policy. Still, most newspapers of the day were scarcely more than the house organs for special interests. Denverites waited to see what would happen.

Neither Tammen nor Bonfils claimed to know anything about running a daily newspaper. The mechanics of gathering the news, converting it into type, and printing and distributing the papers was beyond their comprehension and interest. But they had an unerring, intuitive instinct for what would catch the public's attention—and sell newspapers.

In one of their first staff conferences, Tammen outlined his philosophy about editing a daily. "You've seen a vaudeville show, haven't you?" he asked the city editor. "It's got every sort of act—laughs, tears, wonder, thrills, melodrama, tragedy, comedy, love, and hate. That's what I want you to give our readers."

Bonfils phrased it another way: "Write the news for all the people, not just the rich and important or those who think they are. If you are understood by the busy, simple folk, everybody will understand you."

Tammen added: "If a thing is horrible, explain why it is horrible

After closing the deal for *The Post*, Tammen (second from left) and Bonfils (third from left) were photographed in front of the newspaper office. Others are unidentified. (Denver Public Library, Western History Department)

and leave nothing to the reader's imagination. Nothing is too trivial to interest some reader, and never forget this: that more people are interested in a man's falling and breaking his arm on Curtis Street than are interested in a disaster in Egypt or China."

Bonfils paraphrased that thought in a characteristically more colorful manner: "A dogfight on Sixteenth Street is a better story than a war in Timbuctu."

In other words, anything people were interested in was news, and the neophyte publishers were convinced Denverites were most interested in local matters.

Three days after the new ownership was announced, the paper's name was changed to *Denver Evening Post*. And at the top of the editorial page appeared this statement:

> *The Post* is absolutely fearless and independent. It is always with the people. It is the sincerest friend the people have. It pleads every deserving cause. It is the home newspaper.

Brave words. But they didn't bring in revenue. It took a happy circumstance to turn the tide. A dry-goods merchant had advertised in the other newspapers that he had bought the entire stock of an Eastern firm which he was offering Denverites at a vast saving. One of his competitors, the Appel Clothing Company, had reason to believe this Eastern company had never existed and sought to express its doubts in full-page ads. When the other papers refused to sell him the space, Appel came to *The Post*, where his business was gratefully accepted.

Still, the first year was a rough one and more than once it appeared the newspaper's third owners would go the way of the other two. On one occasion Tammen and Bonfils were prepared to sell their paper for ten thousand dollars, even though taking a loss on an investment was contrary to their basic tenets. Fortunately the intended buyer had second thoughts and failed to show up. The railroads unwittingly helped *The Post* to meet its payroll some weeks. Legend has it that when Tammen heard someone was planning to go to Chicago or Kansas City, he would offer to get him a ticket for half price. Then Tammen would pick up a pass, which the railroads were distributing rather liberally, sell it, and take the money back to the paper.

Lacking newspaper experience, Tammen and Bonfils were bound by none of the profession's restraints. "Always remember, we want Denver to talk about *The Post*," Bonfils said. The result was a brash, astonishingly uninhibited type of journalism that shocked and often outraged the traditionalists. But soon Denverites were indeed talking about *The Post*. "Write what you see and what you think," Tammen advised the professionals in his employ, and he and Bonfils were seeing and thinking a great deal.

Yet, whatever was carried in *The Post*'s columns, they looked much like the dull gray pages of the other newspapers. W. H. (Billy) Milburn, tall and austere in his gates-ajar collars, changed that. He created the pattern for *The Post*'s wild typography and unorthodox makeup that for decades was the despair of journalism school instructors and underscored charges of *Post* "sensationalism." Milburn had come to Colorado from his native New York because of ill health. By the time Tammen and Bonfils took over, he was the thirty-five-dollar-per-week head of the "printing department," where the average wage was twenty-one dollars.

"You've got to make this paper look different," he told the partners. "Get some bigger headline type. Put red ink on page one. You've got to turn Denver's eyes to *The Post* every day, and away from the other papers."

Even on a dull day the big type and red ink suggested startling news developments that only *The Post* knew about. At one time one-column, three-line headlines had the middle line printed in red. Tammen was delighted. Milburn once remarked, "He loved to stand on the street when the paper came out and watch people's faces when they saw the red headlines." (Edmund J. Dooley, *The Post*'s managing editor from 1950 to 1956, recalls that when he first joined the paper in 1946 he was astounded to be told that the rules required a minimum of twenty-one stories on the front page with each headline in a different typeface. *The Post* of the early years with good reason had been described as looking like an explosion in a type foundry. But it demanded and received attention.)

More than a year passed before *The Post* latched onto an issue on which it could prove itself "the sincerest friend the people have." The deserving cause was the price of coal, which was selling for four dollars a ton and up. Only a year earlier the price had been $2.50 to $2.80 and dealers were advertising aggressively as they competed for sales. Then, apparently, there had been a price-fixing agreement. Advertising ceased. On January 21, 1897, at the coldest season of the year, *The Denver Post* published a front-page broadside under the title "So The People May Know." It is worthy of quoting in full:

> Today *The Post* will begin selling Northern coal at $3.50 a ton and will continue to sell coal to all that may desire it—until the Coal Trust sees fit to quit robbing the people. It is not the purpose of *The Post* to go into the coal business, yet at the same time if there is a necessity for it, in order that the people may be able to buy coal at a fair price, it will do so.
>
> In being able to sell coal at $3.50 *The Post* makes no profit; that, of course, can easily be understood when one stops to think that the Coal Trust, banded as they are with railroads and coal mine owners, put such obstacles in the way—that it's next to impossible to buy coal without a conditional contract that $4.00 shall be the selling price.
>
> It is also true—that $3.00 a ton is the right price—$3.25 would be a profitable price—and *The Post* hopes that in the near future the Coal Trust will be satisfied that extortion doesn't go in this town while *The Post* is here.
>
> In the meantime we have opened a coal department and hope all *Post* subscribers and others will favor us with their orders.
>
> Bring $3.50 to *The Post* today and buy a ton of *The Post*'s coal.
>
> It is all well enough for newspapers to kick and expose trusts. *The Post* believes that the practical way is to actually perform a service. Talk is cheap, but to positively accomplish something is *The Post*'s way.

People snickered at the idea of a newspaper selling coal. Bonfils and Tammen were nicknamed "Lump" and "Nut." Coal companies screamed in outrage. But *The Post* sold enormous quantities of coal from mines it had leased through a subsidiary, The *Post* Coal and Iron Company. However, the campaign apparently had little effect on the "Trust," and *The Post* found coal sales not an excessive drain on its finances. In 1909, a dozen years later, the following was published across eight columns at the top of page 1:

Fall Seems to Have Arrived All at Once and We Would Suggest That You Put In a Little *POST* COAL. Price $3.95 Per Ton for Lump and $3.75 for Egg. This, Mind You, Gives You a Full Ton— 2,000 lbs. of the Best Coal From the Northern Field. Come Down to *THE POST* or CALL MAIN 6550, BRANCH 4. Never Mind the Trust or Its Schemes. *The Post* Will See That Coal Is Sold at the Right Price All the Time.

"So The People May Know" became a unique part of an unusual newspaper. Lawrence Martin, for many years *The Post's* managing editor and associate editor, writes in his history by that same name: "That was to be the caption, for many years, under which *Post* campaigns and crusades were conducted. It became a battle flag, a sword, a rapier, a club, a battering ram, to be used both against conditions and men the paper believed to be wrong, and for reforms and constructive programs *The Post* believed were needed."

However, what *The Post* believed to be wrong or in need of reforms often had as much to do with its own economic well-being as with the public welfare. When its advertising salesmen were consistently turned away by merchants, Tammen and Bonfils began to ask questions. They soon discovered that David Moffat, owner of the rival *Times,* banker, financier, and mining magnate, had passed the word the *The Post* was not to be supported.

The Post lashed back with a "So The People May Know" editorial that complained: "Not content with boycotting *The Post* in a body, the big department stores are now sending their emissaries to all of the independent advertisers who still continue to patronize *The Post,* thus further showing their venom and hatred, and their desire to injure *The Post* and destroy it, if possible."

What followed would be called investigative reporting today. *The Post* launched a campaign against child labor in department stores.

"Little girls, poorly dressed and with pale faces, are employed in these sweat shops," one story charged. "As you enter one of them, a little, pale-faced girl opens the door, standing in the dangerous drafts, for people coming and going. This method of employing child labor at starvation wages which are all the way from $1 to $1.50 a week, for which they work from sixty-five to seventy hours a week, may be fashionable in Baxter Street, New York, but we desire to serve notice on these establishments that it will not go in the great West."

Eventually the legislature passed laws regulating child labor. *The*

Post had demonstrated it had clout in addition to wild headlines. The public took notice, and so did advertisers. And Tammen and Bonfils, who unblushingly called their paper "the official organ of the people," continued their attacks against "conditions and men the paper believed to be wrong."

The privately owned Denver Union Water Company soon became a target. With scant regard for public sensitivities, *The Post* followed Tammen's precepts and left nothing to the reader's imagination. "The city has to drink the sewage of Morrison, Fort Logan, Petersburg and numerous ranches, with a slaughterhouse or two thrown in," *The Post* complained. "The site of an old slaughterhouse in Mount Vernon gulch was visited. Water was running through it washing the old bones and eventually finding its way into the city water mains." Before long the city bought out several companies supplying Denver and laid the groundwork for the vast system that today serves the metropolitan area. Next the streetcar lines came under attack. "Conductors robbing little girls of their half fare tickets," a *Post* headline read.

Not all the attacks appeared under the banner of "So The People May Know." Perkin in his book comments that an editorial page "would have been excess baggage since each article in and of itself was a full statement of the paper's passions and prejudices on the subject matter involved."

Perkin adds that "everyone damned *The Post*—and nearly everyone subscribed." When ministers and society women complained about *The Post*'s lurid coverage of crime stories, the publishers invited them to edit the paper for a day. The result was near-chaos. Meanwhile lawbreaking continued to get lavish coverage with a warning that "Crime Does Not Pay" at the top of each story.

Larry Martin writes: "*The Post* never considered that the things it said about a public official one day committed it to support what he did the next. One time Foster Cline, then Denver district attorney, started a roundup of loan sharks who were bleeding their customers white, and *The Post* heartily approved. A page one cartoon showed Cline harpooning a shark, and carried the caption under it: 'Good work, Mr. Cline! *The Post* has been fighting for this for many years. Now don't get cold feet and quit and run away.' Yet only a few weeks later Cline was roundly criticized by *The Post* for spending too much money on office overhead. This was a characteristic procedure. . . ."

Circulation climbed, and the paper even began to make a little money. The ledgers show that in January, 1897, fourteen months after the partners took over, receipts for the month totaled $7,505.90 (including $4,557.21 in advertising), and expenses $7,936.40—a loss of $430.50 for the month. By the end of the year the paper showed a profit of $5,234.99. In October of that same year *The Post* claimed a circulation of 26,405, approaching that of Moffat's Denver *Times,* which Tammen and Bonfils characterized as "old, decrepit and senile," a newspaper whose circulation had dwindled by the thousands until it stood "practically without a clientele except the corporations."

Despite the claim, *The Post*'s circulation, like those of other newspapers of the day, was inflated by the distribution of thousands of free copies. Accurate figures were not determined until 1901, when a committee consisting of G. B. Fishel, G. W. Brooks, and Charles T. Austin, presumably impartial auditors, examined the circulation records of the *Rocky Mountain News* and *The Post* for a six-month period ending April 30.

They found that in February of 1901 *The Post* had topped the *News* for the first time in paid circulation—24,213 to 24,134. It had taken the *News* nearly a half-century to pass the 24,000 mark. *The Post* had done it in less than six years. *The Post* could now boast the largest circulation in Denver and Colorado, and its dominance was never seriously challenged again. (By 1927 *The Post* could proclaim in a page 1 "ear" that its paid Sunday circulation was 267,373— "100,000 greater than total circulation of all fourteen other Sunday papers printed in Denver and Colorado, Wyoming and New Mexico combined.")

Other changes were taking place. On May 29, 1898, *The Post* issued its first Sunday edition—a mammoth sixteen pages—and raised subscription rates to fifty cents per month for daily and Sunday delivery. On January 1, 1901, the word "Evening" was dropped from the title and the paper became simply *The Denver Post.* The following year the *News* bought the faltering *Times,* and soon the G.O.P.-backed *Republican* also would die.

One day in 1908 Tammen said to Bonfils: "Fred, the paper is doing very well. Our circulation is over 83,000—more than that of all our competitors combined. We are making money. The baby's old enough to walk on its own feet. I think it's about time to begin taking a little out of the business for ourselves."

The partners had agreed to pay themselves $7,500 a year, but never had drawn their salaries. Tammen still had his curio business, which was prospering as a wholesale distributor. Most of Bonfils' income came from long-term leases on real-estate holdings in Kansas City. Now, thirteen years after buying *The Post,* they agreed to pay themselves one thousand dollars a week each. They also wrote out dividend checks of one thousand dollars each. Tammen converted his dividend into a sack of twenty-dollar gold pieces which he took home and showered on his wife's lap. Mrs. Tammen treasured the coins and in later years she would give one on a special occasion to someone who meant a great deal to her. Bonfils bought a pair of diamond earrings for his wife. After his death Mrs. Bonfils had one of the stones set in a ring for Anne O'Neill Sullivan in appreciation of her many years of service. The other went into a tiepin. Then after Mrs. Bonfils died, her daughter Helen had the second stone added to Mrs. Sullivan's ring. It is, to say the least, an impressive sight.

Tammen had difficulty adjusting to sudden affluence. One of the legends has it that when Bonfils gave him a thousand-dollar check two weeks in a row, Tammen protested that he'd been paid the previous week and accused his partner of becoming absentminded. "Harry, don't you remember?" Bonfils replied. "I told you we are now getting a thousand dollars a week, each of us." In view of Tammen's acumen, the story would seem to be at best apocryphal. What

With this issue of January 1, 1901, the word "Evening" was dropped from nameplate. Essentially the same title, but without the period, is still in use.

is more important is that two men, destined to cast long shadows across the history of the West, had now established a sound financial foundation on which to build their influence.

What manner of men were they? Dissimilar as they were in habits, background, and temperament, they had in common an ability to attract legends. We shall examine some of them in the next two chapters.

2

THE LITTLE BOSS

A reporter once asked Harry Tammen how he, a successful newspaper publisher, came to own the Sells-Floto circus. Tammen answered: "I had a dog which was trained to turn somersaults. Then I got another dog and a third, and the first thing I knew they were all turning somersaults. Then I decided that was a good amusement so I acquired a dog-and-pony show. The show was small and badly managed. I decided to make it the best possible and equipped it with everything that would make it so."

That story tells much about Harry Heye Tammen. He was a gentle man with a childlike delight in the simple pleasures. He was also an astute, sometimes eloquently profane, hardheaded businessman who built a fortune—and gave much of it away.

Tammen was very successful at something few men could do—get along with Frederick G. Bonfils, his mercurial partner and best friend. Tammen was the balance wheel in this strange and phenomenally successful publishing partnership. "He let Fred do the blustering," one old-time employee recalls. "As long as the machinery was running right, he didn't interfere. But when he noticed some little thing that looked like trouble ahead, he would go into Fred's office and discuss it. Tammen didn't tolerate any foolishness from F. G. Tammen was older, of course, and he seemed to have a quieting influence on his partner. When F. G. would get on one of his tangents, Tammen would tell him to behave himself. Tammen wouldn't hesitate to cuss him out. Sometimes he'd tell F.G. to get out of town for a while and cool off, and usually Bonfils did. I never heard them raise their voices at each other."

Even Tammen's put-downs were gentle. One oft-told story has to do with the picture of a prominent citizen's son who had won some kind of honor. When the photograph wasn't published in *The Post* after several days, Tammen asked about it. One of the editors explained, "We didn't use it because Mr. Bonfils doesn't like the boy's father."

"Son," said Tammen, "how much of this paper do I own?"

"Well," the editor replied, "from what I hear you own half and Mr. Bonfils owns half."

"That's right," Tammen said. "You can run that picture in my half."

He liked to tell stories on himself. One had to do with his brief experience as bartender at the Windsor Hotel. "Whenever someone paid for drinks with a gold coin," he would say, "we tossed it against the ceiling. If it stuck, it belonged to the management. If it didn't, the bartenders would pocket it."

Some years later, when *The Post* had acquired a reputation for riding roughshod over politicians, Tammen came out of the governor's office after a social visit and noticed reporters from the other newspapers watching him. Turning abruptly, Tammen shouted through the doorway, "And I still say not one penny less than ten thousand dollars." Then he slammed the door and stalked off. He had a great time telling about the looks of amazement and curiosity on the reporters' faces.

Tammen was born March 6, 1856, in Baltimore, Maryland. His parents were Heye Heinrich and Caroline Henriette Piepenbruker Tammen, natives of Herdun in Hanover, Germany. Heye Tammen was a pharmacist, but came to Baltimore as an attaché at the Netherlands consulate. Harry was a seventeen-year-old student at Knapp's Academy in Maryland when his father died. There were younger children at home and further schooling was out of the question. Harry set out to seek his fortune. "Go with love and good cheer," his mother said, embracing him. (Forever after, he would sign his letters, "Yours, with love and good cheer.")

Tammen was not more than 5 feet 3 or 4 inches tall and slightly built. In later years he weighed as much as 210 pounds but he gained no more height. Dressed in a homemade suit that his hopeful mother had sewn much too large, Tammen went to Philadelphia, where he worked for a while in a printing shop. By 1880 he had drifted out to Denver by way of Chicago.

Denver was booming from recent silver discoveries at Leadville, Aspen, and the upper reaches of Clear Creek west of the city. Only four years earlier Colorado had been admitted to the Union as the thirty-eighth state. While waiting for a capitol to be built, the legislature met occasionally at the brand-new Windsor Hotel on Larimer

Harry H. Tammen, co-founder of *The Denver Post*, about the time he moved to Denver in 1880.

Tammen (right) in front of his curio store in Denver's Windsor Hotel, where he once worked as a bartender.

Street. Tammen found employment there as a combination bellhop, busboy, roustabout, and occasional bartender. His goal at the time was to open a restaurant because, he once recalled, everybody has to eat. But soon the goal changed. He noticed that almost everyone was interested in mineral specimens, gold-flecked pieces of quartz or just plain chunks of pretty rock. Tourists were flocking to Denver. Why not sell them rock specimens?

In 1881, a year after his arrival, Tammen rented a small space in the Windsor and opened a cluttered souvenir shop crammed with gewgaws and curios. Inkstands carved out of stone were among his first items. His chief curio was to be "Moon-Eye, the Petrified Indian Maiden," the product of an embalmer's art which he acquired from a bankrupt mortician. To his stock of mineral specimens Tammen added beadwork and other Indian items—including scalps and moccasins manufactured in some urban loft—furs, mounted game heads, polished agates, and turquoise jewelry.

After taking time out to marry Elizabeth Evans, also a native of Baltimore, Tammen threw himself into the work of building his business. He established a mail-order department and then a wholesale division that soon overshadowed the retail store. In the period before World War I, visitors to Alaska were amazed to find Indian and Eskimo curios bearing the label of H. H. Tammen Co., Denver. In later years, with Carl Litzenberger running the business while Tammen looked after his many other interests, toys, stationery, jewelry, and giftwares were added to the company's lines.

The Great Divide was launched to build up the glamour of the West and thus help Tammen's business, but he was well aware that the magazine had to stand on its own merits. To introduce it to advertisers in 1889 he sent out hundreds of little plaster figurines which he called Indian idols of good luck, "made and worshipped by the Zuni Indians of Taos, N.M." With them he mailed out the following letter:

> Dear Sir:—Via today's express we forward you The Great Divide God; please note on the red seal one of the commandments of his creed, and we ask you to follow his advice, because it is a sure chance to Divide, and a Great one, the Surplus. Yours respectfully, The Great Divide Pub. Co.

The commandment referred to read, "Feed Me on Advertising—for the Great Divide, Denver, Colo."

A week after the idol was delivered this follow-up letter was sent out:

> Dear Sir:—The first remark usually made by the recipient of a horned toad, tarantula, or any similar present from the wooly West is—"Wonder what the blamed thing eats?" In view of this fact, and through the fear that The Great Divide God sent you may perish, we suggest that you stuff him liberally with well written advertisements for The Great Divide. P.S.—Never change his diet.

Elizabeth Tammen died in 1890, shortly after Tammen built her a comfortable home. Two years later he married Agnes Reid, a cheerful, pleasant, dark-haired girl many years his junior, who as a teen-ager had come to Denver from Virginia with her parents. They were intensely devoted to each other. The marriage ended with Tammen's death in 1924, but after that Agnes Reid Tammen spent many fruitful years carrying out the course that her husband had charted.

Although Tammen had the vision to look and plan far into the future, he liked to assume the role of a fun-loving con man. He enjoyed playing the ignorant bumpkin, yet in his own home he had his meals served on fine china and he knew which of the many silver forks went with which dish. He boasted he was a hard-boiled confidence man, but he was considerate, compassionate, and generous. In later years he often visited the Denver Press Club on Sunday mornings for a drink. When the steward asked why he chose that hour, Tammen replied: "The people who work for me come to the club, their club, in the afternoon. I don't want the boss to make them feel uncomfortable by his presence."

The environment he liked best was the swivel chair in his office at *The Post's* third home, on Champa Street between Sixteenth and Fifteenth. The executive offices were on the second floor, looking out over Champa. The windows opened on a balcony. Tammen had the office to the right as one looked toward the street, Bonfils the one at the left. Between them was a large room, painted a rich red color, shared by their secretaries. This was Bonfils and Tammen's Red Room, known to outsiders as the Bucket of Blood. It served as a waiting room and was used for staff meetings. When some special *Post* promotion was in progress on Champa Street, Bonfils would survey the scene from the balcony like some European monarch. But Tammen was most at home curled up in his swivel chair, a cigar clamped between his teeth. Any employee felt free to take his problems to Tammen. Consoling the troubled, seeking to find solutions, he would say, "Remember, son, everybody always thinks his fire is the biggest."

One day Tammen drove back to the office after lunch and found the street blocked. "What's going on?" he asked a police officer. The officer explained *The Post* was staging some kind of show and no cars were permitted on the street. "But I'm Harry Tammen, and I own the paper," Tammen protested.

"I'm sorry," the officer replied, "my orders are not to let any cars through."

Tammen walked to his office and called the chief of police.

"What do you want me to do?" the chief asked. "Fire him?"

"No," Tammen said. "Send him to see me."

When the officer arrived Tammen commended him for doing his duty and gave him a cigar.

When Aimee Semple McPherson came to Denver, Tammen asked her to stop at his home to pray for an elderly relative. Three women reporters, Frances (Pinky) Wayne of *The Post*, Helen Black of the *News,* and Eileen O'Connor of the *Express,* were following Aimee around. At the Tammen home Pinky went in but the other two waited outside. Presently Tammen invited them in.

Helen Black's story in the *News* the next morning started with a description of the way Tammen had bowed his head in prayer. When she reported to work that afternoon an angry telephone call from Tammen was awaiting her.

"You shouldn't have mentioned me," Tammen fumed. "Why did you put me in your 'lede'?"

Helen replied: "If your reporter was in the same situation, wouldn't you expect her to write the story as I did?"

Tammen saw her logic and broke into a laugh. Soon afterward, when the press persuaded Aimee to drive into the foothills to deliver a "Sermon on the Mount," Tammen sent the three women in his own chauffeur-driven car with box lunches he ordered for them.

Tammen's secretary was the late Sadie Schultz, who became so close to the family that she was named a trustee of the Tammen estate. When she was away, Bonfils' secretary, Anne O'Neill, would fill in. "He would dictate something to me," she says, "and sometimes I made a correction or two because of the English—the construction of a sentence would seem awkward. He'd call me right in. 'Lady'— he always called me that—'Lady, I didn't say that; I'd never say it that way. Now you go back and write what I said.' And I'd have to do it over again."

Intimate friends called Tammen "the little Dutchman," but to the staff he was known as "the little boss" and no disparagement was intended. Jim Hale, who joined the paper in 1920, recalls that Tammen sometimes wandered out into the city room on Saturdays and passed out dollar bills to the employees, saying, "You can have these—they aren't good for anything." Paul Gregg, who came to *The Post* in 1902 and drew cartoons and painted pictures until his death in 1949, once was asked by Tammen to make some sketches for the curio company's catalog. When Gregg wasn't paid promptly for the work, he just forgot about it. Then about six months later Tammen stopped him in the hallway and apologized for the oversight. "Here," said Tammen, holding out his hand, "I want to pay you."

"Oh, forget it," Gregg replied with a laugh. As he turned away he felt something hit his back and heard the clink of coins falling to the floor. Tammen had tossed a handful of twenty-dollar gold pieces at Gregg, who had no choice but to pick them up.

As Tammen's affluence grew, so did his interest in the finer things. In 1908 he bought three lots in the 1000 block of Humboldt

Street, an area of classic Denver mansions close by cool, green Cheesman Park. But for some reason he couldn't seem to get a building permit. Then it dawned on Tammen that one of the home-owners in the block, William E. Sweet, later to be a governor of Colorado (1923–1925), wasn't anxious to have him as a neighbor. Tammen checked the zoning code and discovered that while live-stock and chickens were barred from the area, there was no pro-hibition against keeping other animals. One day workmen began to put up a fence around Tammen's land. When Sweet inquired, Tammen blandly said that since he couldn't get a building permit, he was going to use the property to house animals from his circus—elephants, tigers, lions, and a python—over the winter. Several days later Tammen received his permit. In 1909 Tammen built a hand-some mansion which still stands. The great and near-great were entertained there. One of the features of the home, at 1061 Hum-boldt Street, is the dining room paneled with inlaid Honduras mahogany. The woodwork was installed by craftsmen loaned to Tammen by his friend George Pullman, the railroad sleeping-car builder.

Tammen persuaded Bonfils to buy the Sells Brothers circus at a foreclosure sale in 1903 as an investment for *The Post*—what busi-nessmen these days call diversification—but it rarely made money. The price was $87,500. One is led to believe that the fascination of the tanbark, the wild-animal acts, clowns, aerialists, and stirring band music (as well as the somersaulting dogs and performing ponies) had as much to do with Tammen's interest as the promise of profit. For many years he spent two to four weeks every summer with the circus, overseeing the activities, evaluating the acts, savoring the excitement of show business as a way of relaxing from the more mundane demands of newspapering.

The Post's sports editor at the time was Otto Floto, whose name fascinated Tammen. "Otto Floto," Tammen would say, relishing the way the sound rolled off his tongue. "Otto Floto, what a beautiful name." So it was inevitable that the circus should be named the Sells-Floto show, that being the total of Otto's contribution to and interest in the enterprise. But when Tammen died, he left $25,000 in trust for Otto and his wife.

Floto had a dog-and-pony show when he first met Tammen. He would come by *The Post* to give Tammen a ride home in his pony carriage. Floto knew a good deal about boxing and eventually he

Aside from his newspaper, Tammen's great love was his Sells-Floto circus. Elephants in particular fascinated him.

joined *The Post*'s sports department. He produced a popular column, which he wrote with scant regard for commas, periods, or grammar. More erudite members of the staff had responsibility for taking care of such minor details. (Floto's successor as boxing columnist was Reddy Gallagher, a former prizefighter who could neither read nor write. But he could dictate.) The years caught up with Floto, but he persisted in using at the top of his column a photograph of himself taken in his youth. Frank H. Ricketson, Jr., now a prominent Denver businessman who started as a *Post* sportswriter, recalls that when Tammen was out of town Bonfils would ask: "Does this picture look like Otto to you? Take it out and have a new photo of him made the next chance you get." But Floto would never get around to having his picture taken. When Tammen returned to the city he would say to Ricketson: "I haven't seen Otto's picture in his column recently. What happened to it?" Then Ricketson would have to explain. Tammen would order the old picture restored, and nothing would be said until Tammen left town again.

Tammen was a prizefight fan, but a frugal one. Ricketson remembers that Tammen would take a lunch of cold beef sandwiches to the fights instead of patronizing the vendors.

However, it was Tammen's determination to provide his circus employees with the very best that led in part to its failure. In a period of notably Spartan accommodations, Sells-Floto performers traveled in Pullmans and could demand meals cooked to order if the mess-tent fare did not meet their fancy. Yellowing records show that in two typical years, 1908 and 1909, the circus went into the red by $41,512 and $50,514, respectively. These recurring deficits had to be made up from *Denver Post* profits. Tammen was convinced that the way to make the circus pay was not to cut back on quality, but to produce a better show that would sell more tickets. But World War I led to changing public interests, and the circus was sold in 1920 for $211,445.03, barely enough to pay off its debts.

Among those in Tammen's widening circle of friends was J. Ogden Armour, heir to the Chicago grain and meat-packing fortune. And it was Armour's present to his wife of a fantastically expensive string of matched pearls that led to a long series of generous gifts from the Tammens to the people of Denver. Agnes Tammen admired Mrs. Armour's pearls, as any woman would. Tammen said only a fool would spend so much for baubles, but to himself he vowed that one day he would give his wife an equally impressive necklace.

Shortly before Christmas, 1921, Tammen handed Agnes a check for $100,000, which had just been distributed as *The Post*'s year-end dividend. "For your string of pearls," he said.

Delight and distress mingled on Mrs. Tammen's face. Tammen was quick to sense her moods. "What's the matter?" he cried.

Notably nonathletic himself, Tammen (right) was a prizefight fan. Heavyweight champion Jim Jeffries, who was 6 feet 2½ inches, towers over other unidentified admirers.

(

Agnes Tammen asked her husband to sit down. Then she told him of the Children's Hospital's fund drive. A new wing was to be built and she had been asked to contribute one thousand dollars. The current goal was fifty thousand dollars, and while there was such a need she felt it sinful to spend twice that sum on personal adornment. Would Harry mind very much if she didn't buy the pearls and gave the hospital the fifty thousand dollars it needed?

Tammen gazed back at his wife with love. "You never cease to surprise me," he said quietly. "We will give them the entire one hundred thousand dollars."

The Agnes Reid Tammen wing cost more than $200,000 before it was finished, and the Tammens footed the entire bill. Carved over the entry are the words "For a Child's Sake." Denied children of their own, the Tammens made the welfare of all youngsters their concern. "It's better to give life to a child than to others," Tammen once said, "because the child means more to the community than anything else. I want the child that hasn't a name to have just the same tender care as a child that doesn't have to worry about what it's called—or even better care."

The Tammens continued to support Children's Hospital generously. His will left one-half of his estate to Mrs. Tammen and the balance, after the payment of several hundred thousand dollars in bequests to relatives, friends, and employees, was placed in a perpetual trust with the income going to Children's Hospital. The money was to be used for the care and treatment of children whose parents or guardians were unable to meet such expenses. The trust fund was valued at more than two million dollars, virtually all of it represented by *Denver Post* stock. Thus in effect Children's Hospital became owner of 20 percent of *The Post*. This stock and the parcel left to Mrs. Tammen were, as we shall see, destined to play critical roles in the fight for control of the newspaper long after the founding partners were dead.

As for Tammen, he knew the end was not distant when the Agnes Reid Tammen wing was formally opened in February of 1924. For months he had been troubled by vague abdominal pains. He lost weight and felt so weak that he had to go home to rest at midday before returning to his swivel chair. The sight faded from one eye, but not his sense of humor. One morning he showed up with a patch over his bad eye and on it was printed, "Read *The Denver Post*." "This eye quit working for me so I put it to work for *The Post*." he said. When he returned to the scene of his boyhood,

Tammen's death of cancer on July 19, 1924, resulted in most of *The Post*'s front page being devoted to him. Bonfils wrote the tribute under Tammen's portrait.

Baltimore, and entered Johns Hopkins Hospital, physicians found advanced cancer.

"How long have I got?" Tammen asked. When he was told, Tammen replied, "That's great! Think what a man can do with six months of life." He arranged a party for the nurses who had cared for him, then returned to Denver in Armour's private railroad car. Death came on July 19, 1924. He had lived sixty-eight eventful years. Pinky Wayne, the fiery red-haired girl from the Central City mining camp who had become one of *The Post*'s star reporters, wrote in her boss's obituary:

. . . From the hour the surgeon in the Baltimore hospital told Harry Tammen that his days were numbered, Mrs. Tammen has held a constant vigil by his side until, Friday morning, feeling much stronger, he asked her to perform a business mission for him. Friday night he urged his wife to send the nurse away so they might have an intimate talk.

Of many things this husband and wife talked as the night closed about them. He spoke of friends dear to his heart; of plans for helpfulness to those in need; he treasured his wife's devotion, and told her of his debt to her; he paid tribute to his longtime friend and business associate, F. G. Bonfils, and to his secretary, Miss Sadie Schultz, and then, clutching at his heart, he said: "I have a pain!"

There were further moments and hours, when the pain had gone, and then suddenly tightening the hold on the hand in his, he asked the eternal question:

"What is this thing that is coming to me?"

And the life he loved and filled so full, ended.

For one of the few times in his life Bonfils wept. Then, in his anguish, Bonfils penned a tribute which was published on *The Post*'s front page:

Harry Tammen, my partner for thirty years, has gone into the "Great Unknown." It will not be "Unknown" long to him over there, and they will recognize and know him at once. And they will love him there as we who know him love him here. And he will smile as he looks into their faces, and he will tell them the truth and say, "I had some faults, but I loved my fellowman and I believed in men, women and children."

Over there they will know that a real man has arrived.

He fell asleep like a tired child, and God and His angels showed him the way home.—F. G. Bonfils.

A few days after Tammen's death Bonfils said in a letter to Larry Martin: "More than half of me has gone. I shall never get over it, for Harry and I were so necessary to each other."

Ricketson puts it another way: "One complemented what the other did not have. It is an interesting fact that the two men had few mutual friends."

Bonfils did not know until later that in the long night before his death Tammen had told his wife: "I trust Fred Bonfils. I trust him implicitly. Now that I am dying, you must trust Fred in everything. Never question him. I would not tell the woman I love to trust a man who would be unfaithful to such a trust."

And Fred Bonfils—erratic, irascible, tightfisted and often arrogant

Tammen's favorite portrait,
autographed to F. G. Bonfils:
"To my best Friend and Partner
with love and good cheer,
H. H. Tammen."

Artist Paul Gregg and *The Post*'s poet, C. Wiles Hallock, teamed up for
this page-1 tribute to Tammen's memory the day after his death.

with the arrogance that power begets—remained faithful to his partner's trust.

Even in death Harry Tammen covered his bets. The services were conducted by the Rev. Charles Marshall, an Episcopalian. He was assisted by Rabbi W. S. Friedman and a Catholic priest, Father Thomas F. Malone.

Two days before the funeral *The Post* published a four-column sketch by Paul Gregg on page 1. It showed two grieving angels labeled "Memory" and "Love" standing over an open book that read: "Life of Harry Tammen: Generous, Truthful, Sincere, Honest, Tolerant, Charitable, Unafraid, Forgiving." Beneath the sketch was a verse by G. Wiles Hallock, *The Post*'s then poet laureate:

> *Here passed a man who knew the conqueror's share*
> *Of dreams and deeds, high hopes and honored days*
> *Nor lost his humble heart to pride or praise*
> *Nor met this Phantom Fear with dull despair!*
> *He never knew defeat; for he could bear*
> *The weight of weal and woe with steadfast gaze;*
> *His dearest joys were plucked by peaceful ways*
> *In paths serenely trod—serenely fair.*
> *We called him Chief, and so we hold him dear;*
> *But he was Comrade, too—our common boast!*
> *His rare rebuke was never less than kind*
> *But O, his gentle smile rebuked us most!*
> *For he was true, courageous, just, sincere*
> *In humbleness of heart and strength of mind!*

THE BURIAL OF BUFFALO BILL

After the bison were gone, William F. Cody traded on the glamour surrounding his name by touring with his Buffalo Bill's Original Wild West Show. The show featured cowboys and feathered Indians and sharpshooters who could shatter glass balls in flight, and of course Cody, who had been immortalized in the stories of E. Z. C. Judson, writing under the name of Ned Buntline. "He was tall and straight," a contemporary reporter wrote of Cody, "with an abundance of golden hair falling to his shoulders, like the cavaliers of old. He had large, brilliant brown eyes, brown moustache and goatee, and features as perfect as if they had been chiseled out of marble."

But Cody turned out to be a better showman than businessman. By 1913 he was in such financial trouble from bad investments that he had to let the Sells-Floto circus take over his show. Cody and Tammen were good friends, in fact such good friends that *The Post* largely orchestrated Cody's funeral and selected his burial place.

In January of 1917 Cody, who had been in failing health, went to Glenwood Springs in the Colorado Rockies in the hope the mineral waters would help him. There he suffered what the newspapers called "a grave nervous collapse." He was brought back to Denver to the home of his sister, Mrs. L. E. Decker, where he died on January 10.

Cody was something of a national hero, a noble link with the romantic past, and it seemed important to the American psyche that he be given a proper funeral. Tammen, both showman and businessman, realized the value of enshrining Cody's memory and his remains in a grand tomb. The upshot was that Cody's widow, Louisa, was approached with a request that Denver be permitted to conduct the funeral, after which the body would be interred atop Lookout Mountain, west of the city, with a suitable monument to the memory of a great man. Cody himself had wanted to be buried in Wyoming.

Tammen with his friend and sometime business partner, Col. William F.
(Buffalo Bill) Cody.

The Post reported:

Near the town of Cody, which the famous plainsman founded,
and close to the great Shoshone Dam, is a mountain which the great
scout long ago elected as his burial place. It is the highest peak in
the immediate vicinity and just below is the gorge through which
the Shoshone River plunges after passing the dam. Far away are the
hills leading up to Yellowstone National Park, while to the south and
west are the mesas and benches of the Shoshone River and the plains
now irrigated by the dam. Such was the place Colonel Cody early
selected as his burial place.

"I'll sleep up there," he told his friends. "I'll sleep and be happy.
And when I'm gone, I want my tomb in the shape of a great buffalo,
carved out of the granite of the mountain—I want that to be the
last resting place of Buffalo Bill."

But in the short days before his death, Colonel Cody changed his plans. Wyoming was far, far away, and the lights shone prettily on the region of Colorow Point in the Mount Lookout region . . . And so as the days faded toward the last, Buffalo Bill decided that his resting place should be nearer Denver, the place he practically had called home for years, atop the rounded peak of Mount Lookout.

It was not Buffalo Bill who changed his plans. His grandson, Fred Garlow, who still lives in Cody, recalls that the family was short of funds and Louisa telegraphed Jake Schwoob, president of the Cody Chamber of Commerce. She explained what Denver had offered and asked what the people of Cody could do to honor the colonel's memory. Schwoob replied sadly that the tiny community of Cody was in no position to create a memorial anything like the one Denver proposed to erect.

And so Louisa opted for Denver. With *The Post* publicizing every minute detail, the Elks Lodge was placed in charge of the services. From the rotunda of the Colorado capitol, where Cody's body lay in state, the casket was placed on a caisson for a parade to the Elks Home. Members of the National Order of Cowboy Rangers led the way, and a band played "Tenting Tonight." After nearly two hours of eulogies and orations, thousands filed by the open casket while the strains of "Auld Lang Syne" were heard. Then the casket was taken to a mortuary crypt to await burial atop the mountain on Memorial Day weekend four and a half months later.

The Post announced that the city of Denver would deed the grave site as a shrine as soon as the Cody Memorial Fund Committee picked the precise spot, and schoolchildren throughout the nation would be encouraged to contribute nickels and dimes to pay for a monument. *The Post* had the decency not to mention that such a monument would be a great tourist attraction. Reporter Courtney Ryley Cooper described the site in these words:

Where the first trembling rays of the morning sun gleam upon the flowers and crags and snow of Mount Lookout's summit—there will Pahaska sleep in the last sleep; there will "the long-haired man" rest after his long journey of life. Far above the plains, stretching out to the north and east beneath him, far above where the buffalo once thundered in its massive herds, where the echoing whoop of the Cheyenne and the roving Sioux shrilled in its eerie warning, where the prairie schooner once rocked its weary way through the sands and gorges and arroyas, there will Buffalo Bill slumber in eternity, his hands folded, his work done.

The burial in the granite of the peak was carried out on schedule. Gene Fowler wrote *The Post*'s story:

> A day has passed. With it we have turned a page that cannot be rewritten. But it is all vivid and fresh in our minds—like the vast throng, the many thousands who began a journey yesterday morning to the summit of Lookout Mountain to an open grave. It was the tomb that was to receive the honored body of a modern knight errant, his escutcheon unsullied by selfishness, his record the history of the West.
>
> There where the winds of the wide world meet, where the trails wind upward as if to lead to higher things, there they pressed the earth over William F. Cody (Buffalo Bill), late in the afternoon.
>
> It was a pageant, the like of which has never been viewed before. . . .

It was a pageant indeed, and years later, after Louisa had been laid to rest alongside Cody, tons of concrete were poured over the grave with steel rails for reinforcement to make sure the bodies never would be moved. Many residents of Cody were demanding that Buffalo Bill be returned there. There were other efforts to claim the body. Relatives proposed the remains be entombed in a national shrine to be built in Washington, D.C. Some urged removal of the body to Nebraska, where Cody lived for years. In 1942 an association of Buffalo Bill's kin, by then numbering two thousand members, sought to have the remains taken to Cody on the ground that no memorial was ever erected on Lookout Mountain. No one explained how many nickels and dimes had been contributed, if any, and what had happened to them.

In 1948 the Cody American Legion Post, only partly in jest, offered ten thousand dollars to anyone who could spirit Buffalo Bill's remains "to their rightful burying place in Wyoming." Commissioner J. F. Fitzstephens was quoted: "No more heinous act was ever committed than to purloin the mortal remains of Cody's illustrious founder and sink him under twenty feet of cold concrete in the foreign soil of Colorado for purely mercenary purposes."

Only a modest monument, surrounded by a wrought-iron fence, stands over the grave today. Nearby is the Buffalo Bill Memorial Museum, a function of Denver's Department of Parks and Recreation. The Buffalo Bill Museum in Cody is more impressive by far.

Among the legends attached to this chapter of history is a story that Tammen and Bonfils gave Louisa Cody ten thousand dollars to agree to her husband's burial on Lookout Mountain. Fred Garlow says he is positive no such offer was made and no payment received. Those who knew Bonfils and Tammen well would be inclined to agree. *The Post* was prospering in 1917, but such largesse was completely out of character for its proprietors.

3

HIS OBSESSION WAS MONEY

Walter Walker, the western Colorado newspaper publisher, was disparaging an old political enemy when he declared in a speech, "Frederick G. Bonfils is the only one of his kind in the world and the mold was broken after him."

There was more truth in the statement than Walker may have realized.

Bonfils' controversy-ridden life was filled with Everests demanding to be conquered. At times dark demons seemed to be driving him to excel. He dominated his family, with unfortunate results, and he sought to dominate the society of which he was a part. He pushed himself hard, shunning almost to the point of asceticism the soft pleasures that might hinder his will to succeed. He expected others to share his dedication to work. At staff meetings he liked to tell his *Denver Post* lieutenants: "Everything we do is a struggle. It is even a struggle to live. Let's welcome struggles. They make us better fitted for the next one."

Bonfils drank no liquor, ate sparingly, exercised vigorously. Although he tolerated a series of notorious boozers on *The Post*'s staff —drinking seemed to be something of an occupational disease in those days—he had this to say about them: "A booze drinker is like a fox in Aesop's fable who because he got his tail cut off told all the other foxes it was the fashion and urged them to do the same." Once, when an editor he wanted to talk to happened to be out to lunch, Bonfils demanded, "Does that man eat all the time?" Then he lectured the others in the city room: "All you men eat too much. You don't need any lunch." On another occasion he applauded the Spartan life with this admonition: "Difficult times should not frighten you. Hard times are good times for us. They make us dig more, work harder, and eat less."

Until his last years Bonfils was lean, hard, athletic. In contrast to his partner, Tammen, Bonfils was meticulous about his appearance. Tammen was known to emerge from the men's room with his suspenders drooping from his trousers. Bonfils strode through life like a conqueror, his blue-gray eyes flashing with vitality. His erect carriage made him look much taller than his 5 feet 8 and often he wore a derby hat to add to the illusion of height. Some of his contemporaries remember him as being nearly 6 feet tall, but he was a much shorter man.

If Bonfils had an obsession, it was money. He enjoyed the challenge of making it and accumulated a large fortune. Fowler tells this story:

> In defense of his nickel-nursing policies, Bonfils once told M. Koenigsberg, the famous Hearst executive: "Certain people say I'm stingy. Well, I cannot forget my boyhood back in Troy, Missouri. We were then a large family and very poor. We seldom had meat. My good father once took a piece of steak and cut it up so that each child would have a piece no larger than another child received. I remember him giving my mother *his* share. Then he kept the bone for himself, pretending it was by far the best and largest piece of all. I wasn't fooled, and then and there I decided that I would get a fortune from the world, that my family never would suffer, and that I would *keep* what was mine and let others waste their substances."

There is no way to tell whether this incident took place, or whether it sprang up as part of the legend encouraged by Bonfils himself. The fact is that Fred was born into a relatively well-to-do family at Troy, Lincoln County, in eastern Missouri, about forty or fifty miles northwest of St. Louis.

Fred's grandfather, born Buonfiglio, was a native of Corsica. Fred Bonfils did not discourage talk that his grandfather was related to Napoleon, but in any event Buonfiglio served with Bonaparte's legions.

After the emperor was exiled, Buonfiglio migrated to Salem, Massachusetts, by way of Rome, shortened his name to Bonfils, married Lucinda Alden of the Massachusetts Aldens, and settled in Tuscaloosa, Alabama. There a son, Eugene Napoleon Bonfils, was born. Grandfather Bonfils must have been a man of no little charm to win an Alden for his bride. The charm was passed on to his son, Eugene Napoleon, who also married well, and to his grandson Fred, who was described by more than one woman as "the handsomest, most charming man I've ever met."

Grandfather Bonfils moved to Lexington, Kentucky, where he taught at Transylvania University. Eugene Napoleon was graduated

The barefoot boy in center is believed to be Fred Bonfils and behind him, with moustache, his father, Eugene Napoleon Bonfils. At left are thought to be William (with dog) and Thomas (sitting on porch). Identity of others is unknown.

The four Bonfils brothers about the time Fred (right) moved to Denver in 1895. Others are, from left, Thomas, William, Charles.

from this institution, taught school briefly in St. Louis County, and moved to Troy in 1852 to begin a law practice. There he met and married Henrietta Lewis, Virginia-born descendant of the family that produced Meriwether Lewis, coleader of the Lewis and Clark expedition into the unmapped territory opened by the Louisiana Purchase. Henrietta lived in a colony of transplanted Virginians just north of Troy. The head of the Powell Memorial Library in Troy, Marjorie J. Evans, says Henrietta brought to Eugene Napoleon Bonfils' home "a gracious, aristocratic way of life," stemming from her Virginia upbringing.

Fred was the fourth child to be born of this union. First was Thomas in 1856; then Eugene, who died in early childhood; William, born in 1858; and then Frederick Gilmer Bonfils on December 31, 1860. Fred was followed by Henrietta in 1865, Mary Eugenia in 1867, who died two years later, Nellie in 1869, and Charles Alden in 1877.

Eugene Bonfils served briefly in 1854 as the first editor of the Troy *Gazette,* the first newspaper to be published in the county. He was elected judge, was one of the incorporators of the town of Troy in 1877, helped organize the Farmers' and Mechanics' Savings Bank, and later went into the insurance business. In addition he operated a small farm. It is possible that he had no easy time feeding and clothing his large brood, but it does not seem likely Fred went hungry very often. Rather, the picture is of an idyllic boyhood in the wooded, rolling hills of eastern Missouri, learning to fish and hunt and observing the wildlife that abounded. In addition to his other accomplishments, the adult Fred Bonfils was a competent and energetic naturalist.

When Fred was seventeen he was nominated for admission to West Point by Congressman Aylett H. Buckner of Mexico, Missouri. He entered the U. S. Military Academy July 1, 1878. He left the Academy in August of 1881.

The "official" *Denver Post* explanation has been that he fell in love with Belle Barton of Peekskill, New York, and, as Lawrence Martin has written, because "he could not be at once a bridegroom and a cadet under academy regulations, he resigned and married." The facts are somewhat different. A year and a half after he entered the Academy Bonfils was "turned back" to a lower class. Subsequently he was discharged "because of a deficiency in mathematics" even though he stood third in his class in "discipline." Crushed, Bonfils took a job briefly in a New York bank, then returned to Troy to help in his father's insurance business.

Nearly a year later Bonfils went back to New York. He and Belle were married July 26, 1882, at the home of her parents in Peekskill. Belle is described as a beautiful blonde, although later photographs show a buxom woman with light-brown hair. A few days after the wedding they set out for Canon City, Colorado, where Bonfils had been hired as an instructor in mathematics and tactics at the then new Canon City Military Academy, a school for boys, supported by the Grand Army of the Republic. The Fremont County *Record* of September 16, 1882, describes "Captain Bonfils" as a "competent" instructor and excellent disciplinarian. The same newspaper a month later reported that Bonfils had resigned because of his wife's ill health and had been ordered by the "government" to Troy, Missouri, as a surveyor. Bonfils' first association with Colorado was brief and not particularly happy.

Troy was too small a backwater to keep Fred Bonfils interested for long in any one calling. He worked briefly for the Troy *News*. On an assignment to cover the state fair, he was denied admittance because he had forgotten his press pass. Bonfils slugged the gatekeeper and went in to get his story. He formed the Troy Amateur Minstrel Club and became its president and leading actor. His first daughter, May, was born at Troy in 1883. In 1885 he became a clerk during a session of the Missouri legislature.

Fred moved with his young family to Kansas City in 1886 to go into the real-estate business. His partner was Aldemon E. White, and perhaps it was characteristic that White provided the $2,300 capital to launch their firm. Business was slow, and one story has it that when Fred was too proud to write to his father for money, White gave him fifteen dollars to buy an overcoat. After a year the partnership was ended; and after another impermanent partnership, Bonfils moved into a more speculative and less reputable enterprise. In retrospect it is apparent that a certain ingenuity was demonstrated by the young Bonfils. He decided to take advantage of the enormous interest being generated by the 1889 homesteading rush into Oklahoma Indian territory.

The center of attention was the Santa Fe railroad's Oklahoma Station, later to become Oklahoma City. Federal troops held back the thousands of land seekers until the official opening, and as the fever grew, Bonfils devised a scheme for profiting from it. For six hundred dollars he bought a section of land across the Oklahoma line in Hemphill County in the Texas Panhandle. He platted the land into a townsite, named it Oklahoma City, and returned to Kansas City, where he opened an office called the Panhandle Townsite Co. A month before the Oklahoma Strip was opened to settlers, he advertised lots in Oklahoma City, Tex., at two to twenty-five dollars each. The words "Oklahoma City" appeared in huge block letters, but "Tex." was in much smaller type.

Bonfils' townsite was a square mile of sagebrush and scrub oak, seven miles from the nearest water, thirty-five miles from the nearest town. No railroad, not even a wagon trail broke the prairie's monotony. The entire county of 900 square miles contained a population of only five hundred. And people bought lots in Bonfils' townsite believing it to be the future Oklahoma City, Oklahoma. He allegedly sold some five thousand lots, clearing fifteen thousand dollars before the scheme was revealed as a fraud.

Until the furor died down Bonfils found it convenient to visit his wife's family in Peekskill, New York. There his second daughter, Helen, was born November 26, 1889.

Bonfils' next notable venture off the straight and narrow path of respectability was a foray into the phony lottery industry being practiced in Kansas City, Kansas, while bribed officials looked the other way. The Kansas City *Star* of June 24, 1894, exposed this industry in a lengthy Sunday story which began with this paragraph:

> Less than three miles from the Junction, across the state line in Kansas City, Kansas, there exist and thrive a dozen alleged lotteries which do a business of over 1½ million dollars a year, and which operate in nearly every city, town and hamlet in the union.

Most of the lotteries were concentrated in the Husted Building and the *Star*'s report charged that Bonfils, described as "formerly a Kansas City real estate swindler," was doing business under the following names: "L. E. Winn & Co., Eli Little & Co., The Little Louisiana Lottery Company, The Louisiana Lottery Company, and M. Dauphin." The story also charged that books of lottery tickets were collated in the offices by women employees and distributed to agents in many parts of the country by express since it was unlawful to transmit lottery material through the mails. In one month, said the *Star*, L. E. Winn & Co. paid the express companies eight thousand dollars for services.

The main complaint about the lotteries seemed to be that no one ever won the big prizes, advertised to be as large as fifteen thousand dollars, for the winning one-dollar ticket. Most of the successful ticket holders turned out to be friends or employees of the lottery companies who ostentatiously flashed their winnings to stimulate the sale of more tickets. Some agents also complained that they were required to pay five-dollar prizes out of their pockets on the promise that they would be reimbursed, but they seldom were. The names Little Louisiana Lottery and M. Dauphin were employed with malice aforethought, for at the time there was a legal and legitimate Louisiana State Lottery whose president was M. A. Dauphin. Bonfils already was a man of considerable means. He had deposits totaling $130,000 in Missouri and Kansas banks and he displayed certified statements of this fact as "absolute proof of the good faith and financial strength" of his lottery companies.

Largely under pressure from the Kansas City *Star* and *Times,* the authorities finally cracked down on the lottery operators. The *Times* of December 20, 1894, carried a report that "F. G. Bonfils, alias L. E. Winn, proprietor of the Little Louisiana Lottery," was arrested twice in one day, first for "violating the Kansas vagrancy law by loitering around a lottery and gambling house without visible means of support," and later "for being engaged in the unlawful calling of conducting a lottery." Bonfils posted bonds of one hundred and five hundred dollars and was released. The *Times* of January 18, 1895, then published this story:

LOTTERIES TO LEAVE
The Winn-Bonfils Concern Will Close Up
Tomorrow

The new county attorney, Samuel Miller, has personally notified L. E. Winn, proprietor of one of the most successful of the Kansas City, Kan. fake lotteries, to pull up stakes and move from the city. Winn says he will close up his business tomorrow.

In March Bonfils pleaded guilty to the two counts and paid a modest fine. Shortly afterward came his fateful meeting with Harry Tammen that led to purchase of *The Post.* It was a particularly fortuitous meeting since the lottery business was all but dead in Kansas City, and Bonfils was looking for new opportunities. This circumstance undoubtedly had much to do with Bonfils' willingness to listen to Tammen's one-sided proposal. In any event, anxious to put the Kansas City phase of his life behind him, Fred Bonfils moved his family to Denver and took up residence at 939 Corona Street. His daughter May was then twelve years old and Helen six.

Within weeks after acquiring the paper Bonfils demonstrated his surprising capacity for inconsistency by launching an editorial campaign against the sale of lottery tickets in Denver. Charging that city officials failed to enforce ordinances against lotteries because of "pull and influence," Bonfils accused lottery operators of "reaping rich harvests" from the "hard-earned money of dry goods clerks and overworked mechanics shuffled relentlessly in the enchanting game of chance." Was this change of heart simply a cynical method of

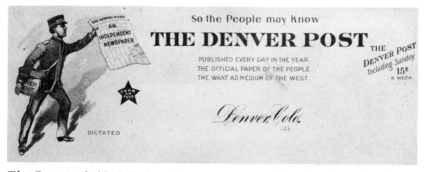

The Post used this letterhead for many years, changing the subscription price as rates were raised.

attracting attention? Or was he genuinely disillusioned and remorseful? At this date it is impossible to determine his motives.

Thus began a new career for Fred Bonfils, and he jumped feet first into the Denver scene with scant concern for the consequences. Perceiving quickly that few persons were paying much attention to *The Post,* he set out to make them take notice. That was to be the lodestar of his philosophy for running a successful newspaper. Of those days Perkin has written:

> Denver was amazed, startled, fascinated, and left waiting, slackjawed, to see what *The Post* would "pull" next. Scandals were exploited to the hilt, and there was a crucifixion of a public official or non-advertising businessmen in each new edition. Everyone damned *The Post*—and nearly everyone subscribed. *The Post*'s owners admitted with frankness that they cared not a whit for the community's respect so long as the community kept buying the paper. "Sure," Tammen conceded, "we're yellow, but we're read, and we're true blue!"

After the campaigns against the coal dealers and child labor in the department stores, *The Post*'s scrutiny and indignation were directed against a long series of community and social ills, real or imagined, significant as well as insignificant. The "trusts," corporations, politicians, the railroads, the streetcar system, all felt the sting of *The Post*'s "So The People May Know" assaults. One observer noted, "*The Post*'s intention was to serve the people, whether they cared or not."

To make sure the people did care, Bonfils and Tammen involved them in its campaigns. On January 9, 1896, this announcement appeared on the editorial page:

$1.00 For An Idea

The Post will pay ONE DOLLAR to any man, woman or child who can suggest an acceptable cartoon for its front page. Suggestions can either be left at our office or sent by mail. We use one each day so don't be afraid to try your hand.

The significance of this promotion has been lost over the years.

Thousands choked Champa Street in front of the *Post* building for a Fourth of July promotion about the time of World War I.

At the time *The Post* was running a daily political cartoon on page 1 criticizing politicians, the fire department, city government, and the like. Often these cartoons were published with no news story or editorial explaining what the situation was about; apparently day-to-day readers were expected to know what was going on. Within

By the mid-Twenties, the building had been doubled in size. The "O, Justice" motto was painted over pressroom windows.

a few days *The Post* announced that "thousands" of cartoon ideas had been received. Some of these were sketched by a staff artist and published with credit.

Bonfils and Tammen soon demonstrated a knack for coining slogans. They called *The Post* "Your Big Brother—The Paper With a Heart and Soul." "There is no hope for the satisfied man," Bonfils said, and these words still appear above the "Open Forum" letters section of *The Post*. In more whimsical moments he composed—and published—this couplet: "I says to myself, to myself says I, *The Denver Post* is the paper to buy." (Bernard Kelly, a veteran *Post* writer, remembers that for years there was painted on the rear wall of the Labor Temple in his native Pueblo, Colorado, this slogan: "She saw it in *The Denver Post* with her hazel eyes." Its significance seems to have become lost with the passage of time.) And one day when visions of grandeur overcame whimsy, Bonfils composed this motto which continues to be part of *The Post*'s flag on the editorial page: "Dedicated in perpetuity to the service of the people, that no good cause shall lack a champion and that evil shall not thrive unopposed."

One other motto requires mention. Painted across the front of the Champa Street building, and over the entrance of the present building at 650 Fifteenth Street, are these words: "O, Justice, When Expelled From Other Habitations, Make This Thy Dwelling Place." How the motto came to be adopted by *The Post* is not known. The same words were inscribed on a stone slab over the entrance to the Boone County Courthouse in Columbia, Missouri, built in 1847 and in use until 1909. Dr. Marian M. Ohman of the University of Missouri says the quotation has been attributed to Dr. William Jewell, who for a time was superintendent of the building. But she adds that conclusive proof has never been offered and scholars have suggested Greek or Roman origin. (Of no significance, but an interesting coincidence, is the fact that Palmer Hoyt, editor and publisher of *The Post* from 1946 to 1970, attended William Jewell College Prep School in Liberty, Missouri.)

It was also in 1896 that *The Post* sponsored what is called "*The Post* Catch Phrase Contest." Miss Emma Dallas won the ten-dollar first prize with "They who read *The Post* always know the most." E. Bogart was the $7.50 second-prize winner with "It's no boast, the facts are in *The Post*"; and Jessie E. Cox was rewarded with five dollars for "*The Post* reaches the masses and pleases the classes." Consolation prizes of one dollar were paid for such contributions as "*The Post* keeps the people Posted," "Come off the fence and lean against the *Post*," and "Ahead of the Times—The Evening *Post*." Perhaps it was efforts of this quality that forced Bonfils to invent slogans of his own.

Even though Bonfils had never completed his college education, he was no stranger to the classics. His longtime chauffeur, Robert Stouffer, remembers that Bonfils enjoyed reciting verse while out walking in the evening, or being driven. His favorite, which tells something of his thinking, was a verse from "Horatius at the Bridge" by Thomas Babington Macaulay:

> *Then out spake brave Horatius*
> *The captain of the gate*
> *To every man upon this earth*
> *Death cometh soon or late*
> *And how can man die better*
> *Than facing fearful odds*
> *For the ashes of his fathers*
> *And the temples of his gods.*

No. 823,100.   PATENTED JUNE 12, 1906.

F. G. BONFILS.
AERIAL BICYCLE.
APPLICATION FILED APR. 20, 1904.

Placards like this were distributed to newspaper vendors. The word "Evening" was dropped in 1901. (John Buchanan Collection)

In 1906 F. G. Bonfils was granted a patent for an "aerial bicycle." This sketch is from the letter of patent.

Bonfils' restless energies and inquiring mind led to many diverse interests in addition to slogans, crooked lotteries, nature study, and newspaper publishing. For example, he was issued U. S. Patent No. 823,100 on an "aerial bicycle," a winged vehicle presumably for use by circus acrobats. The Letters of Patent, issued in 1906, carries this explanation:

> My invention relates to improvements in bicycles provided with wing-like or air-plane attachments, whereby the bicycle after getting a considerable start down an incline, for instance, may sail through the air a considerable distance before again striking the track, it being assumed that there is a gap in the track to permit the machine to make a jump through space. The wings or air planes, which project outwardly on opposite sides of the bicycle frame, enable the machine to take a longer flight than could be accomplished in their absence. To the rear extremity of the frame of the bicycle and centrally located is a revolving wind-wheel which has a tendency to steer the machine during its flight through the air and also adds to the novelty of its appearance. . . . It is further believed that my

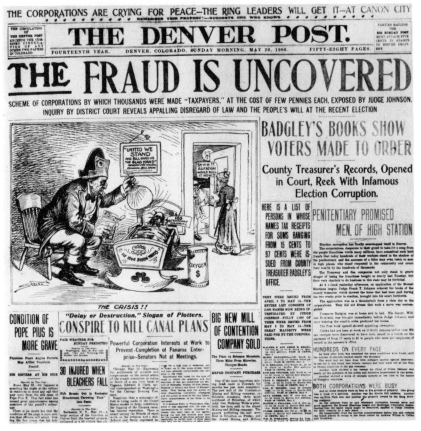

Page 1 of May 20, 1906, with headline reading "The Fraud is Uncovered."

improved machine will be found capable of use in the performance of many feats not heretofore accomplished on a machine of ordinary construction or unequipped with my improvements. . . .

There is no record of Bonfils' actually riding his invention or making money with it. But getting back to the newspaper, over the years Bonfils has been painted as the chief instigator and culprit in the early *Post*'s startling style of journalism, described as being as difficult to ignore as a punch in the nose. However, Tammen as copublisher not only acquiesced but took delight in launching something new in the way of an editorial high jinks, or lowering the editorial boom on a vulnerable foe. Undoubtedly it was Bonfils' more flamboyant style, plus the fact that he outlived his partner by nearly a decade, that led to the placing of the credit or blame, as the case may be. It also seems likely that a basic difference in the personalities of the partners had an important part in the reputation that they left. Remembering the anecdote about the way Tammen threw a handful of gold coins at Paul Gregg, one is inclined to have a warm feeling about his generosity. By contrast, there is a certain maliciousness in stories about Bonfils' penury. Like the anecdote about the time Volney T. Hoggatt, Bonfils' friend, bodyguard, and court jester, went fishing for trout. Hoggatt fell into the stream, narrowly escaped drowning, and returned to the ranch house dripping wet and with a harrowing tale of his misfortune: Bonfils' first comment, as widely reported, was "What happened to my rod you were using? It cost me thirty-five dollars."

Hoggatt was the kind of fellow who could tell Bonfils: "Boss, you keep talking about 'my money, my money.' It isn't your money at all. You only have use of it while you're here and you won't be able to take it with you when you die."

Bonfils did not hesitate to spend money to get the talent he wanted. He telephoned Helen Black at the *News* one day and offered her a job paying considerably more than she was getting. When Helen replied she felt she ought to talk it over with her city editor first, Bonfils said:

"No, you don't have to do that. You have to look out for yourself. Business is a matter of self-preservation."

"But he's been so good to me that I owe it to him to talk to him first," Helen said.

"Look out for yourself first," Bonfils advised.

Then Helen said what had been on her mind all the while: "Mr. Bonfils, I'm afraid you would cut my pay after a few months. You know you've been known to do that."

Bonfils, his hat at a rakish angle, with Volney Hoggatt, his companion, bodyguard, and court jester.

He laughed and promised not to do it, but Helen stayed with the *News*.

In reality, Bonfils demonstrated a deep and often stern sense of paternalism over those close to him, including his employees, but he didn't want to spoil his "family" by excessive generosity. During his earliest years in Denver various members of the Bonfils clan, including his older brother Tom, lived in F. G.'s home. Mrs. Bonfils cooked and washed for them all, and everyone under the roof was subject to F. G.'s fatherly discipline. If Tom wanted to go out for the evening, F. G. expected to be told where he was going and why. F. G.'s practice was to take *The Post* home at the end of the day and study it line by line after supper in preparation for the postmortems at the next morning's staff meeting in the Red Room outside his office. By 9 P.M., when he was ready to retire, F. G. expected every other member of the household to turn off the lights and go to bed, too.

Elmer Strain, who attended many of those daily staff meetings as national advertising manager, remembers that Bonfils seemed to be aware of everything that appeared in the previous afternoon's paper, and that scoldings outnumbered compliments by far. He would dismiss the sessions with a brusque "That's all," rising and leaving the room, and the various department heads would file back to their jobs. Few of them had their characters undermined by large salaries. Meanwhile, Bonfils and Tammen were taking care of themselves generously. The corporate minutes for the annual meeting in 1917 show that they were paying themselves sixty-five thousand dollars a year at the rate of one thousand dollars per week, and thirteen thousand in a lump sum at year's end, plus the dividends.

Perkin tells the story of a poetess who suggested that she ought to be paid for the verse *The Post* had published. "I am amazed," Bonfils replied sadly. "My dear child, Jesus never asked for money." While this account may be apocryphal, Anne O'Neill Sullivan remembers when she "almost" asked for a raise. In addition to working as Bonfils' secretary at *The Post* she kept a record of his numerous investments, clipped his dividend coupons, and kept track of the performance of his stocks. One day he asked her advice about hiring a New York investment broker to do the same work.

"Mr. Bonfils," she said, "do you realize you would be paying him each month what you are paying me in a year to keep track of your investments in addition to all the other work I do?"

"All the other work" included being in the office six days a week, as well as Saturday night, when the Sunday paper was being prepared. "I loved the work," she said, "I wouldn't have stayed if I didn't. But I just wanted to let *him* know that I knew he was taking advantage of my willingness to put in long hours."

And sometimes there was Sunday work. One Sunday she came home and said: "Mama, Mr. Bonfils asked me today what my father died of, and I realized I didn't know. I was only four years old when he died."

Her mother replied tartly, "He died of working on a Sunday—and catching cold."

Yet, such was the magnetism of Frederick Bonfils that he commanded an enduring loyalty among his employees, and they rallied around him when the chips were down. Perhaps they shared a sense of family because *The Post*'s aggressive methods developed many enemies as well as friends. Perhaps they appreciated Bonfils because he demonstrated human weaknesses.

There was the time, for instance, when *The Post* had criticized the architectural skills of Frank E. Edbrooke, who was trying to get the contract for designing a new courthouse. *The Post* was not subtle about suggesting that another of Edbrooke's monstrosities should not be permitted to deface the Denver landscape. Edbrooke took umbrage and demanded a retraction. When no retraction was published, he brought a long Winchester rifle from home and ostentatiously began to clean it in the window of his office, which was directly across the street from *The Post*. Bonfils quickly decided discretion was the better part of valor.

(Many years later, after *The Post* had moved to the corner of Fifteenth and California streets, Gail Pitts and Kay King Conrad were looking out the windows of the women's department when they saw a man brandishing two pistols in a hotel room across the street. The girls were positive he intended to kill Palmer Hoyt, the editor and publisher whose office was just a few doors down the same side of the building. They notified the city editor, who called the police, who sent officers charging into the hotel. It turned out he was a legitimate quick-draw artist practicing for a contest.)

Two men like Bonfils and Tammen could not operate a newspaper like *The Post* in the moral atmosphere that prevailed in the early days of this century without giving rise to rumors of blackmail. Perhaps the most persistent of these stories has to do with the way Bonfils acquired the Leopold Guldman mansion at East Tenth Avenue and Humboldt Street, just west of Cheesman Park, for his home shortly before World War I. Guldman operated the Golden

Eagle department store on lower Sixteenth Street, which specialized in buying up bankrupt stocks and selling them cheaply. He depended heavily on advertising to bring in customers and his business prospered.

In essence, the story is that Bonfils learned about the sexual aberrations of Guldman's son, and Guldman gave Bonfils the mansion in return for a promise not to publish the scandal.

This story is scotched in the recollections of the late Col. Philip S. Van Cise, the attorney who defended the *Rocky Mountain News* against a libel suit filed by Bonfils. In preparing the defense he directed what undoubtedly is the most thorough investigation ever made of Bonfils' background. A manuscript in which Van Cise tells of his part in building the defense contains this amusing and revealing paragraph:

> An alleged clew, which was so generally believed in Denver, that the Denver *Democrat* ran a picture of Mr. X's house on its front page, with the caption "This is the house that 'X' blackmailed 'G' out of" was conclusively proven to be a canard of the first magnitude. The facts were that "G" built the first $100,000.00 house in Denver, had a dispute with his wife about the draperies, met "X" who asked him what was the matter, and recited his troubles to him. The result was a three-cornered deal between "X," "G" and "B" whereby "X" got the house, "G" other property and "B" the Empire building, and the counsel for "G" was to be paid $750.00 as attorney fees by "X." The bill was sent twice, and no answer. Then the lawyer phoned and asked about it, to which "X" responded—"Why, we never pay attorney fees, send over your picture and your write-up and we will run it a few times!" However, he finally received the fee minus the write-up.

"X" of course is Bonfils, "G" is Guldman, and "B" is Horace Bennett, well-to-do real-estate man of the era.

Caroline Bancroft, who started *The Post*'s first book-review section in 1928 and went on to become a well-known Denver historian, heard a slightly different version from Mrs. Bennett. The Bennetts purchased Guldman's home, but before they could occupy it they heard the palatial Wolhurst estate south of Littleton, Colorado, was available. So they bought Wolhurst and sold the Guldman mansion to Bonfils without ever moving in.

Leverett A. Chapin, who joined *The Post* as reporter in 1928 and became one of its outstanding reporters and editors, remembers many occasions when he accompanied Bonfils on visits to Guldman's office in his store. "The relationship between the two men was always warm and friendly," he says. "Guldman knew that advertising in *The Post* was responsible for much of his success, and Bonfils appreciated the fact that Guldman used *The Post*. It was unthinkable that Bonfils had blackmailed Guldman." As a matter of fact, records show that the two men in partnership invested in downtown Denver real estate in 1917 and again in 1926.

Anne O'Neill Sullivan also was asked about the Guldman story. She replied that after Bonfils' death Internal Revenue agents spent more than nine months going over his records with her. Everything was found to be in order and, among other things, the search unearthed the large canceled check with which Bonfils had paid for the Guldman house.

But old tales die hard. Not long after William (Tex) Gressett went to work in 1934 as an advertising salesman, he was told to get some liquor for a *Post* party. Gressett didn't know whether he was supposed to buy it, ask for a discount, or find someone who would donate it. Having heard about *The Post*'s reputation, he decided it would be a mistake to pay the retail price and suggested to the liquor dealer that a discount would be appropriate.

"Discount, hell," the dealer said. "You'll pay full price like everybody else."

Groping desperately for a retort, Gressett blurted. "You know what happened to the Golden Eagle store, don't you? Well, think about it for a while." Then he stalked out. That same afternoon a case of liquor was delivered without charge.

Gressett still squirms as he relates the story.

THE BIG FISH CAPER

F. G. Bonfils was not one either to play or enjoy practical jokes. But he enjoyed fishing for trout, and the bigger the trout he caught, the greater his enjoyment. Thus he might have found a small smile in a practical joke that H. Ray Baker played on the fishermen of Colorado.

It happened many years after Bonfils' death, when Baker was art director of *The Post*'s Sunday rotogravure magazine. Baker also was an ardent fisherman given, as fishermen are wont to do, to fantasizing about giant trout he would hook, play, and land. One day he decided to make his fantasies come true. Together with a couple of coconspirators he ordered the largest king salmon Frank Torizawa at the Granada Fish Company could find among his suppliers in Seattle.

The salmon that was flown to Denver was a magnificent fifty-five-pounder, broad of beam and armed with a great underslung jaw. With his airbrush, Baker painted the salmon's flanks so that it took on the appearance of a fearsomely huge rainbow trout.

On the opening of trout season, a cold, snow-showery spring day, Baker and his friends took their salmon high into the Rockies. They mounted a ski rack on the side of their car and placed the salmon on it in plain view of any motorist they would encounter. Then they began a leisurely drive back to Denver.

What happened along the way was nothing short of chaos. Outbound fishermen slammed their cars to a halt to gape at the giant trout. Some made U-turns on the highway to follow the fish. As the caravan wound through Idaho Springs, townspeople halted in their tracks to stare in awe.

Baker's party drove slowly through Denver and past the *Rocky Mountain News*. Someone in the sports department sighted the fish and dispatched a photographer after it posthaste. Baker managed to elude him by heading for *The Post*. With the salmon slung over his shoulder, Baker walked wordlessly through the city room and out the side door. Someone checked with the director of the state game-and-fish department and was solemnly assured it was possible that monster-sized trout could be lurking in high mountain lakes.

After the joke was over, Baker and his friends ate salmon until they were sick of it.

4

AN EVIL-MINDED MAN AND OTHER SENSATIONS

Faced with four aggressive and established competitors, the new proprietors of *The Denver Post* had to react quickly or go under. In analyzing the early success of Harry Tammen and Fred Bonfils, two reasons become apparent:

—They set out to attract the people's attention by a variety of imaginative promotions and by publishing material of interest to them.

—They hired the best available professionals to carry out their plans.

Page 1 of May 8, 1921, with headline "Dandelion is Mother's Day Flower, Wear It and Squelch the Profiteer."

Fowler expresses it another way: "Underneath all their circus-like activities, *The Post* owners were shrewd businessmen. They made sure of giving the sucker more news and more excitement and more features than it was possible for any competitor to do. That practice guaranteed circulation, and circulation guaranteed advertising."

Fowler was wrong on one count. Bonfils and Tammen never regarded the public as suckers. They didn't hesitate to trample roughshod over those in power, but they needed the people to support their newspaper and their advertisers. Thus the people were respected, entertained, titillated, catered to. The newspaper and its promotions were designed with their interests in mind. Remember that *The Post* was born in the decade of the Gay Nineties, when, despite the Silver Panic and a growing concern about Spanish oppression of Cuba, Americans in general and frontier Coloradans in particular were a provincial, unsophisticated people. Timbuctu was distant and dogfights were very exciting events. Thus when *The Post* published a front-page story like the one that follows, people bought the paper to read it, talk about it, and wonder what sensational item of local news would be published on the morrow. This is the story, published in 1896, in its entirety:

AN EVIL MINDED MAN
Charles Adams Insults a Woman Missionary

Followed Her for Blocks and Is Finally Arrested on Sixteenth Street—The Accused Is a Married Man, 54 Years of Age—Severely Punished

Charles E. Adams, a well-dressed but evil-minded man of 54, the father of a family, was the recipient of deserved exposure in the police court this morning. He was tried on a charge of soliciting, an offense never before preferred against a man in Denver. A few minutes before 6 o'clock last evening Adams, who had been drinking, insolently approached Mrs. Ellen M. McCrae, of 2312 Champa Street, a most respectable woman and an ex-missionary matron of the Crittendon Home. Mrs. McCrae was walking along Champa Street near Eighteenth, when Adams with the assurance of a professional "masher" rudely accosted her and advanced a number of insulting propositions.

Although outraged by his behavior, Mrs. McCrae, not in the least alarmed, determined to teach the disgusting old fellow a richly deserved lesson. Firmly refusing his vulgar requests, and attempting to get rid of him without a scene on the street, she was compelled to humor the aged reprobate and walk with him for several blocks. When opposite the office of *The Evening Post* Mrs. McCrae espied

Patrolman Baughman, to whom she complained of her insulting tormentor. Adams was arrested and hustled off to jail.

When arraigned before Police Judge Webber this morning the aged Lothario was faced by her whom he had imagined would receive his loathsome advances. Mrs. McCrae, who is a handsome woman, occasioned a mild sensation when she testified. That the court might recognize the real character of the foul old man, she practically repeated the remarks which Adams had addressed to her, which were disgusting.

Shamed and cowed by this complete exposure, the old fellow advanced but a feeble defense—he pleaded intoxication as an extenuating circumstance. His plea was unavailing with the court, who after lecturing the depraved prisoner, imposed a fine of $25 and costs.

Mrs. McCrae was complimented by Judge Webber for having the nerve to prosecute such a specimen of aged depravity. Adams languishes in the city jail, where he will remain until his fine is liquidated. The prisoner, whose identity is concealed under the alias of Adams, is a married man, residing in a fashionable part of the city. He has heretofore borne an excellent reputation and was not known to indulge in even ardent spirits. He is physically a wreck, being a chronic sufferer from consumption. His friends will probably intercede with the mayor for a pardon.

When Tammen and Bonfils called their newspaper "Everybody's Big Brother"—sheltering the public's sensitivities by concealing the identity of an "aged reprobate" or trying to force down the price of coal—they were sincere. For a long time the newspaper's telephone switchboard shared space with Bonfils himself in his office. He wanted it that way so he could keep in touch with the thinking of the people. "Write to me personally if you are not satisfied with *The Denver Post,*" he would say.

(*The Post*'s current editor and publisher, Charles R. Buxton, answers his own telephone, a practice which startles callers expecting to fight their way through a phalanx of secretaries. His home number is listed in the directory, and occasionally he receives complaints about delivery, which he dutifully relays to the circulation department. "Call me back if you haven't received your paper in an hour," he says, and subscribers have discovered they rarely have to.)

To draw the public's attention to itself, *The Post* undertook an incredible variety of promotions, virtually all of them at little or no cost to the paper. These promotions were joint affairs involving *The Post* and some merchant or organization that would benefit from the resulting publicity. Some survive to this day. For example, there are *The Denver Post*-Dave Cook Big Trout Contest and *The Denver Post*-Gart Brothers Camping Tips Contest, both cosponsored with leading sporting-goods dealers. *The Post* name gets top billing even though its contribution is limited to news space. Tammen and Bonfils believed this was contribution enough—that the promotion could not succeed without the publicity they provided and for the merchant to bear the expenses was only a fair division of responsibility. Subsequent managements have not had many occasions to disagree.

While every newspaper has its promotions, many of *The Post*'s were unique. The rabbit hunts, for example. Periodically jackrabbits would proliferate alarmingly on Colorado's eastern plains, decimating what crops could survive drought and hail and threatening the livelihood of the farmers. With *The Post*'s encouragement these farmers would round up the rabbits in wintertime drives covering many square miles, clubbing them to death by the thousands. But the meat wasn't wasted. The carcasses, quickly frozen by the cold, would be sent to Denver in donated railroad cars, trucked to *The Post,* and distributed free to queued-up lines of the poor. To stimulate the goodwill of ranchers, *The Post* also offered a bounty on mountain lions which preyed on sheep and cattle. Many a mountain man, smelling pungently of a hunting camp, would make his way to *The Post* with a dead lion in the back of his truck, there to be photographed claiming his bounty.

Under Al Birch, whose job for years was to dream up promotion ideas, *The Post* sponsored cross-country roller-skating contests, had Harry Houdini escape from a straitjacket while suspended upside down from *The Post*'s balcony, and invited local girls to wrestle a troupe of professional women grapplers. Tammen's circus connections led to tightrope walkers performing over Champa Street and a "slide for life" in which a girl in tights, hanging by her teeth, zipped down a wire strung from atop the Public Service Building to the street in front of *The Post*. Birch, a onetime city editor, even planted a modern "Eve" near Rocky Mountain National Park and wrote daily stories about her adventures. Even after Palmer Hoyt took over in 1946, the arrival of the circus in Denver meant Champa Street in front of *The Post* would be blocked off for a noontime performance by waltzing elephants and bareback riders; in July, the Cheyenne Frontier Days Committee would arrive with buckskin-clad Sioux Indians who whooped and danced on the asphalt.

In the heyday of vaudeville the stars and showgirls would visit

The Post as soon as they reached town in hopes of getting publicity. Otto Floto took a particular delight in meeting pretty girls. One day a particularly attractive showgirl dropped by, which was Frank Ricketson's cue to leave the sports department. As he walked out the door, three men walked in, cornered Floto, and earnestly tried to sell him on the idea of publishing a story about a ski hill they planned to establish on Lookout Mountain. They talked interminably while Floto tried unsuccessfully to get rid of them. Finally the showgirl tired of waiting and left. When Ricketson returned, Floto told him, "Promise me, Rick, you'll never write anything about skiing for *The Post*."

In one of the few promotions catering to the "elite," *The Post* in 1907 began to take a trainload of notables to the Frontier Days rodeo and celebration each summer in Cheyenne, Wyoming. The guest list was made up of government officials, advertisers, and friends of Bonfils and Tammen. In time the "*Post* train" developed into a day when tycoons and members of Denver's power structure dressed in cowboy garb and enjoyed an outing at *Post* expense. Being seen on the *Post* train became such a prestige matter that some of the uninvited would drive to Cheyenne in their cars and mingle at the rodeo with official guests. (After 1946 prominent national figures often were invited as Editor and Publisher Palmer Hoyt's special guests. William Zeckendorf, the New York real-estate tycoon who was involved in some major Denver building projects, boarded the train one year. But he was such a busy man, he said, that he had to leave the rodeo at midpoint to catch a plane back to Denver. The next morning the *Rocky Mountain News* published a photograph of Zeckendorf watching a wedding at a nudist colony in the mountains near Denver. He was still in the fancy cowboy outfit he had worn on the *Post* train to Cheyenne.)

With the exception of several war years, the train ran until 1970, after which it was discontinued for a variety of reasons, not the least among them being that the Union Pacific couldn't provide enough diners without upsetting the entire system. The last train consisted of twenty-seven cars (including nine diners) and carried more than twelve hundred guests. Hoyt spent much of the two-and-a-half-hour northbound leg walking the length of the train shaking hands with his guests. In the best Western tradition the booze flowed liberally on these trips and it was the responsibility of *Post* employees to maintain a reasonable level of decorum. A task force was assigned "shore patrol" duty, sweeping Cheyenne bars for *Post* guests and

For many decades *The Post*'s special train to Frontier Days rodeo **in** Cheyenne, Wyoming, was a leading promotion. In 1955 real-estate developer William Zeckendorf (left) embarrassed editor and publisher Palmer Hoyt (right) by leaving the rodeo before it ended to attend a nudist wedding.

persuading them to board the train as departure time neared. One year the shore patrol found a well-known politician apparently in the clutches of a frizzly-haired B-girl. Against her violent protests—she insisted she was his wife—they hustled the politician out of the bar and on the train. When the train arrived in Denver the same woman, still angry, was waiting on the platform. She had jumped in her car and beaten the train back to town, and it turned out she really was his wife.

A somewhat more democratic promotion was the misnamed *Post* Summer Opera which ran almost without interruption every July from 1934 until 1972 in Cheesman Park. These were primarily operettas and musical comedies performed outdoors before as many as twenty thousand spectators a night seated on blankets on the park lawn. The programs were an outgrowth of free lectures on astronomy which were given in Cheesman Park for many summers by Leo Patterson, *The Post*'s full-time astronomy writer at a time when space travel was only a figment of Jules Verne's imagination. Patterson had a way of introducing his lectures with a cornet solo, usually "I'll Take You Home Again, Kathleen." When Patterson's lectures began to pall, musical and ballet programs were substituted as *The Post*'s contribution to popularized culture.

The first all-music program, titled "An Evening with Verdi," was presented in 1934. It included the Prison Scene from *Il Trova-*

tore, the "Quartet" from *Rigoletto* and "Grand Triumphal March" from *Aïda.* But grand opera proved to be a bit heavy for popular tastes, and *The Vagabond King* enthralled audiences in 1936. After that came *The Desert Song, Rio Rita, The Student Prince,* and a variety of Broadway hits, winding up in 1972 with *The Sound of Music* for the third time.

The series began with amateur talent, homemade props and costumes borrowed from the Shriners. Union musicians, stagehands, and electricians donated their work and philanthropist Mrs. Verner Z. Reed donated $212, which covered all expenses. In later years the programs were put on a businesslike basis. Recognized Broadway stars played the lead roles, supported by top local talent. Some of the presentations cost more than $130,000, with the F. G. Bonfils Foundation footing the bills. The versatile Al Birch was the producer, and somehow he doffed his huge old Cheyenne train cowboy hat, a gift from Tom Mix, in time to preside over the stage shows a few days later. Invariably he would preface his remarks with "*Post* operas are completely free; spectators cannot spend one penny for anything."

Most *Post* promotions, however, were of a more pedestrian nature, but there were plenty of them. One annual report by the promotion department lists in excess of fifty of them—an average of more than one a week. These ranged from Easter egg hunt and kite-flying contests to summer picnics at the two amusement parks, a junior cowboy contest in connection with the National Western Stock Show in which the moppet with the best costume won a Shetland pony, a "My Favorite Milkman" contest cosponsored by a dairy, a "Name the Elephant" contest tied in with the Denver Zoological Society, and of course the arrival of Santa Claus. Thousands participated in these events at Big Brother's invitation. When eleven appliance distributors donated one home freezer apiece for a "Freezer a Day" giveaway, sixty-five thousand wrote in to tell judges why they wanted one. Various groups of merchants came up with more promotion ideas—although many were half-baked—than could possibly be used.

But these promotions were only the frosting to make the public aware of the paper and its contents. In the early years *The Post*'s able and unusual news staff was directed by hard-driving Josiah (Joe) Ward, the city editor. His manner was enough to discourage fainthearted cub reporters from pursuing the profession further. Those who survived his apprenticeship joined a fun-loving legion, many of whom went on to lasting fame in New York, Hollywood, and elsewhere. In this volume there is space to name only a few:

Damon Runyon was a *Post* alumnus. He came up from Pueblo as just another guy named Al, better known for his drinking and practical jokes than reportorial skills. Then he went on to Manhattan, dropped the Al, and won fame and fortune as the chronicler of Broadway guys and dolls.

Courtney Ryley Cooper was taken off *The Post*'s city staff to handle publicity for Tammen's circus. His experiences led to a series of well-remembered circus stories for *The Saturday Evening Post* and other national publications.

Burns Mantle was a *Post* linotype operator until one day he filled in for the regular drama critic, who was ill. His knowledgeable comments won him a writing job, but his talents needed a broader field. He was the dean of New York drama critics for decades.

George Creel, a *Post* reporter, later became Denver police commissioner, the U. S. "information czar" in World War I, and confidant of Presidents.

Gene Fowler, briefly a *Post* writer, turned out a series of books and movie scripts and became one of the nation's great storytellers. His drinking made him one of *The Post*'s more brilliant problem children. Ricketson recalls one day in 1918 when city editor Al Birch sent Fowler to cover a war-bond rally featuring Gen. Leonard Wood. Some sixth sense told Birch, a man of Puritanical bent, that Fowler might not be on the job. Ricketson, who was sent to locate him, went straight to a speakeasy called Leona's and found Fowler in no shape to cover the story. But he had his wits about him and dispatched young Ricketson to the rally to pick up some details. Fowler put Ricketson's facts together with his imagination and wrote a colorful story. Next morning there was a note on the bulletin board signed by Bonfils saying Fowler was being given a five-dollar bonus for a great piece of reporting.

Some time later Birch wangled a five-dollar pay increase for Ricketson, then sternly instructed him to bank the raise and demanded to see his passbook regularly.

Pinky Wayne, who as an "untouchable" had a private office in a building adjoining *The Post,* became accustomed to finding Fowler on Monday mornings sleeping off a bender on the floor, wrapped up in her prize Oriental rug. But she had more than she could take when one Monday she found Fowler asleep under the rug together with his lady of the evening. Pinky strode across the city room into

Bonfils' office and demanded that he come to see what she had to show him. By the time they returned to Pinky's office the girl was gone but Fowler was still trying to wake up. A short time later Fowler left for New York. Pinky, who by then regretted having told on Fowler, helped arrange his passage. In those days two tickets had to be purchased when shipping a body by rail—one for the corpse and the other for an escort—and Fowler headed out of town as the escort to an elderly corpse.

There were others of lesser renown, but no less colorful in their way:

Polly Pry (Mrs. Leonel Ross O'Bryan), one of the earliest of the sob sisters, got onto a story and stirred up one of her subjects so violently that he shot Bonfils. The details belong in another chapter.

Pinky Wayne knew the city she covered so thoroughly that she could telephone a few key women and guarantee a turnout at a City Council hearing or a meeting at the Statehouse if the cause she was pushing seemed to need help.

Diedrich Stackelbeck, who spoke with a thick German accent, knew the burial place of countless political skeletons. He was to play a key role in uncovering the Teapot Dome scandal, the Watergate of its day, and Bonfils' strange role in that drama also will be saved for another chapter.

Pudgy, truculent Joe Ward presided over them and scores of others in their ilk, and still found time to write a scholarly book on the archaeology of the Middle East, *Come with Me into Babylon*— a land he had never seen. Perhaps some of Ward's outlook could be traced to ill-fitting dentures which he had a habit of leaving on the shelf in the men's room. Once a reporter replaced them with a set filched from the city morgue, and Ward suffered with them for several days before the teeth were switched back.

(John Buchanan, a latter-day stalwart, helped play a refined form of this same prank on fellow reporter Zeke Scher while both were at City Hall. When Scher proudly displayed a straw hat which he had picked up at a season's-end bargain sale, Buchanan and Ed Oschmann, who covered City Hall for the *Rocky Mountain News,* hurried to the same store and bought two identical hats, one a size larger and the other a size smaller than Scher's. About the time Scher needed a haircut, they would replace his hat with the small one. After Scher visited his barber, they would slip the large one on the press room hat rack and studiously ignore Scher's befuddled look as the straw slipped down to his ears. And occasionally, in Scher's hearing, Buchanan and Oschmann would hold solemn discussions about a friend suffering from a strange malady, one of whose symptoms being that his head seemed to swell and shrink every few weeks. Scher, incidentally, was so determined to become Denver's best-qualified court reporter that he went to law school at night and was admitted to the bar.)

If newspaper people seem to have a special affinity for practical jokes, it may be the result of the nature of their jobs. Short periods of great pressure and concentration may be followed by times when nothing is happening, and agile minds seek relief from utter boredom.

H. Allen Smith remembers that Ray Humphreys, later an ace investigator for the District Attorney's office, filled in many of his spare hours writing Western and detective stories for the pulp magazines. "I suspect he made more money out of the pulps than he got from *The Post*," Smith says. "It was his fancy to use the names of *Post* guys as characters in his stories. He persecuted two of the top men, Joe McMeel and Joe Cook [later a district court judge], unmercifully—the lowest and crummiest cowboy saddle tramps would turn up in his tales bearing their names, slobbering tobacco juice over their chins and talking like morons." One day H. Allen Smith emerged in one of Humphreys' stories as a wandering Englishman with bowler hat and monocle.

Actually, there was a descendant of a genuine Scottish noble on the staff from 1909 until 1945. He was Captain the Honorable Lyulph Gilchrist Stanley Ogilvy, D.S.O. He signed his name "L. Ogilvy." Tammen hired Ogilvy as a writer for *The Great Divide,* which was being revived as a farm magazine. Ogilvy had been known as Lord, and Tammen decided to use "Lord Ogilvy" as his by-line. Ogilvy was credited with many escapades that never happened, but what really took place is fascinating enough. He is entitled to a chapter and will be accorded one.

As for McMeel, he is well remembered for the time a barkeeper, despairing of ever being paid, agreed to cancel a thirty-two-dollar tab if Joe would promise never to return. McMeel, so the story goes, thought about it for a moment, then said, "Chris, the custom is that when a man settles up his bar bill the house sets one up for him. How about it?"

This is a good place to tell the story of Gene Lindberg's headline. Lindberg joined *The Post* in 1929. This episode took place when Lindberg was working for the *News,* just before he moved to *The Post*. It seems a passion play came to Denver. The men who played

Christ and Judas drank too much and got into a fight, and Christ punched his companion through a plate-glass window. Lindberg covered the story and turned it in with this headline: JESUS SETTLES 2,000-YEAR-OLD GRUDGE. Unfortunately it was not used.

H. Allen Smith is the source of another story in which divine intervention of a sort helped a *Post* reporter named Morris Watson to get a story. A Denver clergyman had vanished with church funds and one of his choir singers, and Watson was ordered to get an interview with the abandoned wife. She, naturally, was reluctant to talk to the press. This is Smith's account:

> He went to her house and knocked on the door a long time and then he heard her. She called out through the door that he should go away and then he heard a noise as if she were dropping to her knees and she began praying. "Oh, Father in Heaven," she pleaded, "must I be punished more and more?" She went on a bit and Morris realized that she was a deeply religious type of woman, and gabby religious to boot. He had, in his youth, held membership in seven different churches and he knew a thing or two about praying. So now he dropped to his knees and in a loud voice began imploring the Creator to interpose on his behalf. "Ask this God-fearing woman," Morris prayed, "to speak her mind about that husband who ran away with the money and Miss Crockett. Ask her to tell you, Lord, how it makes her feel!" And inside the door the deserted woman responded, "Oh Lord, my husband is a dirty wretch. Who should know it better than I? From the day I first met him he was a sneak and a cheat and a dirty wretch. And as for that Crockett whore, if I could get my hands on her she would never look the same in this life." And so Morris got his interview.

It was not a significant story, but it made spicy reading and it sold *The Post*. Although we can disagree today with the standards by which Tammen and Bonfils evaluated news, those standards catapulted their newspaper to a preeminent position. Denverites talked about the dirty wretch who ran off with Miss Crockett and they also talked about unfortunate Zeller the cigar maker whom they read about in this *Post* story:

ZELLER'S MAD PLUNGE
While Intoxicated He Falls From a Bridge

While returning to his home in Globeville at a late hour last night, Andre Zeller, a dissipated cigar maker, was the victim of a peculiar accident, which although it fortunately did not result fatally, may render him a helpless cripple. Zeller spent the evening in Denver with a jovial crowd, and for several hours drank heavily. Some time in the neighborhood of midnight, presumably, he started for his home across the Platte River. He was then practically in a helplessly intoxicated condition. Not sufficiently sober to cross the Twenty-third Street viaduct, which affords ample protection for befuddled pedestrians, Zeller wandered along the bottoms until he came to the Union Pacific bridge. This structure is used for railway traffic alone and is not even safe for foot passengers who are possessed of all their faculties. The bridge rises to a height of fully twenty feet, and its abrupt sides are not protected by guard rails.

Into this dangerous structure the intoxicated cigar maker clambered, and with unsteady steps essayed to cross over the bottoms and the Platte. The attempt was disastrous. With his journey half completed, Zeller met with misfortune. He lost his balance and plunged twenty feet below, where he found a resting place on the frozen ground. The shock of the fall did not inflict any appreciable serious injury, or the slightest bruises. There the unfortunate man lay exposed to the chilly air for many hours. . .

The story then went on to tell how railroad workers found Zeller in the morning, with his limbs frozen. Of such grist was much of the news made. When Miss May, a boardinghouse keeper, wearied of the mortal coil and tried to do away with herself, *The Post* of 1896 felt it of sufficient importance to issue an extra. Displayed prominently atop page 1 is the following:

EXTRA   4:15 o'clock

TIRED OF LIFE

Miss May, a maiden lady, one of three sisters who run a very fashionable boarding house at 32 Lincoln Avenue, attempted suicide this afternoon by taking a dose of arsenic. She was found by one of her sisters, and a messenger was hurriedly sent to police headquarters for assistance. Dr. Jarecki promptly responded and is now working over the unfortunate woman. No reason can be assigned for her rash act.

Even when the news was legitimate, *The Post* treated it as if it were the sensation of the century. Witness this story having to do with *The Post* underbidding rival newspapers for the contract to print legal notices:

THOUSANDS OF DOLLARS SAVED
The Taxes of Denver and Arapahoe County
Can Be Reduced $25,000

Newspaper Trust Must Disgorge

Through the Efforts of *The Post* the People Will Have the Public
Printing Done at 300 Per Cent Less Than It Cost

Last Year—In One Item of County Printing
Alone Something Like $8,000 Is Saved
A Gigantic Conspiracy, Worse Than the Water Monopoly
Receives Its Death Blow—Exorbitant Prices Paid
By Denver and Arapahoe County in the Past

The intrusion of *The Post* into the newspaper field has upset a number of calculations by greedy corporations, who think they possess a divine right to all the privileges attendant on the publication of a newspaper. The newspaper trust of Denver, than which there is nothing extant more grinding or oppressive in commercial life, has received its first fall through the lusty operations of *The Post,* and now the taxpayers may know they are in a fair way to get honest value for their money.

The history of this trust in Arapahoe county is a history of grab and grasp. The regulation arrangement between the two morning (*News* and *Republican*) and one afternoon organ (*Times*) of personal interests, ambitions and vicissitudes has been for one of the organizations to appropriate the advertising for the city, another for the county, while all the advertising for state purposes was given à la dog, as a bone to the afternoon organ which is peculiarly and particularly the mouthpiece of the corporations who hesitate not to defile the machinery of the municipality. . . .

This story appeared under the largest headline on page 1, and only by reading much deeper into it could one learn that *The Post* had contracted to publish legal notices at twenty-one cents per column inch instead of the going rate of sixty-five cents.

Not long ago A. C. Rollnick, wealthy owner of a chain of shoe stores and real estate, recalled his boyhood when he hawked *Denver Post* extras. He was in the sitting room of Green Gables Country Club, whose membership is predominantly Jewish. "Most of us newsboys were from Cheltenham School on West Colfax," he said. "That's the area where Jewish immigrants lived. We had to sell papers to help support our families. After school we'd walk all the way downtown and wait for the final edition to come off the presses. If there was something big going on, a man from *The Post*'s circulation department would come to the school and arrange to get us dismissed early. The principal let us go because he knew we needed the money. We sold the paper for a penny and got to keep half a cent." Rollnick looked around the clubhouse and added, "I would guess that ninety percent of the members of this club sold *The Post* when they were kids. And when we grew up and went into business, we advertised in *The Post*."

Vignette

THE FINE ART OF BOOTJACKING

The expression has failed to make its way into the *Dictionary of American Slang,* but "bootjacking" was a practice developed into a fine art during the heyday of Denver newspaper competition.

To understand bootjacking it is necessary to understand how newspapers were sold during the decade or so after World War I. Radio then was a novelty, television was unknown, and newscasting, when it happened at all, was performed by announcers reading items from the papers. Because newspapers, aside from word of mouth, were the only real source of information about what was going on in the world, they published extras at the least provocation. And newsboys raced

Headlines about a burning oil field, bubonic plague, and a stolen baby helped young newsboys sell *The Post.*

down the streets with them, bellowing the headlines unintelligibly—
to stir the public's curiosity—in the-world-is-coming-to-an-end tones.
(The late Benny Bee, a crackerjack *Denver Post* newsy in his time,
is alleged to have been arrested for disturbing the peace and tran-
quillity of Manhattan when he demonstrated to New York newsies
how papers were sold in Denver.)

It was the public's familiarity with extras that made bootjacking
both possible and profitable.

The practice was encouraged by street circulation supervisors,
particularly on days when early editions had not sold well and too
many copies were being returned for credit. The returns would have
to be thrown away unless they could be bootjacked. So the supervisors would sell them to the boys at a discount, three or four copies
for a cent. After dark the boys would swarm over the downtown area
shouting the headlines—bootjacking stale papers as though they were
the latest extras. The darkness was a necessary accessory.

Nate Gart, who went on to found a chain of sporting-goods stores,
recalls that bootjacking ceased to be profitable if practiced more than
once a week. He had a "corner" at Sixteenth and Larimer streets and
there he learned early that *The Post* was a winner. *The Post* was
easier to sell than any other paper.

"Stick with *The Post*," advised his father, a frequently unemployed
immigrant house painter. "*The Post* means success." Nate gave considerable weight to the advice since his earnings were helping to feed
the family.

An alert newsboy can see, hear, and learn many things. Nate
learned to buy watches and rings from his regular customers when
pawnshops declined to loan what they thought the valuables were
worth. He resold the merchandise at a profit. Eventually he accumulated five hundred dollars, invested it all in a store that shared space
with Sam's Coney Island No. One where the specialty was nickel
hot dogs fried in the window, and put bootjacking behind him forever.

At first Gart couldn't afford to advertise but he did business with
The Post nonetheless. Gart bought scrap newsprint gummed into
pads and it was his stationery until he could afford more pretentious
letterheads.

Today, Gart's son Jerry runs a seven-store chain and Nate spends
much of his time running about in a Cadillac with a push button
that rolls back the top. He is one of *The Post*'s largest advertisers and
no one is twisting his arm.

5

CAPTAIN THE HONORABLE LYULPH GILCHRIST STANLEY OGILVY, D.S.O.

Harry Tammen and Fred Bonfils assembled an unusual crew of men and women to staff their newspaper, but none was more remarkable than the tall, bearded Scot named Lyulph Gilchrist Stanley Ogilvy. For sheer color, not even Tam and Bon could rival him. He was born in London in 1861, the second son of David Graham Drummond Ogilvy, eighth Earl of Airlie, a title that goes back to 1639. Lyulph first visited Colorado with his father in 1889. The earl bought the SLW Ranch in the northeastern corner of the state for the twenty-eight-year-old Lyulph and then went home, leaving his son in charge. A dashing, mischievous *bon vivant,* Lyulph became acquainted with Harry Tammen on his frequent visits to the Windsor Hotel bar. Nearly twenty years later Tammen was down at the railroad yards while his circus loaded up when he discovered Ogilvy working as a Union Pacific watchman for $1.50 a night. Ogilvy was no journalist but Tammen knew he would be useful. He was hired as farm-and-livestock writer. In that new career, which he took on at age forty-eight, Ogilvy did as much as anyone to give the raffish *Post* a certain aura of respectability.

The *Post* published a front-page story in December of 1909 announcing that "Lord Lyulph Ogilvy" had been retained "as a special writer on topics connected with the coming horse show, the stock show and stock interests and ranch and range generally." The association, with time out for service in World War I, lasted until 1945, when he retired at age eighty-three because of failing health. He died in Boulder, Colorado, two years later.

Being the second son Ogilvy had no title but he was widely known as Duke and Lord since few Americans could pronounce Lyulph. Tammen selected "Lord Ogilvy" for his by-line and he provided a steady stream of reportage and comment on such subjects as the importance of bloodlines in livestock breeding, irrigation, trends in

Lord Ogilvy, a dashing *bon vivant* who as farm writer brought the raffish *Post* a certain respectability.

the wheat and cattle market, nematodes that bored into sugar beets, the price of farmland, and the vagaries of equine temperament. Colorado's economy, founded on mining, was just beginning to depend more heavily on agriculture and Ogilvy played no small part in furthering the process, first with the weekly *Great Divide,* and later in the columns of *The Post.* Because of his aristocratic connections, Denver hostesses would have liked to rope him in but he studiously avoided them. He once explained that he had a certain amount of the social life in his youth, hadn't cared much for it, and wasn't going to fool with the American brand.

Lord Ogilvy was a man of rare independence who genuinely liked people and probably was as widely known as any member of *The Post* staff. Yet he lived alone much of his life. His son, Jack, now retired after many years as a distinguished professor of English at the University of Colorado, says of Ogilvy's habits, "I rather think he liked solitude, but whether he did or not, he could certainly stand more of it than most people."

Apparently Ogilvy, who was about 6 feet 2 inches tall, had a real affection for the chunky Tammen. With Bonfils, whom he knew for much longer and regarded with a clinical interest, he reached an accommodation. Ogilvy once told his son, "Bon has flaps which automatically come down and close his ears when anyone says something he doesn't want to hear. He seems to be totally incapable of grasping anyone's view if it conflicts with his own." But if someone were to ask him how he could have anything to do with a rascal like Bonfils, he was likely to say, "I like him just as I do you, old man—in spite of his faults." Ogilvy was demonstrating his well-developed Scottish sense of integrity. He enjoyed leaving the questioner with the problem of making what he could of this reply.

Ogilvy brought no formal agricultural training to his career as a writer. But he had acquired an enormous fund of practical knowledge, beginning with the days he spent with the caretakers of the family estate in Scotland, a spread that included two castles eleven miles apart and the land in between. He learned much by observation. While farming near Greeley, he liked to sit around a harness shop in winter and listen to his neighbors talk about crops and dry-land farming methods. He also read voraciously and many times demonstrated an uncanny skill in judging horses and other livestock. One story is that on a trip back home in 1924 his nephew, the then Earl of Airlie, asked him to look over the stables and pick a horse to be entered in the Grand National at Aintree. Lord Ogilvy selected a rawboned horse named Master Robert which was being used for plowing. The earl reluctantly had Master Robert groomed for the race, which of course he won. But all this came after Lord Ogilvy settled down. His youth is much more exciting. Legends clustered around Ogilvy the way barnacles attach themselves to a ship's hull. He, like Tammen and Bonfils, was credited with episodes which may or may not have taken place, although they were of an altogether different nature. Jack Ogilvy, who was very fond of his father and got to know him well, is the source of much of the material in this chapter separating fact from legend.

While he was operating the SLW ranch soon after his arrival in Colorado, Ogilvy and a partner contracted to dig an irrigation ditch near Fort Morgan. Their workmen soon uncovered a series of springs that turned the area into a quagmire. The horse-drawn scoops used for earth moving in those days bogged down and became useless. Ogilvy bought a heavy steam tractor and used the belt drive for power, but it was a slow process and his fortune suffered reverses from which it never fully recovered. This tractor was responsible for an inaccurate but widely repeated story.

One night, so the story goes, Ogilvy as an alcoholic prank stole a steamroller from the Denver street-maintenance department and drove it to Fort Morgan, wreaking havoc on bridges along the way. This would have been a pretty good trick since the distance from Denver to Fort Morgan by today's interstate highway is more than eighty miles, and it probably was a much longer trip when roads meandered over the countryside. Jack Ogilvy says the steamroller of the story in reality was the steam tractor which his father had brought for the ditch-building contract, and he drove it at night to keep from spooking teams off the road. But the bridges did take a beating. Lord Ogilvy observed that they needed rebuilding anyway.

There was a certain abandon to Lord Ogilvy's escapades, particularly where horses were involved and especially when he mixed horses with Scotch. Jack Ogilvy says it has been pretty well authenticated that his father during his bachelor days made a habit of bringing horses into the house. "One explanation for this behavior may be the cruel attacks of homesickness from which most Britishers suffered," Jack writes, without making clear how a horse in the house mitigated those pangs.

"Another may have been that he was drunk. He was certainly drunk when he decided to take his racehorse Trooper upstairs and put him to bed. If the story is true, he did get the horse upstairs and subsequently down again. Whether he actually got him to bed is not recorded. Another of L. Ogilvy's experiments involved getting a horse to jump a ditch while pulling a buckboard. It ended in disaster for the horse, the buckboard, and L. Ogilvy. It seems strange that one so fond of horses should attempt something in which the horse was almost bound to be hurt, but I suppose that one who has no respect for his own neck can hardly be expected to be careful of other people's. Many of these events displayed the perverted ingenuity of the sophomore. For example, his releasing a number of cockerels that were just learning to crow, in the Windsor Hotel at five in the morning. Another feat connected with the Windsor Hotel was his driving two ponies in tandem into the lobby." It is no wonder that Tammen remembered him.

Lord Ogilvy was a skilled horseman who amazed cowboys by riding broncos and using the flat English saddles. Once he encountered an unusually persistent bucker. Lord Ogilvy decided to ride him every day for a month and then give up if he had not cured the horse of bucking. After the first week his first thought when he awoke was "I've got to ride that blasted horse again." After three weeks it was the horse that gave up to become a fairly decent mount. In time Ogilvy sold the horse and it quickly resumed its bucking habits. The horse then was sold to Buffalo Bill for his Wild West Show. He became a very reliable performer which could be counted on to buck at every performance. One day Ogilvy asked a man who had worked for the show about the horse. "How did you get to know him?" the man wanted to know."

"Oh," Ogilvy replied, "I owned him for a while. I used to ride him in a flat saddle." Jack Ogilvy recalls that his father said, "The man looked at me as if he had met Ananias and Sapphira and Baron Munchausen all rolled into one."

After the unfortunate contracting experience Lord Ogilvy sold the SLW ranch and moved to a smaller farm north of Greeley. When the Spanish-American War broke out in 1898 Ogilvy, although still a British citizen, enlisted with what was known as Company D, a cavalry outfit, in Greeley. The unit was moved to Camp Adams, near what is now Denver's City Park, for training. There Ogilvy astonished his comrades by breaking the ice on the horse trough every morning to bathe.

(Jack Ogilvy remembers an old-timer living on the plains east of Greeley who told him: "When we learned that this English dude Ogilvy was coming to stay with us for the roundup, we couldn't wait for a chance to play tricks on him. Well, he turned up with another man. First thing next morning the other fellow went out and smashed the ice on our pond with a fence post, and then Ogilvy came out and took a bath in the pond. After that we were afraid to try any tricks on him.")

Convinced Company D would never see action, Ogilvy and half the members of the outfit transferred to Torrey's Rough Riders. Soon afterward Company D was shipped to the Philippines and engaged in some spirited battles with the Insurrectionists. Torrey's Rough Riders went to Florida to fight mosquitoes, chiggers, and boredom with an occasional battle against the natives when Ogilvy thought they were being overly unkind toward the Negroes.

Before Ogilvy could be mustered out, Britain became embroiled in the Boer War. Lord Ogilvy sold his Greeley ranch and signed to escort a shipload of mules from New Orleans to the British forces in South Africa. Accounts vary as to whether he had 200, 700, or 1,190 mules in his care. In any event he delivered most of them safely after a thirty-two-day voyage, then enlisted with a cavalry unit called Braban's Horse. The outfit was under fire 180 days in a year's time. Ogilvy was awarded the Distinguished Service Order for rescuing some wounded under fire, was promoted to captain, and eventually was shot through the shoulder and invalided out of service.

Ogilvy regarded war as something of a game, as indicated by this anecdote: Once, when required to carry a message through an area under Boer rifle fire, he bet another officer five pounds that he would make it, figuring he would never miss the money if he lost the wager. Ogilvy mounted an especially fast horse and got him up to full speed before reaching the exposed area. The Boer riflemen, who were accustomed to slower horses, found themselves firing behind the rider all the way.

Back home, he decided it was time to settle down. In 1902, at age forty-one, he married Edith Gertrude Boothroyd of Loveland, Colorado, and took her to live on another farm he had bought a few miles south of Greeley. By this time he had quit drinking, announcing he had already consumed his share of the world's whiskey. Two children were born, Jack, whose full name is John David Angus Ogilvy, and Blanche Edith Maude Ogilvy. Some sources say Ogilvy was cut off without a cent for marrying a commoner, but Jack calls this nonsense. His bride was warmly received when Lord Ogilvy took her to meet his relatives, including his niece, Mrs. Winston Churchill. However, by the time of the marriage most of Ogilvy's money was gone. His wife's fragile health was a further drain on his funds. By 1907 Ogilvy sold the farm in order to pay doctor bills and moved his family to Denver. Mrs. Ogilvy died the following year and the children went to live with her mother. For a while Ogilvy was reduced to working as a railroad watchman, and that's when his path crossed Tammen's again. After Ogilvy went to work for *The Post* he bought some land just off Broadway in South Denver, built a small house, and lived there alone. He called the property Hardscrabble and conducted some haphazard experiments in growing alfalfa and various grasses and in breeding hens, hardly his favorite form of livestock but all he had room for.

At *The Post* Ogilvy, who was called Captain by his coworkers, wrote his copy in an almost illegible form of semiprint with a soft pencil. These pothooks, as he called them, were set into type by the one linotype operator who could decipher them. For a while Ogilvy attempted to use a typewriter, but that didn't prove to be much of an improvement. Jim Hale, who presided over the copydesk before he became city editor, was one of the few men who could decipher Ogilvy's writing. One day when Hale was gone, a young employee named Elvon Howe drew Ogilvy's copy and was defeated by a passage that appeared particularly mangled. In some fear and awe, Howe took the copy to Ogilvy for an interpretation. Howe said the old man gave him a look that implied the village idiot should have been able to read the passage, but interpreted it nonetheless. "I know the look well," Jack Ogilvy explains. "It made him look like a wounded eagle. I was almost twenty years old before I realized that it meant he was apologetic."

One year at the Stock Show a Missouri cattleman exhibited several carloads of steers that had been fattened on special feed which he was marketing. Lord Ogilvy wrote that they were good steers but their fat was too soft as a result of excessive amounts of molasses in the ration. After the story appeared the feeder stormed into *The Post*'s offices, canceled his advertising, and demanded Ogilvy's scalp. Lord Ogilvy stood by his judgment but was embarrassed for *The Post* and offered to resign. "Resign, hell," said William C. Shepherd, by then the managing editor, "write the facts as you see them." And that's the way Ogilvy reported the farm news. Meanwhile, in retaliation for the feeder's effrontery, Shepherd ordered that the man's name was never to appear in *The Post.*

Arbitrary banishment from *The Post*'s pages was a practice begun years earlier by Bonfils. Critics of Bonfils or his paper angered him and he would tell his editors, "He doesn't like us. If I were you, I wouldn't run his name in our paper anymore."

When World War I broke out in 1914 Ogilvy resigned and hustled off to Britain to enlist in the Army. He was then fifty-three, too old for the front. The Army Service Corps put him in charge of a training depot. Britain's damp weather aggravated his rheumatism. Ogilvy took a discharge in 1916 and returned to *The Post.*

"In his youth, L. Ogilvy was a snappy dresser, but that was before I made his acquaintance," his son says. "As one gets older, he worries less and less about appearances as a rule, and if he has no woman to keep him in order, as L. O. did not after 1908, he is likely to become downright careless. When I knew him, only traces of former glory remained. He was the only man I knew who owned three dress suits (by Mortimer, *the* tailor for dress clothes). He was vague as to how he had acquired so many. I still have some rather striking vests he wore, one in Ogilvy tartan, another in bright yellow-and-red stripes.

"But his uniform at *The Post* consisted of a blue work shirt two inches too large in the neck—he hated tight clothes—with a World War I surplus olive-drab tie which extended about four inches below the four-in-hand knot. He had several suits by Scott of Blairgowrie, but since he insisted on looseness and filled his pockets with pipes, tobacco pouches, and what-have-you, the fact that they were tailored could easily escape the uninitiated. Being good British cloth, the suits lasted almost indefinitely. When they finally wore out, he found a tailor in Denver to make him suits in a rather similar style.

"Despite the fact that pigskin braces had no elasticity and therefore took off buttons as fast as one could sew them on, he insisted on wearing them, I suppose because he liked good leather. To ease the strain on the buttons he wore the braces very slack; seen from the rear his hindquarters rather resembled those of an elephant, which finds it comfortable to wear his skin loose.

"L. O. wore cotton work socks and high brown shoes, laced about halfway up. Coupled with his beard, unfashionable in those days, this ensemble gave him an unusual appearance, even a startling one to those who met him for the first time. After people got to know him, they more or less forgot about his appearance, partly because of his complete unselfconsciousness. If one worries about his dress, he somehow manages to call attention to it; if he doesn't think about it, others don't pay it much attention either."

One of those who did pay attention was Joy Swift, a pretty young artist whose job it was to select photographs and lay them out for the Sunday rotogravure picture section. Joy took a daughterlike interest in Ogilvy's appearance and fought a long and losing battle to get him to lace up his shoes and look at least halfway presentable.

Tammen's will left Lord Ogilvy $2,500, which he invested in a Model T Ford coupe, his first car. Ever since, the Ogilvy family car was called "HH," for H. H. Tammen, followed by a serial number. The man who was so skilled in handling horses never really felt at ease driving an automobile, perhaps because he expected the vehicle to have horse sense. "L. O. felt a car ought to know enough to stay on the road, so that riding along with him at thirty or forty miles an hour while he studied the crops and livestock on both sides of the road was a bit nerve-wracking," Jack recalls. "Also, he had been used to taking off across country in his buckboard and steering by the stars, and he preferred to follow this method with the car because we saw more country that way than by following the main roads." When Ford brought out the Model A, Lord Ogilvy refused to struggle with the gearshift lever and gave up driving.

In 1922 Ogilvy bought a part of his father-in-law's farm on the Big Thompson River near Loveland, Colorado, so he could go back to raising horses and cattle. He also negotiated the first three-day workweek agreement at *The Post*. Ogilvy told Shepherd that since he could turn out enough copy for the week in three days at the office, he'd like to spend Thursday-to-Sunday weekends at his country place.

Shepherd agreed in deference to the farm editor's long service, and from then on Ogilvy spent most of his time in the country except for Stock Show week in January. Stock Show exhibitors were Ogilvy's friends and he was interested in the animals they showed. Besides, the show was in his field of special knowledge and he felt it his duty to cover it thoroughly. Even young reporters today consider the Stock Show no picnic, for the barns are drafty and dusty and the coldest weather of the winter seems to settle on Denver the week the stockmen are in town. Ogilvy insisted on covering the show even in his declining years and as a result spent much time in a hospital each winter.

In the depths of the Depression *The Post* cut the pay of many employees. One day Shepherd called Ogilvy to his desk and told him his salary had been reduced from fifty dollars a week to thirty-five dollars. Apparently Ogilvy was not surprised. In his most courtly manner, which he often used as a wall of glass between himself and people he didn't like, Ogilvy said, "Thank you, Mr. Shepherd."

Shepherd suspected sarcasm and said so.

"Oh," Ogilvy replied, "I wasn't thanking you for the cut. I was thanking you for telling me."

When Lord Ogilvy died in a Boulder nursing home in 1947, something of *The Post* died with him. His service with the paper had covered thirty-six years. His acquaintances had ranged from British noblemen to raunchy Colorado cowboys. If he was inclined to cultivate any group, it was the first-class workmen in any field—bankers, con men, and even journalists. He had the Victorian habit of respecting the best, and comparing his own achievements with theirs.

THE BROTHERS LEVAND

Bonfils and Tammen were among the sharpest operators in the history of American journalism but it took a former newsboy to show them little tricks that saved them many dollars. His name was Louis (Louie) Levand, one of three brothers associated with *The Post* for a quarter-century before they bought their own newspaper.

Louie Levand knew nothing about publishing when he went to work for *The Post* not long after Bonfils and Tammen purchased it. But he had grown up among people who made a virtue of frugality. Jewish immigrants struggled to save enough to buy a horse and wagon so they could go into business for themselves as junk, scrap-metal and old-rag collectors. There was money to be made in salvaging what the profligate threw away. This is the lesson Levand taught Bonfils and Tammen. He showed them there was a market for steel drums that had contained printing ink, wooden boxes that transported stereotype mats, the outworn rubber rollers from the presses, and the exhausted metal from typesetting machines. You didn't throw away this stuff nor did you sell it to the first junk collector who drove up the alley. You stockpiled it until the market was right and then advertised for competitive bids. You didn't have to pay to have old newspapers hauled away; they could be sold by the ton. Newsprint from the ends of rolls also could be sold as scrap, but it brought more money when it was cut and gummed into pads.

Bonfils and Tammen respected such astuteness. Soon Levand was named assistant to the publisher, in which his duties were indeterminate. Mostly, he looked after things. He did favors for hundreds of Denverites and they felt obligated to do business with him. Louie was the man to see if you wanted a job selling popcorn at the *Post*-owned Empress Theatre or peanuts at the *Post*-sponsored semipro baseball tournament. If you had an overgrown son who needed work, Louie might arrange to have him put on the police force. If you had a daughter looking for a job, chances were that Louie could make a phone call and get her placed as a salesclerk at the Golden Eagle department store.

Bonfils and Tammen used Levand to search out details about real estate they were interested in, rustle up newsprint or other supplies when they were scarce, crack a potential advertiser's hostility. Once in New York Levand couldn't even get in to see the advertising director of a large oil firm until the executive vice-president heard his name and recalled that Louie had helped straighten out an inequitable tax assessment for his father. Levand came out of that meeting with a substantial advertising contract.

But there was another side of Louis Levand. His skills as a fixer-upper and his sharp business practices inevitably made enemies. He brought tales back to Bonfils and the pressure he put on businessmen to buy stationery supplies or advertising from *The Post* contributed to its unsavory reputation.

Louie had three brothers and two of them worked for *The Post*. Max Levand was in the business office and John was known as "King of the Newsies" when he was circulation manager. Max left *The Post* in 1922 to buy the Casper (Wyoming) *Herald*. Three years later he sold it to buy the St. Joseph (Missouri) *Gazette,* where John joined him. All three brothers pooled resources to buy the Wichita (Kansas) *Beacon* in 1928. Louie was publisher, Max the president, and John the circulation director.

There were many brother acts in an organization as large as *The Post*. Among the more notable were the Days—Eddie Day, hired away from the *News* to become managing editor in 1932, and Johnny Day, who came up through the ranks to become a movie-type city editor. They worked together at *The Post* until Johnny died in 1933. Eddie's son, Edward C. Day, Jr., worked in the *News* sports department and the Denver *Catholic Register* while going to law school. He was elected to the Colorado Supreme Court in 1956 and continues to serve. Angelo and Fred O'Dorisio were brothers who worked side by side for some twenty years in the editorial art department until Angie died in 1971. Orin and Ira Sealy served even longer as photographers. But no three brothers left a more lasting imprint on *The Post* than the Levands.

6

TWO-FISTED EDITORS

In the early days of America, newspapermen occasionally had to defend their editorial positions with fists or firearms. By the time Bonfils and Tammen came along such frontier ebullience was largely a memory. Yet the partners soon became embroiled in controversies that led to at least one fight in the streets, threats from armed enemies, and a shooting affray in their Red Room office in which they were seriously wounded. This last encounter, incredibly, involved a certified cannibal, a lionhearted sob sister, two hung juries in what had appeared to be a cut-and dried case, a grand-jury investigation, and ultimately a bribery conviction. Bonfils and Tammen, who started as the innocent aggrieved in this instance, abruptly inherited the villain roles to go along with their gunshot wounds.

The episode begins with Alferd Packer, onetime Army scout and mountain guide, whose misfortunes provided one of the more colorful chapters in Colorado history. In the fall of 1873 Packer was hired to guide a party of prospectors from Provo, Utah, to the Los Pinos Indian Agency in the south-central Colorado Rockies, near where gold had been found. Snow fell earlier than expected and Packer lost his way. The party ran out of food. Packer was the only survivor. He walked into the Indian Agency on April 16, 1874, telling a story of hardship, hunger, and death. Investigators who made their way to Packer's camp found unmistakable evidence of cannibalism. It was never made clear whether Packer had killed his companions, whether they had killed each other or simply had died, but Packer confessed he had lived off their flesh. He was sentenced to be hanged. Granted a second trial by a higher court, he was given forty years in the state prison for manslaughter.

Packer had served about fifteen years of his term when Bonfils and Tammen, shortly after they acquired *The Post,* took on his freedom as one of their campaigns. Polly Pry was assigned to write a series of tear-jerking stories about the kindly old man, unjustly imprisoned, who was living out his life behind bars in Canon City. Early in January, 1900, Polly was approached by a well-known hustler, C. M. Fegen-Bush, who said an attorney named William W. Anderson wanted to talk to her about Packer. As it turned out, Fegen-Bush's angle was that he was planning to start a tobacco stand and Packer would make a first-rate attraction if he could be freed and put in charge of it. Anderson told Polly he had an idea for getting Packer sprung and wanted to talk to Bonfils and Tammen.

Polly arranged the meeting. Anderson explained that Packer's trials had been held in territorial courts although the crime allegedly had been committed on an Indian reservation, which was under federal jurisdiction. He contended Packer could seek his freedom on this technicality. Bonfils replied that the idea was not new, but that he wanted to confer with *The Post*'s attorneys before authorizing Anderson to begin legal action at *Post* expense. Another meeting was set up for the following morning.

Anderson did not keep that appointment. He took the overnight train to Canon City. According to later testimony, he had gone to the penitentiary to inquire about buying some bricks and in the course of his visit asked to see Packer. Anderson told Packer he was a director of *The Denver Post,* promised to see what could be done about getting him released, and accepted twenty-five dollars from Packer as a "docket fee."

Bonfils was furious when he heard about this. He summoned Anderson to the Red Room and, in the presence of Tammen and Polly Pry, harsh words were exchanged. Tammen accused Anderson of going back on his word and shouted, "You are a cheapskate and a liar and I want nothing more to do with you." Bonfils added, "They tried to disbar you for swindling a poor widow out of four hundred and twelve dollars, and *The Post* will see to it that you are disbarred for bunkoing Packer out of the twenty-five dollars."

Anderson, rising from his chair, retorted, "I don't allow any man to talk to me that way."

There is disagreement as to what happened next. Bonfils testified that he thought Anderson was reaching for a pistol and struck the attorney twice with his fist. Anderson said Bonfils leapt at him, grabbed him around the head, and punched his face repeatedly.

Whatever the case, Polly Pry cried, "Gentlemen, gentlemen. Stop it," and succeeded in halting the hostilities for the moment.

Anderson picked up his hat and started out of the office. Tammen sped his departure with "Now, damn you, get out and never come in here again."

Bonfils trailed Anderson out of the office. "I followed him through the hall to the outer door," he testified in court. "As I opened the door Anderson took two long steps into the outer hall, put his right hand in his overcoat pocket, drew a gun, and fired point-blank at me."

Anderson told a different version in an interview published in *The Denver Republican* the day after the shooting: "I sat there with my legs crossed and my hat in my hands, with no more idea that I was to be attacked than you have that I am going to strike you in the face this minute. Tammen called me a vile name, and I said, 'Look here, Tammen, I won't allow you to talk to me like that.' With that Bonfils caught me around the neck with his arm, getting my head in chancery, and began smashing me in the face. I could not do a thing. Then he and Tammen began pushing and shoving me toward the door. Bonfils kicked me then, and, as I reached the door, he kicked me into the hall. That was one kick too much, and I let him have it. Then I went after Tammen. It was funny to hear him roar."

Anderson had a five-shot, .38-caliber revolver concealed in his overcoat pocket. He fired twice at Bonfils. One bullet entered the left side of his chest near the nipple and coursed through the chest cavity to the right side. The second entered the right shoulder blade, ranging down into the chest. As Bonfils fell, critically wounded, Anderson took after Tammen.

Meanwhile, Polly ran to the window, screaming for help. This is her testimony as to what happened next: "I saw Anderson running down the room. Mr. Tammen raised his hand as if to ward off a blow. Anderson was a few feet away, two or three feet. Anderson was in front of Bonfils' desk. I hadn't moved from the window. Anderson shot Mr. Tammen twice. At the first shot I ran. Mr. Tammen had fallen on his side over the valise. One arm was up. Anderson leaned over and shot at him again. I ran, as I said, between them and threw my hands up, like this [she faced the jury and illustrated the action]. I said: 'For God's sake, Anderson, don't shoot again, please don't.' Anderson had his revolver pointed at Tammen. All this time I was standing in front, following with my body the motions of the revolver, imploring Anderson not to shoot. . . . Then he said, 'I'll call the police.' I said: 'Don't call the police, call a doctor. You've done murder enough.' I looked up; the door was crowded with our men employees of *The Post*. I examined Mr. Tammen, found where he was shot and left him in the hands of our

Sob sister Polly Pry: Her interest in freeing a cannibal from prison led to the near-fatal shooting of Bonfils and Tammen. (L. A. Cantwell Collection)

proof readers. I went to go to Mr. Bonfils. Just as I got to the hall I saw Anderson and shouted out: 'Don't let that man go—he's shot Bonfils and Tammen.' None of them heeded me; they let him go."

Tammen had been shot in the left arm, shattering the bone, and in the left shoulder. The second bullet went through the body, but his wounds were not as serious as those of Bonfils.

A doctor was summoned. Meanwhile Anderson went to the offices of a physician nearby to have facial cuts and bruises treated. Police officers found him there a short time later. Anderson surrendered his pistol, which still had one live cartridge and four empty shells in it, and accompanied the officers to headquarters. The shooting had occurred too late for *The Post*'s editions. The following day, January 14, it reported the attack on its owners in a remarkably restrained manner beginning with a two-column story on the left side of page 1:

THE SHOOTING OF
MESSRS. BONFILS AND TAMMEN

A Plain, Straightforward Story
of the Attempt of
W. W. Anderson to Assassinate
the Owners of *The Post*

HE CAME TO THE OFFICE WITH
A PISTOL IN HIS POCKET

Both Men Were Twice Shot, Mr. Tammen
Seriously and Mr. Bonfils
Dangerously Wounded

The Trouble Grew Out of Anderson's Misrepresentations to Alferd Packer, Whose Pardon *The Post* Has Been Attempting To Secure, That He Was a Director in This Paper and Had Full Authority From It to Act as Packer's Attorney and Work for His Release—When Rebuked He Attempted to Strike Mr. Bonfils and the Tragedy Was the Result—Judge Butler Allowed Anderson to Give Bail and He Was Released—Condition of the Wounded Men.

At noon yesterday a brutal attempt to assassinate Frederick G. Bonfils and H. H. Tammen was made by W. W. Anderson, a lawyer, in the office of *The Post*. At 9 o'clock last evening, when one or both men were in a critical condition, when it was beyond human divination whether they would ever recover and the chances of Mr. Bonfils were balanced to a hair, Judge Butler, behind closed doors at The Denver Athletic Club, admitted the would-be assassin to

The Post reported the shooting of Bonfils and Tammen in their office in 1900 with remarkable typographical restraint.

bail in the sum of $10,000, against the vehement protest of the district attorney.

The city had been in a fever heat of excitement all day. The most wild and improbable rumors had floated about on the wings of the wind, to be eagerly snapped up and excitedly discussed, but an array of facts stand out conspicuously. Anderson's name had not been mentioned in the columns of *The Post,* either directly or indirectly. There had been no misunderstanding between Anderson and the owners of *The Post* until Anderson broke faith with them. . . .

Indeed there had been great excitement in Denver. Many, particularly those who had felt *The Post*'s lash, were not in the least sorry for its owners. *The Post's* pointed reference to the fact that Anderson had not been mentioned in its columns would indicate that the editors were aware that some of their stories well might invite violence. A number of leading citizens including F. E. Edbrooke, the rifle-toting architect who had been criticized by *The Post,* hurried to the police station to offer bond for Anderson. The *Rocky Mountain News,* which had been taking its lumps from *The Post* in their circulation battle, became so disturbed by public reaction to the shooting that it was moved to publish a generous and sobering editorial, portions of which are quoted below:

> One of the developments of the Anderson shooting is startling. Almost immediately after its occurrence there was, so far as words went, a strong approval of the act. Scores went to the police station to speak their sympathy to Anderson and give him assurance of support. This, too, without knowledge of all the circumstances which led to the tragedy. It caused Anderson to assume the demeanor of a stage hero and set thoughtful people to wondering whether murder was an approved method with the Denver public for settling personal differences.
>
> Messrs. Bonfils and Tammen publish a newspaper that has established strong public support. It has acquired a large circulation under their management, and its advertising patronage is from the best of Denver merchants and is considerably more than that enjoyed by its evening competitor. It will not do to say, as some malicious hint, that both circulation and advertising has been acquired by terrorizing the public—readers and merchants. If it could be true, it would be a poor compliment, indeed, to the intelligence and independence of Denver and Colorado people.
>
> The fact is, Bonfils and Tammen have made *The Post* a very readable paper. It is wide-awake, and, typographically, a model after which other papers might profitably pattern. It has been aggressive. Here one commences to see the trouble. Its aggressiveness has made it and its publishers enemies. Was it commendable aggression? That will be referred to a little later. . . .

The political fights that Bonfils and Tammen waged were invariably on the side of the people. They were against the greed of Denver corporations, intrenched and fortified with years of uninterrupted sway and the enjoyment of phenomenal profits wrung from a bound and helpless people.

Let the public calmly review these struggles and pass in array the measures and men against and for whom they fought. Stand them out boldly, so that they will cut a cloudless mental vision and note them on memory's pages—public officials who had betrayed in vital public measure their constituencies; public officials who were pledged in honor to resist certain corporate aggressions, and who gave evidence of casting honor aside to accept a corporation's dirty bribes; public officials who were plainly guilty of duplicity and falsehood; public officials who bore the marked visage of the hypocrite and assumed the mask of virtue with which to grossly betray the public; corporations who, with unblushing effrontery, violated contracts, made the public subjects of their extortions; that corrupted electors and hesitated at no crime to carry out their conspiracies— every one of them against the public welfare and for their own lawless enrichment. These were the fights they made, and the *News* wishes this, its opinion, to be carried to them on their beds of suffering—to one of them who, the *News* fears, is on his bed of death.

The editor who thus fights cannot but make enemies—many enemies, of the strong and influential. These enemies will be found in banks, in brokers' officers, in the rooms of directors. Their influence in manifold and far-reaching. Of such a man they speak with bitterness. Almost praying that their prophecies will be realized, they mutter, "Some one will kill that fellow yet." . . .

Of Bonfils and Tammen this can be said: They spurned bribes that were offered. They would not sell their columns for corporation gold. Does anybody doubt—nobody who knows the facts can—that their support would have been bought over to corporations' schemes, that their opposition might be silenced, if they were in the bribe-givers' market? Those for whom they had fought had no bribes to give, they were helpless, even, to help themselves without the support of such fearless men as the stricken publishers.

May not this account in a large part at least for the startling and shameful exhibition of gladness at the tragedy? The hero they would lionize presents a pitiful sight as he, under pretext of representing *The Post,* induces the prisoner Packer to pay him $25 of his savings from the monthly pension which the government pays the once brave and loyal Army guide and scout. Going to an interview at which he had no reason to anticipate violence, if he could explain the questionable episode, he arms himself, and when whatever violence there was is ended, he shoots one of his victims down in the hallway and enters a room and pursues the other into a corner, and shoots him down and would have wounded him further but for the brave resistance of a woman.

Bonfils and Tammen have many faults. They have not published an ideal paper. They in many instances violate accepted newspaper ethics. But they are brave men, and in public matters stood mainly for the right. There are many worse men than they who commanded the smiles and approvals of those who rejoice at their misfortunes. They are generous of heart, impulsive and irascible. Many men can be better spared from the community than they.

Such comment was most welcome and perhaps it was not entirely coincidental that later that year *The Post* endorsed Thomas M. Patterson, editor of the *News,* for United States senator. (The editorial supporting Patterson was warmly laudatory. However, he was well qualified, experienced in politics, had the backing of the Democratic party, and no doubt would have been elected without *Post* support. One of his rivals was Thomas J. O'Donnell, who shortly would have his own clashes with *The Post*. The Patterson-*Post* détente was brief, and their sensational falling-out will be related later in this chapter.)

Elsewhere, much of the press regarded the shooting as something of a joke. Said the *Washington Post:* "In the future the proprietors of *The Denver Evening Post* will keep an eye on those gentlemen who practice law with a revolver." The Santa Fe *New Mexican* said: *"The Denver Post* certainly secured a scoop upon its contemporaries last Saturday when it had a serious shooting affair in its own office. Had not the bullets taken effect its jealous rivals would have been pretty apt to call the affair a fake." The Grand Junction (Colorado) *Star,* no longer in business: "Bonfils and Tammen have been accused of several bad things, but it is evident they don't carry guns." The Baltimore *American:* "If the people of Denver keep on shooting editors between meals, that health resort will not be very popular with newspaper men." The Kansas City *Times:* "That Denver lawyer who tried to slaughter all the proprietors of a newspaper with one revolver found, like the British South African army, that his artillery was insufficient to carry out the extermination contract. If he wanted to stop the publication of the paper he should have demolished the linotype machines and presses with dynamite and then destroyed the printers with a Maxim."

Fortunately for Bonfils and Tammen, infection, which was a major problem with gunshot wounds, did not set in. One of the bullets was removed from Bonfils' side. The other was left in his body. Neither had damaged vital organs. It was touch and go for a while, but in three weeks Bonfils was able to return to his desk, although complete recovery took many months. Tammen's shattered arm was placed in a cast and he, too, was soon back at work.

Anderson was charged with two counts of "assault with intent to commit murder," one against Tammen, the other against Bonfils. It was decided to try the cases separately. The assault on Tammen was set for trial first, in April, three months after the incident. Although it was evident that Anderson's version of events in the Red Room would be challenged by the three other participants—Bonfils, Tammen, and Polly Pry—his attorney chose to plead justifiable self-defense. In his opening statement the defense attorney charged that Bonfils and Tammen together had attacked Anderson in their office, striking him repeatedly.

"There were a number of them, not the two blows the prosecution talks about," the attorney told the jury. "Tammen struck and split his ear open. Blood poured in rivulets down his face. His shirt was torn and his face was bruised and scratched by those blows. That was the aggression. Anderson was dazed, bloody, and beaten when they called him a cur and ordered him out. They hurled him into the hall, and Bonfils let loose of him and kicked him in the rear.

"Anderson put back his hand and it fell on his gun. He had forgotten that he had it. If he could be beaten without cause like that and kicked and driven like some common hound, it was natural that he should think of the gun. . . . Put yourself in Anderson's place and see what you would have done. What was the limit and why was Anderson called there? Was it not natural with the entire force of employees in the building that Anderson should think that they were liable to murder him?"

Most of the twelve good men and true, described in a *Post* headline as "An Absolutely Good Jury Without Suggestions From Anybody," shared the attorney's fears. Following a week-long trial the first ballot was 10 to 2 for conviction. Thereafter the jury was deadlocked 6 to 6. Following a day and a half of fruitless deliberations the foreman reported that a decision was impossible. The judge agreed and dismissed the jurors.

The Post's editorial comment was uncharacteristically judicious:

> *The Post* has no criticism to pass upon the members of the jury in the Anderson case; it does not seek to impugn their motives, to cast aspersions upon their honesty or to insinuate that they or any of them may have been biased. Everyone on the jury is well known in the community. They are, with a single exception, long-time residents and all men of substance and standing. Nevertheless, had the

circumstances been precisely the same in every respect except the vital one that the shooting occurred in a lawyer's, a doctor's or a merchant's office instead of a newspaper office, is there any doubt, with the array of invincible facts presented during the past week, what the verdict would have been, either from the small jury in the courtroom or the much larger jury on the outside, which forms what is known as public opinion? We think not.

The result at the West Side Courtroom yesterday is not alone of individual importance and significance to the proprietors of *The Post*. It was well and adequately named in the legal indictment as The People against William W. Anderson. The offense committed was not alone against the two individuals who were shot, but against every peaceable and law abiding citizen in the county and state. If there were outrage committed, it was not alone upon its immediate victims, but upon the peace and dignity of the commonwealth. If one man is outraged today and the crime go unpunished, some other inoffensive citizen may have his turn tomorrow. Diffused in widening ripples such conditions degenerate into anarchy. Hence it is that the outrage from which the individual suffers becomes the concern of all people, and the man who fails to secure justice is in the long run no worse off than the rest of the people in the community in which he resides.

This is the calm and impassioned view of the extraordinary trial just closed with such a lame and inconclusive decision by the jury in the West Side court. That decision may be just or it may be unjust; it may have been the result of prejudice or of honest conviction; it may, on the one hand, represent the best and calmest judgment of the soundest citizenship, or on the other the bigotry and narrowness farthest removed from justice; but whatever it may or may not represent, it cannot be ignored that it concerns every citizen of Colorado totally irrespective of his connection with, interest in or bias for or against the parties immediately concerned, and to the people, the great and final jury whose judgment is infallible. . . .

In July, 1901, fifteen months after the first trial, Anderson was tried a second time for the assault on Tammen. Once again the jury was deadlocked 6 to 6. It was dismissed amid rumors that Bonfils and Tammen had tried to bribe some of the jurors. The Denver *Times* finally broke the bribery story. It published affidavits from the six men who had held out for conviction in which they said they had been offered up to five hundred dollars each to vote against Anderson. A grand-jury investigation was ordered.

Anderson went on trial a third time on the same charges late in October, 1901. Although the testimony was virtually identical in all three trials, this time he was quickly acquitted. The District Attorney promptly dropped charges of assaulting Bonfils, and Anderson walked out of court completely exonerated.

A month later the grand jury indicted Tammen, Police Magistrate W. J. Thomas, Bailiff Robert Schrader, and a fireman, Daniel Sadlier, on charges of attempting to bribe six members of the second Anderson jury. Bonfils was not mentioned. A series of involved legal maneuvers delayed action on the indictments until the whole sorry mess ended abruptly one day in April, 1903, when three of the accused pleaded guilty.

The *Times* published this story on page 1:

> Golden, Colo., April 25—H. H. Tammen, the editor of a disreputable Denver evening newspaper, Robert Schrader and Daniel Sadlier appeared before Judge De France in the district court this morning and pled guilty to the charge of attempting to bribe the Anderson jury. They were sentenced to serve a day in the county jail of the city and county of Denver and pay fines of $100 each.
>
> Police Magistrate W. J. Thomas of Denver appeared to answer to the same charge and entered a plea of nolo contendere. . . .

Tammen, Schrader, and Sadlier were driven the short distance from Golden to the Denver county jail, booked, locked up, and then released after an hour. Tammen had admitted his guilt, but he was far from contrite. On page 1 of *The Denver Post* of that day he had "A Word to the Public." Describing Anderson's attack on him and Bonfils as a "cowardly, murderous assault, without right and without reason," Tammen wrote:

> I at once set about to do what I could to have him legally punished, and I was engaged in that effort from that time until he was acquitted. The law said he was not guilty; my opinion and feelings, however, have not been modified. . . . It would be useless for me to say to the public what I did in connection with the matter. Those who desire will think evil. Those who are my friends will think good. It is sufficient for me to say that I did whatever I could to bring about his conviction, and whatever I did was done because I was prompted by the sincere feeling that he had attempted to murder me, and I had a right to see that he was adequately punished. . . . I simply reiterate that whatever I have done in the matter, whether good or bad, my conscience is clear, for I have sought but one end —justice. . . . I myself have the consciousness that I have done no wrong. . .

Thus Tammen revealed a strange aberration, also demonstrated by Bonfils in a later incident. They saw themselves as avenging angels. When frustrated in their efforts to seek redress by conventional means from what they considered to be wrongs, they felt entitled to bring about justice in their own way.

As for Packer, a man-eater in the wilderness but an innocent bystander in affairs of the more sophisticated urban jungle, he was paroled January 8, 1901. This was just short of a year after Anderson came to see him and pocketed the twenty-five-dollar fee, and six months before Anderson's second trial. He retired to a little shack in Littleton, now a Denver suburb, and died there April 23, 1907. When Anderson died in 1930, *The Post*'s brief obituary made no mention of the shooting.

The incident involving Bonfils took place during the happy holiday season of 1907. In a singularly uncharitable bit of timing, the *News* on the day before Christmas charged that Bonfils was a blackmailer who ought to be driven out of the community, out of business, or into the penitentiary. To emphasize the point, Bonfils was cartooned as Captain Kidd. The editor of the *News* and its sister paper, the *Times,* was Thomas Patterson, the same gentleman endorsed by *The Post* for U. S. senator seven years earlier. The *News* headline read: "F. G. Bonfils Slanders Businessmen Who Refuse to Be Bled." The secondary headline was: "Foiled in Blackmail Scheme, He Brands Citizens of Unimpeachable Character as Blacklegs and Gamblers." Among the passages in the story was this: ". . . While Bonfils' attack was couched in language that was incoherent to a degree—causing many of those who read it to declare it had been written by a man who was either drunk or insane—it was the most brutally frank demand for blackmail that has ever appeared in *The Denver Post. . . .*"

Obviously *The Post* held no monopoly on rhetoric. It is likely that Bonfils stewed over the editorial attack all through Christmas Day. The following morning Bonfils overtook Patterson near the corner of East Thirteenth Avenue and Logan Street as both were walking to work. Patterson testified in court that he heard someone say "Good morning," and when he turned to reply, he was punched in the face by Bonfils and knocked to the ground. Patterson was then sixty-five years old, Bonfils forty-seven. There was disagreement as to the number of blows struck, but Patterson said his upper plate was broken and his mouth cut. Passersby quickly restrained Bonfils as Patterson struggled to his feet.

There was also disagreement as to what was said by the two editors. One witness reported that as Patterson brushed the dust off his clothes, he said, "You came up behind me and struck me like a coward without giving me any warning."

Bonfils allegedly replied, "You lie. I said, 'Good morning.' "

There are several versions as to what Bonfils said after that. One has Bonfils saying: "Good morning, Senator. So you're going to run me out of town, are you?"

Then, *pow!*

The other and more believable version: "You damned son of a bitch, I won't stand your abuse any longer."

In any event, Bonfils hurried to his office and wrote a bitter "So The People May Know" editorial which was published next day on page 1 over his signature. Here is the full text:

> For twenty years Thomas M. Patterson has run amuck in this community—abusing, vilifying, slandering and libeling every citizen who has disagreed with him. According to this creature there can be no honest difference of opinion. Believe as I do—talk as I do—do as I do—or I will brand you as a thief, blackmailer or grafter. This is the proclamation of this man—and this is how he has applied it. The Supreme Court of Colorado rendered a decision that Patterson did not indorse—and he immediately slandered and libeled them until he was sentenced by this court for contempt and fined one thousand dollars. The policy of Gov. Henry Buchtel does not meet the approval of this man, and he vilifies the governor each day through his awful papers—exhuming old soldiers that have slept for years in the cemetery, and putting in the mouths of these dead men unspeakable lies and epithets against the Governor. Mayor Speer has run Denver according to his own policy, and Patterson daily slanders, vilifies, traduces and disgraces him—and so on down the long list. "You must agree with me and do as I do, or I will hound you out of the community," says Patterson. Having stood the vile assaults of this man until my patience was exhausted, I met him as I was walking to my office yesterday morning. An altercation ensued, during which Mr. Patterson received a well-merited thrashing. Insofar as I am concerned he may keep his tirade about other people—and I have no objection to his endeavor to create as much sympathy for himself as he may choose—but I also desire it understood that I will not sit idly by and allow him daily to abuse me—even though it may help him politically or otherwise, and whenever he does so I shall call him to account where I meet him.
>
> F. G. Bonfils

The following day the *News* replied with a long editorial, two passages of which are significant:

> . . . There is no mistake about what the language [of the *Post* editorial] implies. It is a threat, pure and simple, that whenever

anything concerning Bonfils, that he considers abuse, appears in the *News* or the *Times* he will assault Senator Patterson. There is difficulty about Bonfils' position: He is to be the judge of what is abuse. What is said may be as true as holy writ and affect the public in its most vital parts, yet he may consider it abuse. Then comes the attack. . . .

. . . If what the *Times* or the *News* has said about *The Post* proprietors is untrue, even a fraction of it, they have causes of action against Senator Patterson sufficient to impoverish him and to shut down the papers. . . .

Charges of assault and battery were brought against Bonfils and a trial was begun without delay before Judge Thomas Carlon. It turned out to be a strange hearing in which the altercation became secondary to the question of whether Bonfils was a blackmailer.

Probing for reasons behind the *News'* criticism of Bonfils, his attorney, John T. Bottom, asked Patterson, "And you have had objections to the manner in which he conducted his newspaper, is that the idea?"

Patterson replied: "Yes, sir. I have had objections, as all journalists should, to the style of journalism [of *The Post*] in dealing with men, the businessmen, with officials and with matters that affect the safety and morality of the people of Denver."

Bottom then asked, "In what way does that style differ from the style of conducting the *News-Times?*"

Patterson hesitated a moment, then replied, "In this, I have no question in the world but that Mr. Bonfils and Mr. Tammen have used the paper they control for blackmail purposes."

Bottom demanded specifics: "When if ever did *The Denver Post* or Mr. Bonfils blackmail anybody?"

Patterson said he did not want to mention names. Turning to Judge Carlon, Bottom declared it was imperative to his case that individuals be named. For years, he said, Patterson's newspapers had charged that *The Post* had blackmailed people and called Bonfils "a thief, a perjurer, a blackmailer."

"I say to your honor," Bottom continued, "if Senator Patterson said these things in his newspaper without having any foundation, then under all the laws of humanity this man had a right to meet him and to give him a thrashing, and he would not be a man if he didn't. And on the other hand, if Mr. Bonfils is a liar, a thief, a perjurer, and a blackmailer, then Senator Patterson had a right in his newspaper to say so.

"But there is an unwritten law that protects a man for making an

Bonfils (center) at one of his periodic appearances in court. At left is his attorney, John T. Bottom; at right is Hugh O'Neill, *Post* reporter.

assault upon one who starts to rob him of a good name. I want to show by this witness [Patterson] that he gave this man [Bonfils] justification to assault him."

Under this kind of prodding Patterson replied: "I do not know of my own knowledge that they ever blackmailed anyone. My opinion that they were blackmailers was gathered from reading their paper and from common rumor."

Pressed for details, Patterson testified:

"The first I recall was the case of Edward Monash, who ran the Fair. He had been advertising in *The Post*. He concluded that he would advertise simply in the *News,* possibly in the *News* or the *Times.* Almost immediately upon that occurring *The Post* commenced a series of articles concerning Mr. Monash and the Fair, charging him with violating the child labor law, charging him with cruelties of every kind to the children in his employment, printing the most incendiary articles about Mr. Monash's management of the Fair. It brought Mr. Monash to terms, and Mr. Monash commenced to readvertise in *The Post,* and immediately every attack of that kind ceased."

Bottom summoned Monash as a rebuttal witness. This exchange followed:

Q—How long after the last of the articles with reference to child labor of the Fair were printed before you advertised in *The Post?*

A—About a year.

Patterson also testified that when J. S. Appel, operator of a clothing store, switched his advertising to the *News, The Post* published a series of articles charging him with cheating and mistreating women customers.

Appel was placed on the stand. He admitted he had owed *The Post* $1,423.85 when he received a letter from the newspaper saying, "We wish you would not present any more copy for advertising in our paper until such time as these back items can be straightened up." He then arranged to make weekly payments until the account was settled.

Q—Were your advertisements solicited during the time these payments were being made?

A—No, sir.

Q—Were they solicited during the time any attacks were made on you in *The Post?*

A—No, sir. They knew that I declined to advertise with them, and I always put it on the basis of expense.

Q—Just prior to the time any attacks were made, Mr. Appel, were you solicited to advertise in *The Post?*

A—No, sir, I was not.

Appel then was questioned about stories in *The Post* that he had been arrested for an assault on women.

Q—You had been arrested?

A—I had been arrested.

Q—Then, when they said you had been arrested, they told the truth, didn't they? Didn't the paper tell the truth?

A—No, sir.

Q—You hadn't been arrested, then?

A—I had been arrested.

Q—And *The Post* said you were arrested?

A—*The Post* said I was arrested.

What apparently had touched off Patterson's charges the day before Christmas was a report that Bonfils had tried to coerce two men promoting a stock issue to give him 51 percent in return for newspaper support. The money raised by the sale of stock was to be used to buy Overland Park, south of Denver, and to stage a state fair with horse racing. Bonfils was interested in investing, but only if John

Condon, a Chicago racing figure, would join the enterprise. When Condon decided not to take part, Bonfils also dropped out.

G. A. Wahlgreen, one of the promoters, declared under oath that it was his understanding Bonfils intended to pay for his stock just like any other investor.

"Did Mr. Bonfils demand this stock of you?" he was asked by Bottom.

"He did not," Wahlgreen replied. "He suggested that he and Mr. Condon be permitted to take fifty percent of the stock, provided Mr. Condon would go in with him."

"Were Mr. Bonfils and Mr. Condon to pay for their stock the same as the others?"

"Yes, sir. That was my understanding."

"Did Mr. Bonfils ever demand any amount of stock whatever?"

"No, sir, he never demanded anything at all."

All the Denver newspapers gave the case voluminous coverage with *The Post* and the *News* trying to outdo each other in slanting their stories to support their editors. One *Post* headline read: "Patterson Admits That Malice, Not Justice, Inspired Charges; Is Unable to Produce a Single Fact to Substantiate His Outrageous Accusations." Disturbed by the personal attacks that raged in the press and his courtroom, Judge Carlon sternly lectured both Bonfils and Patterson before passing judgment. "Words of a defamatory or derogatory nature, whether spoken or published, of or concerning a person, do not justify an assault," the judge said. "The truth or falsity of such utterances does not change this rule. . . . Let me suggest to the defendant and to the complaining witness that if you desire to place this community under a deep debt of gratitude, you can easily do so by placing in the columns of your great newspapers matters more beneficial to the community and interesting to the readers than that which it has been thought necessary on the part of the court to call to your attention."

He warned Bonfils that if he should be found guilty of a similar offense, "the sentence ought to be far different from that which the court is now to pronounce." Then he fined Bonfils fifty dollars and court costs.

Although the *News* had suggested that Bonfils should sue for libel, should he not like the *News'* charges, no such action was taken.

Bonfils kept the peace, more or less, for six years. Then he got into another punching scrape. This time his opponent was Thomas

J. O'Donnell, an attorney affiliated with the Denver Union Water Company, and the man who had run against Patterson in the 1900 race for senator. There had been bad blood between him and *The Post* since that time. In 1902 *The Post* had criticized a $17,000 fee O'Donnell collected as receiver when the Denver Savings Bank went bankrupt. A few days later Tammen and O'Donnell had a confrontation at Tortoni's restaurant. "Passing the table where Mr. Tammen was seated," *The Post* reported, "he leered at him in a bloodthirsty manner."

When Tammen ignored the bloodthirsty leer, O'Donnell slapped him with a folded newspaper and drew a gun. *The Post* reported that Tammen knocked O'Donnell to the floor and took the gun away, a pretty good trick for a small man of Tammen's sedentary habits. Whatever the case, Tammen did not press charges.

Bonfils' encounter with O'Donnell stemmed from the privately owned water company's bid for a twenty-year extension of the franchise to serve Denver. *The Post* opposed the franchise with typical vigor, urging municipal ownership in front-page editorials and editorials thinly disguised as news stories.

"The city of Denver can go into the open market at the present quotations for the stock and bonds of the Water company and buy the entire plant, water rights and all, for $9,175,000," one editorial said. "If you vote them a new franchise you will immediately put the valuation up to $14,500,000. In other words, you are unloading on yourselves a burden of $5,000,000 the minute you vote to give them this franchise. Now, that is plain, isn't it?"

In February of 1914 Bonfils had gone to the courthouse at Sixteenth Street and Court Place, a site now occupied by the May-D & F department store, as a plaintiff in a suit against the water company. He met O'Donnell in the hallway. Bonfils later said he saw O'Donnell reaching for a revolver and attacked first in self-defense. This is the way *The Post* described the encounter:

> As O'Donnell slowly pulled his hand from the pocket, Mr. Bonfils saw that he had a revolver, and leaping at O'Donnell, grasped his hand in which was the revolver. Holding O'Donnell's gun hand with his own left, Mr. Bonfils struck him a terrific right-hand blow in the face, and, although it staggered the gun-fighter, Mr. Bonfils noted that he made another attempt to get the gun into full action, turning it against Mr. Bonfils' body and attempting to pull the trigger. As O'Donnell refused to drop the gun and continued trying to get it against Mr. Bonfils' body, the latter again hit the lawyer with his

right hand, and then he grabbed the revolver with both hands and attempted to wrest it from his assailant.

O'Donnell contended he was ambushed and had drawn the revolver to protect himself. The men were separated before any serious damage was done and O'Donnell was charged with assault. *The Post*'s account of the court's decision is a classic, reminiscent of the way Mark Twain described a fight in which he pulled his opponent down on top of himself and firmly thrust his nose between his enemy's teeth. The first two paragraphs of the story, which was used on page 2, were:

> Disregarding the evidence of the witnesses to the attempt on the life of F. G. Bonfils by Thomas J. O'Donnell, and considering the assault as the result of a heated political fight in which he was beaten and discredited, a jury in the West Side court spared Mr. O'Donnell further humiliation by finding him not guilty of assault to commit murder last night.
>
> The jury took into consideration the fact that O'Donnell not only did not succeed in injuring Mr. Bonfils, his intended victim, but that he had received decidedly the worse of the encounter, and that the prosecuting witness' fist had proved more effective than the defendant's revolver, which he tried in vain to use. Mr. Bonfils had proved that he was more than a match for Mr. O'Donnell and that he was able to take care of himself in an encounter of the kind which was forced upon him by the defendant. . . .

What was more important was that the franchise was turned down. The day before the election *The Post* printed this front-page invitation:

> Come to *The Post* Tuesday night at 7 o'clock and help us celebrate the great victory of the people over the Water company. We have made elaborate preparations to get the returns, and you will know the result as soon as anybody in the city. We will have a large corps of telephone operators and anybody who cannot get downtown is invited to call Main 6550 and get the latest news. The new Vocalino or sweet voiced Siren of the Sells-Floto circus will sing songs of the victory while the returns are being flashed on the screen.

The vote was 13,346 against the franchise, 6,824 for.

"WHOOPEE! PEOPLE WIN!" exulted *The Post*'s headline followed by these "decks":

WATER CO. FRANCHISE IS WALLOPED
AND MOFFAT TUNNEL BONDS CARRIED

Denver Now Will Get Municipal Plant; Ready to Buy Out Corporation, if Fair Price Is Made, Without Further Quibble But Will

Build New Institution if Further Attempts to Grab Illegal Profits
Are Made by the Financiers Who Were Repudiated at the Polls

The page 1 "So The People May Know" editorial was typically florid:

> Again, *The Post* salutes the people, the Imperial People, and
> places upon their brow the laurel wreath of victory.
> Again, *The Post* salutes the people with reverence and with love.
> And again, *The Post* dedicates itself to the cause of the people
> forever.
> In the defeat of the Water company yesterday, Denver advanced
> twenty years, and every interest—real, physical, and moral, in-
> creased 100 per cent. . . . It makes every man proud of the name
> American. . .

But under the flamboyance and whoop-de-do, despite the bitterly
emotional personal attacks, there had been genuine accomplishment.
The rejection of the franchise led to municipal ownership of Denver's
water system. This was the key to orderly development of water
resources, perhaps the largest single factor in municipal growth on
the arid eastern slope of the Rockies.

THE NIGHT THE MOB STRUCK

The fifteen hundred employees of The Denver Tramway Company nursed a growing anger that long, hot summer of 1920. The company was threatening to cut wages from fifty-eight cents an hour to forty-eight cents unless the city of Denver allowed fares to be increased from six cents to seven. This the city was disinclined to do. On the other hand the union wanted pay increased to seventy-five cents an hour. The company countered by stating flatly that even with a seven-cent fare there was no possibility of a pay boost.

On the night of Saturday, July 31, about a thousand of the fifteen hundred employees attended a union meeting. They voted 887 to 11 to strike, and the streetcars quit running at five o'clock Sunday morning. The company promptly imported strikebreakers, armed them, and restored partial service.

On Wednesday, August 4, a committee from the Denver Trades and Labor Assembly, backed by a large delegation, called on Mayor Dewey C. Bailey to protest the running of streetcars with armed strikebreakers. Bailey rejected the protest, declaring: "We are going to run the cars. No eleven hundred men or twenty thousand men are going to prevent us from furnishing streetcar service to the public."

The following afternoon's *Post* applauded and asked editorially, "What is the matter with the people, headed by the 4,000 membership of the Chamber of Commerce, marching to our City Hall and indorsing Mayor Bailey for the righteous and fearless stand he has taken in this matter of vital interest to our city?"

Early that evening a mob overturned and burned several streetcars on East Colfax Avenue in front of the Cathedral of the Immaculate Conception. "Let's get *The Post*," someone cried, and a crowd estimated at a thousand persons, many of them curious spectators, started toward downtown Denver. The crowd straggled down Fifteenth Street, turned on Champa Street, and stopped in front of

The Post building. By then it was 9:30 P.M. and darkness had closed in. The only activity in *The Post* was on the third floor, where a small night crew was setting type for the next day's editions, and in the newsroom on the second floor, where a skeleton force was working.

Someone threw a rock through the glass of the locked front door. A long ladder was propped up against the second-floor balcony in front of the building and several men scrambled up. More rocks were thrown. As soon as they realized what was happening—and saw the size of the crowd—those inside the building turned off all lights and fled by a back door.

Now members of the mob poured into the building. They overturned desks in the business office on the first floor, smashed typewriters, dumped out the contents of file cabinets. They ran up the stairs and joined those who had entered the second-floor newsroom by ladder, ripping pictures off the walls and splintering office furniture. The engraving room also was on the second floor. Some of the mob smashed equipment but prudently kept hands off the carboys of acid. The composing room with its intricate typesetting machinery was on the third floor. The vandals were unable to find the light switch and did not enter. The way to the basement pressroom was blocked by a locked door. The heavy mesh screens over the windows were torn off, the glass smashed, and the press equipment attacked with rocks, pipes, and lumber. Unfamiliar with the presses, the mob inflicted little serious damage. A roll of newsprint was trundled into the street and unwound down Champa. The street was so jammed with spectators that police and firemen were helpless. When several fires were set inside the building, a *Post* copyboy mingling unnoticed with the mob stomped them out. His name was Charles T. O'Brien and he went on to become *The Post*'s political writer.

In less than an hour the mob was gone. Damage estimated at twenty-five thousand dollars had been done. Next day *The Post* came out at the usual time. "You bet! Business as usual!" *The Post* announced on page 1 along with a detailed account of the previous night's violence. "Let's go about our usual matters in our usual way, unafraid and undisturbed, remaining tranquil and sane, and so, of course, this week, as usual, with *Post* want ads, not only bountiful results, but unusually attractive presents."

If the above doesn't quite make a proper sentence, despite the abundance of commas, perhaps it can be forgiven in view of the circumstances.

The entire front page of August 6, 1920, was devoted to a strike mob's violence. *The Post* was among the targets, but the paper did not miss an edition.

One of the legends rising from this episode is that Bonfils congratulated O. M. Ethell, his composing-room foreman, on getting the paper out on time after the invasion. Ethell explained matter-of-factly that he had been able to do it without incurring overtime. At that point Bonfils spoiled it all by suggesting Ethell might be keeping too many men on the payroll. Ethell was a tall, spare man whose icy dignity had earned him the privilege of being referred to by everyone as "Mr. Ethell." He was at his iciest when he replied, "Mr. Bonfils, they did it for me. They did not do it for you."

Fearful of further violence, Mayor Bailey called for martial law and two hundred federal troops from Fort Logan, near Denver, and another five hundred from Camp Funston, Kansas, patrolled the streets. Before peace was restored seven persons died and more than fifty were wounded.

(When *The Post* sought to replace its broken glass, every bid was almost identical, causing the newspaper to fulminate against "the glass trust" that was taking advantage of the public.)

In the end the strikers—and the public—lost. Tram fare was raised to eight cents, two rides for fifteen. But the top wage was cut to fifty-two cents an hour because, as the company explained, it was far in arrears in tax and interest payments.

The mob's fury against *The Post* extended even into the men's second-floor rest room. Basins were torn from the walls and doors to the toilet stalls were ripped off. Those doors were never replaced until Palmer Hoyt came to *The Post* in 1946. Legend has it that Bonfils removed the doors in an attempt to minimize the time men spent away from their work. This is not true. Old-time employees say he simply did not replace the doors after the mob had done its work.

7

WAR AND PEACE ON THE
NEWSPRINT FRONT

By 1909 *The Post* was prospering far beyond any dreams the owners harbored when they bought the property fourteen years earlier for $12,500. In 1907 the newspaper had moved into magnificent (by the standards of the times) new quarters in a four-story building at 1544 Champa Street. The next year Bonfils and Tammen felt secure enough to draw salaries for the first time—one thousand dollars a week—and to pay themselves dividends from the paper's earnings. It was time to look for new challenges, and they found one in the struggling Kansas City *Post*.

A Democratic evening newspaper, The Kansas City *Post* held somewhat the same position in its community that *The Denver Post* had occupied in 1895. Both its circulation and influence were limited and it was in financial trouble. The Kansas City newspaper field was dominated by the *Star* and the *Times,* both the property of William Rockhill Nelson, with the *Journal* and *Post* vying for the scraps. J. Ogden Armour, who was to become one of Tammen's closest friends, had a substantial interest in the Kansas City public-transit and electric-light systems and he quietly had been backing the *Post* in return for its editorial support. On October 29, 1909, Bonfils and Tammen announced they had bought the Kansas City *Post*. Armour was a silent partner in the purchase, but that was not revealed.

The Denver Post reported the purchase in a backhanded manner by quoting verbatim a story published by the Kansas City *Journal* rather than writing its own account. The *Journal* quoted Bonfils, who had been interviewed at the Hotel Baltimore, as saying "the price paid by us was $165,000." The *Journal* also reported that Bonfils owned real estate valued conservatively at one million dollars in downtown Kansas City, and this statement, too, was reprinted in Denver. The story was published in Denver under a three-column headline—"F. G. Bonfils and H. H. Tammen Buy the Kansas City

Post"—on the lower half of page 1. But in the day's final edition this story and almost everything else on page 1 was replaced by the news that Jim Jeffries and Jack Johnson had agreed to a heavyweight championship fight. An eight-column headline across the top of the page read: "JEFFRIES AND JOHNSON SIGN." Under it in only slightly smaller type was this line: "Black and White Champs Agree to Fight 45 Rounds July 4."

That afternoon's Kansas City *Post* carried the following statement from Bonfils and Tammen:

> We have bought the Kansas City *Post* and with this issue assume control. It is our intention to make it as good and vital a newspaper as abundant means and our brains can produce.
>
> The policy of the *Post* will always be "the greatest good for the greatest number"—but a "square deal for all." It will try to accurately reflect the hopes, ambitions and achievements of this great city, this great state and this greatest of American territory, the fertile and salubrious West.
>
> The Kansas City *Post* will be similar in makeup, general appearance and ownership to *The Denver Post,* which is generally conceded to be a most remarkable and successful newspaper, but we must stop or you will think we are bragging. In entering this field, we, too, have our hopes, ambitions and ideals—none of which can be realized without your active good will and support—which we want—but only as we deserve them.
>
> We have ordered the best, latest and most complete newspaper equipment money can buy, which will be installed in our new building within the next few weeks, after which we hope to produce for you a real newspaper. Until then we ask your patience and indulgence.

Bonfils and Tammen had every intention of pouring enough resources into Kansas City to repeat the success they enjoyed in Denver. The Kansas City *Post* had only eight typesetting machines; the new owners ordered twelve more. William Randolph Hearst agreed to let the *Post* have a fast Hoe press he had on order and wait four months until another could be built for him. Charles A. Bonfils, F. G.'s personable and mild-mannered younger brother, was named managing editor but it was obvious Bon and Tam would be making policy. Otto Floto, who had developed a considerable reputation as a boxing writer, was dispatched to run the sports pages. Charles Bonfils' wife, Winifred Black, and cartoonist Doc Bird Finch headed a list of staff stars who would shuttle between Denver and Kansas City.

It was not merely hope of profits that motivated the partners. Bonfils had never forgotten Nelson's role in exposing the lottery business which hastened his departure from Kansas City. He yearned to thrash the *Star* as he had thrashed the *Rocky Mountain News* in Denver, and promptly set about to inflict rambunctious *Denver Post* tactics on conservative Kansas City. The *Post*'s screaming red-ink headlines were an astonishing contrast to the staid typography Kansas Citians were (and still are) accustomed to seeing in the *Star*. Circulation climbed rapidly, but the new owners found Kansas City advertisers reluctant to buy space. Nelson, too, chose to ignore the interlopers until 1912, when a full-blown circulation war exploded.

It started when the Kansas City *Post,* distributing nearly one hundred thousand copies a day, cut its price to five cents a week for seven papers. The *Journal* did likewise. Then the *Star* and *Times* announced they would be priced at one cent daily and two cents on Sunday. This was a windfall for the public but newsboys' profits were cut to one-fourth of a cent per copy. When *Star* and *Times* newsboys were ordered not to handle the *Post,* they went on strike, no doubt with the encouragement of *Post* circulation agents. The *Post* screamed when police arrested forty-three of its newsboys "for investigation." Otto Floto was quickly dispatched to City Hall with $10,000 in cash to post bail for them and as many more as might be jailed.

The next major *Post-Star* confrontation resulted in a strange libel suit that dragged through the courts for nearly fourteen years. On November 2, 1921, the last day of an American Legion convention in Kansas City, the *Post* published an editorial charging August Frederick Seested of pro-German loyalties before the United States entered World War I. Seested was general manager of the *Star* and his brother Frank the circulation manager. The Kansas City *Post* alleged that the Seested brothers had contributed thousands of dollars to Germany before the war, that August had lived in the United States forty years but did not apply for citizenship until after the United States went to war against Germany. August Seested saw this personal attack on his loyalty to the United States as an attempt to embarrass the *Star*. Frank Seested promptly filed a suit for libel against the Kansas City *Post,* asking $100,000 actual and $100,000 punitive damages.

It was shortly afterward that Bonfils and Tammen decided they had had enough of Kansas City and it would be wiser to concentrate their energies in Denver. On May 18, 1922, they announced sale of the *Post* to Walter S. Dickey, multimillionaire manufacturer of clay pipe who only a year earlier had bought the struggling Kansas City

Journal for $100,000. The magnificent skyscraper home the Denverites had promised for the Kansas City *Post* had never materialized. Its assets consisted of rented quarters, some well-worn machinery, goodwill such as it was, and a circulation of more than 150,000. For this they received $1,250,000. Thirteen years earlier they had purchased the paper for $165,000.

But they were not through with Kansas City yet. In November, 1926, a circuit court found Bonfils and Tammen guilty of libeling Frank Seested and awarded damages of $200,000. This judgment was appealed to the Missouri Supreme Court, which in September, 1930, affirmed the lower-court ruling but reduced the award to $125,000. The Supreme Court decision, written by Justice W. T. Ragland, said the *Post* knew the article was false and itself concocted the falsehood. "It was apparent from the face of the libelous article the *Post* was striking primarily at the *Star,*" Justice Ragland wrote, "because if it had been effective the *Star* would have had to sever all connection with the Seesteds."

By this time Tammen was dead. The Kansas City *Post* had been sold and the assets distributed, and Bonfils contended the Missouri judgments could not legally be paid by his Colorado holdings. Finally, on September 11, 1935—two years and seven months after Bonfils' death—the U. S. Circuit Court of Appeals in Denver ruled that the executors of his estate must pay Frank Seested. He had retired five years earlier and his brother August had died in 1928.

While the Kansas City *Post* never was as successful as its Denver counterpart, Bonfils and Tammen thought many times of launching a morning paper in Denver. Twice they announced their intentions. Both times they were inspired by changes in ownership of competitive newspapers, although on the first occasion their motive may have been a devious ploy having nothing to do with a new publication. That episode began in October, 1913, when Senator Patterson, then past seventy years of age and weary of his labors, sold the *News* and the *Times*. The buyer was John Charles Shaffer, Chicago financier and philanthropist who also owned newspapers in Chicago; Indianapolis, Muncie, and Terre Haute, Indiana; and Louisville, Kentucky. Shaffer also bought the morning Denver *Republican* and merged it with the *Times*. That left Denver with four newspapers, the *Express* (owned by the Scripps-McRae chain) and the *News* in the morning field, and *The Post* and *Times* in the afternoon. Perhaps Tammen sensed opportunity after Shaffer called to pay his respects. William L. Chenery, then a *News* editorial writer who went on to become editor and publisher of *Collier's Magazine* for many years, tells of that meeting in his book, *So It Seemed*.

"Mr. Tammen," Shaffer said, "I am going to run my paper as Jesus Christ would run it."

"Why, you old son of a bitch," Tammen replied. "I'm going to run *The Denver Post* as George Washington would run it. Now what are you going to do about that?"

John C. Shaffer, referred to snidely by *The Post* as John Clean Shaffer, a gentlemanly patron of the arts, obviously was not cut out for journalism as practiced in Denver. One of his more notable accomplishments was the purchase soon after his arrival of a twelve-thousand-acre ranch in the foothills a dozen miles southwest of downtown Denver. He named it Ken-Caryl after his sons, Kent and Carroll, and spent $100,000 to build a baronial home on a site from which Denver could be seen through a notch in the sandstone ridges. In 1971 Johns-Manville, the industrial conglomerate, bought essentially the same property for $7.5 million as a site for its world headquarters, research center, and a planned community of 5,500 residences.

On February 22, 1914, four months after Shaffer's arrival in Denver, *The Post* in a page 1 "So The People May Know" editorial said Bonfils and Tammen were prepared to publish a morning newspaper "if the great sovereign people of the Rocky Mountain region want or insist." The reason the people might insist, the editorial explained, was "that the *News* and *Times* are unsatisfactory as newspapers, caring nothing for the public good, being violent corporation organs which cater to the few instead of to the public as a whole." Bonfils and Tammen went on to say that forty thousand subscribers would be necessary before they could start the project. A subscription blank for their nonexisting newspaper was printed and *Post* readers were urged to sign their names and send it in.

There is no record as to the number of coupons Bonfils and Tammen received. It seems unlikely that many Coloradans would wish to support a fifth Denver newspaper. Nonetheless the coupons, signed or unsigned, served their purpose in a curious way that requires a bit of backgrounding. While newspapers cover the local scene with their own writing staffs, they depend largely on news-gathering agencies to provide them with material from various parts of the nation and the rest of the world. The largest of these agencies is Associated Press, an organization owned by the hundreds of newspapers which have franchises to use its services. These members of the Associated Press pay assessments to meet the cost of operating it. Unlike United Press (now United Press International), whose services can be bought by any legitimate news medium, Associated Press dispatches are available only to franchise holders. It is understandable that AP franchises are valuable properties.

There are AP franchises for morning newspapers and franchises for evening newspapers. A franchise holder can veto the granting of a franchise in the same time cycle to another newspaper in the same city. *The Post* had the AP evening franchise in Denver, but not for its Sunday-morning editions. And Shaffer owned two morning franchises as a result of buying the *News* and the *Republican*. When Tammen sought to buy the defunct *Republican*'s franchise, Shaffer turned him down.

Tammen then announced that he and Bonfils were ready to start their morning paper. The legend according to Fowler is that Tammen took Shaffer to the window and showed him a *Post* truck loaded with small bundles of paper—allegedly the coupon response to *The Post*'s subscription drive. Thereupon Shaffer agreed to give *The Post* the Sunday AP rights if Tammen would cancel his plans for a morning paper.

Perkin tells us in his book: "Thus *The Post* acquired a franchise worth perhaps a hundred thousand dollars without laying out a cent, and Tammen went back to Champa Street chuckling. He and Bonfils had no intention of starting a morning paper at this time, and all but a few hundred of the coupons in the truck were blank sheets of newsprint cut up to proper size by *Post* clerks."

Whether or not this story is authentic, the decision not to launch a morning *Post* demonstrated good business judgment. *The Post* continued to prosper through the years of World War I. By 1921 *The Post*'s gross revenue was $3,615,000, and its net profit (after deducting income taxes instituted that year) topped a million dollars for the first time. The precise figure was $1,018,000, representing a 28 percent profit on the gross revenue. The profits shown by *The Post* during the next five years are little short of phenomenal:

Year	Revenue	Expenses	Profit After Taxes	% Profit
1922	$3,891,000	$2,416,000	$1,303,000	33.49
1923	4,119,000	2,579,000	1,364,000	33.11
1924	4,108,000	2,689,000	1,247,000	30.36
1925	4,503,000	3,058,000	1,257,000	27.91
1926	4,709,000	3,335,000	1,171,000	24.87

Tammen, whose death came in 1924, did not live to enjoy these superprosperous years. But in 1923, his last full year of life, the partners split a cash dividend of $1,550,000 from their stock in *The Post,* plus profits of $835,000 from investments in securities—a cool $1,192,500 each at a time of relatively modest income taxes. In addition, of course, they were drawing salaries.

Each year until Tammen's death the partners held a perfunctory annual meeting. They would go through the motions of electing Tammen president, Fred Bonfils secretary and treasurer, and Tom Bonfils vice-president. Periodically they would meet to declare dividend payments and Tom, who owned only one token share of stock, would vote dutifully along with the other two. After Tammen died, the Bonfils brothers became a two-man board, with Fred as president and treasurer, and Tom as vice-president and secretary. They continued to meet regularly as required by law, but with Fred doing just about as he pleased. The dividends they voted usually amounted to $100,000 a month, split between Fred and Tammen's heirs. (Agnes Tammen did not join the board until after Bonfils' death.)

A state the size of Colorado (population 939,629 in 1920) hardly could support more than one newspaper so abundantly. Denver had four and three suffered. In the mid-Twenties the *Express* staggered along with a circulation of less than 15,000. The *Times* circulated fewer than 25,000 copies and the morning *News* about 30,000. *The Post* boasted a circulation of 161,000 daily and close to 240,000 on Sunday, when papers were distributed on both sides of the Rockies from the Texas Panhandle to Montana. *The Post* was verily the dominant newspaper in the area, but the disparity in numbers does not necessarily provide a true gauge of the quality of the Denver publications. H. Allen Smith has written of his experiences at *The Post* in that period: "From stem to stern *The Post* was loaded with silliness posing as wisdom, broad inconsistencies that wouldn't fool a prairie dog and bold statements that a certified idiot wouldn't believe—yet the people of Denver either believed these things or simply enjoyed the colorful manner in which they were served up."

Some of the more sanctimonious Denverites looked down their noses at *The Post* as a "libelous, sensation-seeking yellow rag" and professed never to read it. But they had it delivered secretly to their servants' entrance. It was during this period that Bonfils came up with a fiendishly ingenious idea for ensuring the advertising support of socially prominent merchants. Any flagging of their loyalty would result in their wives' names vanishing from *The Post*'s society pages, and the husbands soon got the message. Most merchants, however, could not afford not to advertise in a medium as dominant as *The Post*. Hard selling by *Post* solicitors seldom was necessary. A gently dropped hint that Mr. Bonfils was displeased that a store was running so much linage in a rival paper—and might decide to bar that store's advertising from *The Post* in the future—usually was enough to bring the merchant in line. One day Bonfils cornered Buzzy Briggs, a theater operator. "Briggs," he said, "I see you're buying billboards. Cut it out. All you need is *The Post.*" Briggs told friends he didn't know whether Bonfils was joking or threatening him. Jack Kanner, a boxing promoter who had prospered with liberal publicity in *The Post*'s sport pages, made the error of buying a one-inch ad in the *News* to announce one of his fights. *The Post* immediately dropped its support and Kanner's promotions suffered drastically. *The Post* with its dominant circulation could damage a business or enterprise simply by ignoring it.

By 1926 John Shaffer was looking for someone to buy his *News* and *Times*. The logical purchaser was the newly organized Scripps-Howard chain, at the time forging a nationwide network of daily papers under the dynamic leadership of Roy W. Howard. Scripps-Howard already had a foothold in Denver. The *Express,* the smallest of the dailies, was part of the Scripps-McRae chain, which had changed its name to Scripps-Howard following a reorganization in 1923.

On November 22, 1926, Shaffer and Howard reached an agreement. Scripps-Howard bought the *Times* and the *News* for $750,000 —$300,000 in cash and the balance in assumed obligations. The next day Howard announced the *Times* and *Express* would be merged into a new six-day afternoon paper to be called the Denver *Evening News*. The *News* itself would continue as a seven-day morning paper.

A few days later Howard chose the Denver Chamber of Commerce as the forum in which to challenge Bonfils. He was derisive as he declared the new management was coming to Denver "neither with a tin cup nor a lead pipe." Before an audience chuckling in appreciation of the barbs thrown at Bonfils, Howard declared, "We will live with and in this community and not on or off it. We are nobody's big brother, wayward sister, or poor relation."

Bonfils responded swiftly to the challenge against *The Post*'s dominance. Within two weeks he announced invasion of the morning field. The story, set four columns wide across page 1, read with characteristic bombast:

> *The Denver Morning Post* will soon be issued by the *Post Printing and Publishing Company*. It will be a morning paper without a superior anywhere in the United States. It will be just as good a morning paper as *The Denver Post* is an afternoon paper. That means, of course, that *The Denver Morning Post* will be one of the great morning papers of the world.
>
> *The Denver Morning Post* will have the full and exclusive Associated Press service; the full and exclusive Chicago *Tribune* and *New York Times* news service; the full and exclusive *Hearst* morning paper news service; it will have the Consolidated Press, the North American Newspaper Alliance and, in fact, it will have every news service in the United States that is worth while having.
>
> *The Denver Morning Post* will be produced by an all-star staff, picture makers, special and feature writers, photographers, etc. AND IT WILL BE DELIVERED TO YOU BY MAIL OR CARRIER AT 10 CENTS A WEEK.
>
> *The Denver Morning Post* will be the paper of optimism, of joy, of sunshine and quality. Its policy will be that of *The Denver Post* —constructive to the nth degree, ever standing and fighting for the interests of Denver and Colorado, Wyoming, New Mexico, Arizona, Utah, Idaho, Nebraska, Montana, Nevada, Oklahoma, the Dakotas, western Kansas, and the Panhandle of Texas.
>
> It will be the spokesman for the every day fellow, for the great masses. It will be the champion of every good, and pure, and noble, and holy and righteous cause; and the faithful and unceasing defender of righteousness, justice, decency, law and order; it will be the opponent of every wrong and evil thing, of every form of crime, oppression, greed, selfishness and lawlessness. . . .

This announcement went on to make much of the fact that *The Morning Post* would carry Associated Press stories. Howard, who was building his United Press into a lively, enterprising service, had dropped AP from what he called the two NEWSpapers. *The Post* treated that business decision as an affront to the honor of the West, than which there is nothing touchier: "This greatest city between the Missouri River and the Pacific Ocean, east and west, and from the North Pole to the City of Mexico north and south in this longitude, has been belittled, humiliated and wantonly and willfully disgraced by the selfishly bringing about of the abandonment of the morning Associated Press service in Denver."

That was only the beginning. Day after day both sides fired deafening volleys of ballyhoo and beefed up their staffs for the impending battle of the century. The publicity did not go unnoticed in other parts of the country. *Editor & Publisher,* the newspaper industry's trade journal, in its issue of December 4, 1926, abandoned its editorial neutrality to complain about the "contemptible journalism" of Bonfils and *The Post*. It likened the coming newspaper war as a crusade in which *The Post* would be vanquished by the might of Scripps-Howard, cleansing the souls of all conscientious journalists. A portion of that editorial is quoted at the beginning of Chapter 1.

This is the way the lineup appeared:

Prior to Roy Howard's arrival: *Express* and *News* in the morning field. *Post* and *Times* in the afternoon.

After Howard: *Express* and *Times* merged into a new paper, Denver *Evening News,* challenging *The Post* in the afternoon field. Bonfils then launched *The Denver Morning Post* to challenge the *Morning News*.

The first issue of *The Morning Post* appeared Monday, January 3, 1927, touching off what Bob Perkin has aptly described as "the wackiest slugging match since Punch and Judy . . . newspaper competition as taxes the credulity of anyone who was not an eyewitness." It ran fifty-two pages, the bulkiest morning paper in Denver up to that time. Or so *The Post* thought. Even though editors and reporters of rival newspapers may not speak to each other, members of the mechanical departments have a way of keeping communications channels open. Tipped off in adequate time, the *News* came out with sixty-eight pages. (Next day *The Morning Post* was down to a more reasonable sixteen pages.) The news contained in neither paper justified the ballyhoo of the previous weeks. *The Morning Post*'s lead story under an eight-column bannerline was a not particularly startling development in the Chicago White Sox baseball scandal. And on the sports pages, Reddy Gallagher devoted a column to speculating on whether Jack Dempsey could have licked Gene Tunney the day following his defeat in their championship fight. Gallagher's conclusion: He might have. But a birth of a newspaper could not be allowed to pass without a "Salutatory" which read:

> *The Denver Morning Post* is hereby dedicated in perpetuity to the services of our God, our country, our homes and our fellowman—and may it always be the champion of every good and noble and righteous cause—and the opponent of every evil and wrong thing. May it ever be the defender of the right against wrong, the helpless against the greedy, aggressive, strong; and may *The Denver Morning Post* by and with and thru you, and you, and you, make Denver,

Colorado, and the magnificent Rocky Mountain section the very best, most healthful, prosperous, moral, patriotic, law-abiding and God and home-loving country thruout the Earth.

After that kind of send-off, what more was there to say? The four newspapers proceeded, morning and evening, to belabor each other and the public with news stories blown up all out of proportion and an endless series of promotions and giveaways announced by bomb blasts, red ink, and wailing of sirens borne aloft by that novelty, the airplane. A skid-row murder was important enough to send a taxi-load of reporters racing to the scene of the crime, and for days afterward they would milk the incident for every possible angle. In its second issue *The Morning Post* trumpeted a scandal:

IRA M. DeLONG IS
SUED FOR DIVORCE
Boulder Dry Leader
Was Secret Drinker
Says Mrs. DeLong

The second issue also announced *The Morning Post* would give away "a brand spanking new Nash light-six two-door sedan" (donated by the James-Nash Motors Company) to the most popular and attractive girl in the Rocky Mountain region. All a girl had to do was fill in a coupon printed in *The Morning Post* and send it in with a photograph of herself. Later there were contests to pick the most popular policeman, mail carrier, waitress, streetcar conductor, salesgirl, etc., etc., but there was an angle. Denverites could vote by subscribing to *The Morning* Post for one month. The paper sold for two cents per copy or a dime a week, delivered.

Bonfils knew the value of getting people involved. He offered prizes for the best letter commenting on such diverse matters as "Are Women Becoming Wickeder?," "Mother's Love" for Mother's Day, and "Capital Punishment." When publishers came out with Charles A. Lindbergh's book *We,* about his epic solo flight from New York to Paris, *The Morning Post* offered it free to anyone who came in with four one-month subscriptions. Charley Murray of the comedy team of Murray and Mack (Sennett) came to Denver and it was announced he would leap from a twelve-story building, just like they do in movies, across the street from *The Post*. Nearly twenty-five thousand jammed Champa Street during the lunch hour to crane their necks as Murray, puffing on a cigar, strutted on the parapet atop the building. He waved to the crowd, signaled a team of fire-

Nearly 25,000 persons jammed Champa Street in front of *The Post* to see comedian Charley Murray jump off a twelve-story building, "just like in the movies." A dummy was thrown off the building. Denver newspapers vied with such "promotions" for public attention. (L. A. Cantwell Collection)

men with a safety net into position, and went through the motions of leaping into space. Women screamed as a form hurtled through the air and smashed into the pavement a dozen feet from the net. *The Post*'s headline read: "Spectators Get Thrill and a Laugh When Charley Murray's Dummy Goes Off Top of Foster Building."

H. Allen Smith describes the near-chaos in *The Post* newsroom when he came to work: "Two big fat newspapers were being published in quarters designed for only one. . . . I was escorted to a chair on the rim of the copy desk. I told Morris [Joe Alex Morris] I had never been a copyreader but that I knew what one was and he said not to worry, that nobody in the place knew what anybody else was doing. If a grizzly bear had come down from the mountains and walked into that big room wearing an eyeshade they'd have handed him a soft-lead pencil and put him on the copy desk."

In February of 1927 *The Post* and the *News* clashed head-on over classified advertising. *The Post* was charging twenty-five cents a line. It offered two gallons of gasoline—selling at twenty-one cents a gallon—free to anyone placing a two-line ad in the Sunday edition.

The *News* came back with an offer of three gallons. *The Post* raised the ante to four, headlining its announcement, "You Can't Stop Us, By Cracky!" and boasting:

> Beginning today, Thursday, Friday and Saturday, to those smart men and women, boys and girls, who bring to the office of *The Denver Post* their want ads for the Big *Sunday Post,* we are going to give four gallons of the finest White Eagle gasoline, guaranteed 60 degrees gravity, low initial and end point, assuring quick starting of your engines, and unusual mileage.
>
> This gasoline will be delivered to you at the Barco oil station, Eighteenth avenue and Sherman street, upon presentation of a coupon to be given you by *The Post* when you bring your *Sunday Post* want ad to us.
>
> This is 84 cents worth of gasoline, four full gallons, given to you free with any want ads, little or big, brought in for the big *Sunday Post,* only one coupon to a customer.
>
> What do you think of that?

For those without cars, the offer was three loaves of bread from McGavin's Sanitary Bakers or a half-pound package of Doran's Red Seal coffee. (Giving away gifts for want ads was nothing new. Over the years *The Post* had offered, among other merchandise, two Rocky Ford cantaloupes, a half-dozen doughnuts, a half-dozen lemons, two pounds of California onions, a half-pound of peanuts, glassware,

In cutthroat competition for classified advertising, *The Post* and *Rocky Mountain News* gave away vast amounts of merchandise. At one time *Post* gave four gallons of gasoline (worth eighty-four cents) to anyone purchasing a fifty-cent classified ad. Iron stairway at right led to newsroom.

soap, tooth powder, and "fifty-seven varieties of useful and valuable presents.")

When the *News* upped the bid to five gallons, Bonfils discreetly backed off. Perkin reports that the *News* printed fifteen thousand classified ads that Sunday but suffered a loss of forty thousand dollars. By the following week *The Post* was racing off on another caper. It arranged "The Last Leap of Leaping Lenas" to publicize a new car show. Seventy-five old cars were hauled atop Castle Mountain near Golden, twenty miles west of Denver, by Colorado National Guard tanks and shoved over the edge, one by one. "If you want to see how an automobile looks tumbling over the side of a mountain to mechanical oblivion," *The Post* invited earnestly, "hit the Golden paved road Sunday afternoon and park by the side of the mountain."

But there were also some solid achievements. For instance, in January, 1928, *The Morning Post* distributed its first rotogravure picture section. Edited in Denver and printed in a Chicago roto plant, the section reproduced photographs of the magnificent Colorado scenery with remarkable fidelity. This marked the beginning of *The Post*'s interest in rotogravure. It led to the installation of a roto printing plant when the paper moved into new quarters in 1950 and the founding of *Empire, The Post*'s Sunday magazine.

The frenetic pace of the Denver newspaper war could not go on forever. In 1926, the year before the start of the war, *The Post* had made a profit after taxes of $1,171,000 on gross revenues of $4,709,000. In 1927 revenue dropped slightly to $4,495,000, but expenses soared and net profit plunged alarmingly to $384,000. Scripps-Howard, too, was pouring far more of its resources into Denver than the results warranted. The *News'* morning circulation during this period had climbed from 30,000 to 42,000, the afternoon circulation had doubled to 50,000 and the Sunday circulation was nearing 102,000. *The Morning Post,* starting from scratch, had reached the 33,000 mark. *The Post*'s evening and Sunday papers were still dominant—164,000 daily and 280,000 Sundays. Still, the publishers had proved nothing except their willingness to spend money, and Denverites were becoming sated with a two-ring circus every morning and evening. Bonfils and Howard, both practical men, met secretly to seek a truce. Howard had taken the initiative, and Bonfils welcomed it.

They announced their agreement in their editions of Monday, November 5, 1928:

—*The Morning Post* was "sold" to the *News.*

—*The Evening News* was "sold" to *The Post.*

—*The Morning Post* and *Evening News* would be discontinued immediately by the new owners, leaving Denver with only two newspapers.

—Both *The Post* and *News,* which sold for two cents, were raised to three cents daily, and from five to ten cents Sundays.

—*The Post* agreed to transfer its morning AP franchise to the *News.*

—The *News* agreed not to publish an afternoon newspaper, and *The Post* agreed not to publish a morning paper except on Sundays, for three years without the other's written consent.

What was not announced was that *The Post* agreed to pay the *News* $250,000 to seal the agreement. In this sense it might be said *The Post* had lost the war. However, Scripps-Howard later admitted it had dropped about three million dollars in its sally into the Denver afternoon market. While *The Post* continued to make money, its profits fell approximately two million dollars. *The Post*'s financial picture for the two years of the war and the years before and after it looks this way in tabular form:

Year	Revenue	Expenses	Profit After Taxes	% Profit
1926	$4,709,000	$3,335,000	$1,171,000	24.87
1927	4,495,000	4,050,000	384,000	8.54
1928	4,765,000	4,000,000	673,000	14.12
1929	6,114,000	4,018,000	1,865,000	30.50

Obviously a quarter-million dollars was a small price to pay for an armistice. As for Scripps-Howard, according to Perkin, the money went a long way toward meeting the *News'* losses of $400,000 between 1928 and 1942.

A few days after the announcement a love feast was held at the Denver Chamber of Commerce before another packed audience. Howard appeared in the same suit that he had worn during his appearance two years earlier; he wanted to show, he said, that while he might have lost his shirt, he still had his coat and pants. Bonfils was confined to his bed with a cold and was represented by Major Fred W. Bonfils, his nephew and the paper's business manager. Both were properly gallant and gracious. Howard praised F. G. Bonfils for putting "the benefit to the community ahead of any benefits to himself."

"With two years' fair trial," he went on, "Mr. Bonfils has demonstrated that the type of paper he provides with his *Denver Post* is more nearly attuned to the wants of the evening newspaper field. In the morning field, the *Rocky Mountain News* has met with a fine response and under Scripps-Howard management has enjoyed a re-birth."

Major Bonfils observed that people pay for the privilege of watching a prize fight, "but in this so-called newspaper war, while the spectators cheered from the sidelines, the contestants lost about five million dollars." He said the surviving papers probably would be bigger and better, "and we expect that both of us will spend more time in building up and less in tearing down."

If there was any consternation in Denver over these developments, it was in the staffs of the four newspapers. Suddenly there were only half as many jobs.

Vignette

TELEGRAM TO THE PRESIDENT

On February 20, 1929, twelve days before Calvin Coolidge was to relinquish the Presidency of the United States to Herbert Hoover, a telegram was delivered at the White House. It was addressed to President Coolidge and it read:

> *The Denver Post,* the largest paper in the United States between the Missouri river and the Pacific coast, wants you as its editor-in-chief and as the press states you are considering newspaper work, *The Post* will pay you a salary of $75,000 a year to start. Your policies and those of *The Denver Post* are so entirely in harmony with each other that you would feel at home on this paper. This offer is made in the utmost good faith and a guarantee indorsed by every national bank in Denver will assure you of the earnestness of this offer. Denver is the most healthful and delightful city in the world in which to live and we want you to seriously consider this offer. Frederick G. Bonfils, owner and publisher of *The Denver Post.*

Serious negotiations for high-level employment normally are conducted quietly. But Bonfils reproduced a facsimile of the telegram on page 1 of *The Denver Post* under a two-line, eight-column headline that shrieked:

A job offer to President Coolidge became page-1 news in 1929.

PRESIDENT COOLIDGE IS INVITED BY F. G. BONFILS
TO BECOME EDITOR-IN-CHIEF OF *THE DENVER POST*

The accompanying story, under Pinky Wayne's by-line, read in part:

> For a man in the zenith of his powers, with vision made keen thru world contacts, with sympathies deepened by being the faithful chief of a devoted nation, the task and opportunity offered by F. G. Bonfils to Calvin Coolidge would seem to be made to his own order.
>
> —As editor-in-chief of *The Denver Post,* Calvin Coolidge would have the privilege and opportunity of shaping the destinies of this glorious section of the world. . . .

The next day *The Post* ran another eight-column, front-page banner-line over a story by Bruce A. Gustin which was a remarkable display of wishful thinking in print. Gustin's story began this way:

> Acceptance by President Coolidge of the invitation of F. G. Bonfils, publisher of *The Denver Post,* to become editor-in-chief of *The Post* when he leaves the White House would be the greatest thing that could happen to the Rocky Mountain region and the whole west.
>
> It would give to this wonder section a real leader.
>
> With Calvin Coolidge at the editorial helm of *The Post*—the greatest newspaper between the Missouri river and the Pacific coast —the voice of the west would be heard and listened to in Washington, D.C., and around the entire world. No longer would we have to crawl into the national capitol and ask favors. We could demand our rights and get them. . . .
>
> There wouldn't be any more discrimination against Colorado or other states of the west if we had Calvin Coolidge for our spokesman. We wouldn't have to petition the railroads or the bankers or the industrial combinations or the politicians or anybody else for a square deal. They know and respect and appreciate the strength of Calvin Coolidge and they would go the limit to win the cooperation of the territory for which he spoke.
>
> Calvin Coolidge, as editor-in-chief of *The Denver Post,* would do more for this western country in one hour than the Moffat road will do in forty years. . . .

Calvin Coolidge did not accept *The Post*'s offer. He went back home to Northampton, Massachusetts, to write and think and enjoy his leisure. When he died January 5, 1933, *The Post* published a eulogy on page 1 signed by Bonfils. "In the death of Calvin Coolidge the United States has lost one of its sanest, best and most patriotic citizens," Bonfils wrote. "No president ever possessed that rarest of all qualities, plain common sense, in a greater degree than Calvin Coolidge. . . . His like as a citizen and an official will not be duplicated in generations, if ever."

8

BOODLE-SOILED HANDS

Until Watergate became a household word, the Teapot Dome oil-lease scandal was the standard by which corruption in high federal office was measured. Although not a part of the scandal itself, *The Denver Post* became involved in a curious, indirect manner.

The story begins in 1912, when President William Howard Taft set aside two oil fields in California—Elk Hills and Buena Vista Hills—as a reserve source of supply for the Navy. In 1915 President Woodrow Wilson designated a third reserve, the Teapot Dome field, about fifty miles north of Casper, Wyoming. In 1921 President Warren G. Harding transferred supervision of the oil reserves from the Navy to the Department of the Interior. Soon afterward it was reported that Secretary of the Interior Albert B. Fall had decided to lease Teapot Dome for production because wells in the Salt Creek field just outside the reserve were believed to be draining the Navy's oil pool.

Early in April of 1922 rumors emanating from Washington, D.C., indicated the Teapot Dome lease would go to the Mammoth Oil Company, headed by Harry F. Sinclair. Several companies were hoping to get the award. Reports that Sinclair was to be favored without benefit of competitive bids caused considerable anxiety in the industry. Secretary Fall denied the rumors, but on April 7 it was announced that Sinclair had indeed been chosen. On April 14 *The Denver Post* ran a story on its business and financial page under this headline:

TEAPOT DOME LEASE TO SINCLAIR
THREATENS WYOMING OIL SCANDAL,
PROBE BY CONGRESS MAY BE ASKED

The same day Bonfils was visited by John Leo Stack, an oilman and one-time Colorado Democratic candidate for Congress, whom he had known for some years. Stack showed Bonfils a contract between himself and two oil companies, the Pioneer Oil and Refining Company and Société Belgo Americaine des Petroles du Wyoming. The contract stated that Pioneer and Belgo owned certain valuable oil leases in the Teapot Dome field dating back before it was declared a naval reserve. Further, the contract empowered Stack to seek additional leases from the government on the naval reserve which would wrap up the area in a very attractive package. For his efforts Stack was to be paid 5 percent of whatever the package produced. Now, Stack complained, Pioneer and Belgo had bypassed him and sold their old leases to Sinclair for one million dollars. This sale naturally enhanced the value of the lease Sinclair had been granted by Secretary Fall. In brief, Stack contended he had been gypped out of his 5 percent commission. He didn't care which one paid him, but he felt entitled to a settlement from either Sinclair or the Pioneer-Belgo combine, which was also known as Midwest Oil Company.

Bonfils asked what Stack thought his contract was worth.

Stack replied that, based on estimates of the amount of oil in Teapot Dome, he was entitled to as much as five million dollars.

"Well," Bonfils asked, "what do you want us to do?"

Stack replied, "I want you to join in there and help me realize on this contract."

The upshot was an agreement under which Stack promised to give Bonfils one-half of whatever he realized from the contract "in consideration of your services in aiding me to work out an adjustment thereof." A later agreement provided that the first $50,000 realized from the settlement would go to Stack and the remainder would be divided with 46¼ percent going to Stack and 46¼ percent to Bonfils (which he agreed to split with Tammen) and 7½ percent to their attorney, H. H. Schwartz of Casper.

Sometime later, when the Teapot Dome matter came to the attention of the Senate Committee on Public Lands and Surveys, Stack was asked why he had gone to Bonfils instead of to his personal attorney, Karl T. Schuyler.

"Because I knew I would have to have money to fight the thing through," Stack replied. He explained that Schuyler would require specific payment, and he and Bonfils had retained Schwartz on a contingency fee, with Bonfils putting up the money for travel and other incidental expenses.

"And how much money did you expect it was going to cost to prosecute this action?" Stack was asked. He replied:

"Well, I did not know, did not have the least idea. I figured I was going up against the greatest legal lights in the country, and I figured that they could keep me in court for years and years and I did not know how long it would take, and I wanted somebody who was a fighter and who would go through with me on the financial line."

"You were willing to give him two million, five hundred thousand dollars in order to have him put up money to prosecute the lawsuit?"

"Yes, sir," Stack said.

The chronology of events after Bonfils agreed to help Stack in his search for justice is interesting:

April 15, 1922, the day after Bonfils and Stack signed their agreement— *The Post* published an editorial beginning with this sentence: "After having made an unpardonable and inexcusable blunder in the leasing of the Naval oil reserve in Wyoming to the Sinclair oil interest, purely a Standard Oil company, the Secretaries of the Navy and Interior have issued the statement below, not because it is news but in a feeble attempt to justify the most serious blunder that the present administration has made up to date." The editorial concluded with this sentence: "A few such arbitrary and autocratic deals as this will set the country aflame with protest against these kinds of methods, these kinds of deals, and this kind of favoritism of the Government for the powerful and already completely entrenched oil monopoly."

April 16, 1922— Under the "So the People May Know" banner *The Post* charged that Sinclair and his Standard Oil associates received in the Teapot Dome lease a "gift" from the government of high-grade oil valued at between $250,000,000 and $500,000,000 "through trickery that verges, if it does not encroach, on the bounds of crime. If carried out it will consummate one of the baldest public-land grabs of the century." A marked copy of the paper was sent to members of Congress.

May and June— Diedrich Franz Stackelbeck, an ace investigative reporter, was sent to New Mexico, where Secretary Fall owned a large cattle ranch, to see what he could find. Stackelbeck was gone about a month. He heard that Sinclair's private railroad car had been on a siding at Fall's ranch for many days. He also brought back what Bonfils later described as "shocking and astounding" information from people who asked not to be identified. Testifying before the same Senate committee that had questioned Leo Stack, Bonfils said he had shown Stackelbeck's report to William C. Shepherd, the managing editor, and to John T. Bottom, the paper's attorney.

"We had a meeting," Bonfils testified, "and it was decided that these articles should not be printed because of the great danger of libel; they were libelous if they were not true. If they were true we had to prove that they were true. It is an easy thing to sue a newspaper for libel—get the article and sue on it and then the newspaper has to show it is true. Well, so that was the unanimous idea in causing us not to print these articles, because of this danger of libel, which we thought would follow surely. . . ." So Stackelbeck's report was not published; it simply went into Bonfils' files.

July, 1922— At Sinclair's invitation, Stack and Bonfils took a train for New York. They met Sinclair in his office, where Bonfils outlined Stack's claim. As Bonfils related it, Sinclair replied brusquely: "I don't know why you gentlemen came here at all. This suit is not with me; I made no contract with you. The suit is with the Midwest and its allied companies there, and I don't see how you get me mixed up in it at all."

Bonfils replied, "Well, if that is true, Mr. Sinclair, we have come on a fool's errand, and on a long one. We will go back home."

August, 1922— Stackelbeck went back to New Mexico and uncovered more evidence of close ties between Sinclair and Secretary Fall. After he returned, *The Post* on August 15 published a lengthy "So The People May Know," charging that negotiations to lease Teapot Dome land began in January, 1922, in Sinclair's private car parked at Fall's Three Rivers Ranch in New Mexico. As a result, *The Post* said, Sinclair was given a lease on nine thousand acres with 12½ percent royalty to be paid on the oil produced from this land. Only six months earlier, *The Post* went on, oil firms seeking leases on nearly identical land near Teapot Dome were bidding 25 to 33 percent royalty, plus cash bonus payments averaging one thousand dollars per acre. Since Sinclair had paid no bonus, he had been given a gift of $9 million on that part of the deal alone, *The Post* contended. The editorial also charged that Sinclair was in position to make an enormous profit by manipulating the supply of oil by use of a pipeline he would be permitted to build.

Up to this point the nation's press had paid only desultory attention to the Teapot Dome situation. But as *The Post* hammered away with details, other newspapers began to perk up.

September, 1922— Sinclair asked Bonfils to come to New York again. Bonfils huffily declined and suggested Sinclair come to Denver. Sinclair then replied he was planning to visit oil fields in Oklahoma and he would be happy to get together with Bonfils in Kansas

City. They met at the Muehlebach Hotel. Out of that conference came an agreement under which Sinclair settled Stack's claim by paying $250,000 in cash and turning over a half interest valued at $750,000 to a 320-acre oil lease in Teapot Dome.

Rounding out the figures, Stack personally collected $50,000 off the top, plus about $86,000 for a total of approximately $136,000. Bonfils' share was also $86,000, which he divided with Tammen; so they pocketed $43,000 each. Attorney Schwartz got $15,000 and the balance went for expenses. The complicated lease deal was to be settled within eighteen months.

Suddenly *The Post* dropped its interest in Sinclair. No articles mentioning Sinclair were published in *The Post* between September 15 and December 3, 1922, and after that only news-agency dispatches about routine developments in the Teapot Dome matter appeared in *The Post*.

By this time, however, nationwide attention had been focused on Teapot Dome. The Senate Committee on Public Lands and Surveys, headed by Irvine L. Lenroot of Wisconsin, a Republican, began an investigation, and some startling information came to light.

Testimony revealed that Secretary Fall had accepted $200,000 from a Sinclair source shortly before granting the Teapot Dome lease. Fall had also solicited a $100,000 "loan" from Edward L. Doheny of the Pan American Petroleum Company before that firm received leases on portions of the Elk Hills and Buena Vista Hills reserves in California. Eventually, Fall was convicted of accepting a bribe, fined $100,000, and sentenced to a year in prison. Sinclair and Doheny were acquitted on charges of bribery and conspiracy, but the Supreme Court ruled the leases illegal and ordered them canceled.

Senator Lenroot's committee conducted a far-reaching investigation, and one of the questions it wanted answered was why Sinclair would agree to pay Bonfils and Stack a million dollars. Bonfils appeared voluntarily before the committee on February 8 and 9, 1924.

Lengthy backgrounding established the details of Stack's contract with Pioneer-Belgo and with Bonfils, and the fact that *The Post* had published a number of editorials highly critical of the Teapot Dome lease. Then Chairman Lenroot came to the point:

THE CHAIRMAN: And yet so long as you got your piece out of it, a million dollars, you were willing to become a party to it and stand upon this rotten deal and contract?
BONFILS: I was not. That had nothing to do with it at all.

CHAIRMAN: Is not the contract, sir, based upon this very lease for this 320 acres of land?

BONFILS: Oh, that was part of the deal.

CHAIRMAN: And did you not thereby become a party to this "rotten commercial transaction," sir?

BONFILS: I don't think so at all. I don't think so at all.

CHAIRMAN: Is it not a fact, Mr. Bonfils, that your transactions with Mr. Sinclair were not based upon any supposed legal rights to Mr. Stack?

BONFILS: That is not true at all.

CHAIRMAN: But that this whole deal was for the purpose of Mr. Sinclair purchasing your silence in your newspaper?

BONFILS: That is not true at all. It is as false as it could be; absolutely false.

At this point Senator Lenroot abruptly changed his line of questioning. He began to probe into Bonfils' personal and professional history. Although this had nothing to do with the Teapot Dome scandal, Bonfils felt obliged to respond.

Senator Lenroot asked what line of business Bonfils had followed in Kansas City before moving to Denver. Real estate, Bonfils said.

"Anything besides real estate in Kansas City?" Lenroot asked.

"No, not particularly," Bonfils answered.

Lenroot then asked whether Bonfils had "any difficulties while in Kansas City with the authorities." Bonfils replied, "No, not that I know of."

Next, Lenroot asked whether Bonfils had testified in the trial of Thomas O'Donnell in Denver. Bonfils remembered him well. Ten years earlier O'Donnell had tried to kill Bonfils.

Lenroot went on: "I want to ask you whether in that trial in Denver you testified as follows [reading]: 'Q. You were in the lottery business in Kansas City, Kansas, were you not?' "

Bonfils broke in, "Now, Kansas City, Kansas—now you are coming to it."

Lenroot said, "I said 'Kansas City.' I did not say where, did I?"

Bonfils then explained: "I was in the lottery business in Kansas City, Kansas. I was there two years. At that time there was no law in Kansas City, Kansas, against the lottery business. One could be in the lottery business as legally as in the banking business, as far as the law was concerned."

LENROOT: Yes, well, when I asked you a moment ago about any other business, did you remember then that you had been in the lottery business?

BONFILS: Yes I did.
LENROOT: Why did you not tell me?
BONFILS: Because you asked me about Kansas City, Missouri.
LENROOT: I did not ask you about Kansas City, Missouri.
BONFILS: I thought you did.

When Lenroot continued to hammer away on the point that Bonfils had failed to volunteer information about being in the lottery business, Bonfils retorted, "I should think you would feel very proud of bringing it out."

"There is just one reason, Mr. Bonfils," Lenroot answered. "The committee is very much interested in ascertaining whether this deal that you made with Mr. Sinclair was an honest compromise of an honest debt, or whether it was a deal between you and Mr. Sinclair to purchase the silence of *The Denver Post*. That is the materiality of it."

It is possible to read a great deal into Lenroot's statement, but he did not state in so many words that Bonfils' lack of candor about something that happened thirty years earlier might be a reflection on his current testimony about Teapot Dome. As for Bonfils, he felt that the honor of *The Post* needed defending. He made a rambling statement about Tom O'Donnell's "blind and malignant hatred for years and years" of *The Post,* about the Alferd Packer case that led to the shooting in the Red Room, and about the newspaper's efforts to break the coal trust.

"Now I want to make one more statement, and then so far as I am concerned, I will not raise my voice again in this matter," Bonfils finally said. "You will pardon this allusion that is personal. In the history of the journalistic world there has never been a paper that covers its territory with as complete a saturation as *The Denver Post*. It has 215,000 paid circulation on Sundays and 153,000 paid circulation on weekdays. It has a paid circulation each day of 60,000 more than there are houses in the city, by the water company and the directory. It has each day more circulation than all the other papers printed in Denver, Colorado, Wyoming, and New Mexico combined. It has on Sundays 30,000 more circulation than the papers of Denver, Colorado, Wyoming, and New Mexico. I say that not in the spirit of braggadocio, but in the spirit of gratitude. I would rather see one man coming into my office carrying a dinner pail, than to see a man leaving the finest limousine and coming in. And I am never going to forget my allegiance to the common man. He has made *The Post,* and he has not breathed the scandal, and the lies that have been circulated by the wealthy and the rich in that state. We have sold, in the last twenty-five years, about 15,000,000 tons of coal. And you can buy it there now the same as you could twenty-five years ago. It is now $5.90, or $4.90 a ton, delivered anywhere in Denver. That is the service that has made *The Post* one of the greatest papers of the United States, and one that has a greater per-capita circulation than any paper published anywhere in the history of the world."

He paused for breath and then this exchange followed:

LENROOT: Do you think, Mr. Bonfils, Mr. Sinclair was aware of all that?

BONFILS: I hope he was; and I hope you are aware of it, too.

LENROOT: Now, why do you think Mr. Sinclair was willing to pay you and Mr. Stack $1,000,000?

BONFILS: He didn't pay us $1,000,000.

LENROOT: He paid you $250,000, and he had an obligation to pay $750,000 more, which is an obligation for $1,000,000. Why do you think he was willing to do that?

BONFILS: I think Mr. Sinclair was willing to do that because he had the greatest oil dome in the world, and he thought he was going to make, as he said, $100,000,000, and he thought he had earned it and would pay for it.

LENROOT: Why should he pay you and Mr. Stack?

BONFILS: Mr. Stack had the contract, and I had an agreement with him for a portion, because they paid no attention to him. For a time, I suppose, Mr. Sinclair——

LENROOT (interposing): Why should they pay more attention to you than to him?

BONFILS: In the first place, I think I am a more important man. At least——

LENROOT (interposing): You certainly have a very important newspaper. . . . Do you think that Mr. Sinclair paid you $1,000,000 on the theory that there might be any legal liability there?

BONFILS: I do.

LENROOT: Do you think that, Mr. Bonfils?

BONFILS: I do. Did you ever know of Sinclair giving anything away to anybody? He is about as closefisted a man as you ever met.

LENROOT: I think Mr. Sinclair thought he was was getting value received for whatever he paid to you, sir.

BONFILS: He fooled himself if he did, sir.

The senators were never able to determine beyond doubt whether Sinclair's payment was settlement for a legal liability or whether it was the price of *The Post*'s silence. Robert Perkin in his *The First Hundred Years* tells us that at the Rocky Mountain *News* there was no doubt—Bonfils had been nabbed with his fist in the jam pot.

"The *News* gave it the full treatment—for one series of editions,"

Perkin writes. "Next day, as the hearing in Washington proceeded, it was disclosed that John Clean Shaffer [owner of the *News*] was involved too. Shaffer, who was always pleased when biographers took note of his years as Sunday School superintendent, had written in to the plundering oilmen and suggested mildly that he be placed 'on a parity' with Bonfils. The raiders decided that, viewed as a moral issue, there was merit to the suggestion. The sum of $92,500 was passed along. Joy subsided at the *News*. Staff members were crestfallen. Their own boss was a boodler, too. And a cut-price boodler at that."

There was one additional development that needs recording. At its second annual meeting, the now prestigious American Society of Newspaper Editors (ASNE) took note "of charges which had been made against certain members of the newspaper profession as a result of the Teapot Dome Oil hearings," and ordered an investigation by the Committee on Ethical Standards. Bonfils, Schuyler (the attorney), and Stackelbeck appeared before the committee.

The committee reported its findings to ASNE's board of directors, which on February 9, 1926, resolved: "By a contract of September 25, 1922, entered into with H. F. Sinclair of the Mammoth Oil Company, Mr. Bonfils accepted an interest the value of which depended upon the validity of the Teapot Dome lease to some degree, and that he therefore allowed himself to be placed in a position where he had in prospect a great financial gain by the success of a transaction which his newspaper had condemned and denounced as improper, illegal and perhaps tainted with scandal. Holding that such a dual relation as that occupied by Mr. Bonfils to the oil operators on one hand and to his newspaper and the public on the other is conducive to the weakening or destruction of public confidence in the newspaper press, the Board believes that Mr. Bonfils should be censured and suspended from membership in the Society, and so orders."

No publicity was given to the decision, and Bonfils was notified by mail. He promptly hit the ceiling and threatened to sue the Society and each director for slander. At a subsequent meeting Bonfils offered a deal—if the Society would drop the matter, Bonfils would resign.

Ten months after voting to oust Bonfils the ASNE board met in Chicago and adopted the following resolution: "That after scrutiny of the constitution and by-laws of the American Society of Newspaper Editors, and acting upon the advice of counsel, this Board declared that it is without authority to impose discipline upon members of the Society, and for that reason it hereby rescinds the action taken by the Board in the case of F. G. Bonfils at the meeting in Cleveland February 9, 1926."

And so Bonfils resigned.

Nathaniel R. Howard, then of the Cleveland *Plain Dealer* and later an ASNE president, is quoted in the Society's history: "The fact is that the case established for the whole profession to understand—undoubtedly one of Bonfils' motives—that ASNE did not have the muscle and lacked the authority to punish anyone."

It was a freebooting era and one must suspect there were other sanctimonious editors, like John Shaffer, with boodle-soiled hands they were reluctant to have bared to public scrutiny.

THE PUBLISHER AND THE CROWN PRINCE

After Harry Tammen's death in 1924 F. G. Bonfils accepted the possibility that he would not live forever and began to cast about for the man who would take over *The Post*. The two he looked at most often were William Chauncey Shepherd and Major Frederick Walker Bonfils.

Shepherd was born in New York City September 29, 1874, and moved to Denver in early childhood with his parents. His father was a jeweler and watchmaker. Shepherd's first job was copyboy for the Denver *Republican*. After a brief period with the Denver *Times* he joined *The Post* in 1908 as reporter, then news editor. In 1912 he was made managing editor, a job in which he not only supervised the entire news operation but served as a buffer between Bonfils and the staff, and vice versa.

"Shep, oh, Shep," Bonfils would call from the Red Room when he was displeased or had something on his mind. Shepherd's desk was just outside Bonfils' office. He was a tall, dignified man and when he heard the summons he would heave his bulk out of the swivel chair and hurry inside.

Even though Shepherd was given a good deal of leeway, Bonfils kept a sharp eye on expenses. His eye was sharpest at year's end, when annual reports came across his desk. One year he listed ten news-department people he wanted fired, presumably because they were being paid more than he thought they were worth. (Since the mechanical crafts were unionized, summary dismissals almost invariably hit the news and business departments.) Tossing the list on Shepherd's desk, Bonfils said, "I want you to get rid of these men. We've got to cut expenses."

Shepherd examined the list, wrote his name at the top, and took it back to Bonfils. "I approve," he said, "and I've added to it."

When Bonfils saw Shep's name, he slammed his fist against the desk and cried, "You're the most aggravating creature I've ever had around here. Now get out." And that was the end of that.

Major Bonfils was the son of F. G.'s sister, Henrietta Walker. He was born October 28, 1895—the day Bonfils and Tammen bought *The Post*—at Raton, New Mexico. He attended the U. S. Military Academy, where he played on the same football team as a cadet named Dwight D. Eisenhower, received his commission in 1916, and saw extensive combat in World War I. After the Armistice the Army sent him to Massachusetts Institute of Technology, where he received a bachelor's degree in engineering in 1922. The young officer's career seemed to be assured; he apparently was destined to win a general's stars. But in 1924, when he held the rank of major, Fred resigned from the Army and joined his uncle at *The Post*. Two years later he was appointed business manager.

Without a son to carry on, F. G. persuaded his nephew to change his name from Walker to Bonfils. Was this part of a promise that Major Bonfils would inherit the newspaper? F. G.'s younger daughter, Helen, was not unaware of the possibility. Once she confided to Donald R. Seawell, her attorney, friend, and successor as chairman of the board of *The Post,* that she confronted her father and demanded to know his intentions. "She told me," Seawell says, "that she walked straight into her father's room and accused him of trying by indirection to obtain a son and an heir to *The Post*. He said, 'What are you going to do about it?' And she replied: 'I'm not going to let you get away with it. If you have changed your will, you're going to tear it up and write a new one. If you have not changed your will, you're going to keep it the way it is and I'm going to run *The Post* after you're gone.' Then Bonfils replied: 'Bravo! That's the spirit I wanted you to show. Honey, you have more spunk than I gave you credit for. You have what it takes to run *The Denver Post*.' "

It was also about this time that Major Bonfils was severely reprimanded by F. G. for his conduct on *The Post* train to Cheyenne. It was no coincidence, then, that when F. G. wrote his last will it provided that Helen would have not only her own ownership of the newspaper stock, but would direct his foundation where the ultimate control of *The Post* lay. After F. G.'s death in 1933, Shepherd became editor and publisher and it was Helen, not the major, who joined the board of directors. Helen was named secretary-treasurer. If Major Bonfils was disappointed that he had been passed over, he never spoke of it. He served loyally as business manager until retirement in 1951.

F. G. Bonfils was forever on the lookout for talent to help him run his newspaper. On his travels he recruited a series of bright young men—usually without consulting Shepherd or the Major—who came to Denver with the impression that they were being groomed to become the next editor or business manager and were responsible to Bonfils alone during the training period. But soon he would tire of them, or become aware of their shortcomings, and return to the faithful Shep and Major. F. G. finally made his decision clear in 1932, when he named Shepherd assistant publisher and Eddie Day was hired away from the *News* to become managing editor.

Yet, even as F. G. loosened his grip on the editorial reins, everyone knew he was still the boss. He could be demanding about details. When *The Post* published a story datelined "Tiflis, Georgia," he pored over an atlas of the United States in fruitless search of its exact location. Called on the carpet for letting such an error get into print, copydesk chief Jim Hale had a difficult time explaining that this Georgia was in the Caucasus region of Russia. Bonfils could be erratic. Outraged by something that had happened in the nation's capital, he ordered that no Washington dateline was to appear in *The Post* henceforth. Until he decided to forget the order, the copydesk changed all Washington datelines to Baltimore:

> Baltimore, Md. (AP)—Dispatches from Washington today reported Congress had . . .

But there were also demonstrations of Bonfils' sheer, unorthodox genius for gripping reader interest. One dull Saturday the wire services quoted a London physician as saying an infant goes through a traumatic experience at birth. Bonfils assigned Pinky Wayne to interview Denver doctors and her story was published on page 1 Sunday morning under an eight-column headline that asked: DOES IT HURT TO BE BORN?

"DO YOU BELIEVE IN GOD?" *The Post* asked in two-inch-tall type on page 1 another Sunday. It appeared over a story of a religious census in cooperation with the region's leading clergymen.

When the nation waited with growing anxiety to learn the fate of Comdr. John Rodgers and his crew of four, down somewhere in the Pacific on a trail-breaking flight from California to Hawaii, *The Post* announced their rescue with a bannerline that echoed the public's sentiments: BLESS GOD, THEY'RE ALL SAFE!

When the parched eastern Colorado plains were drenched after

Page 1 of February 5, 1928, with headline "Does It Hurt to Be Born?"

Page 1 of December 5, 1926, with heading "Do You Believe in God?"

a long drought, *The Post* exulted over the "MILLION DOLLAR RAIN."
Many years later, after Palmer Hoyt became editor and publisher,
The Post headlined a "TWO MILLION DOLLAR RAIN" along with a
straight-faced explanation that inflation had doubled the value.

9

F. G.'s LAST HURRAH

After *The Post* and the *News* buried the hatchet in 1928 journalism in Denver became almost sedate compared to the circus days. Editors of some of the smaller papers around the state complained the *News* had become complacent and had abandoned its self-appointed role of badgering *The Post*. This sort of criticism was beginning to get under the skins of members of the *News* staff. Thus there was more than ordinary interest in a story turned in the night of August 10, 1932, by one of their reporters, Maurice Leckenby, later editor and publisher of the Steamboat Springs (Colorado) *Pilot*.

Leckenby had been at the Brown Palace Hotel for a pre-primary meeting of the Jane Jefferson Club when a factional dispute erupted between two Democratic stalwarts, Walter Walker and Edwin C. Johnson. Walker was the retiring state Democratic chairman and publisher of the Grand Junction *Daily Sentinel*, western Colorado's leading newspaper. Johnson was a candidate for governor and later a three-term U. S. senator. Walker picked the occasion to lash out at both Denver newspapers and Bonfils personally, all of which Leckenby reported in his story. Editors at the *News* pondered over it awhile, then decided to print it after removing some of the more pointed comments about their own paper. The story appeared at the bottom of page 1 in this manner.

POST IS ATTACKED
IN DEMOCRAT ROW
Walter Walker and Edwin C. Johnson Rip Into
Each Other and Each Flays Bonfils

Walter Walker, retiring state chairman of the Democratic Party, and Edwin C. Johnson, one of the party's designees for governor gave evidence last night of bitter factionalism which exists within the party on the eve of the primary campaign.

Speaking before the Jane Jefferson Club at the Brown Palace

Hotel, Walker ripped into Johnson and Johnson retaliated, and together they attacked Fred G. Bonfils, publisher of the *Denver Post,* and his newspaper.

Johnson also attacked W. W. Grant, Jr., the Democratic keynoter, and accused him of getting "misfacts" for his keynote address from the columns of *The Denver Post.*

The *Rocky Mountain News* then drew the fire of Chairman Walker. He spoke of a resolution condemning F. G. Bonfils which it was proposed to present to the Democratic assembly last Monday, and implied that the *News* would not have printed this and other facts of a definite news character pertaining to the assembly's action.

By innuendo, Walker charged that Johnson, who received the high designation for governor on the Democratic ticket, was responsible for the failure of plans to give Gov. William H. Adams a rousing ovation at the assembly in recognition of his service at the state house and his fidelity to the Democratic party.

Walker in his remarks defended Grant's speech, but said it appeared that he had some misinformation.

The retiring chairman charged that a "studied attempt" had been made to keep Governor Adams from the platform of the assembly for fear there would be an ovation that would hurt the chances of other candidates for governor. This thrust apparently was aimed at Johnson.

Discussing the Denver publication, Walker declared:

"Despite the boast that *The Post* is advertised by its enemies, we know that the vulture gnashes his teeth and shakes with rage when attacked.

"A resolution condemning *The Post* should have been passed by the Democratic assembly, and it would have been, save for those who truckle and fawn at the feet of *The Post* in order to get their pictures in the news columns and that of the wife in the society sheet.

"The day will come," he continued, "when some persecuted man will treat that rattlesnake as a rattlesnake should be treated and there will be general rejoicing.

"Governor Adams will live long as Colorado's greatest governor, but F. G. Bonfils will be remembered as the vilest man who ever dealt in the newspaper business.

"Bonfils is a public enemy and has left the trail of a slimy serpent across Colorado for 30 years.

"I hope any man on either ticket supported by *The Post* will be defeated. The people have a right to suspect candidates supported by *The Post*. All of us love Ben Stapleton for the great enemy he made. It is lucky Billy Adams and Ben Stapleton were not nominated on the same ticket, because that miserable creature would have died in a rage.

"Frederick G. Bonfils is the only one of his kind in the world and the mould was broken after him.

"His assault on the governor was the foulest, dirtiest, vilest piece of newspaper work in memory and would have been attempted by no other newspaper in the United States.

"Colorado has stood too much from the contemptible dog of Champa Street."

In his remarks concerning Governor Adams, Walker said:

"I regret that Governor Adams is not a candidate again, for I know that I speak for 80 per cent of the people of Colorado when I say they wanted him for their governor for another two years.

"I was sorry that the man who has made a great record in Congress, Edward T. Taylor, was not called to the platform to speak.

"I say now the things I felt like saying yesterday. Certain people did not want an ovation for Billy Adams. People who fawn and truckle before the power of Champa Street."

There were nine more paragraphs to Leckenby's story but with one minor exception they made no further reference to *The Post* or to Bonfils.

Two weeks later Bonfils sued the *News* for libel, charging that its story on Walker's speech had been published "maliciously and with the express and malevolent purpose and intent of blackening the good name and reputation of this plaintiff, and subjecting him to public hatred, ridicule, scorn and contempt." Bonfils contended he had suffered damage in the sum of $100,000 and he asked another $100,000 in punitive damages. He listed five specific passages as objectionable. They are reproduced here with his interpretation in parentheses and italicized:

"Despite the boast that *The Post* is advertised by its enemies, we know that the vulture gnashes his teeth and shakes with rage when attacked. *(Meaning thereby that the plaintiff is a vulture.)*

"The day will come," he continued, "when some persecuted man will treat that rattlesnake as a rattlesnake should be treated *(Meaning thereby that the plaintiff is a rattlesnake, and that he should be killed as a rattlesnake is killed)* and there will be general rejoicing.

"It is lucky Billy Adams and Ben Stapleton were not nominated on the same ticket, because that miserable creature would have died in a rage. *(Meaning thereby that if Billy Adams and Ben Stapleton were nominated on the same ticket, that the plaintiff would have died in a rage.)*

"His assault on the governor was the foulest, dirtiest, vilest piece of newspaper work in memory and would have been attempted by no other newspaper in the United States. *(Meaning that the plaintiff had committed an assault on the governor which no other newspaper published in the United States would have attempted.)*

"Colorado has stood much from the contemptible dog of Champa St." *(Meaning that the plaintiff is a contemptible dog.)*

Charles E. Lounsbury, a former *Post* employee who was then editor of the *News,* was puzzled by the suit. Bonfils had been called worse on numerous occasions by other newspapers. Was the suit an act of harassment that would be withdrawn before it came to trial? Still, a suit for $200,000 was a lot of money and Lounsbury lost no time in summoning the newspaper's counsel, Philip S. Van Cise, the highly respected onetime crime-busting District Attorney, for a strategy session. Van Cise explained what Lounsbury and his assistants already knew: Truth is the complete defense in a libel suit. Then he added: "I think we can find enough around here to prove these allegations."

At that point Roy Howard telephoned from New York. Lounsbury spoke to him briefly and then put Van Cise on the line. Those in the room heard Van Cise say, "I refuse to have anything to do with a compromise. If I go into this case, I'm going in it to win." There was a pause, and then he said, "All right, Mr. Howard, it's agreed that I'm going into this with everything I've got." He said if the case went to trial his fee would be at least thirty thousand dollars and if there were appeals "that might be only the beginning."

Now Van Cise outlined his strategy. There had been reports that Bonfils' anger had been fueled by the loss of key advertisers to the *News.* However, Van Cise preferred to assume that Bonfils was genuinely afraid his assassination was being incited and would press the suit to a conclusion. Van Cise noted Bonfils' claim that he was "well and favorably known" and that his good name and reputation had been blackened; the *News* would be defended by proving Bonfils did not have a good name and his reputation was so bad it was impossible to damage it further. To do this Van Cise would need to know everything there was to know about Bonfils' life; he would need a year-by-year, month-by-month chronology of Bonfils' history. Wallis M. Reef, a sharp and tenacious veteran reporter of the *News* staff, was assigned to work under Van Cise's direction.

Reef, a tall, soft-spoken man with a deceptively easygoing manner, set out to interview Denverites who had been attacked in *The Post* and invited them to tell their side of the story. To his amazement he found no one willing to talk. Some people said they were reluctant to open old wounds. Reef had to assume others had something to hide or the victims were still afraid of arousing Bonfils' ire. And possibly, some of the attacks might have been based on fact.

Meanwhile, Van Cise rented one floor of the Patterson Building next door to the *News* and hired a staff to compare stories on important local subjects published over the years in *The Post*, the *News*, the *Times*, and the *Republican*. Where there was a wide discrepancy between the accounts in *The Post* and the other three, the story was noted for further investigation. At the same time newspapers throughout the state were checked for uncomplimentary names they had applied to Bonfils and *The Post*. An alphabetical list of 188 was compiled, starting with *assassin* and ending with *yellow dog* and *Zulu native*, and including such choice epithets as *blackmailer, cuttlefish, crook, coyote, cootie-covered rat, devil's paramour, felon, ghoul of Champa Street, hyena, jackal, moral assassin, octopus, polecat, recidivist, rattlesnake, skunk, traducer, vermin,* and *vulture*.

When it became evident Reef wasn't going to get much to help the *News'* case in Denver, Van Cise assigned him to retrace Bonfils' steps all the way back to his boyhood in Troy, Missouri. Thus began a remarkable detective job, checking into every lead and rumor, seeking details of every remotely damaging indiscretion that Bonfils might have committed over a period of some sixty years. Reef climbed into his car and headed for Kansas City. The trail led to Oklahoma, Texas, Arkansas—to the shacks of old-timers, to yellowed newspaper files, musty courthouse records and the fading memories of police officers and former officials. After he had been on the road a few weeks Reef's wife, Peggy, joined him. She had been a *News* reporter and her help proved invaluable. Reef dug into the land fraud in which Bonfils had sold worthless desert plots in Texas by purporting them to be in Oklahoma City, into the Kansas City lottery episodes, a police court hearing after a fistfight in Guthrie, Oklahoma. He probed Bonfils' bank records in Missouri in hopes of uncovering evidence of illegal income. After interviewing and poring over records all day he would stay up half the night to write reports to Van Cise. He was working against time to assemble a complete dossier before the libel suit came to trial.

In a letter to Thomas L. Sidlo, general counsel of Scripps-Howard newspapers, Van Cise explained what he was doing:

> This libel case is peculiar in that we made general statements about Bonfils, calling him a rattlesnake, a vulture, contemptible dog, etc. If we had called him a thief the issue would be easy. . . . If a man is called a thief and is one, you justify by giving the court in which he was convicted of larceny, the date, etc. But, when you call him a rattlesnake, or the things we call him, we have to put into

the answer every possible thing that we can find which would justify such a statement. Otherwise the answer is subject to demurrer on the plea of justification, and all that would be left for us would be to go to the jury on the issue of his reputation. Granted that we could not justify, he has such a bad reputation that he could probably not recover anyway but it would be a rather Pyrrhic victory. Hence the reason why the *News* has got to spend a lot of real money in getting up facts on Bonfils from the cradle to the grave, and all of those facts must be set forth in detail in the answer.

Van Cise was astonishingly thorough. While Reef was in Texas he received this letter:

Dear Wally:

I overlooked one thing that is quite essential in regard to Oklahoma City, Texas. Please find out how close it is to water. Is it on the Canadian River, or is there any stream near it, or dry wash, or well, or water of any kind? What is its topography? Is it sand-blown, river bottom, rocky bluff, or what?

If by any possibility there are any rattlesnakes in that vicinity, it would be a "ten strike" if your picture of Oklahoma City, Texas, showed at least one rattlesnake in the near foreground, with a vulture circling overhead and a contemptible prairie dog twittering at you from a nearby hole.

Hastily yours,

Emphasizing the thoroughness of his investigation, Reef recently recalled two rumors that he looked into but could not substantiate. One was to the effect that Bonfils had been horsewhipped in Holdenville, Oklahoma, sometime in 1909 by a Sells-Floto circus roustabout for trifling with his wife. No proof was ever found. The other was that when a boyhood friend of Bonfils' died in Troy, a grieving young Bonfils had chiseled a cherub off the headstone and taken it home. What Van Cise hoped to prove by this bit of intelligence is obscure, but Reef visited the ancient cemetery, located the grave, and found the headstone and its cherubs intact.

Word of Reef's mission sifted back to *The Post* and Van Cise's strategy became apparent. Bonfils, approaching his seventy-second birthday, did not relish the thought of his entire life being laid bare to public scrutiny through the courts and in the columns of the *Rocky Mountain News*. When he was summoned before a notary to make a deposition, Bonfils on the advice of his attorney, Philip Hornbein, refused to give little more than his name, rank, and serial number. Here is an excerpt from the transcript:

Van Cise: What was your father's occupation?

HORNBEIN: We object to that. We are not going into any foolishness here.

VAN CISE: That is the only question I am going to ask about his family.

BONFILS: He knows. What difference does it make? His father and my father were intimate friends. What business is it?

VAN CISE: His father and mother were most excellent people.

HORNBEIN: What are you going into it for?

VAN CISE: I am asking now what his father's occupation was.

HORNBEIN: Tell me what that has to do with this case, any more than what your father's occupation was.

VAN CISE: I wish to have an answer to that question.

HORNBEIN: I am asking you what has that to do with it?

VAN CISE: I am not going to answer.

HORNBEIN: You decline? He [Bonfils] does not decline to state what his father's occupation was, but he takes the position it is immaterial, unless you say in this record what the relevancy is, his father's occupation. It was never asked in any court in this state at any time. We want to know if you are willing to say what the purpose of it is.

VAN CISE: I have asked you what your father's occupation was. Will you answer the question, or not? (No response.) Let the record show that the witness remains mute.

BONFILS: Don't get in any smart things here. Don't pick on my mother or father.

VAN CISE: I am not picking on your mother and father. I thought very highly of both of them.

BONFILS: You better not.

VAN CISE: I knew them in the church, and I am not making any insinuation in any way, shape or form. I simply am asking what his occupation was. I understand that he was a probate judge down there, and I wanted to find out. That is the only purpose of my question.

Hornbein's strategy backfired. Van Cise later admitted he had known comparatively little about Bonfils' past and had only a few questions to ask. But because of Bonfils' refusal to answer, Van Cise was able to go to court for a ruling as to whether the witness could be required to respond. This delayed the suit while Reef continued to amass information.

At a second deposition hearing on November 15, Bonfils again refused to answer Van Cise's far-ranging questions. Hornbein argued that the issue was that the *News,* unable to overcome Bonfils as a competitor in the newspaper business, "conceived the purpose of instigating his assassination." He complained: "Clearly, the examination is not in good faith, not made for the purpose of taking his testimony as a witness. The question of what he was in school, whether he was good in mathematics, or anything of the kind does not show or tend to show the remotest relevancy to the issue which we are here confronted with. Under these circumstances, we will retire."

This was precisely what Van Cise wanted. That afternoon he went to court to ask that Bonfils be punished for contempt. The purpose of the deposition, he said, was to have Bonfils tell about his life from 1881 to the present and "to show thereby the truth of all the statements made about him by Walter Walker." In this petition Van Cise listed forty-three allegations, many of them relating to material Reef had uncovered. By making these allegations part of the court record he made it possible for the *News* to publish them, which it did in three columns of type. It was evident that Van Cise ran out of serious allegations after a while and threw in everything he could think of to complete the list. For example:

> 39. That because of the many and varied transactions in which he [Bonfils] has been involved since 1881, he is subject to violent nightmares and fear that in one of them he may reveal some of the shady transactions of his past and requires a constant companion when asleep so that he may be instantly awakened when seized by such a spasm.
>
> 40. That his reputation is not good, but on the contrary is bad in Denver, Colorado, and the various states of the United States.
>
> 41. That he claims virtue and all good things for himself and his paper, *The Denver Post,* but that he conducts a theater where he shows a burlesque of dancing girls and hootchy-kootchy dancers which is given over largely to raw and lascivious exhibitions and alleged jokes of the smutty variety.

The forty-second allegation was: "That although a millionaire he is penurious and parsimonious with his own family and the members of his household." For some reason the *News* did not publish it.

Bonfils asked for further delay, which was granted. Van Cise gloated in a letter to Sidlo: "Apparently he [Bonfils] is going to do everything possible to prevent being forced to take the witness stand. . . . For the first time Bonfils is put in the position of taking the witness stand in public so that his entire life can be exposed, or quitting cold and conclusively showing that he is yellow. Either action by him will go far to break his power."

As Christmas approached, Van Cise agreed to let Wally and Peggy Reef come home for the holidays with the understanding they would go back on the road to complete picking up depositions. At *The Post,* members of the staff noticed that Bonfils seemed to be deeply preoccupied and more and more withdrawn.

On Thursday, January 26, Bonfils complained of a pain in his ear and left for home early with his driver. Reporters in the city room saw that while his step was firm, he held a hand over the ear. That was his last exit.

Bonfils was confined to bed in his home. On Monday, January 30, physicians performed minor surgery to drain the ear and ease the pain. By early Thursday morning, February 2, Bonfils was dead of was was described as toxic encephalitis, an acute inflammation of the brain. He was seventy-two years old.

The Post that day devoted the better part of six pages to the news of its publisher's death. Only two items on page 1 dealt with a subject other than the death—the weather forecast and Arthur Brisbane's "Today" column. The story that was front-page news in many other newspapers around the country that day appeared on page 8 of *The Post* under a headline that read: "Hitler Opens Drive Against Communists; Party Headquarters Raided by Police Thruout Prussia." On page 1 all the column rules were inverted, but the masthead in unintentional tribute to the paper's cofounder proclaimed: "The Paid Circulation of *The Denver Post* Yesterday Was 147,212. Average Paid Sunday Circulation of January 287,224. The Best Newspaper in the U.S.A."

Ironically, it was a *News* extra that was first with the death story. As rumors of the seriousness of Bonfils' illness filtered out of his mansion, the *News* stationed a deathwatch. Oxygen tanks were seen being taken into the home. Late Wednesday night the Rev. Hugh L. McMenamin, rector of the Cathedral of the Immaculate Conception, entered the mansion. Later, it was learned he had baptized Bonfils and administered the last sacraments of the Catholic Church. In anticipation of the death Wally Reef was summoned to the *News* office to write an obituary. He hammered out a factual summary of Bonfils' life and the impact he had on the history of the state, compassionately omitting the snide and gratuitous remarks that he might have used. The obituary was set in type and press crews held in readiness. Before dawn a reporter telephoned that there was unusual activity at Bonfils' home and it was believed Bonfils had died. The *News* wanted to be positive. A member of the staff telephoned the leading mortuaries, identified himself as calling from the Bonfils mansion, and demanded to know when the hearse was coming.

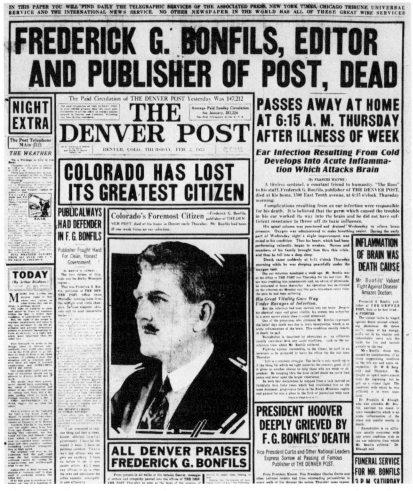

The Post devoted nearly six pages to covering the story of its editor's death, but had to depend on the *Rocky Mountain News* for some details. This was page 1.

When one mortician said his people were on the way, that was all the confirmation needed. Later that morning Lounsbury received a call from Eddie Day, the *News* employee who had gone on to become managing editor of *The Post*.

"Chuck," Day said, "your story on Mr. Bonfils carries a copyright line, but I hope you won't mind if we use some of it to fill out our coverage. You seem to know more about his background than we do." Permission was granted.

After Bonfils' death the libel suit was dropped and the mass of material Reef had gathered—enough to fill four drawers of a steel filing cabinet—was turned over by Van Cise to the *News,* after which it vanished into Scripps-Howard's corporate archives.

For his pains, Van Cise suffered a fate common to those who had affronted *The Post:* His name was banned from its news columns. The ban was not lifted until Palmer Hoyt arrived in 1946 and announced *The Post* wasn't mad at anybody. Hoyt was introduced to leading Denverites at a series of receptions and Van Cise was delighted to be invited to one of them. In 1954 *The Post,* along with the Better Business Bureau and its directors, was named in an eleven-million-dollar suit by Leo Spears, a chiropractor, who charged that articles written by Robert Byers constituted a conspiracy to destroy Spears' clinic and hospital. This time Philip Van Cise and his son, Edwin P., as attorneys for the Better Business Bureau were also called on to defend *The Post.* Spears lost his case, but subsequently the *News* decided to seek other counsel. However, *The Post* management was so impressed by the Van Cises that their firm was retained to handle its libel matters. The relationship continued happily until the younger Van Cise gave up his practice to accept a judicial appointment in 1974.

There is one sad sequel that has to do with Reef, who worked so hard and loyally to bolster his newspaper's defense against Bonfils' suit. He fell ill, possibly in part because of exhaustion from overwork during the four months he was on the road, and was forced to take a leave of absence. He had been paid seventy-five dollars a week as a member of the *News* staff, a substantial salary in 1933. When he went on leave he received full pay for two weeks and half pay for an additional two weeks. After that he was dropped from the payroll. He never returned to the *News.*

In the quiet that descended over Denver following Bonfils' death close friends remembered something he had said a month earlier on hearing that Calvin Coolidge had died. Aware of the encroaching years, physically weary, and filled with anxiety about the libel suit he had instigated, Bonfils remarked: "There are times when I get very tired of this struggle. Sometimes I think it would be easier to step through the door to the supreme adventure."

Thomas Hornsby Ferril, the onetime Denver newspaperman who became a poet of national stature, still remembers Bonfils' office the last time he visited it. There was a large world globe in one corner and behind it was a shotgun. Somehow, it made Ferril think of Alexander the Great who mourned because there was nothing left to conquer.

MANY WHO MOURNED

On the day "The Boss" died his newspaper published brief quotations from sixty-six prominent citizens expressing their shock and sorrow. The headline over the story on page 1 was: "All Denver Praises Frederick G. Bonfils." This was an unabashed hyperbole. Many condemned Bonfils even in death. But there were many others not interviewed, who noted his passing with sadness or warm memories.

Caroline Bancroft remembered him best as the kind, teasing man who lived not far from her home when she was a child touring the block on her tricycle. "Come on across the street, little girl," he called to her one day, "and I'll give you one of my roses."

"I can't," she replied. "My mother won't let me cross the street."

"Well, that's too bad," he said. "My mother won't let me cross the street either, so I guess you don't get a rose today."

Years later he hired her to edit *The Post*'s first book-review section. His managing editor, Shepherd, complained that book-review sections were impractical because publishers refused to advertise, but Bonfils wanted to raise the tone of *The Post*. Miss Bancroft remembers him as a man who had a wide grasp of history, favoring the Napoleonic era, and he could converse charmingly and knowledgeably about classical music, great books, or the flora and fauna of Africa and North America.

Doc Bird Finch, the likable cartoonist who rarely ended any day sober, remembered Bonfils for his compassion. Finch was being paid $125 a week until Bonfils in a fit of exasperation over Finch's drinking cut his salary to $25. What Finch didn't know for a long time was that the other $100 was being sent to his wife each payday.

Despite his roughshod tactics, Bonfils could be something of a philosopher. Something Louie Levand did one day infuriated Lord Ogilvy. The Scot rarely became upset but on this occasion he was ready to smash a chair over Levand's head before several colleagues broke it up. Two or three days later Bonfils called Ogilvy into his office and, without mentioning the Levand incident, remarked, "You know, Captain, at our age anger is a luxury we cannot afford." That was all that was ever said.

Joe Preston, a copyreader, remembered a similar experience. He was sitting in for Joe Ward, by then working out his days as editor of *The Great Divide,* which had been revived as a farm magazine. Bonfils had disapproved of something Ward had used and charged out of his office to bawl him out. Preston suddenly found himself the target of Bonfils' ire. Preston, who had a hair-trigger temper, figured that as an innocent bystander he didn't deserve to be talked to in that manner. He suggested bluntly that Bonfils should "kiss my ass," then put on his hat and coat and walked out.

Next day, somewhat contrite, he marched into Bonfils' office and apologized.

"Son," Bonfils observed quietly, "that was a bit rough to say to your employer, wasn't it?"

Louis O'Brien remembered he had been Bonfils' favorite caddy at the Lakewood Country Club. The club had a rule that caddies were not to be tipped for finding balls hit into an adjoining alfalfa field, a measure designed to discourage time-consuming searches. Nonetheless, most golfers gave their caddies a dime for each ball they retrieved. Bonfils would pay O'Brien a quarter, which was enough to inspire dedicated search but still less expensive than a new ball. Bonfils hired O'Brien as a *Post* messenger boy in 1920 and he was cashier when he retired fifty years later.

Some people snickered in recollection of Bonfils' immodesty about his prowess as a fisherman. In 1932 he hooked a large trout on a Royal Coachman No. 8 dry fly in the South Platte River at the Wigwam Club, a private fishing preserve. He landed it about 11:30 A.M. after an hour's battle. The fish weighed eight pounds, twelve ounces. Details were telephoned immediately to *The Post,* and a story about Bonfils' feat appeared on page 1 that same afternoon. The trout was entered in *The Denver Post*-Dave Cook Big Trout Contest and won the $150 grand prize. If many were amused that Bonfils should win his own contest, others recalled that often he would gently unhook a trout that had given him a particularly courageous fight, kiss it on its slippery snout, and free it to fight another day.

There is another fish story that makes the point that Bonfils was not always penurious. Frequently he would return early from trips to the South Platte and place his catch in an ice chest used to keep

stereotype mats moist and cool. One hot summer day a young stereo-
typer named Emmet J. Wilt neglected to order the ice and the fish
spoiled. Bonfils gave Wilt a blistering he never forgot. A short time
later Wilt sought a three-hundred-dollar loan at a pawnshop to meet
family medical bills. Without telling Wilt, the pawnbroker telephoned Bonfils to check on his employment status. Bonfils summoned

When Bonfils caught a big trout, it was page-1 news.

Wilt and asked why he needed the money. When Wilt explained, Bonfils wrote him a check for the full amount.

Medical research frequently was on Bonfils' mind. Through the Frederick G. Bonfils Foundation he offered prizes for discovery of a cure for tuberculosis, a scourge in those days, and for the conquest of cancer. But eminently more practical was his gift of twenty acres of land, valued at $100,000, as a site for the University of Colorado Medical School. The state legislature had appropriated funds to match a $750,000 gift from the Rockefeller Foundation to launch the school in 1922. But there was not enough money to buy a site. Bonfils owned forty acres between Eighth and Eleventh avenues on Colorado Boulevard—a prime piece of land—and he gave half of it "as an unrestricted gift to the people of Colorado."

Bonfils' actions were marked by many other seeming contradictions. Some people remembered the venom with which he assailed his perennial foes—politicians, the "trusts," and "corporations." Others recalled that he had dressed in a Santa Claus suit to entertain underprivileged youngsters at a Christmas dinner aboard a Union Pacific diner.

Some recalled that Bonfils had proposed that Colorado auto license plate No. 1 should be presented as an "Order of Merit" to "Denver's most useful citizen." The secretary of state went along with the idea and the first year, 1932, the award went to Emily Griffith, founder of a famous vocational education program in the Denver Public Schools. "Henceforth when the car that bears it passes along the streets and highways it will be a sign that one who has achieved nobly rides forth," *The Post* announced. But the following year plate No. 1 appeared on Bonfils' own car.

Those who knew Frederick Gilmer Bonfils could understand. Like money and power and giant trout, License No. 1 symbolized a goal, and Bonfils was constitutionally unable to resist the challenge of capturing each of them.

10

TWO PROUD, WILLFUL WOMEN

Harry Tammen died childless and distribution of his multimillion-dollar estate in 1924 was a relatively simple matter. Half went into a trust for his wife, Agnes. She outlived him by eighteen years and enjoyed her legacy to the fullest, traveling widely and supporting many charities. The balance of Tammen's estate, after numerous generous bequests were taken care of, went into a trust for Denver's Children's Hospital.

The problem was more complex for Fred Bonfils. When he drew his last will on February 4, 1930, his wife, Belle, was not in robust health. A series of small strokes was to leave her cheerful but sometimes forgetful. She and Fred had two daughters. May, the firstborn, was his favorite but when she defied him to marry a man he considered unworthy, Bonfils' affection chilled. Thereafter he concentrated his very possessive love on the other daughter, Helen, who was no less headstrong than her sister and father, but wise enough to remain in his good graces. Whatever her private thoughts may have been, she maintained a "Papa's girl" image.

Bonfils arranged to care for the three women of his family after his death in his own peculiar way. It is important to look into the details because the resentment stemming from his arrangement was to have a profound effect on his newspaper many years later.

May, as we have learned, was born in 1883 and was twelve years old when her father bought *The Post* and moved his family to Denver. She grew into a pretty, thoroughly feminine young woman, her blue eyes somewhat darker than her father's, blond, gently curved, and thoroughly appreciative of the amenities that the family's growing fortune provided. She attended St. Mary's Academy and the exclusive Wolcott School for Girls in Denver (its motto was *Noblesse Oblige*) before enrolling at Brownell School in New York. On her return home she told her father she was going to a dance to celebrate

May was F. G. Bonfils' older daughter. She fell out of his favor when she married against his wishes. (Denver Public Library, Western History Department)

her twenty-first birthday. Bonfils thought she ought to observe the occasion with her family at home and said, "You don't love me, or else you wouldn't want to go out tonight."

"But, Papa," May protested, "I'm twenty-one years old now."

Petulantly, Bonfils replied, "You can go only if you take me with you."

She went to the dance and he went with her.

That incident convinced May she could never assert her independence so long as she lived at home. In 1904 a well-bred twenty-one-year-old girl didn't leave parental bed and board to take an apartment; she lived at home until she married. So May set her cap for a husband. Young and inexperienced, she was attracted by the first eligible man to come along. His name was Clyde V. Berryman, two years her senior, a sometime piano salesman and son of a pioneer Nebraska merchant. A short while later, while Bonfils was away, they eloped to the nearby town of Golden and were married in a civil ceremony. Bonfils was furious when he heard the news but there was nothing he could do but refuse to send May her clothes. The young couple led a wandering existence that took them to Omaha, to Kansas City for several years, then to Wichita, where Berryman ran a music store for seven or eight years. After that the Berrymans moved to Los Angeles and Oakland in California. Helen and her mother visited the Berrymans on a number of occasions during this period, sometimes staying several weeks at a stretch, and Belle sent her daughter money regularly. Bonfils, too, wrote May affectionate letters but could never get himself to accept his son-in-law. Finally, the Berrymans returned to Denver about 1916. May visited the Bonfils home frequently and Berryman would drop by *The Post* from time to time, usually when Bonfils was not in his office. Old-time *Post* employees recall that Berryman was not particularly likable.

Helen also attended Wolcott School. Although May is not mentioned in Wolcott's alumnae book, Helen is listed with the class of 1909. She also attended National Park Seminary in Forest Glen, Maryland. Helen was taller than May, also blue-eyed, and her facial contours more resembled her father's. She was more effusive than May and given to theatrical mannerisms that became more pronounced as she grew older. At home she absorbed a great deal of knowledge about the world of business by listening to her father talk about *The Post* and the securities and real estate he bought through the Boma Investment Company, a family-owned holding company which was also the repository for his *Post* stock. *Boma* is the Swahili word for an enclosure formed by thornbushes as protection from wild beasts; no doubt Bonfils picked it up on one of his trips to Africa and found it appropriate for his fiscal objectives. Although Helen

Helen, the younger, made sure she inherited control of the paper. Both pictures were taken somewhat prior to 1935, when the sisters had a falling-out.

might not have been aware of it, she was gaining the background that enabled her to make some shrewd investments and critical business decisions when she became a Broadway producer and an executive of *The Post.* In her younger days, however, her activity in finance did not go much beyond helping Papa's secretary, Anne O'Neill, to clip bond coupons. Her interests focused largely on the Margery Reed Mayo day nursery and the theater.

The theater was an early love. She often attended matinees at the Tabor Grand and Elitch's, Denver's famous summer theater, with her mother and grandmother. She also played in many amateur productions at the University of Denver's community theater—*East Lynne, Ladies of the Jury, Good-bye Again, Personal Appearance,* and *The Little Foxes,* with one memorable appearance as Sadie Thompson, the naughty girl with heart of gold in *Rain.* She liked to say she made her theatrical debut at a very early age when she rode an elephant in the grand entry at the Sells-Floto circus. One year when the Denver Press Club was trying to raise funds with a benefit show, Helen played a minor role, helped with the direction, and even persuaded advertising salesmen at *The Post* to sell tickets to their accounts.

But over the years Bonfils continued to keep a protective watch over her. He didn't want to lose Helen to another man like Berryman. He suspected that most young men were interested in Helen only because of his money, and with his reputation for ferocity he didn't have to try very hard to frighten away prospective beaux. But Helen outfoxed him. After his death she admitted that for more than ten years she had boyfriends call on her at May's modest home a few blocks from the Bonfils mansion. Even after Helen reached adulthood Bonfils had the gates to their home locked at 10 P.M. Often she had to miss the last act to beat the curfew, but sympathetic servants made sure she was never locked out. It irked Bonfils that Helen was never invited to join the Junior League. One day when Caroline Bancroft talked to Bonfils about publicity for a Junior League charity, he declared flatly he wasn't interested in helping an organization that was too snooty to accept his daughter. Miss Bancroft took the word back to the society girls and eventually Helen was made an honorary member since by then she had passed the age limit. As her acting skills matured, Helen won parts at Elitch's, where talents as diverse as Douglas Fairbanks and Grace Kelly got their start. Helen's first role was in *Men in White* in 1934. It was at Elitch's that Helen met and fell in love with George Somnes, a New York

Helen Bonfils' first husband, George Somnes (left), had a striking resemblance to her father (right).

director and producer who had come out for the summer. Friends noted that Somnes had a striking facial resemblance to Bonfils.

Robert Stouffer, Bonfils' chauffeur who stayed on to work for Helen, recalls that she was introduced to Somnes by a friend in the cast. "I have never seen a man like that," she told her driver. "He has such piercing eyes." She offered to give Somnes a ride back to the Brown Palace Hotel. Stouffer had been accustomed to dropping guests at the nearest convenient corner. When he stopped across the street from the hotel for Somnes, Helen ordered him to go around the block and drive up to the front entrance. Stouffer figured correctly that she was seriously interested in the director.

Helen and Somnes were married in 1936, fifteen months after her mother's death. By then Helen was forty-six years old. Although she maintained her home in Denver, the couple also leased a luxurious New York apartment. As the Bonfils and Somnes Producing Company, they backed a number of Broadway plays, including *Sun Kissed* in 1937 and *The Brown Danube* and *Pastoral* in 1939. Helen also continued her acting, appearing on Broadway in *The Greatest Show on Earth* in 1938 and *Topaze* in 1947 under her stage name, Gertrude Barton. This probably was the happiest period of her life. She and Somnes were in love and the fantasy and glamour and excitement of the theater helped her to forget the heartache following her father's death.

The trouble was rooted in Bonfils' will, directing distribution of an estate officially valued at $14,300,326. In actuality Bonfils was

Helen Bonfils and Somnes produced *Sun Kissed* on Broadway in 1937. One of the main characters was Sylvia, a trained goose. (International News photo)

worth substantially more. But in the last years of his life several of his acquisitions were turned over to Helen so that she owned perhaps a million in her own name. And Bonfils' investments were so varied and extensive that it is likely some of them did not appear on the inventory of his estate.

The will started routinely enough, although it was a sore disappointment to many who had served Bonfils long and well at *The Post.* Major F. W. Bonfils, who once might have had hopes of owning the paper, was left $25,000 plus $10,000 "for the education (exclusively, and for no other purpose) of" his two children. The major's brother, Col. Eugene B. Walker, and Anne O'Neill Sullivan, Bonfils' secretary, were left $10,000 each. William C. Shepherd got $5,000. Bruce A. Gustin, whose job it was to articulate Bonfils' thoughts in an unsigned opinion column titled "That's That," was bequeathed $2,000. Stackelbeck, who had been sent to New Mexico to uncover Albert Fall's role in the Teapot Dome scandal, was given $1,000, as were Pinky Wayne, the star reporter, and Betty Craig, who worked in the drama department and liked to tell other members of the staff she could get away with anything because she was Bonfils' illegitimate daughter. Other cash bequests ranging from $2,500 to

$1,000 were made to numerous nieces and nephews, a few friends and household employees.

The bulk of the estate was left in trust with the Denver National Bank and the First National Bank of Kansas City, with the income to be distributed in this manner:

—$50,000 a year to the widow, Belle Bonfils, for life.

—$25,000 a year to Helen Bonfils for life. After Belle's death, her annuity would go to Helen, making the payment to Helen $75,000 a year.

—$12,000 a year to May Bonfils Berryman so long as she remained married to Clyde Berryman. But if she divorced him, or was widowed, her annuity would become $25,000 a year for life.

—Annuities of $2,400 a year for life to Bonfils' sisters Etta B. Walker and Nellie Barber, and to his brother Charles A. Bonfils. Annuities of $1,200 a year for life to his brothers Thomas L. Bonfils and William D. Bonfils; to a sister-in-law, Gertrude Yard; to a cousin, Emma Bryant; and to Volney T. Hoggatt, his friend and bodyguard. A $600 annuity to Catherine Donnelly, a household servant.

—All the rest of the income from the trust, and the body of the trust itself after the death of the last beneficiary, to go to the Frederick G. Bonfils Foundation, which was instructed to spend the money within ten years.

The Frederick G. Bonfils Foundation had been established in 1927, more than five years before his death, as "a corporation, not for profit, organized for charitable, benevolent, scientific, medical and public educational purposes."

"It will be used 'for the betterment of mankind,'" Bonfils explained at the time the foundation was announced. "Those five words are the ruling and governing spirit of the Foundation. The idea is as broad as the world, yet I have in mind my special love for our people of this great Intermountain territory, particularly the people of the states of Colorado and Wyoming. I want the Foundation to be so administered that it will result in better schools, better and more intelligent people and healthier and happier conditions of life.

"I hope through the efforts of the Foundation to advance morality and a more widespread regard for the love of God and the gospel of Christ. Whatever will achieve this end will have the support of the Foundation. I do not favor hobbies and isms and strange cults. Science, intelligence, morality and true wisdom are the agencies that will help mankind and these I have kept in mind."

The original trustees of the foundation were F. G. Bonfils, Helen, and his brothers Thomas and Charles, Major Bonfils, and attorneys

O. W. Chanute and J. B. Grant. All except Chanute, who predeceased F. G., were also named executors of his will.

What Bonfils had done through his will was to provide liberally for his widow and Helen, and not quite so liberally for May, during their lifetimes with income from his estate. He had not given them any portion of the estate itself, which was made up in substantial part of *Post* stock. He had placed the estate in a trust to be administered by two banks rather than any individual heir, and after the last beneficiary was dead the stock would go to a charitable foundation.

In practice, however, the banks as trustees were obligated to manage the trust according to the wishes of its principal beneficiaries, Belle and Helen. And since Belle was elderly, effective control of the stock was in Helen's hands.

What Bonfils had in mind for the future of his newspaper and why he chose to give Helen control of the *Post* stock through a trust rather than will her the stock outright to do as she pleased with it are secrets that died with him. Helen testified in one of the suits resulting from the will that she had no prior knowledge of its contents.

But there was one technicality that could frustrate the intent of Bonfils' will. It is inconceivable that he would not have been aware of it. Under Colorado law the widow has the option of claiming one-half of her deceased husband's estate if the will does not provide her with as much. Belle Bonfils exercised this widow's option in June of 1933, four months after Bonfils' death, in effect breaking the will. She claimed as much of the *Post* stock as she was entitled to claim, thus making it available to her own heirs instead of having it locked ultimately in the Frederick G. Bonfils Foundation.

May Berryman also was upset by the provisions of her father's will. She had been treated less generously than her sister and she felt this was unjust. Berryman had been in Texas when Bonfils died, but when he came home he persuaded his wife to challenge that part of the will that affected her. Shortly after her mother claimed half the estate, May filed suit, contending that the provision of the will limiting her benefits to twelve thousand dollars while she was married to Berryman was "contrary to public policy and good morals and therefore null and void." The executors of the estate made a routine objection, but Helen said privately she hoped her sister would win the suit. The court ruled May was entitled to the full twenty-five thousand and the estate's executors accepted the decision. Thus, two key parts of Bonfils' will were frustrated.

Later that summer of 1933 Helen and her mother made a trip to Kansas City. What happened during that visit became a matter of dispute—and an important point of litigation—after Belle died in Denver on June 3, 1935. She was descending the stairway at the mansion, preparing to meet Helen at the Margery Reed Mayo day nursery, when she suffered a cerebral thrombosis and died before a physician could be summoned.

Her will, covering an estate whose value was estimated at ten million dollars, also had its peculiarities. It provided that Helen and May should share in it equally. But it also provided that Helen would receive her share outright while May's share would be held in trust and she would receive only the income from it during her lifetime. If May died first, the principal would go to Helen. Further, the will provided that all Belle's holdings in *Denver Post* stock would go to Helen if they did not exceed half the estate, thus cutting off May from the paper. Helen and E. F. Swinney, chairman of the board of the First National Bank of Kansas City, were named executors of Belle Bonfils' will and simultaneously trustees of the trust to be set up for May's share of the estate.

This time May did not delay going to court. Her petition charged that Belle Bonfils had been unsound in body and mind after her husband's death, that she had been under Helen's domination and Helen had used undue influence to persuade their mother to sign a will favorable to Helen. Specifically, she charged that Helen had taken their mother to Kansas City to have the First National Bank there draft the will. Subsequently, the draft was delivered to Denver and Belle had signed it on September 9, 1933, in the office of her Denver attorney with only minor changes. The petition also protested that a conflict of interest would exist if Helen, a major beneficiary of the will, should also serve as executor and as trustee of the proposed trust to be set up for May. Helen, the suit charged, had been "actively antagonistic" toward May and could not be expected to act as an impartial administratrix.

The sisters—somberly dressed, the *Rocky Mountain News* reported—went to court and after a two-day hearing they agreed to a complex "contract of compromise and settlement" which provided:

—May would get seven-sixteenths of her mother's estate outright.

—Helen also would get seven-sixteenths.

—One-sixteenth of the estate would be placed in a Denver bank in trust for May's benefit. After her death, the assets would be distributed to certain Denver charities.

—The final one-sixteenth would be placed in a Kansas City bank in trust for Helen's benefit, and after her death the assets would be distributed to certain Kansas City charities.

—If Helen should have a child, provision would be made for his benefit from his mother's trust. (Helen was forty-six years old at the time, unmarried, and as was noted in the settlement, "has no present intention of marrying, and the possibility of her ever having issue is remote.")

Thus Helen and May agreed to an equal distribution of the fortune their father had amassed, a large part of which was stock in his newspaper. In May's case the *Post* stock had evaded two obstacles to finally reach her portfolio—the trust set up by her father's will, and the provision in her mother's will that would have given the stock to Helen. A "compromise" demanded by one party through court action, and agreed to by the other as the alternative to bitter litigation, did nothing to ease the rancor that festered between the sisters. After 1935 they went their separate ways, their paths never to cross except by accident. The services of attorneys to compromise their dispute cost the estate $225,000. But no attorneys at whatever the price possessed the human skills necessary to patch up the differences of two proud, willful women.

The division of the estate was not completed in time for *The Post*'s annual meeting in January of 1937. At that time ownership of *Post* stock was divided as follows:

Agnes Reid Tammen's personal holdings	1,459.0	shares
Children's Hospital Trust under Tammen will, with Agnes Tammen and Denver National Bank as trustee	1,041.0	"
Helen Bonfils in person	1.0	"
W. C. Shepherd, new president of *The Post* and editor and publisher	1.0	"
Boma Investment Company, proxy held by Helen as president	1,623.7	"
Executors of F. G. Bonfils estate	249.8	"
First National Bank of Kansas City and Denver National Bank, trustees under F. G. Bonfils' will	624.5	"
Total	5,000.0	shares

By the following year the Boma Investment Company had been dissolved and its assets distributed under the compromise settlement between May and Helen. The 1939 annual meeting showed the following stock representation:

Agnes Reid Tammen, personal	1,459.0	shares
Children's Hospital Trust	1,041.0	"
William C. Shepherd	1.0	"
Trustees under F. G. Bonfils' will	806.1	"
Estate of F. G. Bonfils, Helen Bonfils, executrix	249.8	"
Helen Bonfils, personal holdings	438.2	"
Helen G. Bonfils trust	39.8	"
Thomas L. Bonfils	.25	"
Estate of Belle Bonfils, Helen Bonfils, executrix	487.85	"
Total	4,523.00	shares

The total is short of the 5,000 shares outstanding. They were owned by May Bonfils Berryman—437.2 shares held personally, and 39.8 shares in trust for her. Helen held the same number plus one, the qualifying share she voted as an officer.

May did not bother to vote her shares until 1942, when she was represented by her attorney, Edgar McComb.

We must now go back to 1933, to February 15, which was thirteen days after Bonfils died. His will had been opened and enough time had elapsed to make a business meeting appear decent. At 11 A.M. that day all the various owners of *Post* stock or their representatives assembled for a special meeting in the Red Room. Certainly a sense of history hung over the gathering. It was the first time since *The Post* was founded thirty-eight years earlier that neither of the cofounders was present. Thomas Bonfils, who had held the meaningless office of vice-president for most of those, years, now played his last role. He called the meeting to order as chairman and entertained motions to elect Agnes Tammen, Helen Bonfils, and William C. Shepherd as directors of *The Post*. A unanimous vote was cast; and that formality completed, the stockholders adjourned. At eleven-thirty the three directors met to complete the real business at hand. They elected Shepherd president of the company, Agnes Tammen and

Bruce Gustin vice-presidents, Helen secretary and treasurer, and Anne O'Neill assistant secretary and assistant treasurer. They also gave Shepherd a fifty-thousand-dollar contract for one year as editor and publisher.

Shep was now the man in charge of the entire *Post* operation, the man responsible for day-to-day decisions in both business matters and the paper's content, the man who must fill the shoes vacated by the deaths of Fred Bonfils and Harry Tammen. The two women were the principal owners, but they were away from the city for long periods and Shep was the hand hired to watch the store.

Vignette

AT THE TOP OF THE BLACKLIST

Included among the more durable legends about *The Denver Post* is the so-called blacklist of enemies. Bonfils and Tammen considered that the most appropriate punishment for anyone who had crossed them was to keep his name out of their newspaper, and both were good haters with long memories. Woe betide any editor who permitted a verboten name to appear in print.

The responsibility of keeping the news columns pristine was complicated by the fact that there was no official or formal blacklist that could be consulted. The more cautious editors devised their own methods for keeping track of those in disfavor, but like ancient legends the information was perpetuated by word of mouth with the newest cubs learning by a sort of osmosis. What made the problem even more difficult was that the makeup of the out-of-favor list changed from time to time as Bonfils' personal relationships experienced ups and downs and merchants' advertising budgets fluctuated.

It would have been simple if Bonfils had made it a practice to charge into the city room and announce that henceforth Jack Smith's name must never pollute the columns of *The Post,* or that Joe Jones had been purged of his sins and was once again acceptable. But he didn't, and sometimes editors wished for a sixth sense.

When Palmer Hoyt came to *The Post* as editor and publisher in 1946 he decreed that the slate would be washed clean and that the blacklist, existent or not, was no longer operable. But Hoyt hadn't counted on the depth of Helen Bonfils' resentment against her sister, May. Helen insisted that May's name must not appear in *The Post*'s society pages and Hoyt prudently took the attitude that this was a family matter in which the principal owner was entitled to have the final voice. The society section was very important to Helen. Whereas her father had studied the entire paper each night, Helen concentrated her interest on the society and drama sections, reading every item avidly and taking great delight when *The Post* scooped its rivals on a society engagement or published a particularly penetrating review. Whenever May's name did show up in a piece of copy the society editor would refer it to the managing editor, who would refer it to the publisher, who presumably would take it to Helen for a decision.

May was making legitimate news from time to time, mainly with her charities. Loretto Heights College, a Catholic school for girls, was generously favored and the nuns, who were innocent of the feud, embarrassed *Post* writers on several occasions. Society editor Pat Collins attended a luncheon at the college one day and found herself seated next to May, whom she recognized immediately because of her resemblance to Helen. After some small talk May asked Miss Collins, "My dear, are you a teacher here?"

"No, ma'am," Pat replied. After that the dialogue went like this:

"Well, are you a student here?"

"No, ma'am."

"Well, what do you do?"

"I'm the society editor of *The Denver Post*."

That ended the conversation for the rest of the afternoon.

Bernard Kelly as a new reporter also visited the college for a story and was escorted through a building by a proud nun who suggested that certainly *The Post* would be interested in publicizing it since May had endowed it. Kelly dutifully reported her suggestion to the city editor, who thereupon apprised him of the facts of life as they pertained to the Bonfils sisters.

May had never been close to the paper, and although now she shared in its profits she played no role in its management. Meanwhile her marriage to Berryman, which had been rocky at best, deteriorated. (Shortly before Belle's death Berryman had filed a $750,000 alienation-of-affection suit against her and Helen. It was settled for fifteen thousand dollars. "There was no merit whatever in his case," Belle's attorney wrote, "but we made a settlement for a small sum in the hope that we were getting rid of him.") In 1947 May went to Reno and obtained a divorce.

With $200,000 from her inheritance, May in 1937 bought a square mile of rolling farmland between Denver and the foothills of the Rockies. It was a wise investment. In the population explosion that followed World War II the suburb called Lakewood grew completely around her land and its value soared. May called the estate Belmar—the first syllable for her mother, Belle, and the second for her own name, which was properly Mary. She fenced the land and close to a small lake she built a magnificent home modeled after the Petit Trianon in Versailles. She filled it with works of Renaissance art picked up on trips to Europe. The spacious lawn was dotted with marble statuary. Peacocks and herds of deer roamed the grounds, which were kept up by a staff of five gardeners. Wild ducks and geese shared the lake with domesticated swans.

May seldom left her estate but enjoyed entertaining friends at small dinner parties. She loved to play her favorite pieces from Chopin for them and display the jewels that were her passion. Sometimes she would pin a huge diamond to a ribbon and tie it around the neck of a pet dog and laugh when the guests gasped. A frequent guest was Charles Edward Stanton, a third-generation Denverite, who describes himself as a frustrated architect. He had worked in the East as a designer for the Hilton hotels and Raymond Loewy, as well as at a variety of other jobs, then returned home to Denver to head the home-furnishings department of the venerable Daniels and Fisher store. Stanton, tall and ruggedly handsome, soon made himself useful around May's home, which like many new houses didn't quite "work." With his architectural background he was able to suggest changes in the location of doors and light switches and to propose ways to make the kitchen more efficient, the grounds more attractive.

One day May offered Stanton a job, "a lifetime job taking care of my things." She explained that she had accumulated a great deal of valuable real estate as well as other wealth, and since she had no children, she wanted Stanton to see that it would benefit many worthy causes after she was gone. Stanton was unprepared for what came next. May was not looking for an ordinary business manager. As Stanton recalls the conversation, she said: "You know I have had problems with Helen for many years. If anything happens to me, you wouldn't last overnight as manager of my properties. So you will have to marry me."

"I don't think it's possible," Stanton replied in confusion. "For one thing, there's the matter of our ages."

May by then was more than seventy years old. Stanton was at least twenty-five years younger.

"Don't say that again," May scolded. "I may be younger than you in my thinking. Your family is gone and I have no one. Marriage would be the greatest thing in the world for me."

Stanton asked time to think it over. They were married within a year, in April of 1956.

When Helen heard the news she had only one brief comment: "That old fool!"

11

THE YEARS OF PROFITABLE HIBERNATION

Bill Shepherd had been both friend and employee of Bonfils and Tammen. Hired in 1908 and named managing editor in 1912, he had been responsible for *The Post*'s news operations for more than two decades when he was given the imposing title of president, editor, and publisher. But in reality he was still an employee, charged with operating an unusually profitable newspaper for the heirs of its founders.

Shepherd assumed his new responsibilities on February 15, 1933, when he was fifty-eight years old. It was a difficult time. The national economy was wallowing in the depths of the Great Depression and President Franklin D. Roosevelt's desperate efforts to revive it did not sit well with the Republican-oriented *Post*. Colorado simmered on the western edge of the drought-seared Dust Bowl. Parching winds, relentless and restless, flung topsoil into the sky in great stifling clouds that darkened Denver streets at midday. First a few, and then in droves, farmers and ranchers in *The Post*'s circulation area abandoned the tortured plains and joined the pitiful caravans of John Steinbeck's people seeking their promised land in the Far West. For all newspapers, advertising from national accounts was dribbling away. And for the first time that electronic toy, radio, was becoming a potent competitor that could flash the news through the air without the burden of expensive presses and newsprint. Even worse, radio was claiming an impressive share of the advertisers' dollars.

To complicate Shepherd's problem, a people made cynical by the Depression's grinding pressures were less inclined to be enchanted by *The Post*'s traditional showmanship, tantrums, and hyperbole in red ink. Yet that was the kind of journalism he had been brought up on; he had been part of its phenomenal success under Tammen and Bonfils. Tammen and Bonfils, with their intuition for what interested people, would not have hesitated to change with the times. But Shepherd could not, for he was not an innovator but a caretaker. Deep within he felt an overwhelming obligation to continue supporting the heirs in the manner to which they had been accustomed and his instincts counseled against abandoning a successful formula.

Shepherd retained some of Bonfils' arrogance. Thomas Hornsby Ferril recalls dropping in on *The Post* one day while he was handling public relations for the Great Western Sugar Company. Shepherd motioned to him.

"I see where your lawyer has started a new firm," Shepherd said, referring to a prominent attorney who was retained by the sugar company. "Do you know how I found out? From the people on Welton Street [the *Rocky Mountain News*].Why didn't we get the story first?"

Ferril protested that the attorney wasn't a company employee and he had nothing to do with his personal publicity.

"Mr. Ferril," Shepherd said icily, "I have just reached the conclusion you have outlived your usefulness as an employee of the Great Western Sugar Company."

"Shep," Ferril asked in amazement, "are you saying you have fired me? If that is so, I want you to pick up that telephone and tell my boss, the president of Great Western, what you have done."

Apparently it was one of the few times anyone had spoken up to Shepherd. He did not make the call.

To his responsibilities Shepherd brought dedication and native canniness, but none of the craft of his predecessors. After Tammen's death Shepherd had inherited the role of balance wheel to Bonfils' eccentricities; his steadiness had kept the paper on an even keel through its many crises. In fact, it was for these reassuring qualities, rather than for his flair, that he was picked to take over when Bonfils died. In 1950, when *The Post* published a booklet on its history to commemorate the dedication of its new building, author Lawrence Martin could find only two less-than-distinguished incidents to cite as the high points of Shepherd's career. In 1912, when the liner *Titanic* hit an iceberg and sank in the North Atlantic with heavy loss of life, Shepherd supervised the assembling and editing of wire dispatches for a series of *Post* extras that told the unfolding story. He recalled for Martin with some pride that he worked forty-eight hours without a break. Then, in the waning days of World War II, Shepherd joined a group of leading publishers for a red-carpet tour of the Pacific, which by then had been reduced to an American

William C. Shepherd was Bonfils' handpicked successor. He ran the newspaper for the Bonfils heirs and for Mrs. Tammen, whom he also escorted to social functions.

lake. He was aboard the carrier *Yorktown* when it launched its planes for an attack on Japan. In both of his journalistic high points Shepherd, rather than being a participant, was a bystander on the far fringes of the action.

In fact, like many other newspapermen, Shepherd got into the business almost by accident. When he was graduated from high school he thought of becoming a house painter or a streetcar operator. A sympathetic English teacher urged him to apply for a newspaper job. He worked at the *Republican* without pay for six months, carrying a *Rocky Mountain News* route and helping out as an office boy for an attorney to make ends meet.

"One day I got acquainted with a snake charmer who hung out in a cigar store," Shepherd recalled, "and he gave a rattlesnake banquet in the rear of the store. I ate some of the snake and wrote a piece about the dinner, and the city editor didn't believe me until I brought him part of the snake. That story made the front page."

After that he was paid seventy-five cents a week. Eventually his pay was raised to eight dollars a week, and then he moved over to the Denver *Times* sports department before joining *The Post*.

Shepherd hewed to the old idea that a story was not news until it was published in *The Post*. It didn't matter that subscribers had read about a murder in the morning *News* or heard about it on radio, and certainly it was an arrogant policy that refused to accept the fact that there were competitors. The result was stodginess that led inevitably to dullness.

Of Shepherd's stewardship of *The Post,* Martin wrote in the booklet *So The People May Know:* "He was handling not his own but the money and property of others, and his rule was to guard them faithfully and well. Thus on some occasions when the choice had to be made between taking the kind of risks F. G. and H. H. might have taken, or avoiding the gamble, Shep chose the conservative way. *The Post,* spiritually at least, dwelt for a time upon a plateau of rest, though physically it continued to look much the same as always."

And as always, it continued to make money. The following figures start with 1925, the first full year after Tammen's death, proceed through the boom times of the mid-Twenties, the two years in which the fight with Scripps-Howard slashed into profits, and through the grim Depression years and the war period to 1945, which was the last full year of Shepherd's administration.

Year	Circulation Daily	Circulation Sunday	Gross Revenue	Net Profit After Taxes	Percentage of Profit	Dividend Payments	
1925	144,044	224,118	$4,503,000	$1,257,000	27.91	$1,169,000	
1926	145,896	237,037	4,709,000	1,171,000	24.87	1,200,000	
1927	151,224	249,014	4,495,000	384,000	8.54	550,000	BONFILS ERA
1928	162,521	273,756	4,765,000	673,000	14.12	600,000	
1929	161,329	263,177	6,114,000	1,865,000	30.50	1,000,000	
1930	154,714	292,530	5,848,000	1,593,000	27.24	1,200,000	
1931	160,064	309,166	5,586,000	1,543,000	27.62	1,200,000	
1932	155,063	301,087	4,894,000	1,405,000	28.71	1,100,000	
1933	138,487	283,303	4,408,000	1,438,000	32.62	1,200,000	
1934	144,781	300,422	4,811,000	1,737,000	36.10	1,800,000	
1935	154,335	310,862	4,994,000	1,799,000	36.02	1,800,000	
1936	157,258	310,796	5,309,000	1,918,000	36.13	1,950,000	
1937	159,247	303,890	5,357,000	1,908,000	35.62	1,900,000	SHEPHERD ERA
1938	156,439	279,773	4,974,000	1,592,000	32.01	1,600,000	
1939	155,139	269,085	5,038,000	1,631,000	32.37	1,650,000	
1940	156,869	266,378	5,045,000	1,515,000	30.03	1,500,000	
1941	157,123	264,286	4,934,000	1,326,000	26.87	1,350,000	
1942	164,850	276,697	4,887,000	1,162,000	23.78	1,100,000	
1943	175,868	296,133	5,462,000	1,288,000	23.58	1,100,000	
1944	182,213	302,533	6,038,000	1,244,000	20.60	1,200,000	
1945	187,801	306,664	6,062,000	1,332,000	21.97	1,200,000	

It is an astonishing fact that during the Depression, when scores of newspapers were going bankrupt, Shepherd was able to record some of *The Post*'s most prosperous times. In fact, the two most profitable years in its history were 1936 and 1937. In both the net profit after taxes was more than $1,900,000; for every three dollars that were being taken in as gross income, one was being retained as net profit. The largest single beneficiary at this period was Agnes Tammen, who owned approximately 30 percent of the stock. The Children's Hospital Trust owned about 20 percent, with the various Bonfils heirs dividing the other 50 percent. Thus, in a year when dividends amounted to $1,800,000, $540,000 would go to Mrs. Tammen and $360,000 to the hospital.

Dividends on the five-thousand shares outstanding were paid regularly at the rate of twenty dollars per share—$100,000 a month. But so substantial were the profits that the three directors—Mrs. Tammen, Helen Bonfils, and Shepherd—would meet almost every month to declare additional dividends.

Shepherd, who had been issued only one token share of stock to qualify him as a director, was rewarded with a bonus in addition to his fifty-thousand-dollar annual salary. After the first year, when he proved himself to everyone's satisfaction, Shep would be instructed by Mrs. Tammen to schedule a special directors' meeting each December. When all were seated Shepherd would call the meeting to order and ask Miss Bonfils to serve as secretary. What transpired thereafter is best described by the minutes that Helen carefully recorded year after year with hardly a change in the wording:

> Thereupon, Agnes R. Tammen moved adoption of the following resolution, which was seconded by Helen G. Bonfils:
>
> Resolved: That in consideration of the very exceptional services of W. C. Shepherd as president, editor and publisher of *The Denver Post,* the treasurer of this company is ordered forthwith to pay to W. C. Shepherd, in addition to all salary heretofore voted and authorized to be paid to him, the sum of $10,000.
>
> Whereupon, W. C. Shepherd asked that he be relieved from further participation in the meeting and retired. Agnes R. Tammen then took the chair and acted as president, and the above mentioned motion was thereupon put to a vote and unanimously adopted.
>
> There being no further business to come before the meeting, the same, upon motion duly made, seconded and carried, adjourned.

It is not difficult to visualize the three principals solemnly performing the familiar routine each year to satisfy the demands of corporate legality, with Shepherd rising at the appropriate moment to excuse himself and modestly stepping out of the room while his employers voted him a ten-thousand-dollar Christmas bonus. (After Mrs. Tammen's death in 1942 her personal attorney and executor of her estate, E. Ray Campbell, joined the board and Helen took over the initiative of proposing Shepherd's bonus.)

Dividends such as the two women were voting for themselves and the other stockholders could not be paid indefinitely without injuring the business in some way. A study of the table above reveals that net profits were being dispersed as fast as the money came in, and in some years, faster. In the twelve full years of Shepherd's management *The Post* showed a net profit of $18,452,000, of which all but $302,000 was distributed as dividends. During this time nothing was being put aside for future expansion, or to modernize or replace the aging physical plant built in 1907. The weary old presses and other equipment were kept running largely through the wizardry Major Bonfils and his machinists performed with baling wire and tape.

To keep expenses down, drastic economies became a way of life in the newsroom. Expense accounts for entertainment were nonexistent. While photographers were reimbursed for car mileage. reporters were expected to take the streetcar to their assignments. George Eichler, now a Denver public-relations man, recalls that carfare was three tokens for a quarter or ten cents a ride. Reporters routinely bought three tokens but put down a dime for each ride on their expense accounts. Even this petty larceny caught the eye of a business-office cost cutter who ruled that thereafter only eight and one-third cents would be allowed. When reporters protested, the matter was settled by giving an assistant city editor rolls of car tokens which he issued two at a time to members of the staff going out on assignment.

When a reporter had to drive his own car out of town, a rare event, mileage was calculated from the city limits instead of from *The Post*. Eichler contends he was fired as an aftermath of a dispute over whether he could claim reimbursement for four miles of driving from home to office, and four miles from office to home—twenty cents each way at the rate of five cents a mile—when he needed his car to cover his suburban beat.

Authorization from the managing editor was required to make

even a thirty-cent toll telephone call to Boulder. Bill Beardshear, the erudite and kindly assistant city editor, learned to lengthen the life of pencil stubs with rolled cardboard holders, and the habit stayed with him through his distinguished career. Old-timers like Lord Ogilvy as well as young employees suffered pay cuts. Because jobs were scarce few were inclined to leave, and those who left were not often replaced.

Frank Haraway, still a member of the sports department, recalls that he worked at *The Post* without salary during the summer of 1937 in hopes that the experience would lead to a job. The only pay he received was twenty-five dollars for taking down play-by-play accounts of *Post* baseball tournament games for the final edition. Since this covered a two-week period, the pay amounted to two dollars a day. The following spring, when Haraway applied for a job after winning his degree at the University of Denver, sports editor Poss Parsons told him, "Dammit, Frank, you know we can't put on anybody unless some guy dies or gets fired." A few days later William White, now a Denver public-relations man, announced he was quitting to go back East. Haraway was told to come to work June 1 "to brush up a little," and was put on the payroll a month later when White left.

(White had been hired fresh out of the University of Colorado by Poss Parsons to cover college sports. One day Parsons told White: "This Byron White up at Colorado is a helluva football player and we're going to make him an All-American. The way to do it is to build up his publicity. I want you and Bob Gamzey to turn in at least a story a day about what a great guy White is so we'll have a whole book of clippings." *The Post* helped White gain recognition, but he had remarkable credentials of his own. He became the University of Colorado's first All-American, played professionally with the Pittsburgh Pirates, now the Steelers, and Detroit Lions, became a Rhodes Scholar, and is a Justice of the U. S. Supreme Court.)

Yeoman work by managing editor Eddie Day and his successor, Larry Martin, city editor Jim Hale, telegraph editor Al Dix, and others kept the dwindling staff alert under difficult circumstances. Dix could be counted on to walk across the street to the Champa Bar every hour on the hour for a shot of bourbon and a beer chaser, but he never gave any indication he had been drinking. Hale was a stickler for detail. Eichler learned this when as a cub he wrote an obituary beginning with the pertinent facts about the funeral. Hale tossed it back, saying, "Let's have the man dead before you bury him."

The men on the firing line were a dedicated crew, proud and skilled professionals who knew the paper was faltering but without the authority to do much about it. Looking for leadership from the top, they found it lacking. But for a variety of reasons—loyalty to their newspaper, the absence of opportunities to move elsewhere, the comfort of living in Denver—they stayed. "*The Post* went into hibernation and lived off the fat" is the way Hale puts it.

Hale, who had commanded a squadron of U. S. Army Air Corps mechanics in England during World War I, came from Texas in 1920 to joint *The Post*'s copydesk. A near-infallible memory and judicious temperament led to his promotion to copydesk chief. Hale became city editor in roundabout fashion. When John Day died after eleven turbulent years as city editor, Bonfils without consulting Shepherd promptly named state editor Max Hill as his successor. Shepherd was infuriated, but there was nothing he could do. Bonfils died soon afterward and Shepherd as the new boss could find little good in Hill's work. Before long Hill quit and went to New York and landed a job with the Associated Press. He was given a number of choice foreign assignments and was in the Tokyo bureau when World War II broke out. The man Shepherd wanted for city editor was Joe McMeel, then managing editor of the *News*. However, McMeel was disinclined to take what he considered a lesser job, so Shepherd finally offered it to Hale.

It proved to be a wise decision. Hale was a demanding editor who coaxed—and sometimes shamed—the best from his reporters. Taciturn and forbidding, Hale often would take an inadequate story and drop it without a word on the reporter's typewriter, leaving him to puzzle over the reason for its rejection. Alexis McKinney, who succeeded Hale as city editor in 1946, recalls being in the press room at the state capitol when another reporter was telephoned by Hale. "Think," Hale demanded, and hung up. The reporter blanched as his mind raced over every possible error of commission or omission that might have offended his boss. Away from his desk Hale was a warm, compassionate man who enjoyed a drink, poker, and good conversation.

Martin became managing editor after Eddie Day's death in 1938. Lean, acid, dyspeptic, he had impressed Bonfils in 1923, when they shared a stateroom while accompanying President Warren G. Harding on his voyage to Alaska. Martin at that time headed the United Press bureau in Washington. After a disagreement with his bosses over what part of his poker losses on that trip could be included in his expense account, Martin wound up as information officer at Yellowstone National Park. In the summer of 1924 he asked Bonfils for a job and was hired. Martin was a gifted writer and reporter but was soon named news editor to supervise the production of each day's paper. Newspapers have a way of promoting superior writers into administrative and editorial positions for which they have no special aptitude simply because they are competent people. And reporters take these desk jobs because they pay better and offer a more direct path to promotion. Perhaps Martin would have been happier as a writer, although certainly he was a competent managing editor. Indeed, after ill health hastened his departure from the managing editorship in 1947, he continued to serve *The Post* as a penetrating analyst and writer on many subjects.

Still, Shepherd was the boss and he saw to it that the petulant character of the paper changed little from Bonfils' days except for the addition of his own prejudices and idiosyncrasies. Mary Ellen and Mark Murphy, writing in the *Saturday Evening Post* of December 23, 1944, had this to say about Shepherd's *Post:*

> The paper makes no local enemies now, though, saving its squeals —which once were roars—for such menaces as the Japanese in internment camps and the Democrats in Washington. Old Man Bonfils would approve of the paper's policies toward the Japanese, rationing, labor and Democrats, although he would never understand its coziness with the Denver Chamber of Commerce or its continuing failure to interfere in the lives of Denver citizens. . . . Shepherd says that a good paper is one that is successful, and by his standards *The Post* is wonderful, making as it does, more than $1,000,000 a year. Shepherd is pleased to say, "We have the lowest overhead in the country for a paper this size," and his staff agrees. Some of its old members are paid as high as $150 a week, but its average wage is low, as compared with the salary scales of many major newspapers. Shepherd says that *The Post* follows the policy of the New York *Times* in respect to the news, a statement which must make the *Times* proprietors wince. . . .

This was a perceptive appraisal. *The Post* long since had dispensed with its editorial page. It was superfluous since the newspaper's opinions and biases were only too evident in the news columns. And if there was any doubt, *The Post* made its position un-mistakable in Bruce Gustin's unsigned column titled "That's That," positioned on page 2.

Gustin had been a crack reporter who had learned to put Bonfils' thoughts into words. Eventually, sitting at the typewriter, he began to think like Bonfils. In writing he could be blunt, sardonic, didactic. His style was as subtle as a shillelagh. "That's That" seldom reverted to the editorial writer's favorite "on the other hand" ploy of acknowl-edging different viewpoints. In this column black was black and white was white and there were no in-between shades. Yet, in person, Gustin was a gentle, soft-spoken, almost gnomish man, thoughtful and considerate of his fellow workers, an authority on government and many other subjects. "Let's see what the law says under the Gustinian code," other reporters would say. After work he liked to tend his flowers and spent his evenings creating silver jewelry.

The Post's treatment of "the Japanese" was a direct throwback to the bare-knuckle era. One day in April of 1943 Earl A. Best, who had been discharged for incompetence from the federal Heart Mountain War Relocation Authority camp near Cody, Wyoming, came to *The Post* with a splenetic story about mismanagement and hoarding of food.

The 10,300 residents of the camp were not prisoners of war. They were a segment of the 110,000 Japanese American men, women, and children who had been evacuated en masse from their West Coast homes in 1942 as a precautionary measure by Army commanders who were spurred by liberal doses of hysteria. Two-thirds of the evacuees were native-born American citizens, and they had cooperated in their own incarceration and suspension of civil rights because they felt this was one way of demonstrating their loyalty. *The Post* ignored these facts. It saw only bungling New Deal bureaucrats who were coddling "Japs."

Jack Carberry, a veteran reporter whose vivid imagination fre-quently obscured his view of the facts, was assigned to take down Earl Best's allegations. Then Carberry was dispatched to Heart Mountain to confirm the charges.

The camp's newspaper, the *Sentinel*, a weekly with a circulation of 6000, later noted that Carberry had spent a total of eight hours at Heart Mountain, one of which was spent having lunch with some of the administrators. Carberry's first dispatch began this way:

FOOD IS HOARDED FOR JAPS
IN U.S. WHILE AMERICANS
IN NIPPON ARE TORTURED
Three Years'
Supply Held in
Wyoming Camp
Rationed Items Piled Up
That Enemy Nationals
May Wax Fat
(by JACK CARBERRY.)
(*Denver Post* Staff Correspondent.)

Cody, Wyo., April 23—American flyers have been executed—
"murdered" is the accurate word—by the Japanese! Every tenet of
international law and human decency has been flouted.

Thousands of other Americans, soldiers, sailors, marines, and
civilians, men, women and children, are prisoners in Japan—locked
in squalid concentration camps, subjected to daily cruelties, forced
to perform the hardest and most degrading labor and subsisting on
the meagerest starvation rations.

That's the Japanese way.

With President Roosevelt's announcement of the barbarous killing
of our flyers, captured after the raid on Tokyo, still ringing in the
nation's horrified ears, the story of prodigality, waste and extra-
vagance that marks our treatment of Japanese guests in war relocation camps becomes even more striking than it would be normally.

I have just returned from a three-day trip to Heart Mountain, the
war relocation authority's camp twenty-three miles north of Cody.

There I saw the 10,300 Japanese residents, some native-born,
others citizens of Japan, at work—God save the mark!—and at
play. I talked with and interviewed those in authority, including
starry-eyed dreamers, who pamper and pet, coddle and cater to
even the most outspokenly disloyal among their charges.

I visited and checked warehouses, filled to their very eaves with
every type of rationed food, much of which cannot be purchased
for love or for money, with or without ration stamps, by the American men and women who founded and peopled these American
hills. . . .

Carberry's stories went on in similar vein for several days, reporting in one dispatch that he had found "268,293 cans of rationed
vegetables, 114,885 of these the No. 10 cans, and 153,408 the
No. 2 cans. I discovered 141,405 packages of cereals—corn and
wheat flakes, rice krispies, grape nuts, farina, rolled oats and similar
breakfast foods. Stacked to the eaves in the warehouses, and on

pantry shelves in the mess halls were 61,914 jars of jellies and jams—grape, peach, plum, orange, strawberry, apricot and apple butter. . . ."

A columnist in the camp's newspaper remarked puckishly: "I've wondered how a man who comes up here for three days—most of which was spent in Cody—could write fairly about a complex city of more than 10,000 people, and he sure showed his ignorance. In his first article he says our project director is Mr. Robinson, and that Heart Mountain is 23 miles from Cody. Well, he got only two letters wrong in Robertson's name, which makes him 78 percent right there. And he's 10 miles off on the distance, which makes him 56.5 percent right on that figure. If a star reporter is only 78 and 56.5 percent right on simple matters like that, we wonder just how right he can be on a lot of other things he writes about."

Carberry certainly failed to distinguish himself on this occasion, but he was carrying out Shepherd's assignment. Although he is remembered as *The Post*'s sports editor, he probably was at his best as a police reporter. He had hundreds of contacts which enabled him to dig out stories unknown to his competitors. Carberry was in a hospital following an automobile accident when bandits broke into the Wolhurst Country Club, a posh undercover gambling spot, and relieved a gaggle of high-society types of their valuables. The police were extremely closemouthed about their investigation but Carberry knew what was going on. He covered the story day after day by telephone and George Eichler was assigned to interview Carberry in his hospital room, make verifying calls to numbers Carberry provided, and write the story.

At Heart Mountain there was, in fact, considerable sloppy management but it wasn't the fault of the Japanese American residents, who would have preferred to be back home on the West Coast. Federal officials pointed out that Heart Mountain, which almost overnight had become Wyoming's third most populous community, required a lot of food even though the inmates were being fed at a total cost of 36.8 cents per day per individual. What bothered the evacuees most was that *The Post* was lumping them with the enemy and pummeling them in its attacks on the federal bureaucracy. They had a point, as witness this savage commentary in the "That's That" column of April 25, 1943:

> Recently the Denver city council passed an ordinance imposing a curfew on Denver children. Boys and girls under 16 years must keep off the streets after 10 o'clock at night. If such a restriction

can be applied to American-born children of American citizens, WHY CAN'T THE COUNCIL PUT A TWENTY-FOUR-HOURS-A-DAY CUR- FEW ON JAPS AND BAR THEM FROM DENVER STREETS?

Denver streets are just as free and open to Japs now as they are to American citizens. Every Jap you meet on the street has an impudent grin or sneer on his face. He has an arrogant, contemptuous expression. His very smile is an insult. It seems to say, "You Americans had better be nice to your Japanese superiors; we know you are afraid of us."

This war between the United States and Japan is not merely a war between the American and Jap governments. IT IS A FIGHT TO THE DEATH BETWEEN THE AMERICAN PEOPLE AND THE JAP PEOPLE. And the present policy of coddling and petting and pampering the "nice Japs" and the "dirty Japs" who are in this country while their fellow countrymen are abusing and torturing and murdering Americans who are prisoners in Japan is as crazy as taking a rattlesnake to bed with you to get it warm.

A few days later the Heart Mountain *Sentinel* published the following editorial:

"O, Justice, When Expelled From Other Habitations, Make This Thy Dwelling Place."

Emblazoned in letters of gilt, the above inscription appears, of all places, over the doors to the office of *The Denver Post*.

The much-maligned Goddess of Justice would do well to flee this unholy dwelling place and seek new habitation, for with a vicious pack of half-truths drawn from the twilight zone of fact, *The Post* once again is making sardonic jest.

The most notorious of yellow journals has found a convenient tool to promote its anti-Democratic, anti-New Deal campaign, and it makes light of 100,000 innocent bystanders in WRA centers whose futures are jeopardized, for such considerations as fairness are no deterrent to a shamefully perverted sense of justice.

The charges *The Post* makes about excessive stocks of food stored at Heart Mountain are at considerable variance to the figures from the project director. We are willing that an impartial committee investigate to ascertain the facts.

We have no more tolerance for government waste and misman- agement than *The Post*. If there is such mismanagement resulting from incompetence, we, the residents of the centers, are the first to suffer. But there was no such tender consideration in *The Post*'s mis- directed crusading.

Therefore we protest, in the name of the justice that *The Post* claims to espouse, the cruel, distorted and untrue allegations about pampered treatment and our ingratitude. As a frail, small voice re- plying to *The Post*'s thunderings, we protest the viciously editorial- ized headlines coldly calculated to inflame public opinion against loyal American citizens whose only crime was that of being born with Japanese faces.

It must be said for *The Post* that it was not a lone voice fulminating about the Japanese Americans. The Hearst papers, particularly in Los Angeles and San Francisco, and the Los Angeles *Times,* which has matured into one of the nation's outstanding newspapers, were equally rabid on this subject. If Shepherd read the *Sentinel's* editorial, he was unimpressed as he proved when two representatives of the War Manpower Commission called on him. This was one of the federal agencies given the task of helping the evacuees find jobs in inland communities so that the camps would not deteriorate into a new kind of Indian reservation. One of those delegated to ask Shepherd to soften his attacks was Barron B. Beshoar, a former *Rocky Mountain News* reporter. Beshoar knew the futility of his mission even before he embarked on it, but he had a job to do. For his pains he received a royal dressing down and was admonished to mind his own goddam business. Several days later *Post* reporter Robert (Red) Fenwick appeared in Beshoar's office.

"Barron," Fenwick said with some embarrassment, "I've been assigned to find out what you fellows do here at the War Manpower Commission."

Beshoar had been expecting the call. "Red," he said, "I'll tell you what I'll do. There are all those file cabinets against the wall. It's illegal as hell, but I'll let you take every one of them back to your office and you can find out what we're up to."

"Oh, damn," said Fenwick and walked out the door.

The Post was simply being in character when it took after the Japanese Americans. It had assaulted German Americans and Austrian Americans with comparable savagery in World War I. Dr. Lyle W. Dorsett of the University of Denver has made an extensive study of this sidelight of history. His paper, "The Ordeal of Colorado's Germans During World War I," published in the fall, 1974, issue of the State Historical Society's quarterly, *Colorado Magazine,* says both Governor Julius Gunter and Denver Mayor Robert Speer were accused of being pro-German because of their ancestry.

"The influential *Denver Post* refused to take sides until the United States had declared war," Dr. Dorsett writes. "From then on, though, a flood of hate poured from its pages. Raping and pillaging Germans took every woman between the ages of fourteen and thirty with them as they marched through France, *The Post* reported. 'Huns

Sterilize French Youths' to eradicate French manpower, *The Post* continued, and French babies were speared with bayonets and then delivered to 'frantic mothers.' . . .

"In fighting the forces of the devil, the crusaders turned the state into a virtual hell for countless local Germans. . . . *The Denver Post* discovered that one of Gunter's appointees to the State Council of Defense, Ernest Morris, was born in Prussia. 'The Prussian Rat,' as *The Post* labeled the well-known Denver attorney, was depicted in a front-page cartoon complete with Prussian uniform, helmet, and Iron Cross. The editor acknowledged that Morris was a naturalized citizen but emphasized that Germans were allowed to retain the citizenship of their fatherland even after becoming United States citizens. . . . And as soon as it was discovered that the city and county clerk of Denver, Charles Lammers, was a naturalized citizen of German birth, public pressure, guided by *The Post,* forced him to surrender his function of issuing permits for purchasing and handling explosives."

When a mob tied a rope around an alien's neck, paraded him through the streets, and forced him to kiss the American flag, *The Post* published a photograph with this explanation: "Henry W. Deutsch, a native of Austria, who was the victim of a demonstration of patriotism at Hugo, Colo., last night, and the committee of citizens who spirited him away from Hugo and brought him to Denver."

Other newspapers in Colorado and the rest of the United States were guilty of similar excesses, which leads Dr. Dorsett to a disturbing comment: ". . . our wretched treatment of Japanese Americans was not an accidental aberration that grew out of wartime hysteria. Furthermore, it was not simply an extreme case of white America's degradation of a non-white minority. Our treatment of Germans and Austrians during the First World War foreshadowed the Japanese policy of one-quarter century later. The propensity to bury the Bill of Rights and the abstract political theory of the Declaration of Independence was clearly established a generation before Pearl Harbor."

Late in 1945 Shepherd made his decision to retire, but he told no one. He was seventy-one years old, and he had spent thirty-eight of them working for *The Post*. The war was over now. Soon, the newsprint shortage that had restricted *The Post*'s growth would be eased. Men were coming home from distant fronts. Machines and the type metal to be fed into them would become available. Shepherd

This photo was made in 1946 on the day Shepherd (center) announced his retirement. Flanking him are the other two directors, Helen Bonfils and E. Ray Campbell, representing the Tammen estate. Portraits of Bonfils and Tammen graced the wall of Shepherd's office.

realized a strong new hand was needed to guide his mentors' news-paper in the booming years ahead.

Christmas, 1945, was merrier than usual around *The Post*. For the first time in four years there was no war. On the day before Christmas the usual late-afternoon parties were held in the various departments. Shepherd invited the top executives to his office for a drink before they hurried home to their families. Larry Martin was ill that day, and Jim Hale was sitting in for him at the managing editor's desk. Hale noticed that when the last of the guests had departed, Shepherd closed the door to his office. An hour passed by, then another. Hale became worried, and besides he wanted to go home. He knocked on Shepherd's door. There was no response. Cautiously he opened the door. Shepherd was sprawled face down in a corner. Hale thought he had suffered a heart attack and called for aid. But when he knelt over his boss, Hale realized he had just passed out. Shepherd opened his eyes and Hale heard him mutter, "It's all over, Jim, it's all over."

At first Hale did not understand what Shepherd was trying to tell him. Then he realized Shep was saying he had decided to retire. On January 3, 1946, when Helen Bonfils returned from New York City, Shepherd made it official. He told her and Campbell he wished to be relieved and urged them to find a successor by the annual meeting on February 20. William Chauncey Shepherd's newspaper career was nearing its end, but his life went on another twenty-one years.

ENTER THE GUILD

The American Newspaper Guild, a labor union for employees of editorial and other nonmechanical departments of newspapers, was born in 1933 in Newark, New Jersey. It was the result of newspapermen's growing realization that while they considered themselves professionals, they needed an organization to raise pay levels and improve working conditions. In many papers across the land, editorial and business office employees were paid less than those in the unionized mechanical crafts, worked longer hours, and had less job security. Understandably, many publishers regarded the Guild as something of a plague and did not hesitate to share their feelings with their employees.

Word of the Guild's success in winning labor contracts in Eastern cities drifted westward. One night early in 1936 two *Rocky Mountain News* employees, Maxwell G. Greedy and Barron B. Beshoar, climbed into Greedy's car after work and drove to a mine dump outside the town of Lafayette, north of Denver. There, confident that they would not be overheard, they discussed formation of a Guild unit at the *News*. "Pay and working conditions were terrible," Beshoar recalled later. "We were starving." Other discussions followed, and on April 3, 1936, fifteen members of the *News* editorial staff met at the Adams Hotel at the call of George V. Burns and Robert L. Chase. They agreed unanimously to form a Guild unit and seek affiliation with the national organization. Burns was elected president, Chase vice-president, and Frank M. Plumb secretary-treasurer. Dues of one dollar per month were voted for members making more than twenty dollars per week, and fifty cents a month for those paid twenty dollars or less. Burns, who had paid one dollar to the hotel for the meeting room, was credited with dues for one month.

A few weeks later the American Newspaper Guild accepted the

News unit, and the treasurer was authorized to expend twenty-seven cents for a money order and postage to transmit a five-dollar fee to the national body. The next momentous step was to notify *News* editor Charles E. Lounsbury. On April 27 this conciliatory letter was sent by special delivery:

> Dear Mr. Lounsbury:
> We wish to notify you the Newspaper Guild of Denver has been organized, and that the move is entirely friendly on our part toward you personally as well as the Scripps-Howard organization, and was taken only after Roy Howard and Robert P. Scripps participated personally in the Guild negotiations for the Cleveland *Press* and approved the contract.
> The Denver Guild has been chartered by the American Newspaper Guild.
> Because of the varied schedules of members of the Executive Board we are requesting a personal meeting with you outside of working hours as soon as possible. Will you kindly set a definite time and place?
> This move on the part of the *News* editorial staff is taken with the intention of promoting the fullest cooperation between the staff and management.

The letter was signed by the five members of the executive board— Burns, Chase, Plumb, Beshoar, and Greedy. They met with Lounsbury after work at 12:05 A.M. on April 29, and the unit's minutes record that Lounsbury said, "I will be glad to recognize the group and meet with the committee at any time." In the wake of agreements at other Scripps-Howard newspapers, the first contract between the *News* and the Guild was reached after relatively uneventful negotiations.

The situation at *The Post* was somewhat different. It took members of the *News* unit nearly a year to organize *The Post* newsroom in the face of what the minutes describe as "extreme pressure by the management." With the secret encouragement of Jim Hale, who as city editor was a management employee, Fred Warren, Gene Cervi, Walden Sweet, and Eddie Williamson finally got a unit organized after employees voted down a company union 34 to 22. When contract negotiations began early in 1938 the inexperienced Guildsmen found Major Bonfils, the business manager, an exceptionally hard man to deal with. The talks dragged on with hardly perceptible progress. Finally, in July, *The Post* unit voted to strike, 21 to 6. If members of *The Post* staff had any inkling of the kind of profits the paper was making, they might have reached that decision sooner.

But none of them had access to the books and they had only a vague idea that *The Post* was a profitable paper.

The strike decision met with less than enthusiasm at the *News,* where the members were being asked to assess themselves for a strike fund. When Greedy moved a 50-cent assessment for the strike, it died for a lack of a second. Discussion revealed that eighteen members of *The Post* unit were delinquent in their dues but had been permitted to vote nonetheless on the strike issue. The *News* unit then went into caucus and agreed to ask the executive board not to call a strike until a careful survey was made to determine chances of winning.

Meanwhile, Beshoar came up with an idea. He and Burns drove to Colorado Springs, where John L. Lewis, doughty chief of the United Mine Workers, was vacationing at the Antlers Hotel. Lewis had no reason to love *The Post,* which had been highly critical of his friend Josephine Roche when she was a candidate for governor of Colorado several years earlier. (In time, she was to be named assistant secretary of the treasury by President Roosevelt, and she served many years as a trustee of the Mine Workers' pension fund.)

Beshoar and Burns explained to Lewis that the Guild was having difficulty in contract negotiations with *The Post* and a strike seemed to be the only way out.

"What's that got to do with me?" Lewis asked.

"We don't think the other newspaper unions will honor our picket line," Beshoar said. "We won't be able to shut the plant down. But if some of your miners would join us——"

Lewis said he would see what he could do.

Major Bonfils soon got the message. Less than a week later *The Post* agreed to its first contract with the Guild and a two-page document was signed on August 4, 1938. It provided minimum pay of $22.50 a week for beginning reporters and copyreaders, $30 during the second year, $35 during the third year, and $40 for those with three or more years of experience. The contract also provided that a five-day week would be put into effect "at the earliest possible moment." The news editor, city editor, sports editor, editor's secretary, telegraph editor, and state editor would be exempt from the five-day restriction but would not be required to work more than forty-eight hours per week. Overtime was to be compensated by equal time off or in cash equal to the person's regular pay.

The contract, for one year, was signed by George Burns as president of the Guild and William C. Shepherd as president of *The Post*. The Guild and *The Post* went to the mat many times for no-holds-barred encounters on subsequent contracts, but none was more bitterly fought than the first one.

12

CAMPBELL'S MISSION

The responsibility of finding a successor to Bill Shepherd as chief executive officer of *The Denver Post* fell to Ernest Ray Campbell, an attorney who did not pretend to know anything about editing a newspaper. Campbell, as principal trustee of Agnes Reid Tammen's estate, had been named vice-president of *The Post* when she died in July of 1942. From the beginning he could see many things wrong with the way the newspaper was being operated. But as the junior member of the board, aware of his own lack of experience with journalism and out of deference to Shepherd, who was editor and publisher as well as president of the corporation, Campbell at first made little effort to express his feelings. Besides, the United States was gearing up for the ordeal of World War II and numerous economic restrictions made innovations on the newspaper difficult.

Campbell was quiet, thoughtful, and conservative, a thoroughly discreet man. No hint of scandal ever touched him. Few had ever heard him raise his voice. But when he said no in his gently stubborn way, his associates knew he had reached the decision only after careful deliberation and his judgment was seldom questioned. Courtly, genteel, well-read, and almost shy, Campbell was about as different from Bonfils as Bonfils was from Tammen. Yet he brought to his position a background as interesting in its own way as theirs.

Campbell was born in Cameron, North Carolina, in 1895, the older of the two children of Duncan Ray and Catherine Campbell. Duncan Ray died when his son was three years old. Catherine took in boarders to support her family. E. Ray Campbell worked his way through Davidson College in Davidson, North Carolina, and taught high-school science and coached athletic teams in Charlotte for three years until the United States entered World War I. He was accepted for the first officer training course at Fort Oglethorpe, Georgia, was sent to France as an artillery lieutenant, and saw heavy action. While he was in France his mother died in the influenza epidemic that swept the United States. After the Armistice, with shrapnel wounds in knee and chest and his lungs wracked by gas and tuberculosis, Campbell was sent to Fitzsimons Army Hospital near Denver for treatment.

One of Campbell's North Carolina relatives was a friend of Mrs. Crawford Hill, doyenne of Denver society. She wrote asking Mrs. Hill to look in on Campbell, who was without friends in Denver. As his health improved he visited Mrs. Hill's home frequently and became acquainted with her society circle.

Campbell came to like the West. He enrolled at the University of Colorado's law school, completed a three-year course in a year and a half and made Phi Beta Kappa, and joined a prominent Denver law firm. Six years later, after taking on a wide variety of cases, mainly for the telephone company, he was made a full partner. He was named trustee for Mrs. Hill's very considerable estate, and presently Agnes Reid Tammen, Harry's widow, became one of his clients. Campbell also began to take an interest in public affairs. In 1932 he was elected to a six-year term as regent at the University of Colorado. The next year Gov. Ed C. Johnson named him to a committee to study state government reform. He was elected regent for a second term and helped guide Colorado's largest university through a critical period. Thus Campbell joined a distinguished group who had come west in search of health and remained to become community leaders.

It was during this time that Mrs. Tammen, feeling the advancing years, had several long conversations with Campbell about her estate. She still took a lively interest in *Post* matters, attending directors' meetings regularly. (In her later years she found it difficult to climb the long iron stairway to Shepherd's office off the second-floor city room, and an elevator was installed primarily for her benefit.) At one time, she explained to Campbell, she had hoped that some of her nephews might take an active interest in *The Post,* but they chose to pursue other careers. Then a grandnephew caught her eye. He was Richard Crabbs, son of her niece, Jessie Cox Crabbs, who in turn was the daughter of Agnes Tammen's eldest sister. But Richard Crabbs joined the infant Army Air Corps and in 1932 he died in a crash while on a training flight.

Mrs. Tammen's multimillion-dollar fortune was made up in part of her *Denver Post* stock and in part of other securities and real estate. She told Campbell that since her securities and real estate would care adequately for her relatives, and she despaired of finding anyone in the family interested in taking over the newspaper, she was considering willing her 30 percent of *Denver Post* stock to Children's Hospital. Since Harry Tammen already had given Children's Hospital 20 percent of *The Post*'s stock, what Mrs. Tammen had in mind would have given the hospital half ownership of one of the nation's most profitable newspapers.

Campbell was aware of the power represented by newspaper ownership. Possibly because his own family life was disrupted at an early age, he also held deep convictions about family loyalty and solidarity. While he agreed that Children's Hospital was an extremely worthy charity, he urged Mrs. Tammen to consider carefully before willing her *Post* stock outside the family. The upshot was that in 1938 she wrote a will which had the effect of leaving her *Post* stock to a grandniece, Helen Crabbs Rippey, and her children. This is the way it worked.

A trust was to be set up for Mrs. Tammen's *Denver Post* stock with Campbell, Sadie Schultz, and the Denver National Bank as trustees. Income from the trust was to be distributed in this manner:

—Seven-fourteenths to go to Helen Crabbs Rippey during her lifetime, and after her death to her children. (At the time there were two children, Cynthia Reid Rippey and Arthur Gordon Rippey, III. Subsequently there was a third offspring, Bruce Richard Rippey.) Helen Crabbs Rippey is the sister of Richard Crabbs, who died in the plane crash.

—Two-fourteenths to Jessie Cox Crabbs, of Orlando, Florida, Mrs. Tammen's niece and mother of Helen Crabbs Rippey. On her death her share would go to Helen Crabbs Rippey and through her to her children.

—Two-fourteenths to Thomas S. Cox of Denver, Mrs. Tammen's nephew. On his death his share would go to Helen Rippey.

—Two-fourteenths to Arthur Reid Stubbs of Terrace Park, Ohio, Mrs. Tammen's nephew. On his death his share would go to Helen Rippey.

—One-fourteenth to William E. Cox of Arcadia, California, Mrs. Tammen's nephew. On his death his share would go to Helen Rippey.

Since all the beneficiaries except Helen Rippey were of an advanced age, in the natural course of events all the income from Mrs. Tammen's holdings in *Denver Post* stock would go to her. Twenty-one years after the death of the last heir, the trust would be dissolved and the estate divided among Helen Rippey's children. The will also provided that the trustees could vote the stock or even sell it without consulting the beneficiaries or considering their desires in order to promote the best interests of *The Post* and the beneficiaries. This last provision became a critical point of contention in subsequent lawsuits, as we shall see.

(From the other portion of her estate—the non-*Post* part—Mrs. Tammen arranged bequests for more than thirty relatives, friends, servants, and charities. Sadie Schultz, who had been Harry Tammen's secretary and later Mrs. Tammen's secretary, was given $50,000. Shepherd got $20,000, Pinky Wayne $5,000, and Betty Craig $1,000. Mrs. Tammen also established lifetime annuities for six relatives, and willed that the balance of the income from her estate should go to Helen Crabbs Rippey.)

Helen Rippey was living in Birmingham, Michigan, at the time. She had married Arthur Gordon Rippey, an advertising executive, in 1933, and was in not uncomfortable circumstances. She had only a toddler's vague recollections of meeting Harry Tammen, but she knew "Aunt Agnes" much better. In 1930 Helen came to Denver for what was to be a six-week visit. It stretched on to three months, and Agnes Tammen became very fond of her grandniece. After Helen's marriage Agnes Tammen visited the couple at their home. In 1936 Helen Rippey and her husband were invited out to Denver and met many of Mrs. Tammen's friends. E. Ray Campbell was among them, and no doubt he was carefully scrutinizing the young couple that would be inheriting his client's fortune. Following Mrs. Tammen's death, the Rippeys took up residence in Denver and Arthur established what was to become the city's leading advertising agency. The Rippeys moved into the home that Mrs. Tammen had willed them and soon became a part of the community, but their contact with *The Post* was largely through Campbell.

In settling Mrs. Tammen's estate, it was necessary to establish a value for her *Denver Post* stock. Inheritance tax collectors wanted to set a considerably higher price on it than Campbell thought was reasonable. To establish a market he announced that a 250-share block would be sold to the highest sealed bid. A number of offers were received, but Helen Bonfils' bid of $1,735 per share—$433,850 for the block—was the highest. The sale reduced the Tammen estate's holdings from 1,459 shares to 1,209. Helen, who by then owned 706 shares through distributions from her father's estate, increased her personal holdings to 956 shares, or nearly one-fifth of the stock outstanding. The move also reduced the Tammen estate's tax liability substantially. On the basis of $1,735 per share, *The Post*'s value was $8,675,000.

By the time World War II ground to an end in 1945, Campbell knew that a change was necessary in *The Post*'s top management. For years it had been riding along on momentum, and the momentum was about to run out. Or as Jim Hale put it, the hibernating beast had absorbed its fat and the ribs were beginning to show. Up on Welton Street, the *Rocky Mountain News* was showing disquieting signs of life. At one time in the late Thirties its circulation had fallen perilously close to the thirty-thousand mark and Scripps-Howard had sent out feelers to test *The Post*'s interest in buying the paper. Campbell advised against swallowing the *News*. A monopoly situation, he reasoned, was bad for *The Post* and bad for Denver. He also must have sensed overwhelming problems in one ailing management trying to manage a second ailing newspaper. Campbell's answer was to urge some of the department stores to support the *News*. But now, under an enthusiastic young editor named Jack Foster, the *News* was beginning to move.

Its circulation was wavering around thirty-eight thousand when Foster took over in 1940. He had worked for the *News* during the *Post* and Scripps-Howard newspaper war in the Twenties and he liked to recall that when he scored a scoop with a story on Judge Ben Lindsey and his theories of companionate marriage, Bonfils had telephoned to offer him a job. This time he found the *News* in deplorable shape. There was hardly enough money to meet the payroll and little prospect of changing the situation without drastic measures.

"We tried to make the *News* a homey newspaper," Foster recalled recently. "We played up the city and state. My wife Frankie [Frances] and I traveled all over the state meeting people and writing about them. We established a column called 'The Colorado Question Box,' which answered readers' questions about old Colorado."

Foster replaced the familiar eight-column format with the more manageable tabloid size, which also lent itself to a jazzier makeup. And he came up with Molly Mayfield. Frankie was looking for something to do, and Foster suggested she write a lovelorn column to entertain the thousands of young servicemen at Lowry Air Force Base. She adopted the name Molly Mayfield and to get the feature started, she dug up old Denver scandals and loosely camouflaged them in contemporary settings. Soon Molly was being flooded with more mail than she could handle, and businessmen as well as housewives were chuckling about her tart advice over their morning coffee. The column ran until 1972.

Another *News* asset was Lee Casey, probably the most widely read Denver columnist of his time. Casey was erudite without being stuffy, warm without being maudlin, and he did not hesitate to champion unpopular causes. While *The Post* was vilifying the Japanese Americans, for example, Casey took a reasoned stand and the public supported him.

The Post was still the larger paper by far, continuing to make huge profits, but to Campbell it began to appear like a dinosaur doomed because it could not adjust to changing times. His business instincts told him that if the newspaper was to survive, its dividend policies would have to be changed; the directors would have to stop giving it away a bit at a time to some very wealthy heirs. But that would have to come later. The first order of business was to replace Shepherd and improve the product. As it turned out, Campbell didn't have to twist any arms, a chore for which he was poorly qualified. Shepherd made his own move and Campbell, immensely relieved, consulted with Helen Bonfils and then set out to find a successor.

Methodically, as though he were preparing to try a case in court, he weighed his problem. First, he felt *The Post* needed a Westerner as its editor. He had seen enough of big-city editors from the East. He wanted someone with roots in the West, who understood the West and its aspirations. Campbell also favored someone under fifty, so he could serve *The Post* for the next twenty years if necessary, and who had a record of successful newspaper editorship and management. But most important, he was seeking a leader, a man who could breathe new life and inspiration into a weary, flabby old body. "A newspaper," he once observed, "cannot be run like any other business. Unless it keeps its driving spirit, its soul, its unceasing quest for the new, it can quite rapidly fade and disappear." Whether he knew it or not, he was seeking an editor who could restore *The Post*'s old color and flamboyance without the venality.

In a confidential memorandum to Helen Bonfils he noted that Larry Martin, *The Post*'s managing editor, had been expected to move up when Shepherd retired. But Martin was fifty-eight years old and had suffered a serious heart attack, which eliminated him from further consideration. Campbell also wrote that city editor Jim Hale had the ability to take over as managing editor, but his health was uncertain and the managing editorship ought to be filled by someone who in time could move into the top spot. Campbell questioned Hale's qualifications as editor and publisher.

Campbell next consulted the *Editor & Publisher Yearbook,* which carries a directory of newspaper executives, and made up a list of 288 names. He soon eliminated all but thirty-nine because of age, lack of experience as newspaper executives, or because they were owners in whole or in part of their papers. These thirty-nine were from seventeen states, including nine from Texas, six from California and—Campbell stretched his boundaries of the West a bit—five from Illinois and three from Minnesota. Also on his list was one editor from Colorado—Jack Foster, editor of the *Rocky Mountain News*—and one from Oregon, Edwin Palmer (Ep) Hoyt of the *Oregonian.*

Campbell's report on Hoyt carried this capsule appraisal:

> . . . The *Oregonian* is the leading newspaper in the state (Oregon), and has an average daily circulation of 177,327, and a Sunday circulation of 230,071, and was built up by an individual who died about 1930 and who left the stock to his wife and children. The paper was going down hill rapidly when Hoyt was made managing editor in 1933. He is credited with having put it back on its feet. During the war he agreed to go to Washington as one of the top men in the Office of War Information for six months. After completing his term of six months, he went back to his paper. I think this man is the most promising in the whole list. I have been buying from time to time issues of his paper, and making a rough comparison with *The Post.* He is turning out an excellent paper. The fact that this paper is family owned, and may never offer him the opportunity of proprietorship, might make him available to us, if the salary is sufficient.

A few days later he wrote to Hoyt, beginning the letter with this paragraph:

> Dear Mr. Hoyt:
> You do not know me, but we have many mutual friends, particularly in the Chi Psi Fraternity. I do not wish to presume upon the fact that we are Chi Psi's, but mention it as a convenient method of identification.

Campbell went on to explain that he, as trustee of the estate of Agnes Reid Tammen, and Helen Bonfils had control of *The Post* and that they, with the editor, Shepherd, constituted the board of directors. The letter continued:

> Mr. Shepherd has advised us that he wishes to retire as soon as

possible. We had planned for Lawrence W. Martin, our managing editor, to succeed Shepherd, but Martin recently suffered a heart attack, which eliminates him from further consideration, and even requires that he be relieved of his present job, and given lighter work very soon.

We have investigated many newspaper men, and have concluded to approach you first. We invite you to come to Denver, at our expense, for a personal interview with Helen Bonfils, Mr. Shepherd, who has agreed to help us in the selection of a successor, and myself. Should such an interview result favorably, we are in a position to pay you a salary that would justify your leaving Portland and coming to Denver. Furthermore, we believe that, for a man of your caliber, the opportunities here equal, if they do not exceed, those in Portland.

Our paper is published evening and Sunday, and has an average evening circulation of 183,022 and a Sunday average of 303,986. For some years we have been netting well above $2,000,000 before taxes, and $1,000,000 after taxes, per annum. We have great confidence in the future of this part of the West, of Denver and of our own paper.

May we hear from you at your earliest convenience?

Very truly yours,

The letter was mailed to Hoyt's office in Portland. Hoyt was in the East on business and it caught up with him in New York just as he was about to leave for Washington. Bounding along at his customary breakneck pace, Hoyt didn't get around to reading the letter for several days. His first reaction was that he didn't want any part of *The Post*. Hoyt had been in Denver only once. During the drought years he stopped in Denver overnight. Because he knew no one in the city he simply had a cabby drive him on a sight-seeing tour, and what impressed him most were the parks. He remembered that John Gunther had called *The Post* the worst newspaper in the United States, and now he wondered about the inner workings of a daily with that kind of reputation.

Then, because he was moved by Campbell's sincerity, he replied on January 14 from Chicago in a letter written in longhand on Blackstone Hotel stationery. The wording indicates that by then he was showing a more than casual interest:

Your good letter has only just caught up with me.

I have just come in from New York where I attended a meeting of the Associated Press Board of Directors and am on my way home via Los Angeles. Subject to transportation difficulties I should be home by January 19, Saturday.

I am very much interested in the proposition suggested and

would like to discuss it with you and Helen Bonfils and Mr. Shepherd.

As soon as I know exactly when I will be home I will wire you and perhaps we could chat on the phone and arrange the best time for me to come on. I believe, tentatively, I could make it the last week in January.

I am sorry I can't stop over on my way west but I am on such a tight schedule it would be impossible.

Campbell met Hoyt at the depot and was immediately impressed by this man who walked with the rolling gait of a sailor, who laughed and joked and talked in a rumbling bass voice, and whose massive hands, seemingly several sizes too large for his chunky body, enveloped those of anyone he gripped in handshake. He spent the day talking with Campbell and Miss Bonfils, and another day looking over the paper, its physical plant, and the city.

By then Hoyt knew the newspaper could be changed. He had made drastic changes at the *Oregonian*. But he also knew that he did not want to take over *The Post*.

Why? Many years later, when he was interviewed by his assistant, Mort Stern, for a doctoral thesis, Hoyt explained:

"Because of their procedures, because of the fact they had no editorial page, because of the fact they were running their editorials in the news, because it became quite obvious they had, if not a conscious black book, at least people and causes that were not mentioned. . . . So having made up my mind that I was not going to take the job, I had to give reasons. And as I recall I think there were twelve things, twelve reasons that I gave.

"For example, I couldn't think of running a paper that didn't have an editorial page. Their answer: Put one in. I couldn't think of running a paper that had a blacklist as to people and causes. Well, Mr. Campbell and Miss Bonfils denied that they had such a procedure but everybody thought so. I said I wouldn't even think of taking over a property which didn't have the proper physical equipment. I said I felt that *The Post* was a sort of practical, everyday *Police Gazette,* and I couldn't run a paper that was not only operated and displayed in a sensational fashion, but in a sensational fashion that was long since out-of-date. So in other words, everything I raised objection to, as a reason why I couldn't come here, they agreed to, every point. When I got all twelve of my conditions satisfied, then I didn't have any land to stand on. Then it became a challenge."

Hoyt said he wanted to go home and think about it and promised an early decision. Campbell also had some thinking to do. He and Helen Bonfils quickly agreed Hoyt was the man they wanted, but they also realized that for the first time in more than fifty years the paper would be in the hands of someone with no direct ties to its founders. They agreed in principle with the changes Hoyt proposed to make, but they also wanted to be sure they retained control. On January 28 at a special meeting the directors voted changes and amendments in the bylaws which spelled out the editor and publisher's powers and also placed limitations on them.

The objectives of the paper were outlined in the bylaws for the first time: "These objects and purposes are epitomized in our motto, 'Dedicated in perpetuity to the service of the people, that no good cause shall lack a champion and that evil shall not thrive unopposed,' and it shall be the duty of all the officers and of the editor and publisher to honor this commitment and to maintain the paper as a politically independent, public spirited, patriotic and fearless publication."

Article VIII specified that the editor and publisher would be "subject to the general authority of the officers and directors." It also stated the directors must approve:

1—Change of format or general makeup of the paper.
2—Change in the time of publications or number of editions.
3—Change in the price of the paper.
4—Change in advertising rates or commissions paid to advertising agencies.
5—Contracts for the purchase, sale, or exchange of newsprint and ink.
6—Contracts for news or press services or franchises or features or comics, or the discontinuance of any existing arrangements for them.
7—Contracts with carriers or others for bulk hauling and distribution of newspapers.
8—Any contract for the purchase, sale, or exchange of presses, linotype machines, and other equipment and supplies or services costing more than ten thousand dollars.

The next day, after Hoyt had been properly apprised of the changes in the bylaws, the directors met to vote on the contract that would be offered Hoyt. It was for five years, beginning February 20, 1946, and provided a salary of $40,000 the first year, with $5,000 increases each year until he would be paid $60,000 the fifth year. The contract also provided for cancellation for cause without liability to the company and cancellation without cause at any time by pay-

Palmer Hoyt, the man
E. Ray Campbell picked to run
The Post, in a 1960 portrait.

ment of a sum to be approved by Campbell and Miss Bonfils. Shepherd presided at this meeting but did not vote on the contract.

The salary was about twice what Hoyt had been making at the *Oregonian,* but more than the money it was the challenge of turning a paper around that excited Hoyt. He quickly signed the contract and it was agreed the announcement would be made February 5, after Hoyt had notified his employer at the *Oregonian.*

But as many news executives have learned, there is no place like a newspaper office for secrets being leaked. Several days before Hoyt's move was to be announced, the Associated Press bureau in the *Denver Post* building received a message from the Portland bureau. The message said it was being rumored that Hoyt was to be *The Post*'s new editor and publisher, and could Denver please check it out? A member of the AP staff took a copy to Larry Martin's desk in the newsroom. Martin was down on the first floor in Major Bonfils' office, where Guild negotiations were under way. Martin glanced at the message, then passed it wordlessly to Major Bonfils, who immediately adjourned the meeting. Together they started up the long iron stairway to the newsroom and Shepherd's office. Both these men had aspirations to Shepherd's job when he retired, but neither had been given an inkling that a change was imminent. "That son of a bitch, that son of a bitch," someone heard them muttering as they hurried up the stairway.

Vignette

OF STAGGERING IMPORTANCE

Late in 1941, as the nation prepared for war, reporter Gene Cervi left *The Post* to take a job as regional information director of the Office for Emergency Management. At war's end he launched the Cervi News Service, a mimeographed newsletter of information, opinion, and tidbits "circulated privately to clients who require impartial, accurate, timely and significant news reports and analysis."

Articulate and volatile, Cervi had been highly regarded as a reporter at *The Post*. He never lost his interest in that newspaper. On February 7, 1946, he published the following in his newsletter:

> Change in top management of the fabulous *Denver Post* was the most significant economic, social and political news in the Rocky Mountain region this week.
>
> The man who publishes *The Denver Post* can be one of the greatest forces for good or evil not only in the West but in the entire nation. Quality of living in six Rocky Mountain states is immediately and directly affected by decisons made or not made in the red-carpeted front office at 1544 Champa Street.
>
> Editorial direction of *The Post* is going into hands not calloused with the Bonfils-Tammen philosophy for the first time in its 54 years of existence.
>
> Importance of the appointment of Palmer Hoyt as publisher of *The Post* is staggering . . . not so much because of Hoyt's undeniable abilities, but because of the end of the most incredibly enduring, inflexible, self-perpetuating editorial policy in the history of journalism.
>
> Retiring publisher Shepherd was a trustee of the Bonfils-Tammen personality, an administrator of their psychological bequests. He carried on. Trained and nurtured in their school of rough and tumble, arrogant journalism, he made only minor concessions to the changing times and changing styles. Because of his remarkable ability to do things the way his predecessors would have done them, he had an unusually free hand in the running of the paper. The owners rarely interferred [sic], because they could rely on him to make safe decisions.

Thru the years, *The Denver Post* has grown steadily, in depression and prosperity, into greater financial returns and greater public ill will.

Hoyt is in the unenviable position of taking over an enterprise that is phenominally [sic] successful in a financial way, but badly in need of editorial overhauling, if for no other reason than the dangerously low morale of its internal organization.

Essentially, Hoyt's accession to the publishership of *The Post* is far more of a turning point for the institution than were the deaths of Tammen or Bonfils.

In recent years, under Shep's restrictive philosophies, the way was made easier for competition—competition which remained out of Denver only because of the newsprint shortage.

The big question now is whether Hoyt can stem the tide of competition (when newsprint again becomes freely available) . . . whether Hoyt can save *The Denver Post*. Unlike other commercial ventures, a newspaper cannot live on profits alone . . . it must establish an editorial character which justifies its dominant existence in a community.

The newsletter grew into a highly successful weekly business paper, *Cervi's Rocky Mountain Journal,* which, in addition to reports about real-estate transactions and other commercial developments, featured Cervi's pungently expressed opinions. Eventually, Hoyt and *The Post* became one of his favorite whipping boys. Among others were the supermarkets and the Denver Water Board. However, Cervi's vendetta with Hoyt was a case of unrequited malice. Hoyt studiously ignored Cervi, and the more he was ignored the more bitter Cervi's attacks became.

Hoyt says he thinks there were two reasons for Cervi's bile. In 1948 Cervi ran in the Democratic primary against the incumbent, U. S. Senator Ed C. Johnson. Hoyt considered Johnson such a hopeless isolationist and reactionary that he broke his own long-standing rule against editorial endorsement of a primary election candidate and came out for Cervi. Endorsement by *The Post* was still a dubious asset at that time and Johnson won handily. Hoyt believes Cervi never forgave him for this.

Sometime later one of Cervi's sons was picked up on a minor narcotics charge. Hoyt was in New York at the time. When his editors consulted him, Hoyt ordered that the arrest was to be reported in a brief story buried deep inside the paper. Unfortunately the story appeared more prominently than a report on a narcotics arrest seemed to deserve.

There are others who believe that throughout his adult life Cervi

Hoyt and a pair of Johnsons: Senator and Gov. Edwin C. (left), whose isolationism left Hoyt cold, and Lyndon B. (center), in 1960 photo when L.B.J. was the vice-presidential nominee. (Ed Maker)

wanted to become editor of *The Post,* and what he considered to be Hoyt's mistakes and inadequacies infuriated him.

Cervi died following a long illness on December 16, 1970, which was two days after a testimonial dinner for Hoyt marking his retirement.

13

THE ARRIVAL OF PALMER HOYT

Palmer Hoyt's career with *The Post* began on Wednesday, February 20, 1946. He and his wife, Cecile, better known as Brownie, had taken the train from Portland and it arrived in Denver early in the morning. After depositing Brownie at the Brown Palace Hotel, where he had leased an apartment, he hurried to *The Post* to meet his new colleagues.

The top story in *The Post* that day was a demand by Senator Tom Stewart of Tennessee calling on Edwin W. Pauley to withdraw as President Truman's nominee for undersecretary of the Navy for the good of the party and "out of common decency." Secretary of the Interior Harold Ickes a few days earlier had charged that Pauley tried to block a federal suit to get title to tideland oil by promising a $300,000 campaign contribution from oilmen to the Democrats. Another top story reported that communications workers had approved a national telephone strike. But what may have interested local readers most was a page 1 story that Dr. Robert Stearns, president of the University of Colorado, and Mrs. Stearns had announced the engagement of their daughter Marion to Byron (Whizzer) White, football star and campus hero.

Among many of *The Post*'s older employees there was a sense of fear and foreboding as they awaited Hoyt's arrival. Some of them had known Bonfils, and even Tammen, and they were afraid that the new broom would sweep them out in a general housecleaning. But Hoyt's first appearance was reassuring. He walked through the plant shaking hands with everyone, friendly as a pup.

Larry Martin has written of that time: "When Hoyt arrived in Denver, *The Post* was not exactly in a coma, but it was very sleepy. Nobody knew how he proposed to contrive the awakening; probably, thought some members of the staff—with the chill in their bones that always accompanies a change in top management of a newspaper—

there would be wholesale firings as a starter. Hoyt not only didn't fire everyone; he didn't fire anyone. Instead he promulgated the doctrine: 'Do your job well and get a better job.' "

Part of Hoyt's first day was spent at the annual meeting of stockholders. Shepherd presided for the last time. The minutes carry this entry:

> The President, W. C. Shepherd, then stated that on January 3, 1946, when Helen Bonfils had returned from New York he had called a meeting of the Board of Directors telling them he wished to retire, and submit his resignation at this annual meeting, and wanted the directors to know as early as possible so they would have an opportunity to select his successor. Mr. Shepherd stated his retirement was entirely voluntary and on his initiative because he has now passed his seventy-first birthday and wished to take this action in justice to the newspaper and himself. He further complimented the members of the Board, Ray Campbell and Helen Bonfils, on their selection of Palmer Hoyt as being the best possible that could have been made, and stated his firm belief that under his direction *The Denver Post* will move ahead as it has never done before.

Helen Bonfils then graciously expressed the board's appreciation to Shepherd and moved adoption of the following resolution:

> Resolved, That, we the stockholders of the *Post* Printing and Publishing Company have received with regret the announcement of our able, distinguished and beloved president, editor and publisher, that he desires to retire; That in acceding to his wishes and accepting his resignation, we do hereby express to him our sincere appreciation for his services for more than forty years to this company, and for having so ably and faithfully maintained the standards of courage, independence and public services established by its founders, the late Frederick G. Bonfils and Harry H. Tammen.

Helen Bonfils, Campbell, and Hoyt were elected directors, and immediately they went into a meeting of their own. Campbell was elected president, and for the first time compensation was authorized for the officers. Campbell was voted $12,000 per year for his services as president and for "general, ordinary and routine legal advice." Helen Bonfils was elected secretary and treasurer, to be paid $5,200 per year. Hoyt was given a new position on the board, editor and publisher, without additional compensation. Sadie Schultz as assistant secretary and Henry Meier as assistant treasurer were voted $32.50 per week, which would be in addition to their regular salaries. Sadie Schultz, as a trustee of Mrs. Tammen's estate, was working in Campbell's office, and Meier was Helen Bonfils' secretary.

For many reasons Campbell's choice of Hoyt was a fortuitous one. It was a case of the right man at the right place at the right time. Hoyt brought to his job broad knowledge of the editorial side of his craft learned during the course of his rise from the lowest rungs of newspapering. He had taken over the *Oregonian* when it, too, was nearly moribund due to circumstances astonishingly similar to those of *The Post*. And, as Denverites soon discovered, Hoyt had much of Bonfils' flamboyance, flair, and instincts for what interested people in combination with rock-solid editorial integrity.

Hoyt was born March 10, 1897, in Roseville, Illinois, to Edwin Palmer Hoyt, an impoverished but well-read Baptist minister, and Annie Tendler Hoyt, who had taught school. The couple had two daughters before Hoyt was born. Soon after the boy's birth, the Rev. Mr. Hoyt moved his family to Lowell, Massachusetts, and then to Derby Center, Vermont, where he was given a parsonage and paid four hundred dollars a year. By 1906 he moved to tiny Manhattan, Montana, where the pay was one thousand dollars a year, but after a few years he quit preaching to try to make a living as a dryland wheat farmer. It was a bad time to make the change. Drought set in and the elder Hoyt went broke. Leaving his family in Montana, he went to take over a church in Casper, Wyoming. He died there in 1910 of pneumonia, at age forty-nine. Young Hoyt was then thirteen. Annie Hoyt left the ranch and moved to Manhattan, where, like E. Ray Campbell's mother, she operated a boardinghouse.

In the fall of 1911 she sent young Hoyt to Baptist-sponsored William Jewell College Preparatory School in Liberty, Missouri. To help meet expenses, Hoyt sold the Kansas City *Post,* which had been started a few years earlier by Bonfils and Tammen. But after a year, when Annie learned the teachers at William Jewell smoked and chewed tobacco, she withdrew her son and sent him to McMinnville College, also a Baptist school, in McMinnville, Oregon. He spent the winter of 1916 in his mother's homestead cabin near Lewiston, Montana, reading voraciously from his father's library, and occasionally working for wheat and cattle ranchers nearby, returning to McMinnville for his senior year the next fall. With war impending, he enlisted in the Oregon National Guard, was sent to France as an infantryman, and was discharged in June, 1919, as battalion sergeant major. By then he was twenty-two years old and had no idea what he wanted to do with his life. Temporarily he returned to a ranch job in Montana that paid fifty dollars a month plus board and room. Then he learned the state of Oregon was paying veterans twenty-five dollars a month while they went to college. Since he had enlisted in Oregon he was entitled to this largesse, so he enrolled at the University of Oregon at Eugene with the vague intention of becoming a writer. At the time he had no thought of a career in journalism, but soon he became sports editor of the school paper, the *Daily Emerald,* and sports correspondent for the Portland *Oregonian.* In 1922 he got a temporary summer job with the *Oregonian* as a copyreader when a classmate with better credentials turned it down. "I didn't know anything about copyreading," he told Mort Stern, "but I figured if other people could read copy, I could."

The following year he got his first full-time newspaper job, as telegraph editor with the *East Oregonian* at Pendleton, in ranch country and the site of a famous rodeo. When he asked what standards he should apply in picking the day's top story, he was told. "Read the AP wire and put the biggest headline on the longest story, and you'll never go wrong." But he soon found that some of the longest stories were "pretty damned dull," so he began to look elsewhere for interesting material. Some days he found that stories which arrived by mail from the Newspaper Enterprise Association were more interesting than timely wire news, so that's what he used. In recognition of this show of initiative Hoyt was soon put in charge of making up the paper, reading proof, covering sports, and writing editorials in addition to editing wire news.

During this time Hoyt was also writing pulp fiction—sports stories, horror stories, Westerns, and detective stories—but he didn't sell a single one until the fall of 1926, about the time he returned to the Portland *Oregonian* as a copyreader. In all he sold about fifty short stories to the pulp magazines, mostly sports and Westerns. One series of Westerns was built around a cowboy named Andy Snoot who had one glass eye.

(William J. Barker, who for many years had a humor column called "The Wayward West" in *The Post's Empire Magazine,* once made the mistake of printing a piece of fiction in which a glass eye popped accidentally into a bowl of hot vegetable soup and exploded. Hoyt summoned Barker and contended that what had been described could not have happened. He suggested that Barker find a glass eye and drop it into hot soup and observe the results, which Barker did. Hoyt was right. The eye did not explode.)

In 1929 Hoyt was named the *Oregonian*'s movie reviewer. One of the legends of this era is that Hoyt would dispense free passes and invite some of his colleagues to see the movies with him. If the film was dull Hoyt would fall asleep, depending on a fill-in from his friends to write his review. In view of Hoyt's widely known habit of catnapping at his desk—he would snap awake after a few seconds and join the conversation as though nothing had happened—the story is believable. Hoyt was mulling the idea of quitting the newspaper and writing fiction full-time when he was offered the night city editorship of the *Oregonian* with pay of fifty-five dollars a week —five dollars more than he had been making. The security of a steady income—although he was averaging more than fifty-five weekly as a moonlighting writer—and the opportunity of moving into an executive position overcame the dubious romance of free-lance writing. By 1934 he was promoted to managing editor.

Journalism may have lost an outstanding writer when Hoyt went into management. By coincidence, both he and Leverett Chapin of *The Post* are published in a book titled *News Stories of 1933,* compiled by Frank Luther Mott and twenty-seven other journalism educators as representative of "the best news and feature writing" for that year. Chapin's story was "The Homecoming of Charles Boettcher II." It told of the release of Boettcher, thirty-one-year-old scion of a wealthy Denver family, after sixty thousand dollars' ransom had been paid to kidnappers. Hoyt's story was titled " 'Gone Wrong' Does So at the Pendleton Round-up." It began in this manner:

> Pendleton, Or. (Special)—Eleven hundred pounds of equine dynamite known aptly enough as "Gone Wrong" gave the Round-Up's cash customers their biggest thrill today when he bucked across the low arena fence into the track squarely in front of the grandstand and deposited his erstwhile rider, Tommy Zahn of Enterprise, Or., on the seat of his breeches with forceful precision.
>
> Tommy Zahn arose, ruefully, dusted off the back of his horse pants and softly remarked, "He's gone plum wrong."

Editor Hoyt, as differentiated from Writer Hoyt, might have broken the fifty-seven-word first sentence into several shorter ones.

At the *Oregonian* Hoyt walked into a situation that he would find strangely familiar when he moved to *The Post.* Henry L. Pittock, a printer, had acquired the weekly *Oregonian* in 1860 for back wages. The next year he turned it into a daily. In 1865 he hired Harvey Scott as editor. Except for one brief interlude, Scott remained editor until he died in 1910, leaving his 230 shares of the paper to his four children. Pittock, who held the remaining 470 shares, died in 1919, giving two trustees "full and complete" authority to run the paper for twenty years. It is legend that Pittock told his successor, who had been superintendent of the composing room, "Don't let them change anything in the *Oregonian.*"

O. L. Price, who had been Pittock's private secretary, became the surviving trustee in 1929 and took over control of the paper. He realized that something drastic had to be done to modernize the Oregonian. He called in Col. Guy T. Vishkniskki, a former Hearst executive who was in business for himself as newspaper consultant and efficiency expert. Mainly, his technique was based on ruthless cost cutting. Hoyt, who then was managing editor, and the colonel had some notable disagreements about what needed to be done, but in his report Vishkniskki recommended that Hoyt be made general manager, the job Price held. However, Price kept the title until 1938, when the twenty-year trusteeship expired, and meanwhile let Hoyt run the *Oregonian.*

Then, with Pittock's daughter Mrs. Kate P. Hebard in control, Hoyt was named editor and publisher. By then the *Oregonian*'s appearance, and outlook, had changed considerably. Before Hoyt became managing editor, the paper hewed closely to the standards set by Harvey Scott in the nineteenth century. It had never used pictures on page 1 and headlines were never more than one column wide. The *Oregonian* had not shared *The Post*'s venality but it was dull, dull, dull. Hoyt brightened it typographically, although it continued to look conservative, vastly improved the news coverage, and made its editorial voice heard throughout the Pacific Northwest. Perhaps Hoyt's most notable accomplishment, aside from restoring the *Oregonian*'s viability, was in separating the news from opinion in its columns. Shortly after he became managing editor he was asked about the policy on a story, meaning how it should be slanted. Hoyt answered with a question: "What's the news?"

"No, no," the reporter replied. "I want to know what the policy is."

"Well, what's the news?" Hoyt asked again. "Write the news. Write it exactly the way it happened."

The reporter, who was somewhat older than Hoyt, walked away mumbling, "Goddam, this ain't no way to run a goddam newspaper."

U. S. Supreme Court Justice William O. Douglas, a Hoyt friend and admirer from those days, writes in an unpublished manuscript that, when Hoyt became editor of the *Oregonian,* "he launched a revolution in newspaper circles by taking editorial comment out of news stories and putting it on the editorial page. It was a sad reflection on the press that such a move was a revolution. But the American press by and large wrote its news stories to praise or lambast, build up or cut down the person in the news. The news was slanted to meet the editor's predilections."

When he came to *The Post* Hoyt crystallized his editorial credo into a twenty-word statement: "Print the news as fairly as you can; comment on the news adequately, and never let the two functions mix." As much as anything it was this philosophy, assiduously followed, that brought respectability to *The Post*.

But the merit of his philosophy, and his ability to implement it, had been recognized widely long before he moved to Denver. In 1940 the University of Missouri presented the *Oregonian* a citation for distinguished service in journalism which recognized it for:

> . . . its effective divorcement of news and editorial policies; for its conviction in a day when other editorial pages have lapsed into the commonplace or have swung to commercial timidity, that editorials should be the product of sound scholarship, definite research, and careful judgment; for its conviction that editorial leadership is an important journalistic duty; for its promotion of original production of substantial articles and features by writers throughout its own region; for its aim, from which it has never wavered, to cover the news of its territory with competence and fairness; for its sturdy defense of civil liberties that has made it a bulwark against hysterics; for its journalistic enterprise that has made it more than a city newspaper. . . .

By 1943 Hoyt had achieved such stature as an editor that he was asked by Elmer Davis, director of the Office of War Information (OWI), to come to Washington as head of the domestic division. The division was in trouble. It had degenerated into something of a government propaganda agency, cranking out bales of mimeographed news releases designed to make New Deal bureaucrats look good. Hoyt believed the American people had a right to be told the truth about the war as quickly, accurately, and completely as possible within the bounds of military security, and this must be done if the government was to retain public confidence and support. In June he took a six-month leave from the *Oregonian* and went to Washington to see what he could do about it.

Hoyt's appointment was announced as a congressional subcommittee was debating the OWI appropriation. On the day he reached Washington the legislators cut off the domestic branch without a cent. Introduced to the press, Hoyt outlined his thinking about OWI policy and added: "I didn't come down to take a job. I came to do one.

There's a job to be done, and somebody is going to have to do it. I came for six months, and when the job is finished, I'm going back where I came from."

He was as good as his word. One of Hoyt's first moves was to visit friends in Congress, impress on them the need to get the war news to the people promptly and accurately, and persuade them to restore the domestic division's funds before it lost its entire staff. Congress restored less than half the appropriation. Hoyt proved his ability as an administrator by eliminating duplication, ending pamphleteering, reducing the number of regional offices, and giving the news to the media for distribution rather than trying to do it through OWI itself. Eventually he went to the White House for help in persuading the armed forces to release war information already known to the enemy. What Hoyt had done, Mort Stern observes, was to apply "much the same principle he had established at the Portland *Oregonian* and which he would later establish at *The Denver Post*— keeping news and opinion separate—and as the year 1943 ended, the press of America generally showed that it appreciated the effort."

Hoyt was a national figure when he returned to the *Oregonian*. A number of opportunities of national scope came his way. Oregon's Republican Senator Charles L. McNary, the minority leader, had died and Hoyt was mentioned for an appointment to his seat. He had also received feelers about taking the presidency of the Curb Exchange, now the American Stock Exchange; a vice-presidency with the American Broadcasting Company; editorship of the Chicago *Daily News;* and others. But back home Hoyt sensed a certain coolness on the part of the *Oregonian*'s stockholders, especially after he told them he'd like a share in the ownership of the paper.

Richard L. Neuberger, a Hoyt protégé at the *Oregonian* and freelance writer who himself went on to the U. S. Senate, wrote in *Frontier* magazine in 1950:

> . . . Hoyt felt he had taken the *Oregonian* at ebb tide and brought it to a crest of influence and prosperity. Yet he had not been permitted to acquire an equity in the paper. The ownership, on the other hand, had come to regard Hoyt as primarily interested in his own reputation. These stockholders complained that the frequent writeups in the Press section of *Time* eulogized Hoyt but neglected his paper. They held Hoyt to blame personally. . . .

So when Ray Campbell's letter arrived, Hoyt was more ready to listen than perhaps he admitted to himself. He was almost forty-nine years old, the challenge had gone from the *Oregonian,* and after

Campbell and Helen Bonfils agreed to his every demand, he had little difficulty making his decision. Editorially, the *Oregonian* gave him a warm send-off:

> It is complimentary to the *Oregonian,* of course, that the owners of *The Post,* surveying the nation's newspaper operations for a successor to W. C. Shepherd, retiring because of his years, should have come to this paper and to Mr. Hoyt. But it is not surprising—certainly not to our readers, to the Northwest as a whole or to the nation's press. During the period when Mr. Hoyt served . . . the *Oregonian* has more than kept abreast of the times and has progressed dramatically in public acceptance and approval. . . .

The editorial cited some of the *Oregonian*'s accomplishments under Hoyt's leadership, then continued:

> But when all this is said, it is still only the cold black-and-white record. So far as the *Oregonian*'s hundreds of employees are concerned, and Mr. Hoyt's thousands of acquaintances on the outside —all of whom call him "Ep"—he will be remembered longest for his unmatched capacity for friendship. For this he becomes a permanent tradition among the newspaper fraternity of Oregon.
>
> There will be no misgivings here as to his personal and professional success in Denver, or as to his ability to make *The Post* increasingly accepted as the voice of the intermountain states. We wish him the best. And all who know him will envy Denver his company.

There was nothing counterfeit about Hoyt's friendliness. He has a genuine liking for people and an unpretentious, free-and-easy manner that attracts people to him. Nate Gart, the sporting-goods dealer, had approached Shepherd in fear and trembling to ask support for a promotion he had in mind and got such a chilly reception that he was happy to escape. He called on Hoyt and was made to feel important, and has never forgotten it. And there were many like Gart. The friendliness quickly eased the apprehensions of most of *The Post* staff. Hoyt had been told that Larry Martin, Major Bonfils, and the comptroller, Louis McMahon, all had had hopes of becoming editor or publisher. There was so much rivalry among the three that they were hardly speaking when Hoyt arrived. Hoyt met with them separately and asked their cooperation in solving the problems he faced, and he also told them that from what he knew none of them would have been made the top man even if he hadn't taken the job. Then, at the next board meeting, he got pay raises for all three. Journeymen reporters were being paid $60 a week at that time; Bonfils was raised to $310 a week, Martin to $270, and McMahon to $250. "Larry and the major became loyal lieutenants," Hoyt says.

Robert W. Lucas, a veteran newspaperman who declares proudly that as a youth he hitched his wagon to Hoyt's star, describes his style in this manner: "Ep hired good men and unleashed them to do a sound and gutsy job—supporting them against economic and social pressures applied by the displeased. He kept his own mind reasonably free of prejudices—economic, social, political or cultural—thereby conveying the impression that *The Post* was receptive to change as, when and where it occurred in society. And he kept things reasonably relaxed and 'cool' with his own original sense of humor which was a compound of irreverence, the outrageous, the probing wit and the calculated jibe. Hoyt's wit was more instantaneous (therefore subconscious) than cognitive—a fact that made him fascinating to many people including the worshipful deck hands that sailed his paper for him."

Although there were some among Colorado editors who doubted that Hoyt, or anyone, could change *The Post,* their reaction for the most part ranged from friendly to noncommittal. The Omaha *World Herald,* whose circulation area abuts *The Post*'s in western Nebraska, asked, "The interesting question now is, will Mr. Hoyt change, or will *The Post?*" The same question was inherent in a much warmer, challenging, and friendly editorial written by Houstoun Waring in the weekly suburban Littleton *Independent:*

> A stranger was handed the destiny of Colorado this week when Palmer Hoyt of the Portland *Oregonian* received the appointment as publisher of *The Denver Post.*
>
> Our lives and fortunes are to a considerable extent in Mr. Hoyt's keeping, for *The Denver Post*—all jokes to the contrary—is the most influential force in the state today.
>
> If Mr. Hoyt chooses, the well-being of thousands of Mexicans, Spanish-Americans, Negroes, Japanese-Americans and other minority groups in Colorado will be vastly improved.
>
> If Mr. Hoyt puts his power to the drive, four or five lives will be saved daily when Colorado secures a modern public health system.
>
> If the new publisher wills, our antiquated school setup will be altered so that a child in the Centennial state will have an education equal to one in New York.
>
> There are endless "ifs" but Mr. Hoyt has encountered and corrected many evils in his own estate of Oregon, and we believe he can secure equally beneficent action here.

Mr. Hoyt is a man in his forties. That should mean he still has the energy to take on a fight for the people. We trust he has a free rein to accomplish his task.

Waring's editorial was an expression of hope, almost a supplication, that Hoyt would use the power of *The Post* to lead Colorado out of the darkness which in part was the result of the same newspaper's historically irresponsible venom and lack of concern. But as Hoyt contemplated the challenge of Waring's editorial and laid his plans for the years ahead, he was receiving other mail equally sincere but more disturbing. Here is an example:

Dear Mr. Hoyt:

It is with alarm that us readers of *The Denver Post* notice that we will have a new editor.

In the past *The Denver Post* has been the best newspaper that we ever seen anywhere and always put the welfare of the U.S.A. before foreign interests.

It is our sincere wish that just because you are from the West coast, that you do not bring with you any of the internationalistic communist or radical ideas that are so prevalent in the West coast.

It would be with regret that we would look upon such moves, on the part of *The Post* toward being like its opposition paper, the Rocky Mountain *News,* which is nothing but a communist scandal sheet.

In short we want *The Post* to remain as it has in the past. If you doubt that that is what us Coloradoans want just look at the difference in size between *The Post* and the *News.* I can assure you that a very few years ago the size of *The Post* and the *News* was not so much different, but that was before the leftists got control of the *News.*

I do not know anything about you or the Portland *Oregonian,* but I do hope that we shall like you as well as Mr. Shepherd and that you in turn shall be pleased with your new undertaking.

Yours truly,

Hoyt had never tried to please everyone. He was his own man and *The Post* would reflect his thinking. It would be an interesting time ahead.

LEADERS OF THE OREGON GANG

In his search for competent hands to reinforce *The Post* staff he inherited, Hoyt did not discourage defections from the *Oregonian*. There were many who wanted to follow "the boss" to Denver. In fact, so many joined *The Post* during the first year that they were referred to disparagingly as "the Oregon gang." That they stuck together socially, which was natural in view of friendships established in Portland, did not endear them at first to the Denverites.

Early in June of 1946 two Oregonians of remarkable but differing talents showed up in Denver at Hoyt's invitation. They were Charles R. Buxton and Edmund J. Dooley. Buxton was thirty-three years old, Dooley just a month short of thirty-two. Both were graduates of Oregon State University and had been tabbed as up-and-coming members of the *Oregonian* staff before they went into military service.

Buxton had been sports news editor, picture editor, assistant news editor and night city editor before being called into active duty with the Oregon National Guard in the fall of 1940 for what was expected to be a one-year tour. Aside from his competence in each of his assignments, Buxton had impressed Hoyt with his canny business sense. Several of the *Oregonian*'s sports promotions, including a Golden Gloves amateur boxing tournament, were in financial trouble when Buxton was assigned to bail them out. He not only averted disaster, he made money for the paper. In addition, he had managed the family sawmill.

Buxton had been commissioned a second lieutenant through the college ROTC program. He was named aide to the commanding general of the 41st Infantry Division, and soon after war broke out it was dispatched to the southwest Pacific. In two and a half years of service in that theater, Buxton won a Bronze Star and the Silver Star with Oak Leaf Cluster, and worked up to assistant divisional operations officer. The rest of the war was spent in Washington and other stateside posts. He left active duty as a lieutenant colonel, but remained in the reserves long enough to win his colonel's eagles.

Dooley had been sportswriter, general assignment reporter, and in a variety of desk jobs before enlisting in the Air Corps in 1942. By then he had acquired a thorough knowledge of the editorial side of the newspaper business and demonstrated a capacity for handling any kind of job. He and Buxton were close personal friends; Dooley was best man at Buxton's wedding in 1937.

On one of his trips to Washington in the latter days of the war Hoyt saw Buxton and told him he would be *The Oregonian's* next managing editor with Dooley the city editor. But not long after that Hoyt made his move to Denver. Buxton meanwhile had decided to go into the advertising business. Before he could do anything about it Buxton received a call from Hoyt. Major Bonfils, *The Post's* business manager, was expected to retire shortly, Hoyt explained. Recognizing his personal limitations, Hoyt said he wanted Buxton as his own strong man to run the business office, which was responsible for the complex fiscal, mechanical, circulation, advertising, labor, and personnel matters. Hoyt ticked off Buxton's assets: He was loyal to Hoyt, he knew how to organize, he knew how to handle money, he learned quickly, and he was a veteran of the editorial side of the newspaper business. When Buxton protested that his business experience was limited, Hoyt replied, "Chuck, you're a Scotchman and you pinch every penny before you spend it, and that's good enough for me."

At about the same time Dooley was invited to join *The Post's* news staff. While Buxton was told he would soon be named business manager, Dooley received no promise other than that he would be given every opportunity to move up.

The two men drove to Denver together from Portland. Buxton remembers that when he first saw the decrepit *Post* building he was tempted to return to Portland immediately. Dooley went to work temporarily as a copyreader, then was promoted within a few months to assistant city editor, then to news editor. By 1950 he was managing editor.

When Buxton reported, Hoyt summoned Major Bonfils.

"Major," Hoyt said by way of introduction, "I want you to meet your new assistant, Colonel Buxton."

The emphasis on military titles did not escape Major Bonfils. He took Buxton to his tiny office behind the first floor lobby which he shared with a secretary and an assistant, Hugh Shepherd, son of the former editor and publisher.

"Hugh, go find yourself another desk," Major Bonfils said. "Mr. Buxton is going to work here." Then he invited Buxton to Woolworth's basement coffee shop next door.

"Let's level with each other," Major Bonfils said as he stirred his coffee. "Are you here to cut my throat?"

Buxton smiled and replied, "No, I'm here to learn to be a business manager."

Years later Buxton recalled, "He was a great teacher, and we became good friends."

But Buxton had to wait until 1951 for the major to retire.

14

THICK SKIN AND A SENSE OF HUMOR

The Denver that Palmer Hoyt found in 1946 was hardly more than an overgrown cow town. Colorado's population was less than a million and a quarter. Denver, swollen by an influx of war workers, was nearing the 350,000 mark, which made it the largest city between the Mississippi Valley and the West Coast. Even so, its outlook was provincial and isolationist. Although its economy was based in large part on tourism, which had fallen off drastically during World War II, a more substantial reason for its being was as a supply and distribution center for a rich agricultural area. To the north and east, the broad irrigated plain of the South Platte River yielded bountiful crops of sugar beets, corn and other feed grains, wheat, hay, onions, and potatoes. Thousands of cattle flowed each week into the Denver Union Stockyards, which was also the nation's leading sheep market.

While it was mineral wealth that spurred Denver's early growth, the mountains themselves soon attracted many summer sightseers and, in more recent years, skiers when the slopes were blanketed with powder snow. Paradoxically, these mountains, their granite crags rising range on range, also proved a formidable barrier to growth. The earliest westbound caravans carefully avoided Colorado. Rather than tackle the Rockies, they plodded over the Santa Fe Trail to the south or the rutted Oregon Trail to the north, where the high plateaus of New Mexico and Wyoming were more easily traversed.

When it came time to lay rails for the Iron Horse the surveyors followed the wagon masters' routes. In 1867 the Union Pacific announced it would drive steel through southern Wyoming on its way to rendezvous with the Central Pacific, which then was pushing its way eastward from Sacramento. Denver, more than a hundred miles south of the route, appeared doomed to die on the vine. But Denverites persuaded the Union Pacific to install a link to the main line at Cheyenne in return for $800,000—$300,000 subscribed by leading

Page 1 of *The Post* on February 20, 1946, the day Palmer Hoyt took over as editor and publisher.

citizens and $500,000 raised by a county bond issue. The stub line was completed in 1870 and Denver was saved.

Two generations later, at the dawn of the age of commercial flight, Denver faced a comparable problem. The Rockies were too awesome a barrier for the fledgling planes of the day and once more Denver was bypassed. In 1927, when United Air Lines began service over a hippity-hop route between San Francisco and Chicago, Cheyenne again rather than Denver was picked as a stop. It was another ten years, when the "great, new" Douglas DC3 planes came into use, before Denver got on a transcontinental route.

Hoyt found that *The Post*'s long record of tearing down more often than it built up had done little to encourage Denver's civic progress. As a sharp-eyed newcomer, he could see many things that needed doing in the city as well as on the paper. He wanted a major role for *The Post* in community affairs and was itching to act but his plan was to move slowly at first. "I didn't intend to do anything more sensational than go to the toilet for the first three months," he once said. But in one of his first public appearances, a speech before the Chamber of Commerce, he warned Denver businessmen that their city must act quickly if it wasn't to be left in the backwash of fast-moving events. Ticking off the city's needs, Hoyt couldn't resist commenting humorously on Denver's street signs. They were metal posts about four feet tall with the letters reading top to bottom, Chinese style:

E
L
M
S
T.

Even more confusing, the posts were triangular in shape. Since the city was laid out in a square grid pattern, one was never sure what street he was on. Mayor Benjamin Stapleton, who was in the audience, was heard to remark that Hoyt had found his way into Denver by following the signs and they could bloody well show him the way out.

At the paper Hoyt had settled on three broad objectives: to give *The Post* respectability, credibility, and vitality.

To achieve respectability he set out to improve news coverage and the quality of writing.

To achieve credibility, he would restore the editorial page, which had been eliminated in 1911.

To restore vitality he needed a new physical plant to house the staff and equipment required to put out a bigger and better paper. (As depleted as the staff was when Hoyt arrived, there weren't enough chairs, desks, and typewriters to go around in the city room. Sometimes reporters had to stand around and wait for a vacancy before writing their stories. Exasperated over losing his chair whenever he left the office, Al Birch, the promotion manager, chained it to his desk. When someone pulled the chair to an adjoining desk the tautly stretched chain made a formidable hazard for shins and silk stockings. Once when the telephone operators complained the wooden chairs were snagging their stockings, the business office sent them a supply of sandpaper.)

Hoyt's method was to teach by pointing out errors rather than issuing a series of edicts, but his first editorial move was a combination of the two. While he was visiting Denver in January *The Post* ran a long, detailed story about a juicy society divorce case. Hoyt's instincts were outraged by the salacious manner in which irrelevancies from the past were dredged up. The day before Hoyt came to Denver to move into the editorship the court returned an interlocutory decree and once more *The Post* gave the story extensive coverage. Next morning Hoyt called Larry Martin into his office and told him there would be no more stories like that one.

"We will cover the news," Hoyt said. "A divorce involving prominent persons is news, but the event doesn't deserve the kind of attention given this case."

Hoyt also tackled the blacklist issue head-on. He recalled in an interview with Mort Stern: "When I came here, everybody in town and everybody on the paper was watching to see what I would do and listening very carefully to everything I said. I went out to Martin's desk and several people heard me, and it came up about somebody who was in disfavor, and I said that I want you to know, I want everybody to know that from this moment on, *The Post* ain't mad at nobody. We have no blacklist.

"Well, God, that just went all over the plant, from Martin—everywhere—all over town. So that in itself was policy. . . ."

Several days later Hoyt was visited by A. B. Hirschfeld, owner of a large commercial printing business, who for some reason had gained *The Post*'s enmity. Hoyt was on the telephone and waved Hirschfeld into a chair. When he completed the call and looked up, tears were streaming down Hirschfeld's face. "Mr. Hoyt, Mr. Hoyt," he wept in gratitude, "you put my name in the paper!" Before long Black, Hispano, and Japanese American faces appeared in the paper's "Gallery of Fame," a Saturday feature recognizing outstanding service to the community.

As time permitted Hoyt would wander out into the city room, plop into a chair next to a reporter, put his feet on a desk, and talk about anything that came to mind—the day's news, his impressions of Denver, his personal experiences, his philosophy of journalism. Here are some of his thoughts about his profession:

A newspaperman's responsibilities—"If you are doing a good job,

Soon after Hoyt's arrival Larry Martin (dark suit, center) retired as managing editor, leading to many other staff changes. Key editorial men in 1947 were, from left: Heber Smith, assistant city editor; Don Davis, assistant city editor; Gene Lowall, city editor; Jim Hale, Sunday editor; Martin; Hoyt; Alexis McKinney, managing editor; Bill Beardshear, editorial writer; Ed Dooley, news editor.

you'll have fifty percent of the people mad at you, fifty percent of the time. But they aren't going to stay mad."

If you're scooped—"No paper is going to be first with a story every time. Sometimes you'll be scooped, and when you are, you can do two things. You can take the story away from the competition—run away with it by doing a better job. Second, if the story doesn't amount to a damn, you can just play it for what it's worth. But you never ignore it.'"

The difference between reporting and commenting—"Let's say two men are shot to death on Main Street. The reporter reports the facts. He tells what happened right there on Main Street. But you comment separately on the incident on the editorial page. You comment on the situation—poverty, alcoholism, an inadequate police force, or whatever—that led to this unfortunate event. Report and comment must never be mixed."

Dedication to ideals—"If you have an idea you know to be sound and are steadfast to it, your belief will sustain you no matter what."

Hoyt had a way of enumerating his points when he was pressing an argument. "I can give you six good reasons for doing it my way," he would say. Some of his listeners had a feeling that he did not have six reasons when he started to talk, but they developed in his mind as he was ticking off the first three or four. By the time he finished talking he would have six very good reasons. (Stern's thesis quotes Harold W. Shirley, one of Hoyt's classmates at the University of Oregon, in a story that illustrates his quick thinking. In a college debate Hoyt came up with a very apt quotation from Woodrow Wilson to fortify a point he was trying to make. That quotation apparently won the debate, and when Shirley asked him how he happened to remember it, Hoyt admitted he had made it up on the spur of the moment.)

The openness with which Hoyt attacked his new responsibilities quickly won him the staff's support. Most of them, starting with Martin, were delighted to be given leadership by an editor who cared about the product. Little things, like replacing the toilet-stall doors which had disappeared after the tramway strikers assaulted *The Post* in 1920, boosted morale. "It is the reasonable thing to do," Hoyt explained, but beyond simple restoration of privacy the gesture was an indication that change was in the air.

But not everyone took gracefully to change. If degrees of unhappiness could be measured, no doubt stubborn, fiery Pinky Wayne would have been adjudged the most miserable. Long the uncrowned queen of Denver reporters, she had been assigned to write Tammen's obituary in 1924, Bonfils' obituary in 1933, Mrs. Tammen's obituary in 1942. But in her declining years her work had suffered. Hoyt wanted her relieved of reportorial duties. He offered to let her write a column in which her vast contacts would be valuable, and where she could express her opinions without affronting his standards of objectivity. He invited her to name her own hours or even work at home without ever appearing at the office. Pinky first expressed her outrage by joining the Guild, which she had scorned until then. Unable to accept Hoyt, she walked out one day and never returned.

Major Bonfils also found it difficult to adjust to change. At first he insisted the innovations Hoyt wanted tried couldn't be done "because we've never done it that way before." Hoyt would reply, "That's the best reason I know of for trying it," and eventually Bonfils became an enthusiastic convert to the philosophy of seeking new and better ways.

The Guild tested Hoyt on his second day in Denver. A three-man delegation called to welcome him to *The Post* and wish him well. Then the delegation got down to business. It asked for the right to negotiate directly with him at contract-renewal time. It also asked for a closed shop, meaning all editorial employees would be required to be members of the Guild. Hoyt firmly said no to both. While he would have final approval of any agreement, negotiations would be carried on by his labor-affairs department. And there would be no closed shop so long as he was editor and publisher. That established the ground rules. The committee was unhappy, but Guildsmen generally welcomed Hoyt's arrival. Their enthusiasm for the new boss became even more pronounced when he voluntarily raised the fifty-dollar minimum wage for experienced reporters and editors to sixty dollars a week.

Hoyt was astonished to see that while Shepherd had vacated his office, he kept a desk in the newsroom midway between the city editor and the sports department. He was quoted in an *Editor & Publisher* interview: "I'm going to take a desk in the editorial room; I'm going to smoke cigars and keep a keen interest in the news of the day." Campbell had assured Hoyt that Shepherd would have no connection with the paper after he retired. That "connection," however, turned out to be of brief duration. Shepherd hadn't bothered to speak to most of his hired hands when he was boss. Now he found himself totally ignored. He soon shifted his retirement base to the Denver Athletic Club, where he sat in the lobby, smoked cigars, and read the papers. He was ninety-two years old when he died in 1966.

Once Hoyt got his operation in gear he moved swiftly. New faces showed up the newsroom almost every week as he rebuilt the staff. Leverett Chapin, who had been off for several days to nurse a cold, returned to his job as assistant city editor and found himself surrounded by reporters he didn't recognize. "Here, you take this," he said, passing out assignments. "And you take this one. And you look into this."

One of the men looked up in bewilderment and said, "Mister, I'm not a reporter; I'm just the Western Union messenger boy."

(Late one afternoon, when most of the staff had gone home, Hoyt walked out into the city room and saw a copyboy dancing around as he tended the teletype machines. Hoyt thought the boy was a rather energetic sort who deserved encouragement and invited him into his office. "Son, how do you like your job?" Hoyt asked.

(The boy replied, "Oh, all right, I guess."

(Unperturbed by the lack of enthusiasm, Hoyt said, "Well, keep at it, son. One of these days you'll be a reporter."

Copydesk (foreground) and rewrite bank in *The Post*'s city room in 1947.
Open door in background was to Hoyt's office. (Ira Gay Sealy)

(The copyboy replied, "I don't want to be a reporter."

(Hoyt said, "What do you want to be, a publisher?"

("No," the boy answered, "I want to be a ballet dancer.")

During his first week on the job Hoyt asked Martin which of the
local radio stations called itself "The Voice of the Rocky Mountain
Empire." "None," Martin said.

Hoyt ordered it put on *The Post*'s front-page nameplate. There
it replaced the more grandiose and considerably less accurate motto:
"The Best Newspaper in the U.S.A." But Hoyt retained some of
Bonfils' other mottoes. When the editorial page he wanted became
a reality, he carried on it the "objectives" as spelled out in the bylaws: "Dedicated in perpetuity to the service of the people, that no
good cause shall lack a champion and that evil shall not thrive unopposed." Over the letters-to-the-editor "Open Forum" was placed
a saying directly attributed to Bonfils: "There is no hope for the
satisfied man."

It is characteristic of Hoyt that in establishing the Rocky Mountain Empire he could casually lay claim for *The Post* to a thirteen-
state area stretching from the Canadian border to Mexico, from
Idaho in the northwest to Texas in the southeast, from North Dakota
to Arizona—one-third of the continental United States.

"Who does Hoyt think he is, the emperor?" someone asked.

In reality *The Post*'s circulation—193,000 daily, 316,000 Sunday
in 1946—was concentrated in Colorado and Wyoming. A surprising number of papers were sent into western Kansas and Nebraska,

northern New Mexico and the Oklahoma and Texas panhandles, but only a few scattered copies reached the more distant portions of the "Empire." The Rocky Mountain Empire was no more viable an entity than was Bonfils' League of Rocky Mountain States. While Hoyt's action was reminiscent of Bonfils' style, Stern observes that it "served to set Hoyt on a course of his own and to put the public on notice that new goals were being set and changes were under way at *The Post*." Hoyt explained to Stern:

"This area had been known generally as the Rocky Mountain region or the Rocky Mountain states and they had a sort of union— a union of common interests anyway. . . .

"An area such as this needs a voice, a spokesman. *The Post* is the largest newspaper from Kansas City to the Coast and I've always felt that an area is aided or helped out by its newspaper. And since I felt that this area was large enough to warrant having a voice and since nobody else wanted to be the voice, I thought it was a good thing for us."

Hoyt was indeed signaling a change in outlook. Up to then *The Post* despite its claims was interested primarily in Denver. It had done little to promote the state; Denver's narrow interests were pitted against those of the rest of Colorado and the newspapers of the state were aligned virtually unanimously against *The Post*. Now Robert W. (Red) Fenwick was named to cover the Empire. Martin told *Editor & Publisher:* "Fenwick will have a roving assignment. He'll travel throughout the thirteen states, talk to people and see what they are thinking about. He'll line up correspondents and photographers in every city, town and hamlet in the region. He'll be our city editor of the Rocky Mountain Empire—a city editor who will get out and see people."

Under Shepherd reporters had to have an excellent reason for spending the paper's money. But Hoyt made it known that members of the staff should entertain their contacts when the occasion seemed to require it. One of Fenwick's first expense reports carried this entry: "One bottle of booze for Wyoming politician, $5." It was paid without question.

Fenwick's role never developed the way Martin planned. But he roamed the far reaches of the territory for many years, covering the news and making friends for *The Post*. Kentucky-born but reared in Wyoming, Fenwick adopted cowboy boots, frontier pants, Western shirt, and broad-brimmed Stetson as his year-round garb. He had been a cowboy, cavalryman, and telephone lineman in his youth and there was nothing phony about his friendliness or his interest in Westerners and their problems. (Frank and honest, Fenwick once congratulated Hoyt for "a helluva good talk" at a cattlemen's meeting. Then, unaware that Hoyt took pride in writing his own speeches, Fenwick asked, "Boss, who wrote it for you?")

Fenwick's roving assignment was only the beginning of a policy of covering important out-of-town stories with staff writers instead of relying on the wire services. A major issue at the time was a proposal for a semi-autonomous agency like the Tennessee Valley Authority to develop the Missouri River basin. Prior to Hoyt's arrival *The Post,* in a knee-jerk reaction against "bureaucratic regimentation," had opposed the Missouri Valley Authority in Gustin's "That's That" column.

Hoyt wasn't sure whether TVA was good or bad and no one on the staff seemed to know much about it. So he sent Leverett Chapin to dig out the story with no instructions other than to get the facts. Chapin wrote a fifteen-part series in which his conclusion was that TVA was a great thing for the Tennessee Valley where there was plenty of water, but the idea wasn't practical in the Missouri basin, where water rights were heavily committed. For the first time the issue had been put into perspective. *The Post* followed up Chapin's report by making its pages available for a thorough-going debate between James G. Patton, president of the National Farmers Union, who favored MVA, and former Gov. Ralph L. Carr.

Chapin visited a half-dozen large Eastern cities to write a series titled "What's the Matter in America?" Elvon Howe went to Bikini to witness the first postwar atomic bomb tests. Richard Dudman followed a group of European refugees trying to reach Palestine and wrote vividly of their travail. Hoyt's son, Edwin P. Hoyt, who was working for United Press in the Far East, was hired by *The Post* and sent back some revealing dispatches. Palmer Hoyt himself was asked to join leading publishers in a tour of the bombed-out cities of Europe. U. S. policy on European reconstruction was being debated in Washington, and Hoyt wrote a series that helped to crystallize the view that Germany could not be converted into a strictly agricultural nation as proposed in the so-called Morgenthau Plan. When Hoyt returned to Denver and found the paper had been operating just as though he had been in his office, he knew he was making progress.

Of this period, which was before he came to *The Post* as editor of the editorial page, Robert W. Lucas has observed: "Hoyt elevated journalism and *The Post*'s role by endowing it with a sense of high mission in the community—a level of intellectual commitment that placed it on a plane above the reasonable, normal expectations of just another business. And with this came a feeling among his staff that they were something special; that they were watchdogs of morality and probity in public persons; that they were not only the messengers of news and purveyors of entertainment, but also the guardians of ethics, the filters of good and bad in public policy, the public defenders in a grim game in which the public was always confronted with a stacked deck."

In appearance *The Post* was beginning to change, too. Hoyt quickly abolished "jumps," in which stories which begin on page 1 are continued to an inside page. Customarily a dozen or more stories had been jumped in *The Post,* forcing readers to turn time and again from front to inside to front. Hoyt reasoned that most stories weren't of sufficient interest or importance to draw the reader to an inside page. If a story required more space than could be devoted to it on page 1, he wanted it broken into two, with the inside story providing details not available in the first one. Then one day early in 1947 the old *Post* typography was scrapped for cleaner, more modern makeup. Hoyt had a choice of making the change gradually or all at once. He chose an abrupt changeover. Ed Dooley recalls that all hell broke loose as old-time subscribers demanded to know what had happened to their paper. But the new typography, while still bold, was easier to read and more pleasing to the eye and the protests soon died down. A year later Hoyt destroyed another *Post* tradition. For years page 1 (and of course page 2, the back page of this section, and the inside back page) had been printed on pink paper. The pink was dropped after the issues of July 24, 1948. Even this change was protested by some readers who decried the loss of *The Post*'s distinctiveness. Partly to mollify them, a pink tone was printed behind the page 1 nameplate for some years. Eventually that, too, was dropped. Where once red ink dripped all over page 1 of *The Post,* today it identifies only the final street-sale edition featuring the day's late sports news and stock-market tables.

These two experiences with change convinced Hoyt he was right about something he had suspected: People disliked *The Post,* but they disliked change even more. They did not want the old *Post* changed because they could depend on its nastiness. And because Hoyt was the agent of change, there were many who were bitter toward him and those he had brought with him.

Buxton recalls that he attended a cocktail party soon after his arrival, struck up a conversation with an old-time Denverite, and mentioned that he had moved to the city from Oregon. "Who are you with?" the man asked.

"The Denver Post," Buxton replied. The man turned on his heel and strode away. His first Christmas in Denver, Buxton and his wife, Janet, invited twenty couples for a preholiday party. One couple showed up.

Stern relates a revealing incident that occurred the first week of Hoyt's tenure when he made a speech to a local organization. At its conclusion a man rose and said, "Mr. Hoyt, I want you to know I take *The Denver Post*." Hoyt thanked him and the man added, "I want you further to know that I use it to wrap fish in."

Stern observes: "Up to this point the anecdote suggests the resentment that lingered on with some members of the community. But Hoyt's rejoinder also illustrates his own attitude, which soon won over much of the anti-*Post* segment of the community to his side."

Hoyt asked, "Friend, how is it to wrap fish in?" When the man said it was very good, Hoyt quipped, "Keep on taking it, will you?"

It took a thick skin and a sense of humor to take up in the footsteps of the likes of Harry Tammen, Fred Bonfils, and Bill Shepherd.

THE PLUMBER AND
RANDOLPH CHURCHILL

One day early in 1947 Randolph Churchill, a man not noted for either patience or diplomacy, came to Denver to speak to a gathering of the Knife and Fork Club. *The Post* sent reporter Robert Stapp to interview Churchill in his room at the Cosmopolitan Hotel. Stapp found Churchill fuming. He asked a few questions, then went back to *The Post* and wrote this story, which was published on page 1:

Randolph Churchill, son of Winston Churchill, arrived in Denver Saturday evening and within an hour was plunged into as heated a parliamentary debate as his illustrious father ever waged in the House of Commons. It all started over a faulty stopper in the bawth. Churchill summoned the hotel plumber, Althus Willys, and thereafter the conversation went like this:

Churchill: "There's something wrong with the plumbing."

Plumber: "Well, there's something wrong everywhere in the world today."

Churchill: "For four years five million Americans complained about the plumbing in England. What about this? I draw my bawth and when I go out to interview the press the water all runs out. I shave and when I try to rinse my dirty whiskers out the water all stays in. I turned off the radiator an hour ago and it's still pouring out heat."

Plumber: "What are you doing over here?"

Churchill: "I'm lecturing about the Europeans and writing about the Americans."

Plumber: "What's your name?"

Churchill: "Churchill."

Plumber: "Any relation to Winston Churchill?"

Churchill: "He's my father."

Plumber: "Well, I don't like his policy of putting all those kings back."

Churchill: "Which ones do you mean?"

Plumber: "France, Italy, Greece."

Churchill: "Well, the only one that got back was the king of

Greece, and that was after my father got kicked out."

Plumber: "H. G. Wells was the only really intelligent man England ever had."

To that remark, Churchill had no answer, so the plumber completed his mission and departed.

Churchill, who parachuted into Yugoslavia and supervised the ferrying of supplies to Tito's Partisans, will address the Knife and Fork Club Tuesday on *The British Empire and The Modern World*.

He will not discuss American plumbing.

15

. . . AND TO COMMENT
ADEQUATELY THEREON

On March 7, 1911, *The Post* published an editorial urging the Colorado legislature to approve a measure authorizing the state to build a railroad tunnel under the Continental Divide. The bill had been reported favorably by the House Judiciary Committee and *The Post* saw no reason for delaying action by the full House. The tunnel would "put Colorado on the main line of all across-the-country roads," *The Post* said, and "will benefit every Colorado interest—agricultural, manufacturing and mining." (The Moffat Tunnel was finally begun in 1922 with public funds and completed in 1927.)

The next day, March 8, *The Post* published this headline across eight columns of page 1:

> United States Hurls Army and Battleships South
> To Repel Japs or Seize Mexico? Nation Wonders

It appeared over a story about extensive U. S. military exercises along the Mexican border and off the Mexican coast. These actions had stirred rumors that we were about to invade Mexico, or alternatively that Washington was preparing to meet the possibility of Japan's seizing a foothold in that country. In a lengthy editorial *The Post* endorsed "intervention" in Mexico to protect U. S. commercial interests. "The sham battles, the military and naval maneuvers within sight of the Mexican lines have begun none too early," the editorial concluded.

That was the last acknowledged, orthodox editorial to appear in *The Post* for more than thirty-five years.

The following day, March 9, the rattling sabers had been stilled and *The Post* was off on another tangent. At the top of page 1 was this invitation to come downtown to the *Post* Building: "Bring the whole family with you and all the neighbors—it will be worth your while. The tallest man in the world is going to drop turnips off the

Foster Building and Jean Bedini standing on the sidewalk below will catch them on a fork held in his mouth. The first turnip drops at 12:15."

In the place where editorials customarily had appeared—the first two columns of the back page—there was an essay by reporter Winifred Black on John D. Rockefeller's new two-million-dollar home. She said she preferred her cottage with a lilac bush in the front yard and roses in the back. "Keep your two-million-dollar house, Mr. Rockefeller," she wrote. "I don't like the things that seem to go with it, thank you."

On March 10 Winifred Black wrote another column of little consequence for this space. The rest of the page was given over to features. On March 11 even Miss Black's column was gone. Telegraphic dispatches from all parts of the world filled the page. *The Post*'s editorial page had disappeared without one printed word of explanation or regret.

Fred W. White, who had been editor when Bonfils and Tammen bought the paper in 1895, had been writing most of the editorials. Now he diverted his talents to drama criticism. He died in 1917.

The demise of the editorial page did not mean the paper's strident voice was silenced, or that it had ceased making its opinions known. The news columns continued to carry a mélange of fact and opinion under loaded headlines that left little doubt as to *The Post*'s position. To make its opinions even more clear, the paper occasionally carried little boxed "ears" like this at the top of page 1: "93 DAYS has the 'Do Little' legislature been busy DOING NOTHING, and it would be the same story at the end of 993 days. Let's adjourn now." When there was something of particular moment to be said, a page 1 "So The People May Know" editorial appeared. Martin gave Stern this appraisal:

> These were thunderous, and so declamatory that they virtually dared any reader to have an opposite opinion. They indicted, tried and convicted politicians, public officials and special interests to the very brink of legal repercussions. Even when they gave support to some project or idea, they damned opposition to it.
>
> One result of that kind of editorializing was, that in political campaign times, the support of *The Post* was widely regarded as "The Kiss of Death," and many candidates found it just that.

After Bonfils' death the page 1 editorials appeared less frequently. In time the "That's That" column on page 2, written anonymously by Bruce Gustin, passed for *The Post*'s editorials.

Hoyt's first goal, as we have seen, was to restore respectability to *The Post* by improving its coverage and separating fact from opinion in its news columns. Now he set out to achieve credibility by re-establishing an editorial page.

Hoyt believed it was a newspaper's function to inform the public as completely and honestly as possible about the world's myriad happenings. As part of this function the newspaper must have an editorial page. Here the opinions of a variety of columnists would be presented, and it mattered little if they agreed on nothing. Here the public would have its say through publication of letters to the editor and "guest editorials." But most important the newspaper would express its own opinions on this page. The newspaper's opinion might not be popular, and time might prove it wrong, but it would be presented logically, lucidly, and forcefully after weighing all the arguments, pro and con. A newspaper has an obligation to take a position, Hoyt contended, if for no other reason than to stimulate thought and public discussion. In 1974, just before the general election, *The Post* articulated its thinking about its policy of endorsements in an editorial that may appropriately be reproduced here:

> Before each general election, *The Denver Post* does exhaustive research and interviews involving the issues and candidates. Our goal is to share knowledge of candidates, amendments and charter revisions with you—our readers.
>
> We interview, observe at public forums and research the platforms and accomplishments of prospective public office holders. We talk with opponents and proponents of amendments to the constitution. We seek input from staff writers who report on government in the five-county metropolitan area and at the state and congressional levels.
>
> The end result of these efforts is an opinion expressed to the voter as to the best qualified candidate and where we stand on issues. Several basic fundamentals are involved in the process:
>
> No party politics is involved. *The Post* is an independent newspaper. We owe nothing to either political party. We have supported independents, Democrats, Republicans based on opinion as to merit and the welfare of the city, state and nation.
>
> Ideology is not a determining factor in our endorsements. We do not hew to the line of any of the various political philosophies; we do not lean to either the right or the left. Neither do we always seek the center. It is, however, somewhat comforting to have our judgments attacked vigorously from both extremes.
>
> In the early days of this country most newspapers were directly connected with a political party, and their editorials regarding candidates were nothing more than party tracts. A few papers still ad-

here to this outworn conception of a party press, but most nowadays believe an editorial endorsement of a candidate is nothing more nor less than an opinion intended to stimulate public discussion and to give a newspaper's best judgment for its readers to ponder and weigh as they see fit.

On national and state races of wide familiarity, a newspaper endorsement probably adds very little to the balance for or against a particular candidate. In less well-publicized races the expertise and close attention a newspaper staff has brought to an obscure race or issue may render its opinion more meaningful to voters.

Worthy of repeating is our position regarding party nominations and primary elections. With rare exceptions, *The Post* does not endorse in these situations. In *The Post*'s opinion, such choices rest with the political parties and their members. They are responsible for selecting the candidates to bear their party standards. It is time enough in the general election for a newspaper to make recommendations based on the information at our command.

Our endorsement system is not beyond criticism. And we are not out to make friends. We are seeking improved government of the people, by the people and for the people, and so far we have not found a better way to express election opinion than the endorsement system.

Back in 1946, Hoyt's first step in reestablishing an editorial page was to put Gustin's by-line on his column. That happened on February 24, four days after Hoyt took over. This had little effect in moderating Gustin's views, but stripped of anonymity he was no longer the voice of *The Denver Post*. He was simply another columnist saying his piece, and soon he was joined by a diverse stable of syndicated writers with a far-ranging variety of views. In explaining the role of these commentators, *The Post* said editorially:

> Thus we publish the columns of Norman Thomas, the nation's No. 1 Socialist leader—and we also publish the columns of George Sokolsky, whom we regard as a reactionary. In between, there is Marquis Childs, whom we regard as liberal, and David Lawrence, whom we believe to be conservative in his thinking. There are others, many of them, but the opinions they express are their own.

Among others who joined *The Post* stable were Harold L. Ickes, Ernest Lindley, Paul Mallon, the Alsop brothers, Drew Pearson, and many more.

The man Hoyt chose to speak for *The Post* was Fred Colvig, another unusually talented young Oregonian. Like Hoyt he was a graduate of the University of Oregon, where he was editor of the school paper, a light-heavyweight boxer, and Phi Beta Kappa. He

The men who helped Hoyt direct *The Post* in 1948: From left, Ed Dooley, news editor; Leverett Chapin, assistant managing editor; Gene Lowall, city editor; Alexis McKinney, managing editor; Fred Colvig, editor of the editorial page; Larry Martin, associate editor; Bruce Gustin, columnist.

worked briefly for United Press before joining the *Oregonian* in 1939. He was Sunday editor by the time he went to war as a Navy intelligence officer. Colvig had no intention of returning to the *Oregonian*. Although he was a strong advocate of union rights he had been involved in a disagreement over principle with Guild leaders. It became so bitter that he had offered to fight them, one at a time or all at once. He was the only member of the editorial staff who wasn't given a party when he left for service. This anecdote illustrates Colvig's strong-mindedness rather than his truculence; he was of a sunny disposition and in Denver was well liked and well respected. He came to work in Denver early in May, 1946, a month before his thirty-third birthday.

Hoyt considered himself a liberal Republican. At the *Oregonian* he had supported Wendell Willkie enthusiastically in the 1940 campaign against Franklin D. Roosevelt; in 1936 he had been for Arthur Vandenberg rather than the ultimate G.O.P. choice, Alf Landon. Hoyt knew that Colvig was somewhat to the left of his own position but both were comfortable because they trusted and respected each other. Since they had worked together before, and Colvig was familiar with Hoyt's thinking, he required very little direction in establishing the tone of the editorial page. "Fred was brilliant, a good writer and most engaging," Hoyt says. "He could argue the devil out of his horns. He was a sincere, practicing liberal without a touch of radicalism."

The Post's editorial page was reborn May 19, 1946, three months after Hoyt became editor and publisher, thirty-five years and two months after Bonfils and Tammen allowed it to die. Hoyt himself wrote the lead editorial:

> Today *The Denver Post* inaugurates an Editorial Page which will be a part of every issue henceforward. This page will present divergent views of nationally known columnists and public figures, and of its readers. In this, the editorial column, *The Post* will speak for and to Denver, Colorado and the Rocky Mountain Empire.
>
> In this column you will find the views of *The Post*. Those views will not be found elsewhere; not in the news columns, which will present the daily world, national, regional and local scenes clearly, factually and objectively; not in the signed columns which will present the thinking and ideas of the individual writers regardless of whether or not they conflict with those of *The Post*.
>
> This will be your page. You are invited to express your views in the *Open Forum* which will run today and every day. The voice of the people is the voice of the sovereign. It is your voice. That voice needs to be heard in the land.
>
> *The Post* adds an editorial page at a time when newsprint is worth its weight in gold. It does so to fulfill this newspaper's concept of its basic function: namely, to print the news fairly and accurately and to comment adequately thereon.
>
> The Rocky Mountain region is an economic empire of untold wealth and of vast importance to the United States and to the world. Denver, its capital, is a city of certain destiny. To help Denver and the Rocky Mountain Empire keep their appointment with destiny is the prime responsibility of *The Post;* a responsibility which it accepts.
>
> In establishing the editorial page, *The Denver Post* reaffirms its faith in this great city, the region and the United States and rededicates itself to their service.

A ringing statement of faith, but if anyone had taken the time to check through the files he would have found an interesting similarity between it and the editorial published the day Bonfils and Tammen took over. On November 1, 1895, this pledge appeared in the *Evening Post:*

> The new managers propose to make *The Post* thoroughly and emphatically the people's paper—a paper that shall first and always work and fight for the production of the people's good and advancement of their interests. It will be free from entanglements with political parties, corporations or special interests of any kind. Thus it will be free to do for the people and to be vigorously and unreservedly against whatever is against them. The new management ask the people to watch it closely and see if the paper does not well demonstrate its loyalty to them.

The Post, in its renewal of life, will devote special and ceaseless attention to the material interests of the state and to the development of her vast and varied resources. It will seek to so direct its efforts that more acres of land shall be brought under cultivation; that more exchanges of trade shall be made; that more mines shall be opened and profitably worked; that more mills and factories shall be built and more foundries and smelters be put in blast; that capital shall command greater returns and labor secure larger rewards; that, in brief, the cheer of prosperity shall reach a larger share of the people. . . .

The concern of Bonfils and Tammen for the people had taken some strange turns on occasion. How would Hoyt interpret his mandate to serve? The public could only wait and see.

On that first editorial page in 1946 were three signed columns, in addition to Gustin's, and a guest editorial written by Colorado's Gov. John C. Vivian. Marquis Childs produced a gloomy commentary on the problems of the nuclear age. DeWitt MacKenzie, the reigning Associated Press political analyst, wrote on France's perennial problems. And David Lawrence complained that the Iron Curtain made it impossible for western observers to write meaningfully about the Soviet. Governor Vivian provided *Post* readers with a reassuring link to the past. He denounced the proposed Missouri River Authority Act as "one of the most vicious measures ever introduced in the Congress of the United States." He went on: "It is extremely revolutionary. If it should pass and be signed into law, the American way of life, as we have known it, would fast be on the way out."

Hoyt was aware that too abrupt a break with the past would needlessly alienate many readers. On May 24 he found another chance to reassure them. The railroad unions had struck and the nation was virtually paralyzed. In a page 1 "So The People May Know" editorial *The Post* demanded that service be restored to prevent nationwide chaos while federal authorities redoubled their efforts to reach an agreement. But in addition to the editorial, the news columns gave thorough coverage to the issues involved in the dispute and the positions taken by unions and employers.

It was also on May 24 that *The Post* published the first letter to the editor about the new editorial page. It was mildly worded congratulations for keeping alive "the spirit of freedom." No further communications on this subject appeared during the next ten days.

Most of the letters published during this period were quite innocuous, dealing with such subjects as the objectionable noise airplanes made while landing in Denver, the mounting problem of traffic congestion, and the need to save birds from thoughtless boys with air guns. It is not likely that Colvig, out of modesty or some other reason, intentionally did not publish letters commenting on the revived editorial page. What is likely is that the public took a while to react. Over the years *The Post* had published an "Open Forum" letters section on Sunday but it was far from an open forum. It was edited by an elderly employee, Oscar O. Whitenack, who chose to run little else but letters supporting *The Post*'s (and his) point of view. On the rare occasions when he used letters contrary to *The Post*'s position, Whitenack usually appended an editor's note expressing his dissent. Professor Gayle Waldrop, formerly dean of the University of Colorado's school of journalism, contends that 85 percent of the letters published in *The Post* during this period were written by five persons who used various aliases. "I couldn't believe what was going on," Hoyt said when apprised of this.

It took a while for readers to realize that the new "Open Forum" welcomed well-reasoned comments regardless of the viewpoint. Soon it was running a wide variety of letters, including many highly critical of Hoyt and the new *Post*. Stern observes, "If he [Hoyt] had been amazed by the old system, some of the readers seemed equally amazed by the new."

Hoyt reached an early understanding with Gustin. He was told to restrict his comments to local and regional matters, in which he had considerable expertise. In fact, Gustin proved most valuable in providing Colvig with the background of local issues. Gustin was also told he could write in opposition to *The Post*'s official position, which he often did, but only once on each issue. In other words, he must not carry on a campaign against his own paper. Appropriately, his column was anchored at the extreme right side of the editorial page, where he kept his like-minded readers happily enraged.

Colvig took on his new responsibilities with characteristic vigor. In a detailed study of the first five years of Hoyt's administration, Waldrop made this observation:

> In its determination to hold Authority to account, to fix responsibility and speed needed change, the [*Post*'s] editorial page practices the trinity of editorial principles: independence, leadership, and devotion to the public welfare. "It is the duty of a liberal, democratic press to answer misleading institutional advertising" appeared in an editorial September 22, 1947. In October 1948 *Nothing for Something* pointed out that premium-grade gasoline is a waste of money for most car owners. . . .

This practice of independence on *The Post* editorial page extends to political parties. "Political parties are not matters of men alone but also matters of principles and collective ideals," a July 27, 1948 editorial said. . . .

The thread of persistence that "should run through the editorial page like a Wagnerian motif," as Joseph Pulitzer wrote, is present in *The Post*. Its persistence, as indicated in the *Magnificent Obsession* editorial, recalls a line from Justice Louis D. Brandeis, a fighter for the public welfare: "The greatest menace to freedom is an inert people." It was his opinion that the public must be aroused again and again before reaching the point of action. A conspicuous example of persistence and of the practice of aggressiveness in asserting opinions are seen in more than 125 editorials on reorganization of the state highway department between February 1947 and December 1950.

The page respects the opinions of experts as evidenced by the highway department campaign and one recently started to modernize the penal and parole systems of the state. It has respect for facts and a willingness to apologize for "unnecessary roughness," for non-objective headlines in its news columns, and when its editorial writers are caught "red-handed," their facts wrong. . . .

Colvig was no deskbound editor. Driven by a compulsion to see for himself, he traveled widely. Richard Neuberger described Colvig as a "restless intellectual." Ultimately, it was his tireless search for the facts that led to his untimely death. In the spring of 1949 he traveled to Scandinavia to report on the progress of socialism. He had been back in Denver only briefly when he was invited by the Netherlands government to visit Indonesia, where Sukarno's revolutionaries were fighting for independence. It was too big a story to pass up, and Colvig joined a party of fifteen American writers and editors who flew to Indonesia aboard a chartered Royal Dutch Airlines plane. The homeward leg was routed from Batavia (now Djakarta) through Mauritius, a lonely island in the Indian Ocean. The Americans persuaded their hosts to avoid the long overwater hop—this was before the age of jet transports—by flying back through India. Dutch airliners had been barred from India following a political dispute but special permission was granted for this flight. On the morning of July 12 the pilot, preparing to land at unfamiliar Bombay Airport through a driving monsoon rain, crashed into a hilltop. The plane exploded and all forty-five persons aboard died. Among them were thirteen American correspondents. (Two had left the party to travel home on their own.) In addition to Colvig, the victims included S. Burton Heath and H. R. Knickerbocker,

Following Fred Colvig's untimely death, these men successively were editors of the editorial page: Ed Hoyt (left), Robert W. Lucas (center), Mort Stern.

both Pulitzer Prize winners; Nat Barrows of the Chicago *Daily News;* Tom Falco of *Business Week;* William Newton of Scripps-Howard; John Kerkley of *Time;* and Charles Gratke of the *Christian Science Monitor.*

For Hoyt, Colvig's death was a grievous personal loss. Colvig left a wife and four children, all under seven years of age. *The Post* had no insurance program for its executives, no pension plan, and as a result of this experience Hoyt made them a priority item. In memoriam, *The Post* published an editorial that said in part:

> The editorial page of *The Denver Post* was the creation of Fred Colvig, a brilliant young man of inquiring mind, a deep sense of fair play, an inborn hatred of injustice, a sincere belief in the majesty of the common man. . . . The best tribute we can pay to Fred Colvig, we believe, is to try to carry on this page as he would have it, with courage and conviction, hatred for sham and intolerance and firm determination in the principle of freedom of expression.

Colvig had been editor of *The Post*'s editorial page less than three years and three months. In that span he had achieved Hoyt's mandate for credibility. His page, as much as anything, had destroyed *The Post*'s old image of arrogance and capricious irresponsibility. In his brief time Colvig had created the foundation for a courageous and enlightened page on which future editors built.

He was succeeded by Ed Hoyt, the older of Palmer and Cecile Hoyt's two sons. Ed was properly Edwin Palmer Hoyt, Jr. Since his father was known as Ep because of his initials, the younger Hoyt preferred to be called Ed. (In time the older Hoyt dropped his first name and signed himself as simply Palmer Hoyt.)

Ed Hoyt was working for United Press in Korea when his father moved to *The Post*. Korea had become something of a backwater and Ed was anxious for a change. He thought *The Denver Post* would be an interesting paper to work for, but anticipated that his father would not hire him. So Ed wrote an application letter to Helen Bonfils. Amused by Ed's tactics, she persuaded Hoyt to take him on.

Before reporting in Denver Ed Hoyt filed a number of perceptive dispatches from the Far East, Palestine, and the troubled Mediterranean area. He was assigned as an assistant to Colvig. The two were close friends and spent much time talking about their hopes for *The Post*. But because Colvig had the only job young Hoyt really aspired to—and Ed didn't want to compete with his friend—he soon went to the San Francisco *Chronicle*. In six months he was made a relief night city editor. This meant he shared the job several times each week with Pierre Salinger, who went on to become President Kennedy's press secretary.

After Colvig's death the three remaining members of the editorial-page staff—Larry Martin, Leverett Chapin, and Bruce Gustin—urged Hoyt to bring back his son as editor. Hoyt was anxious to avoid any appearance of nepotism. Chapin persuaded Hoyt that he would not hesitate to hire someone else with Ed Hoyt's qualifications, and therefore he should not let their relationship stand in the way.

Ed Hoyt says, "I hesitated to come back to Denver, but on the other hand I really liked that job and knew precisely what Colvig had planned to do with it. So I came back." In 1951 Ed Hoyt rounded up some backing and took over as editor and publisher of the foundering Colorado Springs *Free Press*. Since then he has become a prolific book author.

Robert W. Lucas, another Oregonian, followed Ed Hoyt as editorial-page editor; then came Mort Stern and James Idema. After Hoyt's retirement Stern returned to the position briefly before Robert Pattridge took over.

The editorial-page editor required a particularly close relationship with Hoyt. Lucas describes his working arrangement this way:

"I was never asked to clear my work or that of those under me before publication. Hoyt apparently had complete confidence in my judgment. And our relationship was almost that of father and son —or better, that of the ideal shortstop-second baseman combination; each knew where the other man was, intuitively, and why. And in all the years that I either wrote or supervised the production of thousands of editorials at *The Post*, Hoyt asked that only one be removed from an early edition. It was a lengthy and ably structured piece by Chapin criticizing the federal government for lifting the security clearance of J. Robert Oppenheimer. Hoyt said he simply did not like 'the son of a bitch,' and that was good enough for me. Had he challenged the reasoning of the editorial there would have been a battle. Hoyt never did that."

Ed Hoyt and his father engaged in many intellectual arguments. But on important editorial issues, Ed recalls, "mostly we did not argue because he was the boss."

Stern says Hoyt's technique "was to put some impatient, enthusiastic (and ambitious) young man in charge, give him his head, and then watch with a mixture of amusement and mild pain the uproar that would inevitably follow." Generally the system seemed to work very well. One suspects Hoyt enjoyed the uproar although Stern recalls that one morning the boss summoned him and said with a grin, "Now repeat after me: I am not going to get that nice Mr. Hoyt in any trouble today."

Vignette

TWO PRIZE-WINNING CARTOONISTS

Since the unorthodox plays such a large part in *Post* history, perhaps it was natural that when honors began coming to the paper the scenario should be somewhat improbable. Take, for instance, the matter of *The Post*'s two Pulitzer Prize winners.

In May of 1964 it was announced that Paul Conrad had won the Pulitzer for editorial cartooning in *The Post* during 1963. But by then he was no longer in Denver. Four months earlier he had been hired away by the Los Angeles *Times*. If this seems to indicate *The Post*'s inability to recognize—and retain—talent, witness what followed next.

As Conrad's successor Hoyt picked Pat Oliphant, a young Australian who had never lived in the United States. Three years later Oliphant's political cartoons won a second Pulitzer for *The Post*.

It was something of an accident that Conrad came to work for *The Post* at all. In February of 1950 Paul and his identical twin, Jim, who had studied commercial art, were graduated from the University of Iowa. Paul had done some editorial cartoons for the school paper and he sent samples with a job application to a number of editors. The replies were not encouraging. *The Denver Post* said it would be happy to have Paul drop in for an interview if he happened to be in the neighborhood. Iowa winters being what they are, the brothers headed south with their sample books, visiting newspapers along the way. By the time they reached Florida they had just about exhausted both money and job prospects. The brothers flipped a coin and Paul won. Then he sent a telegram to *The Post* saying he was on his way. Managing editor Ed Dooley wired back: NO JOBS OPEN, DON'T COME NOW.

Paul tore up the reply. With their pooled funds Paul bought a one-way ticket to Denver while Jim started for home. When Paul showed up at *The Post* Dooley asked if he hadn't received the tele-

Self-portraits of Paul Conrad and Pat Oliphant and Punk.

gram. "What telegram?" Paul said. Ed Hoyt, by then editorial-page editor, was impressed by Conrad's work. Palmer Hoyt at the time was trying to replace an editorial cartoonist who wasn't working out. "We'll put you to work for six months or so as a retouch artist," Hoyt said. "Ever operate an airbrush?"

"Hell," Conrad said, "any artist can handle an airbrush." But he had never learned to use one, and never became good at it. "So, for the first half year at *The Post*," Conrad recalls, "I was painting brassieres on photographs of native girls that Wally Taber was sending back from his African safari, and retouching the offensive equipment off pictures of prize bulls." Jim eventually made it to Denver, where he is a successful advertising artist.

Paul Conrad is tall and angular, a fey character who moves with all the vigor of an Anglo-Saxon Stepin Fetchit. When life pleases him, which is often, he reacts with high-pitched laughter. At his drawing board Conrad wields his pen like a stiletto dipped in vitriol; after work his greatest pleasure is his Little League baseball team. One of Conrad's best-remembered pranks at *The Post* nearly back-fired. To celebrate the elderly Betty Craig's birthday, Conrad and Stanton Peckham, now the book editor, bought a cake, and studded it with candles. They lured Betty out of her office and lit the candles. But Betty had vanished. Before they could find her the candles had fused into a blazing pyre that incinerated the cake and nearly set the room afire.

Early in 1964 the Los Angeles *Times,* in the process of rebuilding its staff, invited Conrad to come out for an interview. He was offered about one hundred dollars more per week than he was getting at *The Post,* plus very favorable terms through the Times-Mirror Syndicate when his contract with the Register & Tribune Syndicate expired. Conrad was not enthusiastic about moving to Los Angeles. He would have remained if *The Post* could have come close to the *Times* offer. But there was no counter offer. He was told it was against *Post* policy to engage in a bidding contest. *The Post,* however, continues to buy Conrad's syndicated cartoons and uses them frequently.

Pat Oliphant, then twenty-nine years old, was working as political cartoonist for the Adelaide *Advertiser* when he read in *Time* magazine about Conrad's move. The *Advertiser* had sent Oliphant around the world a few years earlier to broaden his understanding. Oliphant fell in love with the United States and was looking for a way to return as a permanent resident.

Oliphant's application for the job was among more than fifty received by *The Post*. Mort Stern, then editor of the editorial page, sifted through the various samples but kept returning to Oliphant's. What excited him was the freshness of Oliphant's ideas, his humor, the boldness of his strokes. With some misgivings, because Oliphant was a stranger to the American scene, Stern told Hoyt the Australian was his first choice. To Stern's surprise Hoyt told him to hire Oliphant. Presently Oliphant received a letter offering him the job at two hundred dollars per week, which was fifty dollars above the Guild scale. Oliphant paid the transportation to Denver for himself, his wife, and two children.

"It took a lot of courage for *The Post* to hire me," Oliphant says. "They knew nothing about me. Nobody in America was using my style."

Slim and affable, Oliphant was able to fit in smoothly despite minor idiosyncrasies like eschewing meat. He arrived in the middle of the 1964 Presidential campaign and delighted Stern with his quick grasp of the issues. Oliphant describes his style as a distillation of more than twenty different influences, mostly European and Australian. A little penguin named Punk, who makes pithy remarks and enables Oliphant to inject a second statement, is his special trademark. Within a year the Times-Mirror Syndicate began distribution of his cartoons. (Conrad was still with the Register & Tribune Syndicate.) Oliphant's work appears in some 260 newspapers—more than any other political cartoonist—and at least a half-dozen American artists have paid him the ultimate tribute of adopting a style similar to his.

Early in 1975 Oliphant, too, left *The Post* but not Denver. He joined the staff of the Washington *Star* with a contract that enables him to live in Denver much of the time. His syndicated cartoons, like Conrad's, continue to appear in *The Post*.

16

CRIME AND POLITICS

Ep Hoyt had determined early in his journalistic career that a good newspaper must take a vigorous role in the life of its community. It must do more than report the news of interest to its readers. In addition it has the responsibility of taking an active and constructive part in shaping its community for the better.

Not long after Hoyt's arrival *The Post* injected itself with great vigor and impact into two totally dissimilar events. Whether *The Post*'s role in either instance was consistent with Hoyt's ideals will be left for the reader to judge.

The first was the mayoralty election of May, 1947. Denver has a nominally nonpartisan, strong-mayor and city-council type of government. The incumbent, Benjamin Franklin Stapleton, was a judge when first elected mayor in 1923. He was reelected in 1927 and 1931. In the 1935 campaign *The Post* under Bill Shepherd trained its big guns on Stapleton. A few days before the election the "That's That" column charged: ". . . you will find Judge Stapleton the most incapable and utterly incompetent and extravagant mayor this city has ever had." Stapleton lost to George D. Begole because of a strange multiple-choice ballot which since has been replaced. Voters were permitted to cast ballots for first, second, or third choice—the idea was to avoid runoff elections—and the winner was the candidate with the largest total. Stapleton received 41,124 first-place votes but only a handful of second- and third-choice designations. Begole won 27,393 first-place votes, plus 14,386 for second and 3,872 for third. His total was 45,651 votes to Stapleton's 44,661. In a "So The People May Know" editorial *The Post* crowed:

> The defeat of Stapleton Tuesday was the most magnificent victory ever won by the people of Denver. Every so-called club in the city, the senile Chamber of Commerce, the Junior Chamber of Commerce, all the predatory corporations, every unfair and oppressive interest

in the city, all the criminal crews of bootleggers and gamblers who had been enjoying special privileges under the Stapleton regime were united to keep Stapleton in City Hall. But the little taxpayers who are the heart and soul and brains and backbone of every community joined with *The Post* in winning a glorious victory.

Ben Stapleton, Jr., now a prominent Denver attorney, is the source of an anecdote that may help to explain why *The Post*'s attacks seem to have gone beyond its chronic hostility toward any incumbent. Shortly after Stapleton was elected in 1923 the head of his department of weights and measures asked: "Mayor, how many pounds are there in a ton of *Denver Post* coal?"

Stapleton replied: "Why, two thousand, just like in anybody else's ton."

Several days days later Stapleton received a telephone call from F. G. Bonfils complaining about harassment by a weights-and-measures inspector. Bonfils invited the mayor to come to his office to discuss the problem. "Not under these circumstances," Stapleton replied, "but you're welcome to come to my office at any time."

Ben Stapleton, Jr., says his father refused to let *The Post*'s editorial criticism get under his skin. He often said he considered the intemperate attacks an asset. But his wife was much more sensitive about them. One day when she complained *The Post* was being unfair the mayor said he would cancel their subscription to spare her the ordeal of reading the paper. Thereafter *The Post* was delivered each afternoon to the Stapleton home together with a small printed note: "Compliments of F. G. Bonfils."

Mayor Stapleton was a soft-spoken, almost shy man whose personal integrity was never successfully questioned. The so-called Stapleton machine was made up largely of City Hall employees who owed their jobs to him and were intensely loyal. Perhaps Stapleton's most fortuitous accomplishment was purchase of land, in the face of bitter opposition by *The Post* which charged cronyism, that was developed into Denver's municipal airport. Then, it was far out on the prairie. Today Stapleton International Airport is a major facility conveniently close to downtown Denver.

The people returned Stapleton to office in 1939 and 1943. The salary was the same as it had been in 1923—six thousand dollars a year. By the time the 1947 campaign rolled around Stapleton was seventy-seven years old but reluctant to yield his comfortable chair in the mayor's office. Hoyt, and many others, were convinced Denver needed a younger mayor with fresh ideas to meet the problems of postwar growth. But who? Hoyt found an answer one June night in 1946. Supreme Court Justice William O. Douglas had come to Denver and Hoyt hosted a dinner for him. Among the guests was Quigg Newton, a thirty-five-year-old Yale-educated attorney, scion of a socially prominent Denver family, a Navy lieutenant commander in World War II. Newton had been Douglas's law secretary when he was head of the Securities and Exchange Commission. The talk got around to Denver politics and Hoyt said what the city needed was an able young candidate who could defeat Stapleton. Douglas suggested Newton was just the man for the job.

Hoyt looked into Newton's credentials and liked what he found. One day he tried the idea on E. Ray Campbell. "That callow youth?" Campbell retorted. "All right," Hoyt replied, "find a better man." Campbell soon admitted he could not. The next step was to persuade Newton to run. He had a solid law practice with promise of much bigger things and he was reluctant to take on the hurly-burly of a political campaign. Eventually Hoyt impressed on him his opportunity for great service to his city and won his approval.

Acutely aware that any candidate bearing *The Post*'s stamp at this point in history would be heavily handicapped, Hoyt quietly planted the idea of Newton's candidacy at key places around town. George V. Kelly in his book on Denver politics, *The Old Gray Mayors,* reports that by September of 1946 Sam Lusky, the Rocky Mountain *News* political writer, had heard several rumors about Newton's possible availability. "Sam pounded out copy that speculated on those reports," Kelly writes, "and the *News* gave it good placement. Over at *The Post,* Hoyt was happy with Lusky's story because his tracks had been covered by Sam's scoop. Lusky—and the *News*— didn't collect much credit for the item until eight months after the story appeared, but following Quigg's election, the *News* proudly publicized Sam's reporting as the type of illumination one could expect from the local branch of the Scripps-Howard lighthouse."

Newton announced his candidacy on February 22, 1947, a Saturday, so that both *The Post* and *News* would have an equal break on the story in their Sunday editions. Kelly, then *The Post*'s City Hall reporter, was sent to interview Newton. Writing of his experience in the third person in his book, Kelly says:

> . . . a *Post* reporter, unaware of the maneuvering that began at the Douglas breakfast [sic], was told he was going to participate in a political first. The reporter was sent to the second floor of the Colorado National Bank for an interview: The subject: James Quigg

Newton, Jr. . . . After the interview, the reporter had no doubt of Quigg's political potential. Aside from his physical and personal assets, he would get *The Post*'s support. The warm, friendly treatment pervading the interview and the fact *The Post* reporter was the first media man to question Newton as a candidate were strong indications, the reporter mused, that Quigg had the newspaper in his hip pocket, or vice versa.

When he returned to *The Post* city room, the reporter, still unaware of his publisher's role in the Newton candidacy, found the main news story about the announcement had already been set in type. He was directed to write the interview and a biographical sketch. . . .

The Post played the announcement "straight, almost low-key," on page 1, Kelly says. The *News* reporter was ushered into Newton's office after Kelly left, and he was followed by radio newsmen. All the media gave Newton excellent coverage.

Newton was soon joined in the race by Stapleton and U. S. Attorney Tom Morrisey. Stapleton and Morrisey were Democrats, Newton an independent who some years later declared for the Democrats. Newton was endorsed editorially by both *The Post* and *News,* although all three candidates continued to receive extensive coverage. There was one piece of news about Stapleton, however, that did not get into *The Post*. On May 1, just a few weeks before the election, the Denver Bears baseball team opened its Western League season. The honor of throwing the first pitch went to a young California congressman who happened to be in Denver, Richard Milhouse Nixon. Mayor Stapleton was the batter. Nixon threw a pitch, Stapleton took a lusty swing, missed, and sprawled flat on his face. Floyd McCall, a *Post* photographer, snapped a picture at that moment.

Hoyt decided against using it. He felt it was excessively unkind to the old mayor. He also wanted to avoid charges that *The Post* was picking on Stapleton. But *Life* magazine gave the picture a full page over the caption, "Mayor Strikes out."

The election was a runaway for Newton. He drew 79,695 votes to 35,080 for Morrisey and a meager 17,640 for Stapleton. Newton polled some 21,000 votes more than the other candidates combined. Stapleton took the defeat in good grace. He had done the best he could. It was a heady victory for Newton—and Hoyt. And Newton upheld the voters' hopes by cleaning out the deadwood in City Hall, installing up-to-date procedures, and bringing in many bright young men to help him administer the city and plan for its future needs.

Elderly mayor Ben Stapleton swung the bat on opening day, missed, and fell. *The Post* was opposing Stapleton but Hoyt refused to publish this photograph by Floyd McCall. *Life* magazine did.

Not least among the recruits was restless, innovative Henry A. Barnes, a Michigan traffic specialist, who was given the job of un-snarling an ever-worsening problem. He converted downtown Denver into a grid of one-way streets and installed the "Barnes dance," in which all vehicular traffic is stopped while pedestrians cross an inter-section in any direction, including diagonally. The genius of the Barnes dance is that cars are not obstructed by pedestrians when it is their turn to move, particularly those making right turns. After six years of Herculean work Barnes went on to tackle Baltimore's traffic woes, then moved to his ultimate challenge in New York City, where he died in harness.

The day after the election Newton called on Hoyt to express his thanks for the paper's support. "Ep," Newton said, "you've done it. If there's anything I can do for you, just let me know."

Alexis McKinney, who was at the meeting, recalls that Hoyt replied: "Quigg, there's only one thing you can do for me or for anybody—that's to be the best damn mayor Denver ever had. And that's what I'm sure you're going to be."

During his early years in office Newton conferred frequently with Hoyt, whom he regarded as something of a mentor. Kelly, who continued to cover the mayor's office for *The Post,* and later for the *News,* writes of this period:

Hoyt apparently never exacted any favors from Newton, despite their affinity. The publisher was content to listen to city problems described by Quigg, discuss them and offer suggested solutions. When criticism required, *The Post* supplied it, but not in the muckraking vein of the Stapleton days. . . . Only rarely was a *Post* reporter given a news break by Newton. When it did happen, it was intended to further the timing or the planning of some project, especially if it were believed city council might harbor some opposition. In the latter instance *The Post* would run a news story one day and follow it the next with strong [editorial] support. In the face of such double-barreled strength by Newton, council usually succumbed to the mayor's wishes. . . .

Perhaps this is too sanguine an appraisal. There were disagreements over policy, particularly after Hoyt's son, Edwin P. Hoyt, took over the editorial page following Colvig's death. Generally, however, relations between Newton and the paper were warm and cooperative.

Newton was reelected by a substantial margin in 1951 but the honeymoon with the electorate was ending. In the face of setbacks to a number of bond issues for capital improvements which he favored, Newton announced he would not run in 1955. Kelly says that in the eight years of Newton's administration he and the councilmen and cabinet members working for him "accomplished an impressive list of achievements unmatched before or since by a single administration."

The second event in which *The Post* became more than a disinterested reporter chronicling developments as they happened began with a four-paragraph news item published near the bottom of the back page on Wednesday, November 10, 1948. The story reported that Theresa Catherine Foster, an eighteen-year-old freshman engineering student at the University of Colorado in Boulder, was missing. Boulder at that time was a peaceful little college town about an hour's drive northwest of Denver, located in a spectacular setting just where the Rockies leap out of the plains. The previous evening Theresa had attended rosary services at the Newman Club, an organization for Catholic students. She left the meeting alone at 10:15 P.M. but failed to return to the home of a professor, about a mile from the club, where she worked for her board and room.

On Thursday her body was found by a hunter. It appeared the girl had been slain elsewhere, then the body dropped off a small bridge on a little-used road about a dozen miles south of Boulder. An overnight snowstorm had nearly covered the body, the lower half of which had been stripped. The head was battered almost beyond recognition and the girl's identity was established by the clothing scattered nearby.

Theresa was one of eleven children from a Colorado farm family. She was described as quiet, studious, and religious. She had a steady boyfriend back home, and apparently had dated no one on campus.

The autopsy showed Theresa had been raped. The medical examiner also said he believed the killer was not the "usual type of sex maniac." The beating had been administered by someone "who intended to kill." The skull was fractured in three places and fifteen scalp wounds were counted, but strangulation was ruled the cause of death. The killer apparently had seized the girl by the back of her topcoat, which was fastened at the throat by a metal button, and she had choked to death as blows were rained on her head.

There were some eight thousand young women on the University of Colorado campus. The thought of a psychopathic sex killer loose in Boulder sent a chill through the administrators. Coeds were warned not to be out alone at night. The regents, expressing "deepest sorrow and regret" over the girl's death, announced a ten-thousand-dollar reward for information leading to the arrest and conviction of the killer or killers. President Robert L. Stearns felt obliged to tell anxious parents that the university would "leave no stone unturned to clear this mystery and provide a safe environment for young men and women engaged in collegiate study." The police, who had found few clues, announced that some five hundred male students who had missed classes Wednesday and Thursday would be questioned, with special attention to those owning a car which might have been used to transport the body.

In the offices of *The Post,* Hoyt viewed the situation with growing concern. He feared the authorities were bungling the case. He had also heard vague reports of a homosexual ring involving a few members of the faculty and he wondered whether some of the authorities were dragging their feet to protect campus friends who might be exposed by a thorough investigation. He wanted action.

No one now seems to remember who first came up with the idea of *The Post* retaining Erle Stanley Gardner, creator of the fictional lawyer-detective Perry Mason, to help the investigators, but Hoyt bought it. He instructed Ed Dooley, by then executive news editor, to find Gardner and sound him out. Dooley got on the telephone, located Gardner in New York City, and explained the situation. Gardner indicated interest and suggested that Dr. LeMoyne Snyder, an authority on forensic medicine, also be retained. The fee Gardner suggested stunned Dooley but he promised to see what Hoyt would say.

On Saturday, November 13, two days after Theresa Foster's body was discovered, *The Post* announced on page 1 that Gardner and Dr. Snyder had been hired. The story read:

> In response to appeals by officials of Boulder county and the University of Colorado that all possible assistance be extended to local authorities toward solution of the Theresa Foster rape-slaying, *The Denver Post* Saturday retained the services of two of the world's top men in the trade of crime detection to assist in the investigation.
>
> They are Erle Stanley Gardner, acknowledged as one of the world's masters in criminal narrative, and Dr. LeMoyne Snyder, medico-legal authority on technics of criminology, associated with the Michigan Crime Detection Laboratory and Michigan state police.
>
> These two men, working together in close coordination, will place themselves at the disposal of Boulder county authorities investigating the crime.
>
> Gardner, who began his career as prosecuting attorney in California and is recognized in legal circles as one of the top minds in that field, will report in *The Denver Post* his interpretation of the evidence, procedures and developments in this, one of the most tragically bizarre murders in the criminal annals of Colorado.
>
> Gardner arrived in Denver by plane from New York City early Saturday. . . . Dr. Snyder, unable to make direct plane connections from Detroit due to storms, made a fast auto dash through Michigan Friday night to Chicago where he boarded a plane bound for Denver.
>
> The two men were scheduled to meet Saturday afternoon at Boulder, where Gardner already was on the scene. . . .

Dooley and city editor Gene Lowall met Snyder at the airport in the middle of the night, took him to the Brown Palace Hotel, and filled him in on the case. Reporting an actual homicide story for newspapers was not new for Gardner. A few years earlier he had covered the sensational Sir Harry Oakes murder and trial in the Bahamas. Working swiftly, Gardner had a copyrighted story ready for *The Post*'s Sunday editions:

> Boulder, Colo., Nov. 13—Twenty-four hours ago I was in New York City in conference with the president of my publishing company. The telephone rang and the editors of *The Denver Post* asked me to fly west immediately to see if my analysis of the murder of Theresa Catherine Foster would perhaps help the investigating officers.

I immediately called Dr. LeMoyne Snyder at Lansing, Michigan. Dr. Snyder has been working with me on some of these cases *Argosy* magazine has been investigating, cases where innocent men have been convicted of crimes, have exhausted all their legal remedies, are without funds and have given up hope.

He is one of the outstanding criminologists in the country, his book *Homicide Investigation* is the most authoritative on the subject, and he has just returned from a series of lectures at Harvard University.

Dr. Snyder was not interested until I explained that we were being retained to assist the authorities. He is to give the officials who are working on the case the benefit of his experience and technical knowledge. I am to try to present to readers of *The Denver Post* the situation as it might appear to the eyes of Perry Mason, the fictional lawyer detective who has solved so many cases in my books.

We are not employed to solve the case but to give the authorities any assistance within our power. . . . Accustomed as I am to encountering official jealousy, it came as a pleasant surprise to me to find the attitude of Sheriff Arthur T. Everson and District Attorney Hatfield Chilson. These men were frankly glad to see me, and they were eagerly awaiting the arrival of Dr. LeMoyne Snyder. . . .

District Attorney Chilson had lunch with us and placed everything in his office at our disposal. He likes to describe himself as "merely" a country lawyer. But he impressed me as one of the shrewdest and most honest men I have met in a long time, and it is a source of gratification to me that Perry Mason won't ever have to try a case against him. . . .

News was being made elsewhere in the world, but in Denver and Boulder interest was riveted on the search for the killers of Theresa Foster. That week in London a son was born to Princess Elizabeth and her husband, the Duke of Edinburgh. Elizabeth would become queen on the death of her father, King George, and the baby, Prince Charles, probably would become England's next king. On the other side of the world an Allied military-war-crimes tribunal decreed death sentences for Japan's Hideki Tojo and many of his colleagues. And in Boulder, Erle Stanley Gardner wrote on Monday, November 15, that "the murderer of Theresa Foster can be apprehended, convicted and executed if the readers of *The Denver Post* will cooperate with the sheriff and district attorney" by uncovering clues.

Gardner named three things to look for: anyone "who has been suspiciously active in washing and cleaning a car" since the victim, either dead or dying, apparently had been transported some distance before she was dumped off the bridge. Someone with a wound on his hand, probably the outer side of the left hand, because the girl had put up a furious struggle before she was overpowered. Anyone seen burning or burying garments. The killer's clothing was probably stained with blood. Notify the authorities immediately, Gardner urged.

His appeal for the public's help resulted in scores of calls. Discarded clothing, bloodstained boulders, broken glasses, lengths of rope were turned up in a wide radius around Boulder and each find had to be checked. *The Post,* meanwhile, set up a command post in a Boulder hotel. City editor Gene Lowall moved in and directed a task force of up to seven reporters covering every aspect of the investigation. They turned out reams of copy day after day, most of it dealing with hot clues which turned out to be false. These stories shared space with Gardner's daily dispatches detailing his own investigation, now supported by Leonarde Keeler, an expert on the then new polygraph "lie detector" machine. *The Post* led the way in the amount of coverage but the *News,* the Boulder *Daily Camera,* and the radio journalists were not far behind.

It was predictable that there should be adverse reader reaction. One letter charged *The Post* with "treating the sordid Foster story like a circus." The newspaper replied editorially: "When a mad dog is loose, the public needs to be on guard." Some students declared the story was being handled without conscience to promote circulation. *The Post* responded: "If there is a sensation, it is in the record of the case itself." *The Post*'s circulation in Boulder County (population approximately 48,000) was 6,500 daily and 9,000 on Sunday; in the city of Boulder (population approximately 20,000), the circulation was 3,100 daily and 4,000 Sunday. Most of this circulation was home-delivered—street distribution is a minor part of *The Post*'s total—and saturation coverage of the Foster murder did not boost sales appreciably.

The daily hammering ultimately had its effect. Shortly after noon on Sunday, November 21, ten days after the body was found, Eleanor Walker, twenty-five, walked into the sheriff's office and told a startling story. On the night of November 9, the night Theresa Foster disappeared, her husband, Joe Sam Walker, left their home in a small settlement outside Boulder, saying he was going out to buy a magazine. Mrs. Walker said she dozed and was awakened by a pounding on the door. When she opened the door she found her husband dripping with blood. He told her he had stopped at a tavern for a beer, met a man and a young woman he didn't know, and they had driven around together.

The two men quarreled and then got into a fight. Mrs. Walker said her husband told her he had clubbed the man with the butt of a pistol he was carrying, and then had broken away and come home. She also said Walker had burned his bloody clothing, painted over blood in the trunk of his car, and thrown away the pistol. Then she read of the murder and her suspicions were aroused. She read every word in the newspapers, she said. Finally, when the pressure became too great, she left the house on the pretext of seeing a doctor and went to the police.

Deputies quickly picked up Walker. He was a slim, dark-haired, thirty-one-year-old metalworker. He was running a fever from a badly infected cut on his head. The details of Walker's arrest, although he was still unnamed, were carried in the *Rocky Mountain News* Monday morning. By that afternoon *The Post* was able to report that the suspect voluntarily had submitted to lie-detector tests administered by Keeler and Dr. Snyder. Generally he told the same story as his wife. *The Post* said: "Dr. Snyder said the suspect reacted positively on the machine at three points. These were in preliminary questioning when Theresa Foster's name was mentioned, when the gun believed to be the weapon with which the girl was beaten to death came into the questioning, and when the area where the girl's school books were found was discussed." Because of antibiotics administered to fight the infection, Walker's reaction to the lie detector was described as sluggish.

Questioning was resumed next day in the presence of *Post* reporters. Abruptly he was asked, "Did you have her in the trunk?"

Walker rose to his feet, tore off the polygraph apparatus, and declared, "I refuse to submit to any more of this until I've talked with an attorney."

Walker was charged with murder. He continued to maintain his innocence, blaming the killing on a husky blond youth who was with the girl at a tavern when they asked him for a ride. The youth produced a pint of whiskey, Walker said, and the two men drank most of it. They argued about who was to drive. A fight followed and Walker was beaten unconscious. When he came to, the man was gone and Walker said he found the car trunk open and the girl's feet protruding. She appeared to be dead so he pushed the body all the way into the trunk. Terrified, he drove around aimlessly before pushing the body off the bridge.

In his final report Gardner explained his role and the role of the press in apprehending Walker:

. . . In a murder case of this nature, the press has a distinct service to perform. Without the aid of publicity, the murderer in this case would, in all probability, never have been apprehended. Even as it was, despite the horrible nature of the crime, it was some twelve days after the crime had taken place before the tortured wife reached a point where she could no longer live with her husband and at the same time abide with her own conscience.

In the eyes of some, the steady psychological pressure exerted by the press in continually pounding home to its readers the nature of the crime was merely sensationalism, but the expert criminologists who knew the psychology of the sex fiend realized that this man must be living somewhere near the scene of the crime, to all outward appearances a friendly, normal, likable young fellow. . . . Publisher Hoyt, with dogged insistence, adhered to that one basic principle. "Keep turning on the heat," he instructed. "Gardner, we want you to analyze what must have happened. Keep analyzing, keep pounding it home. . . ."

At our first conference Dr. Snyder pointed out that this would necessitate keeping the interest of the public sufficiently aroused so that the tension on the murderer, his family and his friends who might be protecting him would mount to a climactic point.

Veteran criminologist that he was, he pointed out to Publisher Hoyt that this might lay *The Post* open to some criticism; that some readers might feel attention was being devoted to the case long after it had passed its point of legitimate reader interest. In an editorial huddle Palmer Hoyt considered the various factors involved and then gave his order. "Never mind the criticism. We'll stand that. You men start the investigation and keep it up until I tell you to stop. Keep a constant pressure on the public. . . ."

On May 9, 1949, Walker was found guilty of second-degree murder and sentenced to a term of eighty years to life in the state penitentiary.

The Post followed up with an editorial campaign for a central state crime-detection bureau with a capably manned laboratory. It also urged that the University of Colorado open a training school for police officers, and that a medical examiner system replace the elected county coroners. Eventually the state established the Colorado Bureau of Investigation to assist local law-enforcement officers.

Not long after the Walker trial Lowall was named *The Post*'s national crime reporter, an assignment that took him around the nation to investigate and write about organized crime. Later he served as an investigator for the U. S. Senate's Kefauver Committee, and an investigator for the Denver District Attorney's office before joining *Argosy* magazine.

Meanwhile, Walker began a long series of legal moves in an effort to get his conviction reversed. By 1966, when he had succeeded in getting his sentence reduced to forty years, he won a hearing on his complaint that pretrial publicity had deprived him of a fair trial. Hoyt was among the witnesses. He testified he had hired Gardner, Dr. Snyder, and Keeler because "it seemed to us a public service to make these men available." Hoyt also disclosed their services had cost *The Post* $4,555.15.

Walker's appeal was denied. But in 1969, after Walker had served twenty years, the Colorado Supreme Court in a majority decision ordered his conviction reversed. The lower court was instructed to grant Walker either a new trial or his freedom. Walker's appeal was based on the U. S. Supreme Court's 1966 ruling that a Roman carnival atmosphere in the courtroom during Dr. Samuel Sheppard's trial for his wife's murder had deprived him of a fair hearing. Although no such atmosphere prevailed during his trial, Walker contended in his appeal that "massive and inflammatory pretrial publicity" had prejudiced his defense.

Walker was freed. Exactly a year later he sued *The Post* for two million dollars. Before the suit could be brought to trial Walker's attorney, Francis Salazar, was disbarred in connection with an unrelated case. In January of 1976, nearly five and a half years after Walker filed suit, the case was dismissed on the ground that no action had been taken by the plaintiff for more than a year.

Vignette

THE COW AND THE FARM EDITOR

Late one February day in 1949, a Hereford cow belonging to Bill and Carl Mach gave birth on their farm near Yukon, Oklahoma, which is out on the plains not far from Oklahoma City. The calf was born dead. The cow expressed her disappointment and grief by charging Bill Mach. Bill leapt aside. And the cow disappeared.

This was because Bill Mach had been standing by a silo and behind him was an opening in the silo wall. The hole was 25 inches high and 17 inches wide—about the size of a newspaper page. The charging cow's momentum had carried her right through the opening.

Once he got over his surprise and the cow's ire had cooled, Bill Mach climbed into the silo after her and found she hadn't been hurt. But getting her out that same hole posed a problem.

The news services got wind of the cow's, and Bill Mach's, plight and sent amusing little stories to papers all over the world. Before long Mach had received ideas for freeing the cow by mail and telephone from forty-five states and Canada. Most of them suggested enlarging the opening. That was impractical because it would weaken the structure, and the Machs would rather sacrifice the cow than the silo. Farmer Mach tried some of the other suggestions, but nothing worked.

In Denver, Ralph Partridge, *The Post's* farm editor, read some of the stories. "I'll bet I know how to get that cow out," he mused. "She went in; it stands to reason she can come out."

He told managing editor Alexis McKinney what he had in mind. McKinney, who once had sent a reporter to determine whether a prize cat named "Mr. Rocky Mountain News" was indeed a mister, told Partridge to go ahead. Partridge got on the telephone and persuaded Mach to let him try to free the cow. In preparation for the great experiment, he instructed Mach to take the cow off feed and water so as to reduce her bulk. Then he and photographer David

Mathias caught a plane for Oklahoma City. They showed up at the Mach farm early next morning, which was five days after the cow had become imprisoned. By then she was getting a little bored with life inside an otherwise empty silo.

Partridge stepped through the opening—no problem because of his lean, spare frame—and made the cow's acquaintance. First he haltered and milked her, which as a farm boy he was capable of doing. Then, because the bottom of the opening was eighteen inches off the silo floor, he built a ramp with an old door and some feed sacks. Finally, he smeared the cow with about fifteen pounds of axle grease and tied ropes to her four hooves. Partridge and several volunteers shoved her head through the opening by brute force. They got the front legs partly through. At that point a local veterinarian gave her a shot of Nembutal to relax her. Some of the volunteers pulled on the ropes while Partridge and his crew pushed. The cow began to slide through. She got hung up once on her belly and again when the bony portion of her hindquarters scraped the top of the opening. But moments later she popped out.

The jubilant Mach brothers scrubbed the cow down with detergent. Then they nailed the opening shut. Partridge washed up, had some of Mrs. Bill Mach's doughnuts, and headed back for Denver.

By then Partridge was a celebrity. The story of his feat was flashed around the world and brought welcome relief to newspaper front pages somber with reports of violence and foreboding. Even the "Voice of America" broadcast the story in dozens of foreign tongues.

There is one small postscript to this anecdote. John Randolph, an obscure young reporter, had just been put in charge of the Associated Press's Oklahoma City bureau. He handled the cow story with such finesse and aplomb that his bosses up the line took notice. Quickly he was promoted to a job in New York. When the Korean War came along a year later he was dispatched to Tokyo as bureau chief. That's how one foreign correspondent got his start.

17

HOW TO BUILD A NEWSPAPER PLANT

Within days after his arrival in Denver, Palmer Hoyt plunged into the third phase of his plans for *The Post*—to provide adequate facilities from which to revitalize the newspaper. That meant a new building to replace the one first occupied in 1907, and new equipment to replace the limping old presses and typesetting machinery.

The critical question was where to go. The venerable *Post* building at 1544 Champa Street was only a half-block off Sixteenth, the city's main shopping street, and there were many advantages to remaining in the heart of the downtown area. On the other hand, outlying real estate was less expensive, and a plant on a railroad siding would save much time and money in handling the hundreds of tons of newsprint used each month. Hoyt and Campbell, usually accompanied by Major Bonfils and Buxton and sometimes by Helen Bonfils, spent many afternoons driving around to inspect various sites.

Their ultimate decision was to keep the plant in downtown Denver, such as it was. The core of the city was a motley collection of nondescript buildings, the newest of which had been built in 1928. Downtown had taken on a tacky look and many merchants were considering moves to suburban shopping centers then just beginning to take shape. If the center of the city—and its tax base—were to be held together, something had to be done to restore faith in its future. So *The Post,* which was heavily dependent on the advertising support of downtown retailers, decided to stay in town. But where downtown?

Even before that question was answered *The Post* committed itself to an expansion program by ordering nearly a million dollars' worth of new equipment. On July 2, barely four months after Hoyt took over, a contract was signed with the Goss Printing Press Company for twenty-four Headliner press units and six folders. The price was $966,000. Delivery was to be made within twenty-eight to thirty-two months.

Inspecting stereotype plates for the new Headliner presses: Campbell, Hoyt, business manager Maj. Fred W. Bonfils.

Campbell stumbled on an answer to the site problem when he learned one day that the Home Public Market and the adjoining five-story Temple Court office building were for sale. Losing no time, he put down some money for an option to purchase even before consulting the other directors. The Temple Court Building was on the corner of Fifteenth Street and California Street, catercorner from the Denver Dry Goods Company, a major department store, and only two and a half blocks from 1544 Champa. The market stretched from the Temple Court Building three hundred feet along California Street to Fourteenth Street. The two properties together covered one-half of a city block.

Temple Court was an undistinguished old structure whose gray sand brick was relieved by a lot of gingerbread. It had a number of small retail shops on the ground floor, one of which was Louie Greenwald Liquors, Inc. None of the tenants had long leases and Campbell figured moving them out would be no problem. Home Public Market offered interesting possibilities. It was a cavernous one-story structure with a high vaulted ceiling, looking somewhat like a hangar for blimps. Stall holders sold fresh fruits, vegetables, meats, and grocery items and the atmosphere was redolent with the aroma of dill pickles, salami, roasting coffee, and baked goods. Engineers who examined the structure suggested the possibility of removing the heavy concrete street-level floor, anchoring the huge, two-story-tall presses in the basement, and letting them protrude up into the building. After a little dickering *The Post* bought the two buildings for $608,750.

Locating downtown proved to be an excellent decision. Encouraged by *The Post*'s move, others decided to put new structures in the core city. A building boom followed. The newsprint supplier agreed to pay the cost of trucking the paper from the railroad yards to the plant, and a developing freeway system made it possible to deliver the printed papers to suburban areas without excessive delay.

On December 30, 1946, *The Post* announced the purchase and plans for converting the properties into "one of the most modern newspaper plants in the world." T. H. Buell & Company, a Denver architectural firm, and William Ginsberg, a New York consulting engineer for newspaper plants, were retained. The announcement said Temple Court would be remodeled extensively and house the business, advertising, editorial, and executive offices. The market, described as "one of the most sturdily built buildings in the city," would be given a second story and a new roof. All the mechanical departments were to be located in this part of the complex. Work on the project was scheduled to begin by late spring, 1947.

Problems quickly arose. Home Public Market turned out to be anything but "sturdily built." Engineers had planned to take off the roof and remove the huge wooden arches preparatory to adding a second floor. But in the dismantling process one of the arches collapsed and shattered into splinters. The other arches were found to be in similarly fragile condition, and ultimately the entire building had to be torn down and replaced.

This led to a new idea. Why not demolish Temple Court Building also, and erect a brand, spanking new plant from scratch? The architects came up with sketches for a handsome, eighteen-story, steel-and-glass "communications center." In addition to *The Post,* it would house the news-service bureaus and office space would be rented to advertising agencies and radio stations. It was a beautiful dream. But there was no money for that kind of a project in *The Post* treasury. All those lavish dividends paid out during the Depression and war years had left little in reserve. And Campbell, nurtured on a philosophy of conservatism, insisted *The Post* must not borrow to finance its expansion. The cost of the new plant must be met from current income. There would be no eighteen-story communications center.

There was never any doubt that Campbell's conservatism would prevail, but postwar inflation clinched the issue. In October of 1948 the Goss Printing Press Company not only hadn't delivered the presses, but notified startled *Post* directors that under an escalation clause based on increased labor costs the price had to be boosted 45½ percent! Suddenly drastic cutbacks were in order.

The Post promptly pruned its press order from twenty-four units to twenty, from six folders to four, and cut the cost of the new contract to $1,228,800. The decreased capacity of the new plant was something that would have to be lived with until there was enough cash to buy the additional units. An air-conditioning system for the Temple Court Building was dropped. (It was installed later at a substantially greater cost.) Even the white-tile facing to cover the gray brick—and match Temple Court's appearance with the new mechanical building—had to be deferred. Hoyt later recalled that some architect had persuaded Campbell he could save money by having just one common men's room for the entire building. Hoyt rebelled at that; he knew it would create all kinds of morale problems.

Campbell and Miss Bonfils had expected that the entire expansion project could be handled for a few million dollars. Ultimately it cost seven million, a jolting blow to people who had been taking money out of the paper without putting aside anything for the future.

One delay followed another and progress on the newspaper's new home proceeded at a snail's pace. Meanwhile, Campbell was trying to make the best deal possible for the old building on Champa Street. On February 15, 1949, he sold it for $700,000—$91,250 more than was paid for the new site. The buyers were assembling land for what was to become a block-long Woolworth's store, at that time the world's largest Woolworth's. The old *Post* building was of no use to them and was demolished soon after it was vacated. Campbell had bought a much larger piece of land, excellently located, plus a serviceable five-story building, for less than the selling price of the old property. Bonfils and Tammen would have been proud of him.

The new *Post* building covers half a city block. Low portion in the foreground houses the mechanical departments. Five-story building in background is a converted office building.

By mid-1949 it was finally possible to set the following May as the target date for occupying the new building. But a new roadblock arose, albeit a minor one. It happened this way. S. Arthur Snyder owned the lease on the space in the Temple Court Building occupied by the Louie Greenwald liquor store. He sublet the space for $175 a month to the liquor store's owners, J. Cohen and Morris C. Cox. Snyder extended his rental agreement with the liquor store through January 1, 1951, without consulting *The Post,* which by then owned the building. This was seven months beyond the time *The Post* planned to occupy the entire building. Cohen and Cox contended they had a legitimate lease and refused to move their store for less than a payment of forty thousand dollars from *The Post.*

Buxton considered this sum exorbitant and notified Cohen and Cox that *The Post* was proceeding with plans to make it the only newspaper in the world with a retail liquor store in the middle of its front lobby. Then he ordered workmen to tear down all the other walls on the first floor, leaving the Louie Greenwald company in splendid and dusty isolation. Before long Cohen and Cox were happy to accept $2,500 and vacate.

(Several years later *The Post* inadvertently became landlord for apparently unconnected gambling and prostitution enterprises. This came about when the paper, in anticipation of an expansion project, bought the ancient Roslyn Hotel. It was located across the alley from the loading dock at the rear of the plant, where truckers picked up copies of the paper for distribution. The circulation department used a loudspeaker to direct trucks into the proper slots and, all in all, the area would become rather noisy on Saturday nights when the Sunday paper was delivered. *Post* officials had known gamblers operated out of the hotel because the mechanical departments reported that employees sometimes would drop their entire paychecks there. But they had no idea what else was going on in the hotel until one Monday morning, when a lavishly painted woman showed up in the business office to protest that all the late-night activity on the dock was disturbing her clients. She got very little sympathy and was urged to rent quarters elsewhere. Soon afterward the hotel was torn down.)

Any event as momentous as a new home for *The Denver Post* would have to be celebrated with appropriate fanfare, and Red Fenwick, the Rocky Mountain Empire editor, became the central figure in an unprecedented promotion. His assignment was to deliver one solid silver, gold-trimmed spur to the governor of each of the thirteen states of Hoyt's Empire. The matching spur would be presented when the governor attended the dedication ceremony in Denver. What complicated Fenwick's mission was that he had to ride up to each of the state capitols on horseback.

For his mount Fenwick borrowed a handsome, three-year-old,

Robert (Red) Fenwick was assigned to ride up to thirteen state capitols to publicize opening of *The Post*'s new building.

tan-and-white pinto gelding named G-Boy. The horse had a white mane, black tail, white stockings. Fenwick's spur-delivering uniform was a cowboy outfit embellished by white Stetson, chaps, and a handsome leather vest. Together they cut a striking figure. The main problem was getting G-Boy from one capitol to the next.

Fenwick decided to put G-Boy in a trailer and haul it with his 1949 Lincoln two-door sedan. With unusual foresight Fenwick negotiated an agreement with the paper calling for payment of 12 cents per mile, all repairs, and an overhaul job on the Lincoln after successful completion of the journey. The overhaul bill amounted to $475. Fenwick's expense account may have been one of the few in journalistic annals to include hay, oats, and livery-stable charges in addition to the usual motel rooms, meals, laundry, and booze.

The route Fenwick laid out led eastward from Denver to Lincoln, Nebraska. From there he would swing south to Topeka, Kansas; Oklahoma City, Oklahoma; and Austin, Texas, to take advantage of spring warmth. Then he planned to head westward to Santa Fe, New Mexico, and Phoenix, Arizona, before heading north to Salt Lake City, Utah, and Boise, Idaho. After that he would swing east to Helena, Montana, and Bismarck, North Dakota; then south once again to Pierre, South Dakota; and finally home by way of Cheyenne, Wyoming.

It was an epic journey and it started in epic fashion. G-Boy, Fenwick, and his then wife, Vi, left Denver one late-winter morning in a driving snowstorm. Sliding and skidding on icy pavement, they drove ninety-one miles to Brush, Colorado, before giving up for the day. G-Boy, who was unaccustomed to long-distance trailer travel, had to brace his legs against the lurching trailer floor and was exhausted. Next day they encountered a dust storm near Lincoln. Fenwick located a motel for himself and Vi and a corral for G-Boy. He washed and curried the horse, then rode up the capitol steps to deliver a spur to Gov. Val Peterson.

It rained in Oklahoma and it was unseasonably hot in Texas. At Austin the Texas Rangers told Fenwick there was an old law which prohibited anyone from riding up to the capitol grounds on a horse, a throwback to days when political disagreements often were settled by gunfire. Sorry, they said, they had no choice but to enforce the law. So Fenwick, in cowboy regalia, walked.

The Post expedition encountered a sandstorm in Arizona that blasted the paint off one side of the Lincoln. Outside Nampa, Idaho, they ran into another fierce snowstorm. There was a broken-down shed inside a corral in back of the motel where Fenwick stopped. He put the horse in the shed, then spent the next hour looking for loose boards under the snow. He didn't have a hammer and nails so he tied the boards with baling wire over holes in the shed to give G-Boy a bit more protection. There was more snow in Montana and the trip was beginning to get on G-Boy's nerves. He put on a beautiful bucking exhibition on the capitol lawn at Helena and Fenwick had to call on all his riding experience to keep from being thrown. From Montana into North Dakota the travelers plowed through miles of mud where the road was under construction. Finally they bogged down and had to be pulled out by a tractor. That ordeal cracked the car's frame and it had to be welded.

At Bismarck Fenwick spent the better part of a morning getting G-Boy cleaned up for the ride to see the governor. Just before they were to start out, G-Boy decided to roll in the mud. For a second time, Fenwick walked.

Floodwaters from rain and melting snow covered much of South Dakota. Fenwick drove mile after mile over water-covered highways by steering between rows of fenceposts. Where the water was flowing he would stop and wade ahead to make sure the road was intact. In Cheyenne he found the governor indisposed and walked up to his home at night to deliver the spur.

The final delivery was in Denver, where the capitol is only a mile or so from *The Post*. By this time G-Boy's nerves were thoroughly frazzled and Fenwick thought it prudent not to try riding a skittish horse through Denver traffic. So he borrowed a gentle old mare to mount in the procession to the executive offices of Gov. Walter Johnson. Included in the parade was a flatbed truck disguised as a hay wagon and loaded with bathing beauties. Not until later was it discovered that someone had planted several of Denver's better-known call girls aboard the truck.

Where did Fenwick find the kind of dedication it took to carry out this assignment? He had been city editor of the now defunct Casper (Wyoming) *Times* when his wife gave birth in 1938 to a son, Bob. The child had a birth defect which doctors said would prove fatal within days without specialized treatment. Fenwick borrowed some money and a car and raced with the infant to Children's Hospital in Denver. Since he had to hurry back to work, Fenwick went to the Associated Press office in the *Post* building to ask if someone wouldn't check with the hospital every day and include a medical bulletin along with the news being sent to Casper on the wire. Somehow Shepherd heard of Fenwick's trouble and invited him into his office. When Shepherd had the full story he told Fenwick, "Harry Tammen's money helped build that hospital, and nothing they can do there is too good for a newspaperman's child." Before long Fenwick's son was being given twenty-four-hour nursing care. It took three months before little Bob Fenwick was ready to go home.

Back in Casper Fenwick wrote a story headlined "What Greater Gift?" telling how his son's life had been saved. Someone sent a clipping to Shepherd, and he had the story reprinted in *The Post*. Shepherd also offered Fenwick a job. Reluctantly, Fenwick declined it to go to Washington as secretary to Senator Harry Schwartz, but late in 1942 he came back west to join *The Post*. The Tammen Foundation took care of the Children's Hospital bill and Bobby Fenwick grew up to become an outstanding amateur boxer and serve in the U. S. Navy. Fenwick was still paying on the doctor's bill a little at a time from his forty-five-dollar-a-week *Denver Post* salary when managing editor Larry Martin heard about it. "Forget it," Martin told Fenwick. "*The Post* can take care of it for you." Fenwick had a number of opportunities to better himself after that, but he remained loyal to the paper that helped save his son.

Fenwick's long ride proved less than fruitful. Only four of the thirteen governors showed up to claim a second spur—A. G. Crane of Wyoming, J. Bracken Lee of Utah, Thomas Mabry of New Mexico, and Colorado's Johnson. But as a promotion the ride attracted national attention to the three-day dedication celebration that drew a bevy of government dignitaries, newspaper publishers, and industrial and business leaders.

Instead of publishing the customary special edition jammed with congratulatory advertising for the occasion, *The Post* ran several ads of its own. One listed the names of 3,700 local firms that had advertised in *The Post* during the previous year, with words of thanks for their support. A second ad spoke directly to the readers and listed the names of people who had been subscribers for fifty years. "Some of you have read *The Post* since you were children," the ad said. "To many of you *The Post* has been an essential part of your daily life down through the years. But whether you've been a lifelong subscriber or one who started just last week, it is to you that *The Denver Post* gratefully dedicates its new building—and this page." The third ad listed the names of *The Post*'s 922 employees and invited the public to visit their new home.

Blindfolded Justice atop *Post* building soon disappeared, as did the *Post* sign in deference to Denver's sign code.

When Helen Bonfils left the old *Post* building on the final day she stepped into the elevator and did not look back. She was putting a lifetime of memories behind her. "I couldn't bear to look around for the last time," she explained to a friend. "I know it's stupid and foolish, because the world moves on and we must move with it or we're left behind."

But as a reminder of the old days, a large conference room on the third floor next to her own offices was furnished with belongings from the Bonfils mansion. Even after her death, when *The Post* was badly cramped for space, the Bonfils conference room was left intact.

Hoyt had a sheet-metal statue of the blindfolded Justice moved from the old building and mounted atop the new. And the old slogan, "O, Justice, When Expelled From Other Habitations Make This Thy Dwelling Place," was painted anew above the front entrance. (Eventually Justice became so decrepit she had to be taken away.)

Columnist Marquis Childs attended the dedication and a portion of a philosophical piece he wrote about the occasion, syndicated to scores of newspapers, is appropriately reproduced here:

> . . . A newspaper that is merely a catologue of advertisements is not a newspaper at all. If it is to live up to the function conceived for it by Thomas Jefferson and the founding fathers, then it must reflect not merely the flow of the news but the competition of ideas in a free society.
>
> To do less—to give out merely the private prejudices of one small group or even one individual—is to fail. And failure can contribute more than most casual newspaper readers realize to the decline of the democratic system.
>
> These thoughts are occasioned by an important event just held here [in Denver]. With senators, cabinet members, governors, and assorted grandees present, *The Denver Post* dedicated a handsome new building with new presses and new equipment.
>
> In the clear Colorado sun on the speaker's stand in front of the new building we listened to the speeches in tribute to a free press and to Palmer Hoyt, publisher of *The Post*. Several speakers sounded the familiar theme—it is not just the physical entity, the marble, the steel and the stone; a newspaper is more than that.
>
> That is so true it cannot be repeated often enough. And it is also a truth that is frequently overlooked except on these ceremonial occasions.
>
> *The Denver Post* is an interesting example of a newspaper with character and vigor. In the old days of the wild and wooly West, *The Post* was wilder and woolier than any of them. Its flaming headlines and its blazing sensations were part of the tradition of the West of that other day.
>
> Now in another age Hoyt is seeking to keep the vigor while shaping the policy of *The Post* in line with the swift currents of change sweeping across the world. The West is an integral part of America, and America is inextricably and forever bound up with the rest of the world. This is reflected in both the news and the editorial policy of *The Post*.
>
> To get back to the hard facts of the business office, the new building, with presses, cost something more than six million dollars. Since *The Post* is a prosperous paper, this was paid for out of revenue.
>
> That figure is a measure of certain realities behind the phrase, "freedom of the press." It is a far cry from the days of Tom Paine and the pamphleteers when a man with a hand press could have his say in more or less equal competition with the rich and well-born Tories who opposed the dangerous radicalism of America's revolutionaries. A man standing in the village square could, with the sound

of his voice, reach most of the influential men of his community.

The technology of modern communication costs fabulous sums. I have heard the cost of Marshall Field's newspaper ventures in New York and Chicago estimated as high as thirty million dollars. The newest medium, television, absorbs capital as the desert sands drink up water, and a practical, working basis to support this prodigious new child is not yet in sight.

In my opinion these harsh realities put an even greater responsibility on those who own and direct America's newspapers. The very fact that competition is possible only at a cost almost prohibitive makes it more urgent that there be no monopoly of viewpoint or prejudice. The press has privileges that rest on the noble concept of freedom of inquiry and freedom of ideas. The mere huckster may claim those privileges for a time. But ignoring the duties and responsibilities that go with the privilege, the hucksters will in the end lose all.

In connection with the dedication *The Post* published an eighty-page booklet titled *So The People May Know*. Two-thirds of it was devoted to a narrative of *The Post*'s history, written by Larry Martin and cited as a source in several of the early chapters of this book. Of particular interest was the preface which appeared over Hoyt's signature. In it he said:

> Today, *The Post* not only rededicates itself to the people, but rededicates itself to the task of giving the people the basic information which is sorely needed in an atomic age which confronts man with his greatest opportunity and his potential doom.
>
> It is the belief of *The Post* that slanted journalism, the practice of mixing news and editorial opinions, is dishonest and should be relegated to the dead past.
>
> We wish to say again that you will find our news in the news columns, our editorials in our editorial columns. And it is our pledge that we will never attempt by emphasis, omission or commission to mislead the public because of an editorial "policy." . . . As you view the giant presses only so recently born in the heat of the foundry, you will know that they represent an earnest on *The Post*'s pledge and desire to serve the people to the ultimate of its ability. . . .

On the page above this pledge were the smiling faces of E. Ray Campbell, president of *The Post,* and Helen Bonfils, its secretary and treasurer. It was unmistakable that they endorsed Hoyt's promise to break with what he termed the practices of the dead past; a past of which they had been a part.

Vignette

THE SILVER DOLLAR CAPER

Impressed by the rising payroll, managing editor Alexis McKinney some months after Hoyt's arrival came up with an idea for dramatizing the impact that *The Post* had on Denver's economy. He suggested that on the next payday all the employees be given their wages in silver dollars instead of checks, and that fact be publicized in the newspaper. The theory was that soon the silver dollars would be circulating all over town, and anyone who handled a cartwheel would realize that *Post* money was getting around.

Hoyt liked the idea. The following week employees lined up to receive their pay in silver. Journeyman reporters were being paid only sixty dollars, but even that was quite a load, more than most employees wanted to cart home. They quickly found a way to solve the problem. They streamed into the Brass Rail bar next door to trade their silver for paper money and perhaps invest in a quick beer while they were at it. Soon the Brass Rail had silver dollars stacked halfway up the mirror behind the bar and it began to look as though most *Post* employees spent their pay at the saloon.

This anecdote has an interesting sequel. It begins with the fact that after the silver was delivered to *The Post* by armored truck someone had to wrestle the heavy bags to the various departments. The copyboy who was given this assignment thought it was a bum idea and said so. A management official then suggested the copyboy would be wise to look for other employment. The boy considered this a violation of his rights and took his grievance to the Guild representative, George V. Kelly. Kelly listened carefully, sympathized, but reckoned it was within management's rights to fire a copyboy who refused to do what he was told.

Some five years later—the night of the first Thursday in October of 1951—city editor Willard Haselbush entered the Denver Press Club and sat down at the bar. He had just put the finishing touches

To publicize size of *Post*'s payroll, employees one week were paid in silver dollars. Reporter Eva Hodges (left) claims her pay. At right are Louis McMahon, comptroller, and Miss Bonfils.

to a thirteen-part series that documented some gross irregularities at the state penitentiary, where long-time warden Roy Best was something of a law unto himself. Haselbush had delved deeply to expose Best and was understandably happy to have his stories ready for publication. To all within earshot he announced that *The Post* on the following Sunday would kick off a series that would blow Best right out of the water, and further his stories were safely written and in the cab waiting outside to bear him home.

One of those within earshot was the former copyboy who had never forgotten what he considered to be his unjust treatment by *The Post*. He slipped out and persuaded the cabdriver that Mr. Haselbush had sent him to pick up the package on the back seat. Then, with the package under his arm, he disappeared into the night.

At 1 A.M. George Kelly, by then assistant city editor of the *Rocky Mountain News,* ended his shift and went home. His wife was waiting up for him. "A man called a few minutes ago," she said. "He said he had something important and was bringing it out to you."

The doorbell rang a short time later. Kelly recognized the man as the former copyboy. He said he remembered Kelly's kindness at *The Post* and now wanted to repay him. Together they unwrapped the package. It contained a foot-high stack of documents on top of which were a number of stories typed on the kind of copy paper used at *The Post*. Kelly read the first one and immediately realized it was the opening gun in a well-conceived *Post* campaign to clean up the mess at the penitentiary.

Under questioning the former copyboy told how he had gotten the package. Kelly sent him home and then sat down to examine the material and decide what to do with it. In the stack were scores of letters, copies of purchase orders, vouchers and receipts to prove Haselbush's contention that Best was selling the products of prison labor and buying goods for his personal use with prison funds.

"I couldn't sleep the rest of the night," Kelly recalls, "because I knew I had—illegally—a valuable asset that belonged to the opposition paper."

When morning came he called his editor, Jack Foster, at his home. "Jack," said Kelly, "I know what the lead story in the Sunday *Post* will be."

Foster answered, "If you know, write it today and we'll run it tomorrow and take the edge off their story."

Kelly replied, "I not only know, I have the original copy of a thirteen-part series, plus a bundle of backup material."

He took the package to Foster's home and together they pondered the next step. Briefly, they considered rewriting the material and printing it, but soon decided the honest thing to do was to return everything.

Haselbush, meanwhile, had awakened from a brief night's sleep and discovered his loss. Frantically, he retraced his steps in his mind. He located the cabdriver, got a description of the young man who had taken the package, questioned the Press Club bartender, and finally went to the District Attorney to file charges.

While all this was going on, Foster telephoned Hoyt. They agreed to meet in the lobby of the Brown Palace Hotel. Television had come to Denver for the first time that fall and the lobby was jammed with people watching the Yankees and the Giants in the World Series. The package changed hands in front of the cigar stand.

When either of Denver's two dailies has an exclusive story for its Sunday paper, the editors customarily save it for the final home-delivery edition going to press about midnight. This prevents the opposition from writing a hurried story of its own on the subject. In this case even though it was known that the *News* had seen Haselbush's series, *The Post* waited until midnight to publish it.

Haselbush's revelations led to strong public demand for a house-cleaning. Best was suspended for two years by the Civil Service commission. On the day his suspension ended, Best died.

18

THE YEAR THE GENIUS WENT
OUT OF IT ALL

The first five years of Hoyt's administration sped by swiftly. It was a productive and purposeful time. Under Hoyt's leadership *The Post* with seeming ease achieved his goals—respectability, credibility, and finally, vitality through completion of its new plant. The new *Post* was no longer held up in journalism schools as a horrible example of the misuse of newsprint and printer's ink. Rather, it was studied as a demonstration of the way a vigorous and enlightened management could turn a newspaper around.

Hoyt himself was anxious to talk about the new *Post* and what it was doing. He made hundreds of speeches, accepting invitations, as someone remarked, at the drop of a hint. The paper took on one campaign after another. In addition to helping elect a new mayor and shaking up the state penitentiary, *The Post* exposed Denver's unsanitary and inefficient system of trash and garbage collection, demanded a cleanup of mountain-stream pollution, and an improvement in the Denver mass-transit system. One of the paper's major campaigns was for improved highways throughout the state. Other parts of the country were building fine thoroughfares in anticipation of vastly expanding needs. Colorado's highway department was asleep. *The Post* ran pictures of the state's poor roads and was attacked by officials who contended that the bad publicity would keep tourists away. Hoyt answered, "What's worse—telling them about it and getting something done, or letting the tourists come here, find out how rotten the roads are, and then go back and tell everybody else to stay away?" Then, to show that *The Post* was anxious to promote the state, Hoyt had a film made titled *Westward the Course of Empire* and showed it at luncheons for civic, industrial, and business leaders in New York, Chicago, Detroit, and other key cities.

Hoyt's personal prestige, resulting from his career at the *Oregonian* and enhanced by his accomplishments at *The Post,* placed even greater demands on his time. Following his tour of Europe in 1946 he was asked by President Harry Truman to serve on a top-level Air Policy Commission to chart the nation's aviation future in the jet age. For ten weeks Hoyt served with the Commission in Washington, commuting back to Denver on weekends to attend to *Post* problems. During this period he was also on the executive committee of the Conference of Christians and Jews, a director of the Associated Press, on the Pulitzer Prize board, a director of the Advertising Federation of America, head of the Denver Community Chest campaign, and on the Freedom of the Press Committee of the American Newspaper Publishers Association. He was also elected a Fellow of Sigma Delta Chi, the society of professional journalists. On January 1, 1948, *The Post* opened a bureau in Washington, D.C. Barnet Nover, who had been a Washington *Post* columnist, was put in charge. To announce the bureau, Hoyt held a cocktail party. Nineteen years later Nover wrote to Mort Stern of that event:

> . . . the reception held in the ballroom of the Statler is still remembered. In the middle of it Diemel, the Statler's maitre d'hôtel, came up to the receiving line and said: "Mr. Hoyt, I've been with this hotel from the beginning. I've never seen a more distinguished crowd."
> Among those present were fifty-two members of the United States Senate including Senator Brien McMahon who had given up an important appointment in New York to be with us; seven members of the Truman cabinet and practically all the top members of the President's staff (the President later regretted that he had been unable to come); seven members of the U.S. Supreme Court including the Chief Justice; practically the entire Chiefs of Staff; many House members and top officials of the Executive Department and practically all the top journalists in Washington.

The Post was improved in many other ways. Shortly after Hoyt arrived he started a Sunday magazine printed in Chicago by the rotogravure process. Up to that time *The Post* had a magazine in the "penny dreadful" style, featuring syndicated stories about haunted castles in Scotland, gruesome murders in Paris, and the marital woes of Hollywood personalities. The new *Rocky Mountain Empire Magazine,* in eight-page, seven-column format, focused its attention on *The Post's* circulation area, telling the stories of its people, their history, problems, and accomplishments. Rotogravure provided better reproduction of photographs. And since rotogravure required a higher grade of paper, it was possible to divert scarce newsprint from the old magazine to the daily paper. As rudimentary as it was, *Rocky Mountain Empire Magazine* helped foster a new interest in the West.

The new *Post* building also included a rotogravure plant, the only one between the Mississippi Valley and the West Coast, and in time it became a major operation. In October, 1950, when the plant opened, *Rocky Mountain Empire Magazine's* name was shortened to *Empire,* and it was given a true magazine format. *Empire* went on to become nationally recognized, a circulation builder for the Sunday *Post* and a financial success.

In 1947 *The Post* also restored a Sunday book-review section for the first time since Caroline Bancroft left following F. G. Bonfils' death. Jane Sterling was hired to write an advice column and run a radio program featuring the accomplishments and opinions of teenagers. Robert W. Chandler, now president and editor of the Bend, (Ore.) *Bulletin* and president of several other small Oregon dailies, was put in charge of a program to promote and recognize good soil-conservation practices. News bureaus were opened in Albuquerque, New Mexico, and Colorado Springs. On a fishing trip Hoyt met F. Wallace Taber and his wife, Helen May, a young couple running a dude ranch. In addition to being an expert hunter and fisherman, Taber was a naturalist deeply concerned with wildlife conservation and ecological problems. Hoyt hired him to write on these subjects long before most newspaper readers were aware the problems existed.

In the Presidential election campaign of 1948—a four-way dogfight among Republicans, Democrats, Dixiecrats, and Henry Wallace "Progressives"—Nover and other staff writers were assigned to cover the conventions. But in addition Hoyt arranged for Norman Thomas, the Socialist leader, to write from the Democratic, Republican, and Wallace conventions, and for James Wechsler of the liberal New York *Post* to cover the Wallace campaign. But on the editorial page *The Post* endorsed Republican Thomas E. Dewey.

One day late in 1949 Taber asked McKinney, the managing editor, for permission to accompany some Denver sportsmen on an extended African safari. Because the trip would be lengthy and expensive, McKinney took up the matter with Hoyt. "Well, if he wants to go, let him go," Hoyt said. "It might produce some interesting stories." About the same time Leverett Chapin was sent to England, with the Universtiy of Denver's Social Science Foundation as co-sponsor, to write a series on the effect of the Labour Party's takeover of government. When the Korean War broke out in June of 1950,

Bill Hosokawa went to the front as *The Post's* first accredited war correspondent.

But all was not well on the home front. For one thing, Hoyt's marriage was falling apart. Cecile Hoyt had never adjusted to life in Denver. In June of 1949 she filed suit for divorce after twenty-seven years of marriage. She charged incompatibility and asked for division of property and alimony. The news was carried in a three-paragraph story on page 3 of *The Post.* The headline read: "Mrs. Palmer Hoyt/Asks for Divorce."

Hoyt was also having difficulties with the Newspaper Guild centering around Oscar Liden, who was news editor, a key job in putting the paper together each day, at the time Shepherd retired. Liden had joined *The Post* in 1929, had worked up through the ranks, was well liked by his coworkers, and had been an active Guildsman since its inception in 1937. Liden was responsible directly to the managing editor in his job of deciding what stories to place on page 1, and how to display them. When Hoyt complained about page 1, Liden would be blamed. Eventually Hoyt decided Liden could not adjust to his methods and ordered him transferred to a lesser job.

Some months later a copyreader, James Ashe, brought to Hoyt's attention some leaflets attacking him personally. Ashe charged that they were written by Liden and printed in Liden's home. Hoyt called Liden into his office for a discussion about Guild-management problems as well as the leaflets. Liden said he thought Hoyt was misinformed about many Guild matters and denied having anything to do with the attacks.

Later, Liden told his friends, "I may have been an inept Guild officer, and, as contended, an incompetent editor during my twenty years with *The Post,* but I was never a scandalmonger and I was dismayed, shocked, and angered when Hoyt told me I was reported to be spreading gossip about him."

Meanwhile *The Post* and Guild were unable to arrive at a new contract and a strike was threatened. Agreement was reached before the strike deadline, however, and tensions eased. Some months later managing editor McKinney and Ashe had a conversation. When the nature of this meeting became an issue, McKinney said he merely had asked Ashe for a memorandum on grievances still bothering members of the Guild. Ashe charged that McKinney had asked him to inform on Guild activities, citing what had happened to Liden as an example of the treatment other Guild activists could expect. Soon afterward the Guild filed unfair labor charges against *The Post,* charging espionage in Ashe's case, and discrimination because of union activity regarding Liden.

A National Labor Relations Board examiner criticized both Ashe as an "eager volunteer" of information, and *The Post* for accepting his information. The examiner also ruled Liden had been treated unfairly. *The Post,* contending the shifts in Liden's responsibilities were part of a pattern of overall change after Hoyt became editor, took the case to the National Labor Relations Board itself. The Board sustained the examiner's findings, 2 to 1, and ordered Liden reinstated to a job comparable to that of news editor. *The Post* then appealed to federal court, but the case was dismissed on the basis of a Supreme Court ruling in a somewhat similar case.

Both Ashe and Liden left *The Post* long before the matter was settled. Ashe moved to the Detroit *News* and died in 1950. Liden went to San Jose, California, and was managing editor of the *Mercury* when he died in 1970. He and Hoyt shook hands before he left, and Liden made it a point to drop in when he visited Denver. In a letter to Stern after he had attained management status, Liden warned against a "tendency of many managements" to be tough on editorial employees elected to positions of union leadership, thus robbing the industry "of many level-headed and rational people in key positions." Liden also observed that both he and Hoyt were victims—"he the recipient of bad information and advice from schemers, and I the victim of poison tongues." Many years were to pass before the scars of this labor-management encounter healed over. One result was that a peculiar negotiating practice was discontinued. A committee of *Rocky Mountain News* Guildsmen had negotiated with *Post* management on behalf of *Post* employees, and a *Post* Guild committee negotiated with the *News* management on behalf of *News* employees. The idea behind this arrangement was that it protected Guildsmen from delicate encounters with their own employers but it led to what was described as "secret and frequently unsuspected psychological booby traps being planted."

A third problem facing Hoyt was, from the viewpoint of his *Post* stewardship, the most serious of all. He had become editor and publisher after a twelve-year period during which the paper had paid unprecedented dividends. *The Post* had been able to show such impressive profits only because virtually nothing was being plowed back either to maintain or improve the property. Immediately after he took command Hoyt had to spend liberally to bring pay scales up to competitive levels, to augment a depleted staff, to improve news coverage, and finally, to build an expensive new plant from current earnings. Under Hoyt's leadership gross revenues increased steadily and net profits also remained at a high level. But ever-rising expenses, fueled by postwar inflation, caused the percentage of profit to tail off rapidly. During the Depression years, as we have seen, Shepherd had been able to retain as profit one of every three dollars taken in by *The Post*. Even during the war years the net profit, after taxes, had never dropped below 20 percent of the gross income— one dollar in every five taken in.

The net profit after taxes in 1946, the year of Hoyt's arrival, was 26 percent of gross revenue. In 1947, his first full year in Denver, the profit percentage dropped to 19.34. In 1948 it fell to 13.77 percent, then recovered slightly to 14.44 in 1949. Then in 1950 the percentage of profit tumbled to 7.54.

This probably would not have alarmed the stockholders too much if it hadn't been accompanied by a drastic slash in dividend payments. From 1929 until 1948—a twenty-year span—*The Post* had never paid its stockholders less than one million dollars a year. In 1936, dividends had totaled $1,950,000, and the following year they had amounted to $1,900,000. Each year from 1944 to 1947, *The Post* had paid $1,200,000 in dividends—$100,000 per month.

In 1948, preparing to meet the cost of the new plant, dividends were trimmed to $1,050,000. The real crunch came the following year. In 1949 dividends were reduced to $200,000—less than one-fifth of what had been paid the previous year. Even during the two years of the costly war against Scripps-Howard in 1927-1928, *The Post* had managed to pay $550,000 and $600,000.

Hoyt and Campbell knew they had no alternative but to slash dividends if the new plant were to be paid for from current income. They also knew that the profits Shepherd had been able to show were unhealthy and improvident. But their logic did not still the cries of anguish from some of the beneficiaries who had become accustomed to the lavish payments. Campbell, as president of the corporation as well as trustee for the beneficiaries of approximately half the stock, was cast in an anomalous position. He had to support Hoyt's efforts to produce a superior, and costly, product while at the same time protecting the interests of the stockholders. And Hoyt, as the man in charge, was placed under increasing pressure to cut expenses, to hold back, to modify some of his big plans, to bring in more money so as to return profits to a more acceptable level.

It is possible that Hoyt, while keenly aware of this demand, did not fully understand its significance. Whatever the case, when Campbell put the issue on the line, Hoyt was stunned by both the manner and the substance. It came about this way:

Hoyt's divorce was finalized in due course. Helen Bonfils, a devout Catholic, was distressed but she considered his private life his own affair. Then on November 7, 1950, Hoyt married Helen May Taber, who meanwhile had divorced her husband, Wallace, *The Post*'s wildlife and ecology writer who had gone off to Africa on assignment. Hoyt and his bride were in Hawaii on a delayed honeymoon early in 1951 when he received a remarkable letter. It was from Campbell, speaking for himself and Helen Bonfils, and ran ten single-spaced typewritten pages. In addition there was an eight-page appendix. The letter opened with this paragraph:

> Dear Palmer,
> As we come to the fifth anniversary of your service as Editor and Publisher of *The Post,* we deem it appropriate to give you this candid and confidential estimate of your services, first as Editor and then as Publisher. Also, we outline here the general terms and conditions under which we hope your employment as Editor and Publisher may be continued. We speak with the utmost candor, imposed upon us by both the obligations of friendship and our own trusteeship.

The letter went on to say that as editor, "in all major respects, you have done an excellent job. You have carried out our fundamental objective, which is to print the news truthfully, as completely as possible, and without mixing news and editorial opinion." The letter listed Hoyt's accomplishments in improving the paper and noted, "*The Post*'s reputation for unbiased, unprejudiced and objective coverage of the news has been greatly enhanced in the last five years." Then, in the following words, Campbell proceeded to chide Hoyt about the publicity he had engendered:

> You have been accused of trying to convert the Paper into your personal organ, and of publicizing yourself in its columns and through its various promotions, for the purpose of attaining some high political or government position. We reject these accusations, but their basis is understandable. The dedication of our new plant necessarily put all of us in the public eye perhaps too much. You have taken a very active and worthwhile part in civic and state affairs, and you have made some significant addresses on important public issues. It would be false modesty, of course, to have your name and picture deleted from the news accounts of these events.

At the same time, it may be that some of your admiring employees have overplayed you. Certainly it is a fact that you and the Paper are being criticized on that account. As Trustees, we, of course, owe a first duty to see that the Paper's prestige is advanced and not that of any personality. . . .

For that reason, we believe that all *Post* functions and invitations thereto and all advertisements and all promotions carried on by the Paper be in the name of the Paper, and that all of us practice a little more anonymity. . . .

Both of us have received complaints from time to time over the past five years that you, the Editor, have not been available for presentation of facts and points of view by persons vitally affected by your editorial policy. . . . Your absence from your office for repeated and considerable periods of time during the past five years has been a serious detriment in this and other respects to the Paper. . . .

Campbell is dead and cannot explain his thinking on this point. His widow, Bertha, an exceptional woman in her own right who made it a point not to intrude into his professional concerns but knew his innermost personal thoughts, provides some insights. "Ray was torn by these matters," she says. "He knew *The Post* needed a new image and it could be presented best by a personalized approach through Ep. But Helen Bonfils revered her father and resented the thought of Ep taking his place. In Ep's view, he was *The Post*. Helen wanted *The Post* first, uppermost, with Ep as simply another employee. Ray felt that when you employ someone to take charge, you give him the freedom to act until you can't go along with him anymore, that you mustn't stifle his creative instincts. But in the end Ray sympathized with Helen's feelings for her father."

As Hoyt read Campbell's letter he realized for the first time Helen Bonfils felt he was usurping the position she had reserved for F. G. Bonfils. Hoyt was a man without pretensions; he would take a can of polish out of his desk drawer in the middle of an important conversation and shine his shoes and think nothing of it. But he also felt that the editor and publisher was in effect the paper, that if the boss was not dynamic and active in public affairs, the paper would not be, and that he as the head of a great newspaper must also play his role. "If the publisher is not respected, how can his paper be?" he asked, with good reason.

In his letter, Campbell went on to praise the new editorial page. However, he suggested the department was overstaffed and that its cost of eighty thousand dollars a year could "be reduced without damage to the page." That brought up the matter of the Washington bureau. Campbell noted that the bureau was costing about $25,000 per year. Features and syndicated columns for the editorial page had cost $11,511.50 and, Campbell wrote, between them they "cover Washington very completely. We believe that this coverage by these columnists, plus the coverage we get through AP, UP and INS, and other such services, justifies the abandonment of the Washington Bureau." Prior to 1946, Campbell reminded Hoyt, *The Post* had retained a man in Washington for forty dollars a week and his services had been considered adequate.

Campbell then moved on into Hoyt's performance as publisher. He cited figures to show "that the ratio of our earnings before taxes, as well as after taxes, has been declining over the past five years at an alarming rate. . . . Obviously, unless we can reverse this trend by cutting expenses in areas other than newsprint, wages of the mechanical crafts and taxes, we are not going to be able to continue our present dividend, to say nothing of purchasing certain additional equipment asserted to be necessary. . . ."

Campbell pointed out that between 1945 and 1950, advertising income for newspapers in fifty-two U. S. cities rose 75 percent, *The Post*'s rose 90 percent, but the *Rocky Mountain News* showed a 232 percent gain. *The Post*'s circulation had increased 20 percent daily and 17 percent on Sunday, while the *News* had grown by 121 percent daily and 137 percent Sunday. Further, he said, while *The Post*'s circulation income had increased by 39.5 percent, expenses in this department had risen by 207 percent.

The promotion department was Campbell's next target. In 1945, he said, "Al Birch, with the part time assistance of one clerk and with the occasional help and cooperation of a few editorial employees," had carried out the promotion program. "In 1945 and prior years," Campbell wrote, "there were many lively and interesting promotions sponsored by *The Post* in collaboration with merchants and others, who bore all of the out of pocket expense and expected *The Post* only to furnish proper publicity in its columns. For some reason this kind of promotion has been allowed to lapse, and in its place there has been instituted a type of promotion that not only occupies the full time of a large highly paid staff and expensive space in our news columns, but also considerable out of pocket expense to *The Post*." The department had grown to twenty, which in 1950 cost about $75,000.

Campbell concluded by saying that at the annual meeting Hoyt would be reelected a director, and that the new board would negotiate his reemployment, "on fair terms, and such as will make you happy in your work."

Hoyt had prepared a report to be delivered at the annual meeting that predicted earnings in relation to gross income "should, from now on, rise slowly but steadily" as revenues were increased together with "a substantial lowering of expenses." However, he was understandably stung by Campbell's letter and declined to enter into talks about a new contract. He also put his head together with Buxton to respond to Campbell's criticism.

More and more, Buxton was serving as Hoyt's strong right arm. Hoyt seldom made a key decision without "running it by the Scotchman," as he described it. When trouble developed in the advertising department, Buxton moved over as its director, but it was evident by this time that Major Bonfils soon would retire and Buxton would move into the job he had been promised when he came to Denver, The upshot of his conferences with Hoyt was a letter to Campbell a month later pledging that *"The Post* will continue to get its share of Denver's advertising dollar, and will spend that share wisely." Hoyt expressed his appreciation for Campbell's frankness and support, pointed out that "the position of editor and publisher is indivisible with the individual who occupies it," but promised to see what he could do about cutting down the publicity, and proceeded to refute some of the figures. Here Buxton's fine hand was visible.

If advertising in *The Post* had increased by 231 percent as the *News* had done, Hoyt pointed out, *The Post* would have ranked second nationally in total advertising "instead of thirty-second which is a more logical figure due to size of market and advertising rate structure." Such an increase in advertising would have required 10,250 pages of space and 20,500 more tons of newsprint, he went on, which would have been impossible to obtain. Hoyt also asserted that if *The Post*'s circulation had increased at the same ratio as the *News,* it would now have "519,236 daily and 871,030 Sunday" distribution, "not at all commensurate with the increase in population which the city and state have enjoyed." In other words, the *News* had started from a much lower base and a relatively small actual increase would appear as a large percentage in growth. Campbell quickly admitted he had been caught in a statistical trap.

The exchange, rather than eroding, strengthened the personal ties between the two men. Hoyt asked Campbell to provide him annually with "thoughts, criticisms, comments and suggestions concerning our operations, for which we are jointly responsible," instead of at five-year intervals. No one "won" and no one "lost," but both men emerged with a better understanding of the other's aims and problems. One other outcome was that for the first time in its history *The Post* adopted a comprehensive budgeting system whereby an effort was made to look into the future and plan accordingly. Such a system hadn't been necessary in Shepherd's time and no one had insisted on instituting one when Hoyt took over. Buxton was named chairman of the budget committee, which gave him enormous power in charting the course of the corporation. The business of running the financial side of a newspaper had become an extremely complex operation and Buxton's keen eye for figures would become indispensable.

While Hoyt was working without a contract, he mulled the idea of leaving *The Post*. He knew Campbell wanted him to remain. He also knew that during the next five years he would have nothing like the freedom he enjoyed during the first five. And although to all appearances his relationship with Helen Bonfils was as cordial as ever, he sensed a certain coolness developing.

About this time he had an opportunity to buy the *Globe-Democrat*, the strong second paper in St. Louis, but in the end he decided to stay in Denver. Five months after his contract expired, Hoyt signed a new five-year agreement extending through December 31, 1955. Its principal feature was an incentive bonus giving Hoyt a percentage of the paper's profits. His base salary was reduced to fifty thousand dollars annually, but in at least two years he more than doubled it with his share of the profits and even in the leaner years he did very well.

Hoyt had been known as a spender among editors. Now he became more acutely aware of his responsibilities as a publisher. Many *Post* old-timers recall what took place after the annual meeting as "the downhold of 1951." About half the columns being purchased by the editorial page were canceled. United Press service was dropped. Red Fenwick was brought in from the far reaches of the Rocky Mountain Empire and put on the rewrite desk. Drama critic Alex Murphree and Gene Lowall, who was investigating organized crime, also had to put in time on rewrite. All overtime was banned. In later years, when asked *The Post*'s primary objective, Hoyt sometimes would answer, "To remain solvent." There was logic to it. A bankrupt paper could not remain in business. Yet that was not what one expected to hear from a dynamic editor.

Some of the fire, the verve, the exuberant enthusiasm that causes newspapermen to call their profession a game seemed to go out of *The Post* as Hoyt became increasingly concerned with fiscal burdens. In his first five years Hoyt had lifted *The Post* on a steeply ascending line to a high level of journalistic excellence. Now it seemed to have topped out on a plateau from which its editorial endeavors would rise only occasionally to new peaks of distinction for the remainder of his administration. Perhaps, given its setting and its resources, *The Post* had reached limits beyond which it could not go, but for many those limits were not enough.

Edwin P. Hoyt, Ep's son, makes a harsh estimation: "The decisions that were made that year forced the abandonment of editorial expansion at a crucial point. Sure, later they hyped up the editorial page, but it was too late. By that time the fervor was gone. Before that time Dad was the most up-and-coming editor in the business as well as a publisher. After 1951 the genius just went out of it all."

When the opportunity came to take over the Colorado Springs *Free Press* later that year, Ed Hoyt in his words "went charging down on my stallion, ready to joust with all comers and make my fortune." Ep gave his son a piece of advice before he departed: "One thing you will have to learn if you are going to run a newspaper successfully is this—you will have to grow icicles around your heart." But neither of the Hoyts was able to do it. The *Free Press* soon ran into more financial problems than Ed Hoyt could handle, and without a Buxton to support him, he foundered.

Under the new stringent business practices instituted by Buxton, *The Post*'s gross income continued a steady rise—from $11,634,000 in 1950 to $36,528,000 in 1969, the last full year of Hoyt's administration. Only once in those years did income drop, and that amounted to only $12,000 in 1960. But expenses rose correspondingly in that span and the percentage of profit dwindled progressively. In 1969 only 1.6 percent of the more than $36.5 million taken in remained as after-tax profit.

Hoyt yielded the helm in the fall of 1970 and that proved to be the worst year of all—gross income of $39,507,000 and net profit of only $198,000 after taxes, for a 0.5 percent margin of profit. Although the profit ratio improved, the soaring cost of doing business, common to virtually every sector of industry, made it impossible ever to return dividends to the lush heights of the Shepherd era. Ultimately it was stockholder dissatisfaction with the return that plunged *The Post* into a cataclysmic battle for its independence. And leading the defense was Helen Bonfils with roughly half the stock—either owned outright or in trusts in which she had a voice—ready to risk her personal fortune to retain ownership of the paper in Denver.

Vignette

SMOKE GOT IN OUR EYES

A cigarette manufacturer's somewhat blatant advertising campaign had been irking Edwin P. Hoyt for some time. One day in October, 1950, he wrote an editorial about it. There were some interesting repercussions. The editorial began in this fashion:

> For several months one of the great cigarette companies in the United States has been carrying on an expensive and novel advertising campaign.
> Take a puff of our cigarette, the tobacco hucksters cry. Then take a puff of your own brand.
> Which is milder?
> Your brand is milder, the unwitting dupe always has to admit. My brand is stronger.
> Naturally, say the tobacco hucksters. And of course you are not connected with our company in any way nor are you being paid for saying this, are you?
> No, replies the dupe. I do this of my own free will.
> So, of his own free will the poor jerk helps the hucksters peddle their wares.

The editorial went on to say that a certain person had his fill of this kind of advertising and made a test of his own. He persuaded his father-in-law, mother-in-law, and wife to join him in an experiment. Ed Hoyt reported in his editorial:

> All the family group did as the hucksters had asked.
> First each sucked a mouthful of smoke into his mouth. Then he honked it out through his nose (without inhaling). Then he tried the second brand.
> In each and every case the result was the same, just as the hucksters had said. The second brand was harsher.
> There is a postscript to the story. Our friend had reversed the order of cigarettes, and the huckster's brand proved harsher than the others. This proved only that the second puff of smoke through

the nose was harsher than the first, he reported gleefully, just as he had always suspected.

You don't believe it? Then try it yourself.

Denverites read the editorial and chuckled. Ed Hoyt went on to other things and forgot about it.

Not so with Chuck Buxton. Lately named *The Post*'s advertising director, he was in New York on a get-acquainted visit with the agencies responsible for buying space in newspapers. One morning he walked into the agency handling this cigarette company's advertising and suddenly became aware of a chill. It was the first he had heard of the editorial.

The president of the cigarette company was sailing that day for Europe. Buxton hurried down to the *Queen Elizabeth* on the New York waterfront to try to mollify the tycoon. For his pains he was firmly escorted off the ship. The cigarette company's district manager wrote his superiors suggesting that *The Post* really hadn't meant what it had said. He was fired.

The company canceled a thirty-thousand-dollar advertising contract with *The Post*. But within a year their ads were back in the paper.

19

THE POST VS. SENATOR
JOSEPH McCARTHY

The Associated Press filed a dispatch out of Salt Lake City on Saturday, February 11, 1950, which *The Post* ran under a one-column headline on page 1. The story began as follows:

> Salt Lake City, Feb. 11—(AP)—Senator Joseph McCarthy (Rep.) of Wisconsin hopped across the nation by air Friday, leaving a trail of accusations that the State Department is employing Communists, many of whom hold influential positions.
>
> In Washington the senator's charges brought from State Department press officer Lincoln White the assertion that "we know of no Communist member in the department and if we find any they will be summarily discharged."
>
> The Wisconsin senator fired his first blast Thursday night in a Republican Lincoln Day dinner in Wheeling, W. Va. He waved a paper and said:
>
> "I have here in my hand a list of 205 that were known to the secretary of state as being members of the Communist party, and who nevertheless are still working and shaping the policy in the State Department."
>
> Newsmen missed the senator as his plane stopped in Milwaukee but they found him in Denver where he scoffed at White's denial of his charge. He said he had a complete list of 205 "bad risks" still working in the State Department and if Secretary Acheson wanted to call him later in Salt Lake City, he'd read the list. . . .

The Post for some reason had published nothing on McCarthy's speech in West Virginia. But in the February 11 issue, in addition to the Associated Press story on page 1 there was on page 2 an interview with McCarthy during a thirty-minute stop in Denver en route to Salt Lake City. McCarthy was quoted as saying the State Department knew the names of fifty-seven employees who were "card-carrying Communists." He offered to show reporters the names of the fifty-seven, then said he had left his list in his baggage. He also said his information came from "various sources, including the un-American activities committee."

Hoyt was a staunch foe of Communism. He had seen it try to gain a foothold in the United States during the Depression, and had viewed with concern the rise of the Iron Curtain in Europe after World War II, increasing Soviet obstructionism in the United Nations and growing evidence of Soviet espionage and subversion throughout the world. This, combined with a low opinion of the State Department fortified during his wartime service in Washington, caused him to look on McCarthy's charges with more than ordinary interest. After all, it was a member of the U. S. Senate talking, and presumably he had access to the facts.

McCarthy continued to make sensational charges, but failed to produce proof. Hoyt began to have doubts, particularly when the senator kept reducing the number of alleged Communists in the State Department. *The Post* asked Nover in Washington and the wire services to see if they could get specific information about the accusations McCarthy was making. They could uncover nothing. What bothered Hoyt was that McCarthy was voicing extreme charges through the press without providing enough facts for the public—and editors—to make a judgment. This outraged his sense of fair play. On March 14, a little over a month after McCarthy made his West Virginia speech, *The Post* published an editorial that was the first of a steady barrage against what Hoyt called the evil of mccarthyism—which he insisted on spelling in lower case. It was titled "Call off the Dogs" and is reproduced here in its entirety:

> Senator McCarthy's blunderbuss charges against the State Department, and his branding of individuals without evidence sticks in the craw. Here is more headline hunting, these actions shout.
>
> This is the kind of thing the nation has grown to expect from the Un-American activities committee of the House of Representatives. Americans have become accustomed, but not hardened, to name-calling, mud-slinging and character assassination by that body.
>
> In the beginning, it looked as though Senator McCarthy was adopting a different and enlightened approach to searching out the disloyal.
>
> True, on the protected floor of the Senate he made the sensational announcement that the State Department was overrun with Communists. But he said he would not blacken characters and name names; that the proof rested in the files of the department.
>
> Now, we have the old game of witch-hunt in progress again, with Senator McCarthy as chief witch-hunter, albeit a wordy and indefinite witch-hunter. He's charging key State Department officials

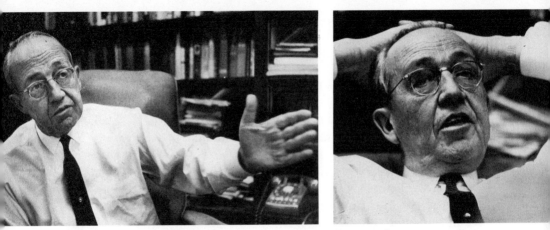

Palmer Hoyt, a shirt-sleeves editor, was never reluctant about expounding his views. (Carl Iwasaki)

with Communist activity. The charges are made in big words, but without an iota of proof, to date.

This kind of irresponsibility is just as inexcusable today as it ever was. It must make Americans wish the laws of libel and slander applied to utterances on the floor of the Senate.

This is the kind of news that makes the headlines. Are the newspapers to blame? Not when a United States senator makes a flat statement that other high government officials are not loyal to their own government. That, brother, is news.

In Arabia, in olden times, they used to boil people in oil. To punish others, they could cut off an arm or a nose or an ear.

Nowadays, though, certain members of our Congress have a more painful method of torture. Persons they do not like, they accuse of "Communism" on the floor of the Congress. They are protected then, but the victims are boiled in the vitriol of adverse publicity, and their characters are slashed to ribbons, slowly and surely, like the death of 1,000 cuts.

Then (and the torturers of old would have marveled at our cruelty), the victim is allowed to live, to live out his life in the sneer of suspicion.

The worst of this torture is that innocence is no defense, nor is truth. Once the blotch is cast, it spreads, and cannot be removed.

Senator McCarthy is indulging in this unworthy game. He made wild charges, and is now called on to prove them. If he can prove them he has not yet shown it.

Rather than drag the names of more Americans through the mud without proof or even adequate evidence, the senate should call off the dogs, and hold up this investigation until the State Department files have been opened to them and examined.

If any other major American newspaper tackled McCarthy head-on prior to this time, there is scant record of it. That part of the nation's press not enthusiastically in support of McCarthy was largely mute. To understand the significance of *The Post*'s editorial it is necessary to be aware of the nation's doubts and fears at that point in history.

Late in 1948 Alger Hiss, a former high State Department official, was indicted for perjury after he denied charges that he gave secret documents to Whittaker Chambers, a onetime editor of *Time* magazine, for transmission to a Communist spy ring. The jury failed to reach a verdict in his first trial but a second jury convicted Hiss in January of 1950.

In September of 1949 the Soviets touched off their first atomic explosion and thereby broke the West's nuclear monopoly. Less than a month later eleven leaders of the U. S. Communist party were convicted after a nine-month trial of advocating the violent overthrow of the American government. That same year the Chinese Nationalist government of Chiang Kai-shek, our ally in World War II, fled to Taiwan as Chinese Communists with Soviet materiel support swept over the mainland.

All of these events made sensational newspaper headlines. The Soviet was seen as a malevolent threat to the United States and, the expression went, many Americans were seeing Communists under every bed. A people in such a state of mind were willing, if not anxious, to believe Senator McCarthy's charges of Communists entrenched in the U. S. government structure. Within weeks after McCarthy made his speech in West Virginia, a British physicist, German-born Dr. Klaus J. E. Fuchs, who at one time had worked at the Los Alamos, New Mexico, nuclear center, pleaded guilty in Britain to charges that he had given valuable atomic secrets to Russian agents. Not long afterward the Federal Bureau of Investigation arrested David Greenglass, who accused his sister, Ethel Rosenberg, and her husband, Julius, of selling nuclear secrets to Soviet agents. The Rosenbergs were convicted and executed in 1953. Greenglass turned state's witness and received a fifteen-year sentence.

In such an atmosphere of fear, uncertainty, and suspicion, it is understandable that most newspapers supported what appeared to be McCarthy's patriotic one-man crusade to root out the Communists in government. To them he was a latter-day Paul Revere shouting alarums to awaken the nation. If some editors had doubts about his methods, many felt they were justified by the circumstances. *The Post* took a different view. Two weeks after the first editorial condemning McCarthy's tactics, *The Post* published another one titled "From Moscow to McCarthy—With Kisses." It said in part:

> Senator McCarthy has done irreparable harm by shooting off his big mouth without sufficient facts to warrant any character smudging at all. The only good thing to come out of the whole investigation is an airing of the State Department personnel policies, which in the past have inclined to the queer. Even that is small consolation for the harm being done at home and abroad. . . .
>
> To get the full impact of the McCarthy episode, Americans must put themselves in the position of those accused.
>
> How would you like to be working for the State Department right now? How would you like to have your name dragged through the mud for no other reason than you once associated with a man who was suspected to be a Communist? . . . Put on a personal basis like this it is easy to see what Senator McCarthy and these few others are doing to our nation. For one thing, they are threatening to dishonor our government service for all time. They must be stopped.

When Haldore Hanson, an employee of the State Department, was named by McCarthy on the floor of Congress as having "pro-Communist tendencies," *The Post* published virtually the entire text of Hanson's rebuttal "in the interests of truth and justice." About the only thing McCarthy had on Hanson was that he visited Chinese Communist headquarters as an Associated Press correspondent after World War II.

The Post observed editorially: "Unfortunately, however, the charges always seem to stick longer and harder than their refutation. It's much easier to blacken a man's name than it is to whiten it. Seemingly, too, all one has to do nowadays is call a man a Communist, and presto-chango, in the eyes of a great many people, he is a Communist—no matter to what the facts attest."

Hoyt was in a quandary as to how to handle the news that McCarthy was making. His sense of objectivity made it necessary to report what McCarthy was saying. Yet it was obvious that many of McCarthy's charges, particularly those made under Congressional immunity, were unfounded, unproved and damaging to the victims. How should the press publish McCarthy's pronouncements as a matter of news coverage without being used by him?

Hoyt rarely wrote memos or gave direct orders to his staff, but he did set down detailed guidelines for managing editor Ed Dooley. It is published here in full:

> In view of the mounting tide of mccarthyism, I would like to re-

view with you certain precautions which may be taken to guard against loose charges, irresponsible utterances and attempts at character assassination by "spokesmen," official or otherwise.

First: Instruct the news staff always to evaluate the source of the charge.

Second: Ask the news staff to weigh the story and see what they would do with it if official immunity were lacking.

Three: Discuss with the news staff the general proposition of whether or not *The Post* can withhold publication of this particular moot story until proof or a qualifying answer can be obtained from the person, organization or group accused.

Four: Ask the news staff whether they of their own knowledge know a doubtful charge to be false, and to apply any reasonable doubt they may have to the treatment of the story.

Five: In connection with banner lines or other headlines on this type of story, ask the news staff to determine whether wording is used as shock treatment or to summarize facts.

It is obvious that many charges made by reckless impulsive officials cannot and should not be ignored, but it seems to me that news stories and headlines can be presented in such a manner that the reading public will be able to measure the real worth or value and the true meaning of the stories.

For example, when it is possible and practical, we should remind the public in case of a wild accusation by Senator McCarthy that this particular senator's name is synonymous with poor documentation and irresponsible conduct and that he has made many charges that have been insupportable under due process.

In connection with the play of the story which cannot be ignored, it is possible that it can be played down. For example, it might be placed in the middle or lower part of page one, or inside the paper and given smaller headlines. If it must be given a large display I would advocate, and I wish you would consult with your staff as to the advisability of this procedure, the addition of a kicker line such as "Today's mccarthyism" or "McCarthy charges today."

Please advise your staff that *The Denver Post* is alert to the problem of mccarthyism and we are anxious to take every possible step to protect the innocent and give everyone under the fire of McCarthy or other "official" spokesman every possible chance to defend themselves. If possible, we want to give them that chance in the same story, but in any event as quickly after as possible and with the same news emphasis. I wish that you would instruct the news staff that *The Post* will not consider any story complete and covered until rebuttal and answering statements are printed. Also, please remind the news staff that it is our policy to request of the press associations rebuttals from those under attack, and to ask the associations to use every possible effort to move these mitigating or diluting statements in time for proper play in connection with any McCarthy or similar attacks.

There are, of course, many similar devices which may be used in connection with one-sided stories, and which will be a matter of judgment on the part of the news editor; such as, a blackface precede or a drop-in in a particular story of accusation saying that similar charges have been made by this source but that no proof has ever been submitted, or calling attention to the fact that those attacked have not had the opportunity to answer or disprove the charges.

As far as *The Post* is concerned, the accused will be given every opportunity to prove his case and *The Post* stands ready to print rebuttal or comment.

Hoyt's memo was widely noted and applauded among newspapermen. He made it clear the principles of fair play enunciated in it applied to any situation where anyone's reputation was damaged unfairly. After McCarthyism tapered off, Larry Martin wrote a memorable series on the "faceless informers" who behind the cloak of official immunity deprived citizens of their rights.

The Post's attacks on McCarthy did not go unnoticed and he put the paper on an earlier version of Spiro Agnew's "enemies list." Hoyt replied editorially:

> Senator McCarthy of Wisconsin has classified *The Denver Post* as one of several newspapers which never say "anything good about anyone who fights Communism."
>
> This is about as inaccurate a statement as the senator has ever made—and his statements have included some masterpieces of pure invention.
>
> If he had said that *The Post* never has "anything good to say about people who fight Communism by the McCarthy method" he would have been entirely correct and we would have been highly complimented.
>
> *The Denver Post* does not yield to the pop-off senator or anyone else in its distaste for Communism and in its desire to see it defeated and exposed as the diabolical system of totalitarianism that it is.
>
> The only way the senator knows to fight Communism is to stand up in the halls of Congress—where he is immune from charges of slander—and make reckless statements that large numbers of people are Communists or Communist sympathizers.
>
> The senator has never had any qualms about smearing the innocent along with the guilty. His method is a sort of verbal pogrom which is un-American and denies to many of the accused their fundamental rights under our duly constituted legal system.
>
> We cannot agree with the senator that the way to fight Communism is to tear down the American concept of fair play and the protection of the innocent from outrageous accusations. The McCarthy method of fighting Communism by making irresponsible de-

nunciations on a scattergun basis smacks of the totalitarianism that is a part of Communism itself.

The United States, we believe, will gain nothing if it defeats Communism in its midst by setting up a rule of fear administered by McCarthy and his gumshoe agents.

In 1954 Hoyt was chosen for the University of Arizona's first annual John Peter Zenger Freedom of the Press Award. The citation is named in honor of the editor who in 1735, by his defense against a charge of criminal libel, established the newspaperman's right to print the truth no matter how unpalatable it might be to the subject of the article. "In the fight to protect the community from infiltration by subversives," the citation read in part, "Hoyt has simultaneously fought to safeguard due process and individual constitutional rights. *The Denver Post,* under Hoyt, has fought for both safeguards as essential to survival of the free American way of life." Hoyt in his acceptance speech on November 21, 1954, lectured the press in these words:

> It is true that the number of newspapers critical of McCarthy has grown during the last year or two. But there are still many of them who are his supporters, his apologists, even his devotees.
>
> Those newspapers, the Chicago *Tribune,* the Hearst press, and others like them, are, from the long-run point of view, as short-sighted as they are self-destructive. McCarthy is not and never has been a believer in a free press. Proof of this is to be found in the way he has tried to smear every journalistic critic as Communist or pro-Communist. They are all part of what he calls the "left-wing press, or branches of the *Daily Worker,"* a category in which he includes the New York *Times,* the *Christian Science Monitor, The Denver Post,* the St. Louis *Post-Dispatch,* and latterly, the Scripps-Howard newspapers.

A few days later, at the culmination of a lengthy and often acrimonious hearing, the Senate by a vote of 67 to 22 condemned McCarthy for conduct "contrary to Senate traditions."

There is a striking parallel between McCarthy's performance in the early Fifties and the actions of certain members of Congress— A. B. (Happy) Chandler, J. Parnell Thomas, John Costello, E. V. Robertson, Leland Ford, John Rankin, Tom Stewart, Martin Dies— with regard to Japanese Americans in World War II. In both instances demagogues with an ax to grind made wild, unsubstantiated charges, and most of the press accepted those charges without question, helping intentionally or unintentionally to stir public passions instead of cooling them, failing in their obligation to seek out and publish the truth. The old *Post,* as we have seen in Chapter 11, was in league with the witch-hunters. The new *Post,* in a startling turn-about, took the lead among the nation's newspapers in challenging demagoguery, demanding the facts, and warning its readers about techniques of the big smear.

Ep Hoyt never made any pretense to being an intellectual. He operated largely on gut instincts based on certain strong principles of justice and fairness, and in this case his instincts could not have been more right.

THE BURBANK OF THE BARNYARD

The collect telephone call near the end of the day was from a mortician in rural Nebraska. A prominent local citizen had died and he wanted to tell *The Post* about it. Leonard (Buzz) Larsen, now chief of the *Post*'s Washington bureau but then newly assigned to the rewrite bank, took the call. The connection was bad and soon Larsen found himself shouting to the mortician to speak up. Suddenly all typewriters in the city room were stilled as everyone listened to Larsen's side of the interview, with some of the other rewrite men encouraging him with rude remarks.

All right, Larsen said to himself. If these guys are so interested, I'll show them a story. He wrote two stories. One was a straightforward obituary as he received it from the mortician. The other was a product of his imagination. He passed the second story to Bernard Kelly at the next desk. Kelly read it and chuckled heartily in appreciation. Jim Kelley, editor of the predated edition that was delivered to the far reaches of the Rocky Mountain Empire, also read the piece and laughed uproariously.

The straight obituary was passed routinely to copy editor Hugh Kane, who would have one of his men check it for style, accuracy, grammar, and punctuation before writing a headline. And because Kelley figured Kane would enjoy Larsen's little flight of fancy, he also tossed the second story in the basket.

Somehow, that second story was read and a headline put on it. Somehow the story was set in type. Next morning, somehow it appeared in the first edition.

Bob Pattridge, now editor of the editorial page, happened to see it as he was checking first copies of the edition for errors. Jim Kelley saw it just about the same time. Both leapt out of their chairs and raced to stop the presses.

This is the way Larsen's story appeared in a few thousand copies

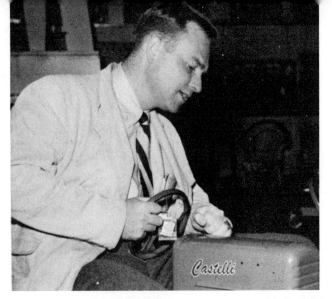

Buzz Larsen on assignment in 1953. Larsen is now chief of *The Post*'s Washington bureau. (Dean Conger)

of the paper, with only the name changed to protect the memory of the innocent:

CALLAHAN DEATH

CASTS PALL OVER

FARM COMMUNITY

GREELEY, Neb.—This bustling western Nebraska farm and ranch community was under a dark curtain of gloom Thursday as relatives prepared funeral rites for Mitchell B. Callahan, the 83-year-old "Luther Burbank of the farmyard."

Callahan, who came here with his parents as a small boy and remained to become one of the world's leading authorities on cross-breeding of domestic animals, died Wednesday.

Callahan was best known for his experiments in crossing pheasants with farm fowl, retaining the best qualities of each. He had successfully matched the pheasant with the chicken, producing the "Phicken," the pheasant with turkey, producing the "Phurkey," and the pheasant with the duck, producing the "Ring-necked Farm Fowl."

Larsen has accepted full credit for the tale but actually, he says, he embroidered on a story that Earl Pomeroy, *The Post*'s resident humor columnist, had told a few days earlier. Pomeroy had talked to a young lady at the State Agriculture Department who told him about crossing pheasants with domestic fowl, producing the phicken and the phurkey. Pomeroy said when he asked what they called the one produced from the pheasant and the duck, she replied, "Oh, we just call him Joe."

20

S. I. NEWHOUSE COMES TO TOWN

There are two slightly differing versions of this next episode, which was to lead to an intensely traumatic dozen years in the history of *The Post*. They are told by the men who had a direct part in the event, and each recollected it for the author to the best of his memory. The conflict in their stories is not important. In this instance what resulted is of much greater consequence than how it happened.

As Ep Hoyt remembers it, he received a telephone call early in 1959 from May Bonfils Stanton, the estranged sister of Helen Bonfils. Hoyt says he is sure of the circumstances because in the thirteen years he had been editor and publisher of *The Post* he had never met or spoken to Mrs. Stanton even though she owned a substantial share of the paper. Mrs. Stanton angrily complained to Hoyt that *The Post* had failed to give adequate news coverage to prizes won by her livestock in an important show.

She charged Helen had ordered that her name was not to appear in *The Post* and scolded Hoyt for carrying out those orders even to the extent of refusing to mention her prize animals. She wound up the conversation, which apparently was largely one-sided, by threatening to do something which would make Hoyt very sorry. Hoyt had no idea what this might be. Since he was accustomed to getting angry calls from subscribers, although rarely from stockholders, Hoyt soon dismissed the matter.

The other version is told by May's husband, Charles Edward Stanton. According to his recollection it was an obituary published in *The Post* that touched off her angry call to Hoyt. Clyde V. Berryman, May's first husband, whom she had divorced in 1947, died on July 30, 1959, at age seventy-eight. The next day *The Post* published his obituary, which was seven paragraphs long. There were five obituaries that day and Berryman's was next to the last. All five were of approximately the same length and they appeared close by the paid funeral notices on page 46, hardly a prominent position in the paper. Ed Stanton recalls that his wife became upset when Berryman's obituary was brought to her attention, complaining that there was more in it about their marriage than about Berryman himself. "They're airing all that dirty laundry again," she cried.

In reality, only two of the obituary's seven paragraphs had to do with Berryman's first marriage. One said: "He was the former husband of May Bonfils, daughter of the late Frederick G. Bonfils, cofounder of *The Denver Post*." The other: "He was born May 8, 1881, in Central City, Neb. He was married to Miss Bonfils November 7, 1904 in Golden. The couple was divorced in 1947."

Assuming that the purpose of a newspaper obituary is to report the high points of a person's life, it would seem this was essential information. In any event, Stanton remembers his wife was quite distraught when she telephoned Hoyt to complain that the publicity was unwanted and it probably was all her sister's doing. "You have maligned me," she stormed at Hoyt. "This is the last straw. You are going to regret this story."

Later, Stanton asked what she intended to do. "Get rid of my *Post* stock," she replied. "Sell it. In fact, I'd give that stock away to spite that miserable man. I don't want to have anything more to do with the paper."

It was not the first time sale of her stock had been discussed, but apparently on this occasion she was determined to let it go. As we have seen, May, in the compromise agreement reached with her sister in 1935 under threat of long-drawn litigation, came into possession of approximately 15 percent of *The Post*'s stock. The stock had proved astonishingly lucrative. In the fourteen years between 1935 and 1948 *The Post* had paid $19,800,000 in dividends; May's 15 percent share brought her $2,972,000 in that time, an average annual income of more than $212,000. Although she lived lavishly, much of the income had been invested shrewdly in blue-chip stocks, land, works of art, and jewels; and her fortune grew.

But, as we also have seen, the dividends were slashed in 1949 to pay for the new *Post* plant and they never returned to previous levels. In the ten years between 1949 and 1958 *The Post*'s dividend payments totaled $5,354,000. May's share was $803,100, an average of $80,310 per year. Having nothing to do with the newspaper's management, watching her income dwindle even as inflation bit into its buying power, it was difficult for May not to believe the newspaper was being mismanaged by Helen and the man she had employed,

Hoyt. On a previous occasion when May's attorney pointed out that her enormous holdings in *Post* stock—worth several millions at least—weren't bringing in as much as they should, she replied with some rancor, "I suspect my sister is charging a large part of her living expenses to the paper." May was asked whether she would consider selling the stock. No, she replied. She said she was afraid Helen might find a way to get control of it if the stock were put on the market. May had fought Helen for the stock and was determined to keep it from going back to her. In fact, while May's last will and testament instructed the executor to liquidate her estate as soon as possible, there were specific instructions that this was not to include "any stock that I own in *The Denver Post,* Denver, Colorado, which stock shall not be sold during the lifetime of my sister, Helen Bonfils Somnes, or during the lifetime of her husband."

But now, angry at Hoyt, she called on old friends of her father for advice about selling the stock. Among them were Louie Levand in Wichita and E. K. Gaylord, the venerable Oklahoma City publisher. They told her the most likely buyers were owners of expanding newspaper chains who were on the lookout for properties to pick up, and probably the best way to get in touch with them was through a newspaper broker.

Ever since F. G. Bonfils' death in 1933 there had been rumors that *The Post* would be sold, and hardly a month went by without some broker inquiring about its availability. Helen had rebuffed them all. Papa had demonstrated his independence, and she vowed his paper would remain independent. She would run it the way he would have, and Campbell was in full accord.

Campbell's files contain a number of letters from brokers asking whether *The Post* could be purchased. Of particular interest is one dated March 11, 1958, from Allen Kander of the firm of Allen Kander and Company with offices in New York and Washington. He wrote to Campbell expressing the interest of chain publisher Samuel I. Newhouse in buying *The Post*. The letter went on to say Newhouse had paid $18 million for a newspaper in Birmingham, Alabama, and indicated a comparable price might be paid for *The Post*. The letter also stated that if Newhouse were to buy the paper Campbell could expect to remain as its president and attorney. Before filing Kander's letter, Campbell attached the following notation to it:

> Showed this letter to Henry Meier and he assured me it was not
> necessary to call it to Helen Bonfils' attention and that her oft-ex-

Chain publisher Samuel I. Newhouse (right) wanted *The Post* in the worst way. He is shown here with Nelson Rockefeller. (Associated Press)

pressed determination not to sell her *Post* stock, which she owned individually or as a trustee, still remained. Accordingly, I am not answering the letter—it is just another one of those feelers on the part of newspaper brokers.—E.R.C.

Kander was a free-lance "finder" of newspapers and television and radio stations for sale. He had been Newhouse's broker in the purchase of a half-dozen papers beginning in 1939. Since he worked on a commission, Kander kept busy bird-dogging properties that Newhouse or other wealthy investors might be interested in. However, in a deposition taken in connection with a subsequent lawsuit, Newhouse revealed that he had become interested in *The Denver Post* "some years before" May Stanton decided to sell her stock. "I studied newspapers in the country," Newhouse said, "and I felt it [*The Post*] was a great newspaper, and I felt that I would like to own it if it was possible to buy it."

Newhouse had approached Helen Bonfils directly as early as 1959. He arranged an introduction through Leonard Lyons, the Broadway columnist, and called on Helen at her River House apartment in New York to tell her he wanted *The Post*. In his deposition Newhouse reported that he said to Helen: "Without having access to any figures and knowing anything about it [*The Post*] I would pay you at least twenty million for the paper, and if you will show me some figures I might be willing to pay you considerably more." He was talking about 100 percent of the stock which, of course, Helen did not have. She told him she would let him know, and a short time later Lyons relayed word to Newhouse that she wasn't selling.

Thus, when in the spring of 1960 Kander asked Newhouse whether he was interested in buying May Stanton's minority interest in *The Post,* he found a warm reception. Newhouse asked what price she had set. Kander said $240 per share for about 15 percent of the stock. Newhouse said he wouldn't quibble about paying the price.

Meanwhile May Stanton and her husband were also talking to other prospective buyers, among them a representative of the Knight chain (Miami *Herald,* Detroit *Free Press,* Philadelphia *Inquirer* and *Daily News,* Akron *Beacon Journal,* Charlotte *Observer* and *News,* etc.). But when Kander was able to assure the Stantons that his client was willing to meet their price, Newhouse was invited to come to Denver. At that time he owned more than a dozen newspapers (Long Island City [New York] *Star-Journal,* Birmingham, [Alabama] *News,* St. Louis *Globe-Democrat,* Jersey City *Journal* and Newark *Star-Ledger,* Syracuse *Herald-Journal* and *Post Standard,* Portland *Oregonian*) plus many nationally distributed magazines and his quota of television and radio stations.

Newhouse later said he went to Denver on May 27, 1960, to work out a sales agreement. At that point the Stantons were still uncertain about whether they wanted to sell to Newhouse. What had impressed May was Newhouse's record as a publisher. At newspapers he acquired the editor was retained and editorial policy left in his hands. However, Newhouse men took charge of the countinghouse. They supervised the advertising, circulation, and mechanical departments, slashed expenses, and almost invariably increased profits. May wanted to punish Hoyt, and she thought that Newhouse would force him to tighten up the business operations. But when she met Newhouse, she found another and less hardheaded reason to justify her decision. She took an immediate liking to Newhouse because he seemed to be of the same stamp as another man she admired and trusted, Harry Winston, the famous jeweler from whom she bought many of her diamonds. Both men are short and slight and she saw many similar mannerisms which reassured her. "Mr. Newhouse simply charmed her," Ed Stanton explains. (Among May's gems was the seventy-carat Idol's Eye, once part of the Turkish crown collection. After May's death the diamond was sold for $375,000, approximately half what she paid for it, according to Victor Argenzio, the Denver jeweler. It was worth considerably more, but there isn't much of a market for gems that large, he says.)

The Stantons were not sure what *Post* stock was worth as none had been sold since settlement of Mrs. Tammen's estate, and perhaps they were surprised that Newhouse would meet their suggested price so readily. In any event, the sales agreement they negotiated included a provision that if Newhouse bought additional *Post* stock at a higher price within the next two years, he would reimburse the Stantons for the difference. Newhouse also agreed he would not sell any of May's stock to any of the then stockholders while either she or Helen was living. May must have smiled a little over still another provision— meaningless except as it humiliated her sister: If and when Newhouse gained the majority of the stock, she would be named honorary chairman of the board.

In later years May said she had never expected Newhouse would try to seize control, but she was being naïve. From the beginning Newhouse had intended to control *The Post,* just as he had bought control of every newspaper in which he had invested. Purchase of the May Stanton block was only the opening wedge. He knew that at the $240 price he was willing to pay, dividends amount to only a bit more than 2 percent. In one of his depositions he testified: "At that time there were a group of trusts [which owned *Post* stock] . . . and because of the nature of the trusts, I had the feeling that sooner or later the trusts would want to increase the income that the trusts received, and that if a satisfactory offer were made, that they would be willing to sell it." On another occasion he said: *"The Denver Post* stock is not held by one individual, but held by many trusts who have a fiduciary relationship; eventually it is going to charity, and under the laws, as I understand them, a charitable trust must get the most income it can from its assets, it must distribute that income. And I felt, under these circumstances, that I would eventually be given an opportunity to bid on the stock."

In addition to approaching Helen Bonfils directly in 1959, Newhouse had his agents making overtures toward other owners of *Post* stock even before the transfer of May's shares was completed. On April 29, 1960, the records show, Keith Anderson, a Denver attorney working with Kander, wrote to the bank which following a merger was now called Denver U. S. National Bank, trustee for Children's Hospital: "On behalf of Mr. S. I. Newhouse and certain corporations controlled by him, we are authorized to offer $240 per share for stock in *The Denver Post."*

At this point another key personality enters the long list of characters in *The Post* story. He is a slim and dapper Southerner, Donald Ray Seawell by name, courtly in manner and polished in appearance. He was a New York attorney specializing in international and corporate law, but it was his interest in the theater that caused his path to cross that of Helen Bonfils. But to begin at the beginning, Seawell was born on Colorado Day—August 1—in 1912 to Justice A. A. F. and Bertha Smith Seawell at Stanford, North Carolina. This is only eight miles from E. Ray Campbell's birthplace, but since the two men were of different eras they did not meet until Seawell came to Denver. Don Seawell received his bachelor's degree from the University of North Carolina in 1933 and his law degree from the same school in 1936. He was admitted to the North Carolina bar and three years later went to work in Washington for the Securities and Exchange Commission that President Roosevelt was revamping. In 1941 he was married to Eugenia Rawls, a budding young actress whose career in subsequent years carried out the promise of her youth. When war came Seawell was commissioned as a counterintelligence officer on Gen. Dwight D. Eisenhower's staff.

After the war Seawell became a partner in the law firm of Bernstein, Seawell, Kaplan, and Block with offices in New York and London. Through his interest in the theater a number of Broadway figures became his clients—Alfred Lunt and Lynn Fontanne, Tallulah Bankhead, Noël Coward, Lindsay and Crouse, and many others. Through the Lunts Seawell became active as a producer. By the mid-Fifties he was a member of the board of the American National Theatre and Academy (ANTA). Another board member was Helen Bonfils, who together with her husband, George Somnes, was producing plays and musicals on Broadway, and they got to know each other casually.

Sometime after Somnes died, early in 1956, Helen Bonfils and her partner, Haila Stoddard, came to Seawell's office for legal help with a play they were planning to produce. "There were some problems connected with the show which I managed to solve," Seawell recalls, "and Helen took a very flattering view of the way it was done. The ladies came back to my office and one of them said, 'Look, we want you as a partner, not just as a lawyer.' "

Seawell explained he couldn't be both partner and lawyer because there might be a conflict of interest.

Miss Stoddard said, "Well, we want you as a partner, and let somebody else handle the legal work."

Almost immediately Helen said, "But I need you as a lawyer, too, to handle other matters."

She went on to explain that Campbell had been advising her in a very faithful way, but he was growing older and she felt she needed help with her personal affairs.

One of the matters Seawell helped her with was her will. Helen Bonfils and Hoyt had been studying plans for eventual employee-ownership of the paper, something she favored because she was without children and felt the employees who had made *The Post* great and prosperous ought to share in its prosperity. In any event, she was determined to leave *The Post* in local hands when she passed on.

Helen, Haila Stoddard, and Seawell set up a corporation called Bonard Productions which produced several shows on Broadway and in London. Later, Helen and Seawell formed a partnership known as Bonfils-Seawell Enterprises, which produced a dozen or so shows starting with *A Thurber Carnival* in 1960. Seawell also found himself becoming more and more involved in Helen's *Post* matters. In 1958 he came to Denver to work with a local firm on details of the Employees Stock Trust, a device to enable employees to buy shares in the paper.

Seawell was in London early in 1959, setting up a production for Bonfils-Seawell Enterprises, when he received an urgent telephone

Seawell (left) and Miss Bonfils (right) produced the first U. S. tour of the Royal Shakespeare Company in 1964. With them are guests Lynda Bird Johnson, Defense Secretary Robert McNamara, Mrs. Lyndon Johnson, and Mrs. McNamara. (Associated Press)

call from Helen in New York. As Seawell got the story, Newhouse had called on her and asked her to set a price for *The Post*. When Helen told him the paper was not for sale under any circumstances he insisted that everything had its price and urged her to name a figure. Because he seemed so determined, Helen urged Seawell to hurry back to New York to make it clear to Newhouse she had no intention of selling, ever. Seawell rushed home as fast as he could and had several meetings with Kander. Then he made some discreet inquiries of his own and discovered Helen had reason for concern. Newhouse was said to have $500 million available for newspaper acquisitions and had been heard to declare he was prepared to spend it all if necessary to get *The Post*. *The Post,* he reportedly had said, was to be the "crowning jewel" of his diadem of newspapers.

Kander tossed out some figures and a quick mental calculation indicated to Seawell that Helen could get as much as $50 million for *The Post* shares she owned or controlled at the time. In addition, Seawell understood that Newhouse wanted Helen to remain as chairman of *The Post*'s board as long as she lived, while Seawell could make himself two million dollars and have a lifetime position on the paper if he could deliver controlling interest.

Helen scorned the proposal. She didn't need money and Papa's paper was the most important thing in her life. The theater was important to her. So were the church and her charities. But at this state in her life the newspaper had become her primary concern and she was determined to keep it independent. Thereafter she leaned increasingly on Seawell. "Before I knew it," says Seawell, "I had the job of saving *The Post* from Newhouse."

Helen told Hoyt that she wished him to consult with Seawell on any major decision affecting the paper. Seawell attended the annual stockholders' meeting in 1959 and every directors' meeting when important matters were to be discussed. "Ep was good about briefing me on everything," Seawell says. "He would be on the phone to me almost every day. Soon I was completely familiar with everything going on at *The Post* even though I was in New York most of the time."

At no time in Seawell's conversations with Newhouse's representatives was it indicated that May Bonfils had agreed to sell her *Post* stock. However, the persistence with which Kander pressed Seawell made it almost certain that if Newhouse had not approached other stockholders, he soon would. Even so, Helen and those around her

Donald R. Seawell, now president and chairman of the board of *The Post*, first caught Helen Bonfils' eye with his legal skill, got the job of holding Newhouse at bay. (Bill Johnson)

were astounded when they learned that May had indeed sold her stock.

The news reached her in a curious, roundabout manner. Hoyt and Buxton were in New York in April of 1960 for the annual meeting of the American Newspaper Publishers Association, a clambake and brain-picking session for members of the top echelon of the newspaper hierarchy. Buxton and some friends were on the way back to their hotel one night from a performance of *The Sound of Music* when they ran across another West Coast friend who was in a somewhat befuddled condition as the result of a convivial party. Buxton volunteered to escort him back to his hotel. En route they stopped at one of the posh watering places on Lexington Avenue for a nightcap. They were at the bar when Buxton felt a tap on his shoulder. It was an attorney for one of the larger newspaper chains. "I hear Newhouse owns a piece of your newspaper now," he said.

"What do you mean?" Buxton demanded.

"Don't you know? I get the word one of the Bonfils sisters sold her stock to him."

Buxton quickly invited the man to sit down, ordered another round of drinks, and proceeded to pump him for information. The attorney didn't have a great deal, but his grasp of details convinced Buxton he knew what he was talking about. Hurriedly Buxton got in touch with Hoyt, who was staying at the Park Lane Hotel. Hoyt called Helen Bonfils at her New York apartment and she in turn telephoned Seawell. Next morning Buxton was aboard a plane back to Denver. He had a lot of conferring to do with Campbell about ways to block Newhouse from gaining any more *Post* stock.

Helen was furious. "How could May do this?" she demanded. Then: "I might have known. She is being vengeful."

In reality, Buxton's information was somewhat premature. May might have made up her mind to sell, but the sale agreement wasn't signed until May 27, 1960. The sale was closed on June 9. May sold all but ten of the 14,734 shares she owned or had held in trust for her. The price, at $240 per share, was $3,533,765.13.

(In 1954 The Post Printing and Publishing Company was merged with the Continental Investment Company. Post Printing and Publishing was the corporation that operated the newspaper. Continental Investment had been the newspaper's property-holding arm and its stockholders were the same as the stockholders in Post Printing and Publishing, owning shares in virtually the same proportion as their holdings in the parent corporation. The new, combined corporation is called The Denver Post, Inc. To accomplish the merger, the 3,108 shares of Continental Investment and 5,000 shares of Post Printing and Publishing were recalled and 94,015 shares of stock in The Denver Post, Inc., issued in exchange. This accounts for the fact that May owned 14,734 shares instead of the much smaller number mentioned in earlier chapters. However, the percentage of her holdings—15.67 percent of the shares outstanding—had not changed, nor had it changed for other stockholders. At the rate of $240 per share, which Newhouse paid, *The Post* was worth more than $22.5 million.)

May once wrote that "Newhouse cannot gain control of *The Post*." She was right, but she had no inkling of the single-mindedness with which he would pursue his goal, nor of the cost in time, money, and energy her father's newspaper would have to expend to maintain its independence. She was to know nothing of all this, for she died in March of 1962, long before the seed she had planted with her sale blossomed into two bitter, debilitating lawsuits. May Bonfils Stanton was buried in a bronze-lined mausoleum of Carrara marble, of Tudor-Gothic architecture, as she had directed in her will. The will also specified that the crypt was to cost not less than $50,000 and not more than $75,000. When Helen was notified of her sister's death, she also was in a hospital for treatment of various ailments including diabetes, phlebitis, and a weakened heart. Without a change of expression on her proud, patrician face, she replied, "There has been nothing between us for a long time." She did not attend the funeral.

May left one-half of her estate, including the magnificent Belmar home, to her husband. Stanton out of courtesy invited Seawell to tour the home. Seawell thought it prudent to check with Helen before he accepted. Her response revealed the woman in her. "Yes, you'd better go," she said, "and come back and tell me what it was like." On another occasion she asked Seawell to find out what was being offered in the sale of May's jewelry. But aside from these instances she never mentioned her sister.

Some years later Stanton donated the home to the Roman Catholic Archdiocese of Denver to be used for church-related purposes. But without funds to maintain it, the mansion deteriorated and eventually it was torn down. A huge shopping center was built on some of May's property. A portion of Belmar was bought by the city of Lakewood for a park, and much of the rest of it is being developed commercially and for housing. The land is held by the Bonfils-Stanton Trust with a large number of public service organizations as beneficiaries. Recently the real estate and other assets in the trust were valued at thirty million dollars.

In life, May had contributed liberally to Loretto Heights College, to a Catholic chapel at the Air Force Academy, to establish an ophthalmology clinic at the University of Colorado Medical Center, and to many other charities. After her bequests to Stanton, some of her liquid assets were put into a trust for the benefit of the Order of Friars Minor of the Province of the Most Holy Name. Stanton also inherited the ten remaining shares of *Post* stock.

On the morning of June 9, 1960, two related meetings were held in different parts of Denver. At one, before a battery of attorneys, the sale of May Bonfils Stanton's stock in *The Denver Post* to S. I. Newhouse was completed. The other, which had been scheduled several weeks earlier, was the annual meeting of *Post* stockholders. Campbell announced that Newhouse was now a minority stockholder in the newspaper, and for publication he stated: "Control of *The Denver Post* remains unchanged and this newspaper will continue to be operated in the interests of Denver and Colorado and the Rocky Mountain Empire."

Newhouse lost no time in seeking to enlarge his holdings. After completing his business with May Bonfils Stanton, he was escorted by attorney Keith Anderson to a lunch with officers of the Denver U. S. National Bank. There, with his eye on the Children's Hospital holdings, Newhouse announced he would be interested in buying all the *Post* stock held by the bank's trust department.

After lunch Newhouse called on Campbell, who asked Hoyt and Buxton to join them. The meeting was brief, cool, but proper. Newhouse asked to see the plant and Buxton took him on a tour. It was the first and only time Newhouse set foot in *The Post*.

(In one of his depositions, Newhouse said he could not remember whether he stayed overnight in Denver after closing the deal. He was asked, "Why would you not have stayed overnight in Denver after you made this three-and-a-half-million-dollar purchase?" Newhouse replied, "A three-and-a-half-million-dollar purchase was not a very significant one. I didn't stay overnight if I didn't have to." In 1962 he paid $42,700,000 for 99 percent of the stock in the New Orleans *Times-Picayune*.)

Newhouse's arrival was a dark cloud on an otherwise brightening horizon. Hoyt had reported at the annual meeting that net earnings were the best in ten years and that *The Post*'s daily circulation within the city zone (170,000) was greater than the total circulation of the rival *Rocky Mountain News* (165,000). Hoyt also noted that as an indication of *The Post*'s growing prestige and stature, it had been ranked seventeenth in one survey of the nation's top newspapers, and twelfth in another.

The sale of May Stanton's stock did not go unnoticed at Children's Hospital and in the home of Helen Crabbs Rippey, beneficiary to 18.8 percent of *Post* stock under Agnes Tammen's will. Over the years one in every five dollars of *The Post*'s dividends had gone to support the hospital, and almost as large a share had been paid to the Rippey family. Income of this kind was very easy to become accustomed to. But lately the hospital board and the Rippeys, like May Stanton, had viewed the drop-off in dividends with growing concern. Despite the high sentimental value attached to Tammen's blessed memory, some members of the hospital board suggested the trustees should explore the possibility of replacing *Post* stock with more productive investments. If Newhouse would pay $240 per share for the 19,754 shares in the Tammen trust, the hospital would realize nearly $4,700,000 to be reinvested in more profitable securities! Mrs. Rippey also was urging Campbell, as principal trustee for Mrs. Tammen's estate, to sell the *Post* stock. She had met several times with her attorney to discuss the wisdom of filing a lawsuit to force Campbell to sell. But she was reluctant to sue, and finally decided to hold off when higher dividends were indicated.

Considerable correspondence about this matter flowed during this period between Keith Anderson and Charles Goldman, Newhouse's attorney in New York. In one letter Anderson reported Mrs. Rippey's attorney might sue to force Campbell's resignation as trustee and require the trust to sell the stock at the best possible price. Goldman wrote back to suggest a court-supervised auction of the stock. Anderson replied, "I talked over your suggestions with Mrs. Rippey's attorney this morning. He rather likes the idea of a court-supervised auction. . . ."

While Mrs. Rippey was getting gratuitous coaching from the sidelines, Campbell adamantly refused to sell for two reasons. He regarded *Post* stock as a sound investment which soon would return to paying good dividends. He also believed it was incumbent on him as a trustee, and as president of the corporation, to protect *The Post* as a viable, income-producing organization, and the best way to do that would be to make sure that neither Newhouse nor any other outsider seized control.

But keeping Newhouse at bay would not be easy. If he succeeded in getting the hospital stock his holdings would rise to 36.4 percent. And if he bought the Rippey stock, he would have control of the paper with 54.7 percent!

This possibility was only too apparent to directors of *The Post.* In an effort to block Newhouse, they agreed to offer the Denver U. S. National Bank $245 per share for the Children's Hospital block. The offer was communicated on July 5, less than a month after May's sale to Newhouse. That same day the bank's executive committee rejected the bid and countered with a price of $260 per share. The committee also notified Keith Anderson that he had an hour and a half to submit a new offer on behalf of Newhouse improving on the $240 submitted April 29.

Campbell did not hesitate to agree on the $260 price. When the deadline passed and nothing was heard from Anderson, Campbell and Cris Dobbins, representing the bank, shook hands on a deal involving more than five million dollars. Two days later Campbell, Helen Bonfils, and Hoyt convened a special directors' meeting. The minutes carry this succinct report:

> Mr. Hoyt summarized the numerous advantages accruing to The Denver Post, Inc. and its stockholders, which would result from the acquirement by *The Post* itself of any stock of the Com-

pany coming on the market, and particularly the 19,573.6475 shares of The Denver Post, Inc., now held by the Denver United States National Bank, Trustees for the Children's Hospital Association. He urged strongly that *The Post* itself buy this stock at the best possible price obtainable from the Denver United States National Bank, in order to guarantee the continued local ownership of *The Denver Post,* which would not only be, in the long run, for the best interests of the present stockholders but, likewise, for the future best interests of Denver and the people in the area of *The Post's* circulation.

Helen G. Bonfils expressed the desire and determination to have *The Post* remain locally owned, as it was and dedicated to the best interests of Denver, Colorado and the Rocky Mountain area which it serves.

Ray Campbell expressed concurrence with the views of both Palmer Hoyt and Helen G. Bonfils.

The three thereupon formally agreed to pay the bank $260 per share for all the stock in the Tammen trust, a total purchase price of $5,089,148.35. The news reached Newhouse almost immediately. Charles Goldman dictated the following memorandum, dated July 7, 1960, to his employer:

> I had a telephone talk with Keith Anderson and Struve Hensel today over the telephone. The bank has declined to give them any information except to tell them in general terms that they are selling stock to *The Denver Post* but refused information as to price or any other details.
>
> The attorneys have the view that probably no deal has been consummated. They also have a feeling that Campbell intends to set up some sort of pension trust for the employees and to buy these shares for the pension trust, and in the meantime to secure financing through the guaranty of Helen Bonfils.
>
> Keith Anderson advises that his firm cannot inject themselves in the situation insofar as it involves the bank. They have therefore suggested the name of an attorney . . . through whom they will act and will make formal demand concerning the business of *The Post* and a specific demand concerning the proposed purchase of the stock. Also they propose to contact the trustees of the Children's Hospital and try to get them to intervene with the Bank on the ground that they are not getting the best price.
>
> They urged that an offer be made even if it is based on the condition of an examination of the facts and securing information in any way that you want it, and they think that this offer should designate a price. As I understand it, in effect they want you to say that you will pay so many dollars in the event that the information you get as a result of your inquiry, within a limited time, will support that price in your opinion, but that you will not do any bargaining.

At the bottom of the typed memo the following was written in Goldman's hand: "Phoned S. I. [Newhouse] at St. Louis. He won't bid for the stock or try to stymie purchase by Campbell; doesn't wish to take hostile attitude; believes his bid will merely increase price C. will have to pay. Bank wants to deal with C.—not S. I. I reported to A. K. [Allen Kander] in Washington."

Later, Newhouse explained he had three reasons for not pursuing the matter. He didn't want to make a bid until he had detailed information about *The Post*'s financial health. He didn't want to set a price unless he knew it would be accepted, that is, he didn't want the bank to go to Campbell with Newhouse's offer and let Campbell buy it for a slightly higher price. And finally, he understood *The Post* was strapped for funds because of building expansion, that buying the stock was "a very unwise investment" in view of the paper's cash position, and "as a minority stockholder I won't increase the price."

The Post paid one million dollars in cash and signed notes for the balance together with an agreement to limit its spending and dividends until the debt was paid off. Keith Anderson was right about what *The Post* intended to do with the stock. The purchase was the first step toward making stock ownership available to employees. The stock from the Children's Hospital Trust would be returned to *The Post*'s treasury until a plan could be drawn up for its resale, and this provision was carefully written into the bank's sales agreement.

There was much rejoicing in *The Post*'s boardroom, for it appeared that Newhouse had effectively been blocked off with only his 15 percent. Now, all the rest of the stock was owned by Helen outright, or was held in trusts and foundations controlled by Helen and Campbell, and they were united in their determination to keep ownership of the paper in Denver. But time was to bring disastrous changes. An unusual notarized affidavit in *The Post*'s minute books a year later, signed by Helen, Campbell, and Hoyt, indicates they were aware that something still could go awry. It reads:

> The undersigned, each being first duly sworn on oath, depose and say:
> At the conclusion of the ordinary business of the stockholders at their meeting held July 14, 1961, but before they dispersed, Mr. Keith Anderson, proxy-holder of The Post Standard Company, owned and controlled by Mr. S. I. Newhouse, stated to the stockholders and officers of The Denver Post, Inc.:
> "I recently called on Mr. Newhouse in New York, having gone there on other business. Mr. Newhouse asked me to convey to *The Denver Post* stockholders that he, Mr. Newhouse, has the highest

respect for *The Denver Post* and its management; that he bought his *Denver Post* stock as an investment." Continuing, Mr. Anderson stated that Mr. Newhouse "has no intention of regarding his purchase of *Denver Post* stock as other than an investment and desired to make this point clear to *The Post* board and management."

Mr. Newhouse, according to Mr. Anderson, "considers *The Denver Post* a good newspaper operation and would be glad to be of assistance if called on. Mr. Newhouse said, however, that he would not offer his services unless requested." Mr. Newhouse, according to Mr. Anderson, "felt that there had been some misapprehension about his [Newhouse's] purposes in buying the May Bonfils Stanton stock in *The Denver Post*."

This position was so different from what the directors knew, or thought they knew, about Newhouse's intentions that they felt it wise to note it for the record. If indeed Newhouse had changed his position, it soon would be changed again, for there is nothing to indicate that he ever abandoned his determination to control *The Post*.

SAVE THE HORSE

Perhaps it was inevitable that a newspaper involved in getting the U. S. government to recognize Save the Horse Week should discover and become the chief publicists for Elijah.

The story begins with Harry Galbraith, sometime reporter and impoverished pulp-fiction writer. In Galbraith's declining years sympathetic police officers in Colorado Springs permitted him to use the back seat of any convenient patrol car in the police garage as his bedroom.

Harry had a singular passion, and that was to honor the horse, which had played such a large part in the development of the West. Now that horses seemed to be destined for extinction in the face of onrushing mechanization, Galbraith spent a large part of his meager income writing to all and sundry advocating a Save the Horse Week.

Most recipients of his pleas ignored them. Red Fenwick of *The Post* did not. Fenwick encouraged Galbraith and even mentioned his crusade on occasion in his "Ridin' the Range" column.

The U. S. Department of Commerce in those days published a list of various days, weeks, and months designated for special or commercial observances. Galbraith despaired of ever getting the bureaucrats to recognize his cause. Then, one year, with Fenwick's encouragement, Galbraith sent a telegram to the secretary of commerce demanding to know why Save the Horse Week was not on his official list. Pretty soon Galbraith received an acknowledgment together with some forms to complete. The next year, 1952, the second full week of October appeared on the calendar as Save the Horse Week. Alas, Galbraith did not live to see his triumph. Some days earlier he had been found dead in his bed in the back of a patrol car.

Galbraith had named Fenwick as a cosponsor of the Save the Horse week and he was so listed. Soon Red was getting hundreds of letters from horse lovers around the country. He carried on a lively correspondence with them about the virtues of horses until he tired of it all.

The story now shifts to George McWilliams, for many years a pillar of *The Post*'s rewrite bank. He was a crackerjack newspaperman but enjoyed deprecating his talents by remarking, "I'm not a writer, but I'm as good as anybody in the business in reporting 'John Jones, age fifty-five, was struck and killed by a truck at the corner of Fifth and Main today.' " One day early in 1956 he heard a strange story from a friend in the Colorado Air National Guard. A couple of small-plane pilots in the town of Gunnison, Colorado, had sighted a horse high on a desolate ridge between 14,420-foot Mount Harvard and 14,196-foot Mount Yale in Colorado's Collegiate Range. High winds kept the ridge clear of snow, but massive drifts apparently prevented the horse from descending to more hospitable areas. To keep the horse from starving, the pilots, Wallace Powell and Gordon (Rocky) Warren, were dropping bales of hay on the ridge several times a week.

McWilliams telephoned Warren, who verified the information and provided additional details. "Incidentally," McWilliams said as he wound up the call, "have you a name for the horse?"

"No," Warren replied. "I guess every horse is entitled to a name. If you can think of a good one you're welcome to tag it on him."

McWilliams turned to a fellow reporter and asked, "Who was that fellow in the Bible who was fed by ravens?"

"Elijah," the reporter replied.

McWilliams hammered out a delightful feature story about Elijah, the hermit horse, who was being kept alive by a couple of winged, latter-day Samaritans.

Newspapers all over the world picked up the Elijah story. Children mailed in nickels and dimes to buy hay for the horse. Television cameramen hired Warren and Powell to fly them over the ridge.

In Colorado Springs Bill and Al Turner saw the pictures and thought they recognized the horse as theirs. The Turners were guides for trips into the high country and the horse, which they called Bugs, was one of two pack animals that had escaped the previous fall from a mountain pasture.

"If Elijah is Bugs," the Turners wrote, "he has quite a history. He hates parked cars and women in skirts, which would certainly be motive enough for heading for the high country."

The Post then published a straight-faced editorial suggesting that

Elijah, after his rescue. (Dean Conger)

the attention focused on the hermit horse was "a hideous invasion of privacy." The editorial went on to say: "If Elijah is an unclaimed nag of uncertain history, then rescue efforts must continue. But if Elijah is really Bugs, leave him alone. He's using his good horse sense in seeking solitude away from a noxious civilization."

When at last spring reduced the snowdrifts sufficiently McWilliams joined the Turners in a rescue expedition. The horse was indeed Bugs and he was escorted down to a gala homecoming in Buena Vista, population 783. The high-school band led a parade down the Main Street and Elijah/Bugs rode in a trailer. Later he was brought to Denver, displayed in the lobby of the Brown Palace Hotel, and introduced along with the thoroughbreds at the Centennial Race Track. Elijah was adopted as the moscot of the Colorado Dude Ranchers Association and today a plaque bearing his likeness hangs in the National Cowboy Hall of Fame in Oklahoma City.

McWilliams died of cancer in 1959. The Denver Newspaper Guild perpetuates his memory with an annual George McWilliams Award for Outstanding News Reporting.

21

AN EQUAL OPPORTUNITY EMPLOYER

Despite the old *Post*'s racist policies, it became one of the earlier "equal opportunity" employers among newspapers. Soon after his arrival Ep Hoyt opened the editorial page to local Black and Hispano columnists who had something to say. Meanwhile he was searching for able men from minority backgrounds to add to the staff. They were hard to find, of course, because few had been given an opportunity to gain newspaper experience. The stories of two who joined *The Post* deserve special mention.

George L. Brown, with a brand-new diploma from the University of Kansas journalism school, in June of 1950 sent a job application to *The Post*. He had a good education and a certain maturity to offset his lack of experience. Commissioned in the Air Corps in the waning days of World War II, he had flown patrol missions in Europe just before the German surrender. *The Post* invited Brown to Denver for an interview.

The first impression Brown got of *The Post* was less than reassuring. When the receptionist saw his black face, she refused to let him in the second-floor city room despite his protestations that he had been asked to come in for a job interview. The janitors were being hired downstairs, she told him brusquely. Brown displayed reportorial ingenuity. He returned to the lobby and joined a group of visitors just beginning an escorted tour of the building, peeling off when the party reached managing editor Ed Dooley's desk. Brown was hired as *The Post*'s first Black reporter and was promptly accepted without question by the rest of the staff as just another cub. With the public, the fact that he represented *The Denver Post* was credentials enough to overcome the surprise of seeing a Negro. In fact, Brown was embarrassed on many occasions after he became better known when people asked that he be assigned to cover specific stories.

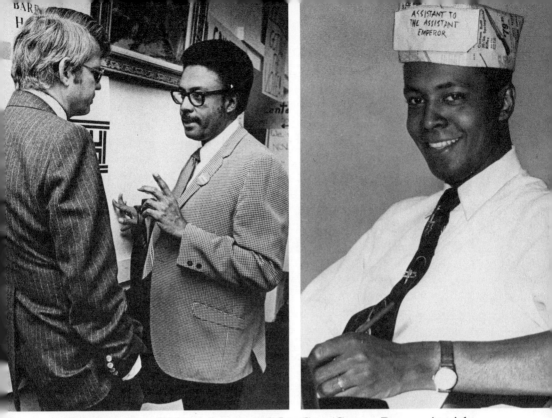

Colorado Gov. Richard Lamm and Lt. Gov. George Brown. At right,
Brown as a cub reporter. (Duane Howell, left photo; Claude R. Powe,
right photo)

Brown was born in Lawrence, Kansas. His father had been an
insurance salesman until the business was wiped out by the Depression. After that he eked out a living as a small farmer, doing odd
jobs, running a restaurant and finally working as maintenance foreman at the University of Kansas.

George Brown soon found that a beginning newspaperman's salary
was hardly adequate for the good life. He and another ambitious
young reporter, Leonard Larsen—the author of the Luther-Burbank-
of-the-barnyard story—moonlighted together as cabdrivers and
clerks in Harry Hoffman's huge liquor store to supplement their
incomes.

About a month after Brown joined *The Post* he received a telephone call from May Bonfils, who asked him to drop by her home.
Brown had only a vague idea about May's connection with the paper
and no knowledge at all about her strained relationship with her
sister. When he showed up May said she would like to offer him
a job.

"Doing what?" Brown asked.

"Oh, I'm not quite sure," she replied, "but we'll find something for you to do. The pay will be a lot better than what you're getting at *The Post.*"

Confused, Brown said he'd think about it and let her know.

Brown and his wife were living in a two-room, third-floor flat and sharing the kitchen and bathroom with the people downstairs. He was walking to work to save carfare and periodically pawning one of his two electric razors for spending money. May Bonfils' mysterious offer, whatever it was, was tempting, but he telephoned her a few days later to say he had decided to stay with journalism, for better or for worse. Then, because he could not understand what May's motives were, he told no one about the incident until recently.

Brown's ambition and ability did not remain unnoticed outside the city room. In June of 1955 he was appointed to fill a Democratic vacancy in the state House of Representatives which he accepted with *The Post*'s blessings. The next year he decided to run for the state Senate. It was an at-large seat and there was considerable doubt among political observers that a Black, and a relatively inexperienced and impoverished one at that, could be elected. By that time Brown had been advanced to *The Post*'s rewrite desk. The rewrite men were relaxing late one afternoon when Brown told them of his decision to run. His friend Thor Severson, who sat across from Brown, slipped a sheet of paper into his typewriter and drafted a press release for Brown announcing his candidacy. Severson went on to become an executive of the Bee chain of newspapers in California.

Brown's election in the 1956 race made him the first Black state senator in Colorado history. He was reelected in 1960, 1964, 1968, and 1972. During his first term Brown took a leave of absence from the paper without pay while the legislature was in session but found it was impossible to get along on the lawmaker's then salary of fifty dollars per month. Hoyt authorized him to work nights at *The Post* while sitting in the legislature during the day.

"At no time did Mr. Hoyt, or anyone else at the paper, say anything to try to influence my vote," Brown declares. "As it was, we weren't on different sides very often. I had the good fortune of working for a newspaper whose philosophy agreed on most issues with mine."

(What a contrast this makes to an unsigned column published in *The Post* of December 6, 1912, under a photograph of Jack Johnson, the controversial Black heavyweight champion, and his White bride, Lucile Cameron. Said *The Post:* "The above is a photograph of the culminating outrage of the Twentieth Century. It marks the wreck of our boasted civilization. One look at it brings the blush of shame to the cheek of every right-thinking American. Is there any other country under the sun that boasts of its civilization that would permit such an affair to take place? The thoughts that go surging through your brain as you glance at it make you want to shout out at the top of your voice against the outrage."

(The column went on in similar vein for some length, calling Johnson "this demon," "unthinkable brute," "this monster," and "this fiend." *The Post* pledged "never again to mention Jack Johnson or any of his doings," and explained it was publishing the photograph "believing that it will so arouse the people that such a crime can never happen again."

(In view of the popular hostility of those times against any Black who refused to be kept "in his place," *The Post*'s tirade probably was not exceptionally vicious.)

Brown was *The Post*'s night city editor in 1957, when Arkansas's Gov. Orval Faubus defied federal integration laws and ordered National Guardsmen to bar nine Black students from Central High School in Little Rock. *The Post* took a vigorous pro-integration stand, which resulted in many angry telephone calls to the editors. As night city editor it was Brown's responsibility to listen to these complaints and placate the callers as much as possible. One night, as Brown listened patiently, a particularly bitter woman ended her tirade with the classic racist question: "How would you like to have your daughter marry one of them?" Brown's gentle reply is well remembered around *The Post*. "She probably will," he said. And Brown's daughter Gail did indeed.

Six years later, when Martin Luther King chose Birmingham, Alabama, for a massive confrontation with Southern racial bigotry, *The Post* sent a two-man team to cover the story. One was Brown. The other was a Mississippi-born White man, John Rogers, who in time was to become *The Post*'s managing editor. The two flew to Birmingham together, but they quickly realized the temper of the city when a White cabdriver at the airport refused to let the two of them ride together. Brown found a motel room on the Black side of the line the confrontation had drawn through the city and Rogers checked into a hotel on the White side. Each covered his half of the front, pretending not to know the other. At day's end Brown would find a way to reach Rogers and feed him information, which was relayed to Denver. They produced a memorable eye-witness account of the rioting and the violence that was wreaked by firemen with hoses and Police Commissioner Eugene (Bull) Connor with his dogs. On their return to Denver Rogers and Brown collaborated on a penetrating series titled "Whirlwind Over Alabama." For the series, and for their on-the-spot coverage, Brown and Rogers were awarded certificates of recognition from the National Conference of Christians and Jews.

(Rogers, who at the time was considered *The Post*'s resident expert on Southern bigotry, also covered James Meredith's effort to enter the University of Mississippi at Oxford. Melting easily into the local scene, Rogers trotted over the Ole Miss campus with Gen. Edwin Walker and the red-necked mob challenging the majesty of the U. S. government, picking up quotations as quickly as they issued from the general's mouth. Later, when Walker sued newspapers which had published an Associated Press account of the night's events, Rogers became the defense's primary witness verifying the accuracy of the story. The suit was never brought to trial.)

In 1965 Brown left *The Post* to become assistant director of the Denver Housing Authority. In 1974 the Democrats nominated a young liberal, Richard D. Lamm, for governor and Brown as his running mate. Some predicted Brown would prove a millstone around Lamm's neck, but the team was swept into office in the Democratic landslide. On a technicality—polls in Colorado close an hour earlier than in California due to the difference in time zones—Brown became the first Negro in history to be elected lieutenant governor. The second, by one hour, was California's Mervyn Dymally, a native of Trinidad. (During Reconstruction days after the Civil War, South Carolina and Louisiana had appointed Black lieutenant governors and another Black, P. B. S. Pinchback, served as the appointed governor of Louisiana for forty-three days in 1872.)

"My years at *The Post* taught me something most politicians never learn," says Brown. "A reporter has to let others talk in order to get his story. As a reporter I learned to listen."

That Larry Tajiri came to *The Post* was one of the newspaper's happier accidents. California-born of Japanese immigrant parents, Tajiri had been working in the New York bureau of the Asahi newspapers of Japan when war broke out in 1941. The U. S. government closed the bureau and Tajiri drifted back to the West Coast in search of work. He spent the war years as editor of the *Pacific Citizen*, a weekly newspaper published by the Japanese American Citizens League out of Salt Lake City. The *Pacific Citizen* of that time is still held up as a shining example of militant and competent journalism by a minority group. In 1952, with many of the League's battles won, Tajiri left the *Pacific Citizen* hoping to hook up with *The Post*. Unfortunately, *The Post* was still reeling under the downhold of 1951. Tajiri then went to Colorado Springs to function simultaneously as sports editor, news editor, and editorial writer under Ed Hoyt at the struggling *Free Press*. Every few weeks he would drive the seventy miles to Denver to ask Ed Dooley whether the situation had changed, and each time Dooley would assure Tajiri that he would be the first man they'd hire when there was an opening.

Ed Hoyt was hardly able to pay a living wage, there was one staff reduction after another, and it appeared his tenure as publisher was limited. Tajiri couldn't wait forever for a job at *The Post*. He sent out some application letters and finally received a favorable response from a newspaper in Washington, D.C. In June of 1953 he drove to Denver one last time to thank Dooley for his consideration and report he was leaving for Washington. Dooley was a taciturn sort rarely given to speaking unless spoken to. On this occasion, before Tajiri could open his mouth, Dooley declared, "Larry, I can't keep you on the hook any longer. You can come to work Monday if you're still interested." Tajiri quickly turned down the Washington job and moved to Denver. Three weeks later the Washington newspaper went out of business.

Tajiri, a chunky pipe smoker whose thick glasses gave him an owlish look, started on *The Post* as a copyreader. Soon it became evident that the job of sharpening the writing of others and composing headlines was not utilizing his talents fully. He had a remarkable memory where he filed away obscure and interesting facts and knew sports so well that sportswriters learned to ask him about details of long-ago events. Tajiri also had such a fine grasp of national and international issues that he would have made an excellent editor of the editorial page. What's more, he was an inveterate moviegoer and a perceptive critic of the drama.

When Dooley resigned in 1956 to start his own business news weekly in San Francisco—which unfortunately foundered on financial shoals before long—Hoyt surprised everyone by naming thirty-year-old Mort Stern as managing editor. Not long earlier Stern had returned to the paper after a year of study as a Nieman Fellow at Harvard and was working as an assistant on the regional news desk. It was Hoyt's style to toss new responsibilities at his men with only the briefest of briefings; they were expected to know what the boss

Larry Tajiri, the widely
respected *Post* drama critic.
(Bill Johnson)

wanted done and how to do it. One of Stern's first challenges was to
come up with a competent editor of the entertainment section, a
particularly sensitive position because of Helen Bonfils' interest in
the theater.

Stern made some inquiries and finally tapped Tajiri for the assignment. After that he had to convince Hoyt that Tajiri could get the
job done. When Hoyt relayed news of the appointment to Helen, her
response was: "Larry who?"

A few days later Tajiri encountered his severest test, an opening
at the Bonfils Theatre, a community playhouse that Helen had built.
She read Tajiri's review and remarked, "Whoever he is, he's good."
After that she insisted that he be on hand for her Broadway openings
and he reviewed them with characteristic honesty. Until then *The
Post* had depended largely on wire-service and New York *Times*
syndicate reviews. Tajiri brought an impressive fund of expertise to
his section and his chatty, newsy "The Spectator" column, as well as
his signed reviews, attracted a large and loyal following.

"Larry had a fantastic way of pulling rabbits out of unlikely hats,"
Stern recalled recently. "Picking him for drama editor was one of
the luckiest decisions I ever made."

Tajiri was a nationally respected drama critic when he died at age
fifty following a stroke in 1965. It is a measure of the esteem in
which he was held that friends organized the Larry Tajiri Memorial
Foundation to recognize outstanding work in community theater in

The Post's circulation area. Bronze statuettes, called Larrys, were designed by Tajiri's brother Shinkichi, a sculptor living in Holland, and these are presented annually at a glittering awards dinner.

Both Brown and Tajiri made significant contribution to *The Post*'s stature as a newspaper. But it is also important to note that years before opportunities for minorities became a national concern, *The Post* gave them the chance to demonstrate their abilities outside the limited confines of ethnic ghettos.

Vignette

THE SCIENTIFIC POET

The Russians put *Sputnik 1* into orbit around Earth on October 4, 1957. This 184-pound sphere, the first man-made satellite, circled the globe every ninety minutes, winking in the early-night sky to herald the birth of a new era in science.

There was enormous public interest in *Sputnik*. The wire services filed reams of material but for *Denver Post* readers the clearest, most satisfying stories were coming from the typewriter of a lean, lank-haired *Post* reporter named Gene Lindberg. From the drawers of his desk Lindberg resurrected stacks of clippings from scientific journals which he used as references for his lucid explanation of what had happened.

Lindberg had performed with similar competence on a memorable occasion a dozen years earlier. On hearing a radio news flash that the U.S. had dropped something called an atomic bomb on Hiroshima, Lindberg rushed to the office. Others were confused but Lindberg knew exactly what had happened. He had read about nuclear fission in an article titled "The Atom Gives Up" by William Laurence in the *Saturday Evening Post* back in 1940. That story had told much more about harnessing nuclear energy than the U. S. government wanted known, once the effort got under way, but a copy was in Lindberg's desk. He went directly to it. The news flash also helped to make other things clear. Lindberg had heard rumors that something very big and hush-hush was going on at Los Alamos, New Mexico, at the University of Chicago, and at a place called Hanford in southeastern Washington. Now he realized all were part of the attempt to unlock the secret of atomic energy. The story he wrote for *The Post* was probably the most complete explanation of the atomic bomb published that day outside of the New York *Times*.

Lindberg had become a newspaperman only because trouble with his eyes had frustrated his hopes of becoming an electrical engineer. He attended the University of Colorado and joined the staff of *The Silver and Gold,* the student weekly. In the spring of 1920, in connection with the initiation rites of a journalism honorary fraternity, the staff put out a "scandal" issue lampooning the faculty, administration, and students. Although mild by contemporary standards, the issue horrified certain administrators who feared it would jeopardize state appropriations for university expansion. Fourteen students were suspended. Ten of them were reinstated quickly. Suspension of the other four was made effective for one year. This denied them graduation. What made the punishment particularly unjust was the fact that the copy had been approved by the faculty adviser, Lee Casey, who had left the *Rocky Mountain News* temporarily to teach. Casey resigned in protest and three of the four students quit school. In addition to Lindberg they were Hal Borland, who went on to become an author and nature columnist for the New York *Times,* and Harvey Sethman, for many years information officer for the Colorado Medical Society. Lindberg went home to Pueblo, Colorado, to work briefly for the *Chieftain* before joining the Denver *Times.* He moved to *The Post* in September of 1929 as a general assignment reporter. A few weeks later he was stopped by Bill Shepherd in the men's room.

"Lindberg," he said, "I hear you write poetry."

"Oh, I dabble at little jingles and verse," Lindberg replied. "I don't know that you could call it poetry."

Shepherd explained that he was looking for someone who could write verse to fit Paul Gregg's Western paintings, which had been published in color each Sunday since 1913. He asked Lindberg to look at the picture Gregg was working on and see what he could do. The painting was on a theme Gregg loved—a pioneer woman on the seat of a covered wagon with rifle on her lap, child cowering at her skirts, as she scanned the horizon for hostile Indians. This is the verse Lindberg wrote:

Our Pioneer Mother

War bonnets riding from a distant hill—
War cries thru desert silence—savage, shrill
Flinging their cruel challenge of the wild
Down on a lone defender and her child.

Somewhere her man is seeking horses, strayed.
No time to call him now. Her only aid

Is courage none but mothers can command—
Courage, and musket, steady in her hand.

Hers was the heart to trail the setting sun.
Hers, then, the glory of the West she won,
For desert plains thru which she dared to go
Are gardens now, because she willed them so.

We are beneath that wagon!—You and I,
We of this West for whom she dared to die,
Our very lives, and all that makes life dear,
We owe to her—this mother pioneer!

Shep liked the poem, and so did F. G. Bonfils. It was published
October 27, 1929. Gregg continued to paint a picture a week until
he died in 1949. More than eighteen hundred of his oils are stored in
The Post's basement. And for each painting that Gregg produced,
Lindberg wrote a verse—approximately a thousand in a twenty-year
span. Often others would watch in fascination as Lindberg would sit
down at his typewriter, take a wad of gum out of his mouth, and roll
it thoughtfully in a ball between thumb and forefinger. And sometimes in fifteen minutes, sometimes in an hour, he'd have a homey,
appropriate verse. Lindberg had many favorites, but the one he likes
best was published October 27, 1940, to go with a picture of a young
pioneer couple building a cabin on their homestead:

Housing Act of 1859 . . .

There wasn't any architect. No banker made a loan
To solve their housing problem. They were strictly on their own.
They didn't sign a mortgage and they didn't buy a lot;
Just stopped the covered wagon at a likely looking spot.

No lumber yards were running. They cut timber in the hills
And hewed it into beams and joists and doors and window sills.
They had to hand-saw every plank and quarry every stone,
But finally they got it done—a home to call their own.

No mansion, but a sturdy house their own strong hands had
    made,
It stood on fertile acres that had never been surveyed.
No warranty. No abstract fee. No red tape legal fuss.
They just came out and built the West and left all that to us.

On his retirement in 1971 Gene Lindberg gets a commemorative plaque from editor and publisher Charles R. Buxton. (Bill Johnson)

After Gregg's death Lindberg wrote verses to accompany unusually appealing photographs for *The Post*'s *Empire Magazine,* meanwhile continuing to function as a general assignment reporter and science specialist. In time the University of Colorado got around to expunging the record of Lindberg's suspension, and in 1960—forty years after he quit school—he was presented with an honorary bachelor's degree in journalism. He retired in 1971, at age seventy-two, after forty-two years in *The Post*'s employ.

22

THE DOMINANT MAGAZINE
OF ITS AREA

It is not likely that any new publication ever promised so much and delivered so little as the first issue of *Empire,* the Sunday magazine of *The Denver Post. Empire* was to be the fruition of Palmer Hoyt's dream of publishing a great regional newspaper magazine. It was to be printed in *The Post*'s new rotogravure plant in conjunction with the opening of the new building in 1950.

As the first step in creating this magazine, Hoyt soon after his arrival in 1946 abolished the existing feature section which was so little thought of that it was called simply *Weekly Magazine.*

Hoyt replaced it with *Rocky Mountain Empire Magazine,* printed in rotogravure in Chicago. Because the section was new and interesting, it built up a substantial readership. Unfortunately the section was never a commercial success even though merchants who advertised in it got unexpectedly good responses. The trouble was that not enough merchants wanted to be in the section. The long deadline necessitated by the rotogravure printing process discouraged them. They weren't accustomed to sending in an advertisement and waiting five weeks for it to appear; the merchandise they were advertising might be all sold out by then. And the few merchants who did buy space in the magazine felt so exposed and lonesome that, somewhat like sheep, they soon returned to other sections of the Sunday *Post* where they could be in the company of their competitors. Without advertising support, growth was out of the question for this section and it seldom escaped its eight-page minimum size.

Little matter. As the new building and the new rotogravure plant neared completion, *The Post* crowed: "In the four years *Rocky Mountain Empire* has been published as a unique, home-edited regional newspaper magazine, a sturdy foundation of experience has been built to meet the challenges and opportunities now posed by *The Post*'s own rotogravure presses." The buildup went on to say the staff's "search for rich and authentic tales about the people of an empire has produced a wealth of stories, many of which have been given national and international circulation by the *Voice of America, Reader's Digest* and other digest magazines. The best of these grass-roots Americana have been collected by Doubleday and Company in a book to be entitled *Rocky Mountain Empire*. It will be released nationally in conjunction with the forthcoming appearance of the new *Empire Magazine*. making it an event of double significance."

The new *Empire* was described as "new in format and outlook, dressed up with lavish use of color." Readers were promised that the new *Empire* "will continue to probe far and near for stories about people and things and events; these may be common in vintage but they must be uncommonly readable and interesting. Whatever the subject matter, *Empire*'s new mechanical facilities will enable *The Post* to present its unapproachably colorful homeland in its true glory as never before."

Unfortunately there was much more to rotogravure than starting up the presses. Rotogravure is an extremely complex process affected even by such factors as the humidity in the air and the chemical purity of the water used in some of the steps. Few local technicians knew much about roto. The men brought in from places like Chicago couldn't make the plant operate the way it was supposed to. What's more, Major Bonfils against expert advice had installed a nine-unit press in the interests of economy. A nine-unit press is something like a seven-cylinder automobile. It could be made to function after a fashion, but it wouldn't work nearly as well as a ten-unit press. The quality of printing in the first issue, October 22, 1950, was frightful. And because the magazine looked so bad, it could have carried stories by Ernest Hemingway, Norman Mailer, James Michener, and William Shakespeare and readers still would have thought it was a miserable issue. The fact that the content failed to live up to expectations didn't help matters.

Slowly the technicians learned to handle rotogravure. And little by little the editorial staff, almost all of them recruited from *The Post*'s city room, became comfortable with the demands and possibilities of a magazine format. Other organizations, notably Standard Gravure Corporation of Louisville, Kentucky, generously gave *The Post* technical and editorial encouragement and assistance. Standard Gravure, a subsidiary of the *Courier-Journal* organization, was a pioneer in the business of printing newspaper magazines. Its management took the enlightened view that if it could help any segment improve, the entire industry would benefit. Even though it was obvious *The Post* would in time be competing against Standard Gravure, *Empire* was invited to take part in the annual meetings for editorial and advertising directors of the various magazines printed in Louisville.

Early in the game the editorial staff of *Empire* reached an understanding that their product was a magazine—not a newspaper, not a supplement, not a feature section, but a magazine with all the challenges and opportunities that implies. It would be the showcase of the Sunday *Post,* excelling editorially because it was not a slave to daily deadlines, excelling in appearance because of the rotogravure printing process, and commanding a premium rate for its advertising. In fact, excellence was the only justification for assigning a large staff to the magazine, using a higher grade of paper on which to print it, and making liberal use of costly color. Hoyt gave the magazine staff a substantial measure of independence from the newsroom, so that it operated semi-autonomously, a wise move since its problems and objectives were quite different from the daily newspaper operation.

Many Sunday magazines in their earlier days were hardly more than inflated feature sections, a dumping place for stories not quite interesting enough to get into the daily paper. Their weekly menu was made up largely of 250-word features about little old ladies who painted chinaware, the man who made hooked rugs for a hobby, the gardener who grew the sunflower larger than a dinner plate— all revered clichés of the newspaper business. *Empire,* on the other hand, set out to make itself the dominant magazine in its circulation area. This was no pipe dream because, being distributed with the Sunday *Post*—and a high percentage of Westerners subscribed to *The Post*—it went into many times more homes in the area than national publications like *Reader's Digest, Life, Saturday Evening Post,* and all the others. All that needed to be done was to dig out interesting regional stories, write them well, illustrate them in a striking manner, package the material nicely, and print it beautifully. Eventually these goals were achieved.

Bernard Kelly, named assistant editor of *Empire* in 1957, attended the Louisville meeting one year and was astounded to hear a speaker urge Sunday-magazine editors to concentrate on fluff that would appeal to women readers. Take advantage of rotogravure reproduction to load the pages with pretty pictures, he said. Use the "Four F" formula, he urged—food, fashions, furniture, family.

Kelly rose to point out that anyone could thumb through such a magazine in a few minutes, and it would get thrown out with the rest of the paper Sunday afternoon. He told the group *Empire* had chosen another approach. In a typical issue *Empire* carried well-researched, well-written stories on sports, history, crime, adventure, the great outdoors, and heavier (but no less lively) material on education, medicine, social problems, agriculture, industry, and economics—all with a regional angle. One of *Empire*'s best-read columnists, Kelly reported, was Red Fenwick, who wrote about hard-bitten cowboys and people who got drunk and often did illegal and immoral things but did them in an interesting manner.

Kelly recalls: "The reaction I got was part amusement, part incredulity. This might suit the people of Denver, but folks elsewhere wouldn't read such a magazine, they indicated. But in the end, as we know, all or almost all locally edited Sunday newspaper magazines have had to come to this approach that *Empire* pioneered."

Thus *Empire* became a magazine that its readers looked forward to, enjoyed, talked about, frequently clipped, and often passed on to friends and relatives in other parts of the world. Here is a sampling of some of its more memorable stories.

—One day in the summer of 1954 staff writer William J. Barker came back to the office with an unbelievable tale. There were a couple of no-nonsense businessmen in Pueblo, he said, who had been experimenting with hypnotism. One of their subjects, an attractive thirty-year-old housewife, under hypnosis had been taken back, back, back through her life to her earliest childhood. Under hypnosis she recalled many details of her life that she couldn't remember otherwise. And then the hypnotists had taken her back even further, before her birth, to a previous life when she was Bridget Murphy who lived in Cork, Ireland, in the first half of the nineteenth century. Under hypnosis she spoke at length of long-dead friends and relatives, obscure towns, little shops, forgotten customs and manners, using quaint words no longer familiar, and the hypnotists had her account of those times on tape!

Since time immemorial people have asked whether we live more than one existence, whether our present lives are only one of many we have enjoyed on earth, whether death is merely a waiting period between incarnations. The hypnotists, Morey Bernstein and Bill Thomson, may have opened a crack into the unknown through which we might get an inkling about answers to these questions.

Barker wrote a three-part series titled "The Strange Search for Bridey Murphy," which *Empire* published with a cautious disclaimer —"publication does not necessarily mean endorsement"—and almost overnight her name became a household word. To protect the identity of the subject, Barker called her Ruth Simmons. It was a fortunate precaution. Reporters from all parts of the country tried to find her. She was denounced as a fraud, offered a movie contract, sought for radio and television interviews. As interest in Bridey Murphy continued to build up, *The Post* sent Barker to Ireland to check musty records for people, places, streets, and shops she had mentioned. His findings, which were not conclusive, were reported by *The Post* in a special supplement. Bernstein went on to publish a book on Bridey.

Seventeen years after Bridey Murphy burst upon the national scene *Empire* published a two-part series on the woman who had been Bridey. Staff writer Olga Curtis persuaded Virginia Morrow to identify herself as the subject of the experiments in hypnotic age regression, and to reveal the many strange things that had happened as a result of the Bridey publicity.

—From its inception *Empire* took a deep interest in Western history, for its region's robust and exciting past is still close in terms of both time and sentiment. Most notable in this area was a ten-part series written by the late Jack Guinn in 1966 under the general title "The Red Man's Last Struggle." The series told of the last great Indian struggle, from the Indians' point of view, to protect their land from the White man's encroachment during the twenty-eight years between 1862 and 1890. It was a struggle marked on both sides by savage bloodletting, perfidy, heartbreak, and courage. Guinn, a student of Western history since the Thirties, when he was a student at the University of Texas under Walter Prescott Webb and J. Frank Dobie, wrote the series with great skill and understanding. Because of numerous requests for reprints the series was reproduced by *The Post* in pamphlet form and it became required reading in many college and high-school history classes. The series won a Western Heritage Award from the National Cowboy Hall of Fame in Oklahoma City. Guinn, a onetime Associated Press foreign correspondent and *The Post*'s city editor for several years, also was the author of the *Glory Trail* series on the history of the cowboy, filmed for National Educational Television.

—A series of somewhat similar significance was produced by Cary Stiff when he dug into the untold story of the part played by

Blacks in the pioneer West. He found cowboys and badmen, political leaders and agricultural colonists, each contributing in some way to the buildup of the nation's Western heritage. This was the first time the role of Blacks in the westward movement was told in meaningful fashion, and this series also became required reading in ethnic-studies classes. Stiff also wrote an *Empire* series on death and dying, a subject that might be considered hardly suitable for Sunday-morning reading but which was widely acclaimed as a sensitive, enlightening, and useful report.

—Among Colorado's less admirable citizens are Alferd Packer, the convicted cannibal who had an indirect part in the wounding of F. G. Bonfils and Harry Tammen, and two brothers with the unlikely names of Chauncey and Clyde Smaldone, kingpins of Denver's Prohibition-era underworld. Red Fenwick produced entertaining in-depth stories on these subjects, in both cases separating fact from folklore and thereby coming up with material that was all the more fascinating because it was true.

Empire was also keenly aware of the present, giving magazine-type treatment to issues in the news:

—A number of Air Force Academy cadets were expelled in 1967 in a major cheating scandal. Many were kicked out for technical violation of the Honor Code, meaning they personally had not cheated but had failed to report knowledge of cheating by others. The Honor Code was much in the news, with extensive discussion about whether it was fair, realistic, or necessary, but the daily papers failed to explain adequately what it was all about. Bernard Kelly wrote a penetrating report under the title "Honor—That Controversial Code." It was so well done that the Academy asked permission to use it in explaining the code.

—At a suburban, middle-class bridge party a mother confessed she was giving her unmarried teen-aged daughter birth-control pills to prevent pregnancy since it was evident she couldn't maintain chastity. This resulted in a report by Olga Curtis titled "Sex and the Single Teen-ager." This was in 1963, some years before permissiveness became an accepted fact of American life, but the story was a forecast of changing moral values. Mrs. Curtis also wrote a deeply moving story of her own bout with breast cancer long before the operations of Betty Ford and Happy Rockefeller became page 1 news.

—H. Ray Baker, *Empire*'s art director for several decades, also wrote well. He delighted consumers, and angered his targets, with stories about how to "shop" for money when in need of a loan, and how to have your car repaired without being cheated.

As *Empire* broadened its horizons beyond the regional scene, "foreign" stories entered its pages.

—In the summer of 1965 a high-level seminar on a world food policy was held at the Center for Research and Education at Estes Park, Colorado. This led to a story by Bill Hosokawa titled "The Coming War on Hunger," which pointed out that chronic U. S. grain surpluses were disappearing rapidly in the face of worldwide food shortages. Although fragmentary reports had been published on the changing picture of U. S. surpluses, this was probably the first comprehensive story to appear. The American Freedom From Hunger Foundation, organized by President John F. Kennedy's Food-for-Peace Director George McGovern, awarded *The Post* a special citation for the story.

—*Empire*'s longest single story was a twenty-thousand-word article putting Red China's so-called Cultural Revolution into perspective. Late in 1967 the newspapers were full of reports about a violent upheaval on the Chinese mainland as teen-agers of the Red Guard denounced the old veterans of the Chinese Communist revolution. But no one seemed to be able to explain why it was happening and what it all meant. Palmer Hoyt sent Hosokawa to find out. Americans were not permitted to enter China at that time, but Hosokawa visited with nearly twoscore China-watchers of four nations on the perimeter of the Asian mainland. His findings were titled "The Real Story of Red China's Upheaval." In introducing the story Hoyt wrote: "This is not the kind of material normally found in a Sunday newspaper magazine. It is, however, a prime example of the deep-probing, significant reporting necessary for an understanding of our complex world in these troubled times—and a measure of the growing stature of Sunday magazines as a source of information as well as entertainment."

Having the printing plant right on the premises enabled *Empire* to do things that would have been impossible under other circumstances.

—A numbing cold wave gripped the Rocky Mountain Empire in December of 1964. Cattle froze on the unprotected range. Traffic was paralyzed. And in northwestern Wyoming the natural-gas pipeline supplying the five thousand residents of Cody burst when the intense cold set up unequal contraction strains on the metal pipe.

The temperature dropped to 31 degrees below zero that night as Cody, deprived of its only source of fuel, slowly congealed. Before gas service was restored next day, the strain on the electrical supply resulted in power outages in many parts of town. Yet, so widespread was the cold that Cody's ordeal received but brief attention in the news stories. In *Empire's* offices the staff wondered how Cody had coped with the disaster. What had happened at the hospital? Had there been panic? How was suffering averted? The impact of this story would be lost if publication were delayed; it had to be rushed into print. Bernard Kelly and John Rogers spent most of that day on the telephone interviewing Cody residents. Meanwhile, a Cody photographer was assigned to take pictures and put the film on the first plane out of town. While arrangements were made in the roto-gravure plant to add a four-page pullout section to the issue ready for printing, Kelly and Rogers hammered out a dramatic story of "The Night Cody Froze."

—Astronauts Neil Armstrong and Buzz Aldrin became the first men to walk on the moon on July 20, 1969. Millions watched their shadowy figures flitting across TV screens in a telecast directly from the surface of the moon. During their twenty-one hours on the moon's surface, in addition to collecting samples of soil and conducting scientific experiments, they took scores of photographs. The raw film was part of the precious cargo sped back to Earth aboard the *Apollo 11* spacecraft. Soon after *Apollo* was hauled aboard the aircraft carrier *Hornet* in mid-Pacific on Thursday, July 24, the film was removed and rushed to NASA headquarters in Houston for development. Four-color photographs were released to the press late Tuesday, July 29. Dan Partner, *The Post's* veteran aerospace reporter, picked up the pictures in Houston and dispatched them to Denver, where they were received the morning of Wednesday, July 30. In the roto plant decks had been cleared to process them. The copies of *Empire* distributed four days later, August 3, carried reproductions of the first color photographs from the surface of the moon in the clear, true-color fidelity of rotogravure. *Life* magazine appeared later that week with the same photographs.

These were the exceptional features, but week after week *Empire's* stock-in-trade was interesting stories from the far reaches of the Rocky Mountain Empire. Writer Zeke Scher and photographer George Crouter teamed up to specialize in fascinating material from distant places. One week they might explore the Rainbow Bridge controversy, explaining in text and pictures that the rising level of Lake Powell behind Glen Canyon Dam wasn't going to be an environmental disaster. The following week there might appear a story about snagging the long-snouted, prehistoric paddlefish in the Missouri River in Montana. Indefatigably, they took *Empire* readers over rarely traversed trails to mountain heights and canyon depths not often seen.

As *The Post*'s understanding of rotogravure improved, the plant took on commercial jobs, printing magazines for other newspapers. The first two were the Seattle *Times* and the Portland *Oregonian*. It is one of the quirks of the printing business that it makes financial sense to transport paper by rail from the Pacific Northwest, where it is manufactured, to Denver, and truck the finished magazines all the way back. In 1968 *The Post* purchased the Pacific Neo Gravure Division of Cuneo Press in Los Angeles. This operation, a wholly owned subsidiary of *The Post*, was renamed Gravure West. Together, the two plants print more than nine million magazine copies each week. The Denver plant, in addition to *Empire*, prints magazines for the Kansas City *Star*, Seattle *Times*, and Oklahoma City *Sunday Oklahoman*. The Los Angeles plant prints for the San Jose *Mercury-News* and Los Angeles *Herald-Examiner*. In addition, it prints about three and a half million copies of *Parade* and two and a half million copies of *Family Weekly*, both of which are syndicated magazines distributed by Sunday papers. Donald C. Cieber, a reporter who early in his career moved over to the business side, is manager of *The Post*'s rotogravure operations. In 1974 he was elected president of the national Gravure Research Institute.

Empire took a long time to attain editorial stature, but even longer to achieve economic maturity. Despite improved printing quality, merchants remained reluctant to advertise in it.

Two developments helped change that situation. In 1956, with the intention of blunting the inroads of color television, Hoyt decided to distribute *This Week,* then the largest and most prestigious syndicated Sunday magazine. *This Week* was probably in its greatest glory at this point, providing a glossy, readable, if not particularly exciting product. But it soon began to go downhill, its skid greased by an editorial diet of pap and blandness. Not only did it fail to attract much of a readership but it hurt *The Post* by siphoning away national advertising that could have gone into *Empire*. Hoyt and Buxton were dissatisfied with *This Week* almost from the beginning but they waited until 1963 to cancel it. By that time several other newspapers had come around to agreeing that *This Week* was flat and uninteresting and they, too, canceled.

A few weeks before *The Post*'s cancellation was to become effective on July 1, 1964, Hoyt took a calculated risk and boosted the single copy price of the Sunday paper from twenty cents to twenty-five cents. Customarily a newspaper offers a new section or new features to sweeten such a price increase. Instead, Hoyt eliminated a section, and so little was it valued that there was hardly a ripple among subscribers. Before much longer *This Week* went out of business. Three months after dropping *This Week* Hoyt appointed Lewis W. Schaub as the full-time sales manager for advertising in *Empire*. Schaub was completely sold on *Empire* as an advertising medium and his enthusiasm proved contagious. In 1963 *Empire* was thirty-third among sixty-five locally edited Sunday-newspaper magazines in total advertising linage. (Denver ranks twenty-seventh

A prize-winning cover for the No. 2 magazine.

Sunday *Empire*
JANUARY 21, 1973
THE MAGAZINE OF THE DENVER POST • VOICE OF THE ROCKY MOUNTAIN EMPIRE®

An inviting place for students
page 24

in population among U. S. cities.) After Schaub took over, the following year *Empire* climbed to twenty-fifth. By 1967 *Empire* was ranked sixth.

The secret was not salesmanship alone. Traditionally, newspaper editorial and advertising staffs go their separate ways almost as if they were proud strangers rather than members of the same team. On *Empire,* the advertising and editorial sides built a rapport under which they could cooperate to solve mutual problems without feeling imposed upon or forced to sacrifice their integrity.

The increase in advertising also boosted the amount of space available for editorial features, enabling the editors to put out a more interesting package, which in turn brought in even more advertising. In 1973 and again in 1974 *Empire* was second only to the New York *Times Magazine* in total advertising, with such giants as the Chicago *Tribune* and Los Angeles *Times* magazines trailing. It was also in 1973 that *Empire* won the *Editor & Publisher* magazine's first prize for creative use of editorial color in newspaper magazines. The prize-winning feature was a cover and pictorial layout, photographed by Crouter, on the University of Denver's new law library.

Empire had made a faltering start as a modest Sunday supplement. It developed into the widely respected, well-read profitable magazine of *The Denver Post*.

Vignette

THE ELEVEN-MILLION-DOLLAR LIBEL SUIT

Leo L. Spears founded the eight-hundred-bed Spears Chiropractic Hospital in Denver and built it into a lucrative business by telling the world about his skills as a practitioner of the healing arts. Between 1951 and 1955 he invested more than a million dollars in advertising. Some of it was spent in newspaper ads, but much went to publishing a tabloid-size newspaper which was widely mailed to "Occupant" and post-office box holders. His paper published almost nothing but testimonial letters from former patients, with photographs, telling how Dr. Spears had relieved or cured them of such ailments as the paralysis of polio, multiple sclerosis, cancer, the aftereffects of strokes and heart attacks.

Spears made a major error when he visited *The Post* one day seeking publicity for what he called a blood test he developed which could be given on a mass basis and detect cancer in its earliest and curable stages. *The Post*'s medical writer, Robert N. Byers, checked around and found that what Spears was doing was a poor approximation of an earlier test developed elsewhere, and discarded as inaccurate. Byers declined to publicize Spears's test until he could see evidence that it worked.

Spears then offered to let Byers go through his patient files without supervision, picking patients at random, looking up the test results, and drawing his own conclusions about the test's accuracy. Byers accepted the offer. He spent two weeks in the record room, but instead of picking files at random he went for the folders of patients whose "cures" were advertised in Spears' paper. He found evidence that Spears knew some of the patients were dead when their testimonials about a cure were published. He also found evidence that some testimonials were produced in exchange for cancellation of hospital bills. In all, he checked eighty-three patients treated for cancer at the Spears hospital and found sixty dead; of the twenty-three living, eighteen had diagnosis of cancer only by the Spears hospital and not by medical biopsy.

Byers wrote in detail about his findings and his stories in *The Post* led to an invitation to appear before a grand jury probing medical quackery.

Spears responded by filing a suit for eleven million dollars. He charged the Better Business Bureau, which was investigating misleading advertising, and *The Post,* of conspiring to destroy his business. He named some ninety defendants including the BBB, its directors and manager, *The Post* and Byers, and the Colorado State Medical Society. Col. Philip S. Van Cise, who was attorney for the *Rocky Mountain News* when Fred Bonfils sued for libel in 1932, was the chief defense counsel, aided by his son, Edwin P. Van Cise.

It was the largest suit in which *The Post* had been involved, but it was one of Spears' lesser efforts to collect for what he considered to be damage to his reputation. Previously he had sued *Collier's Magazine* for $24 million for mentioning him in a story on cancer quacks. When Walter Winchell on his radio program urged his listeners to read the article, Spears sued Winchell for $25 million, his sponsor, the Richard Hudnut Company, for $25 million, and the American Broadcasting Company for $12 million.

The *Collier's* suit was tried first and a New York federal jury found the magazine had not libeled Spears. Shortly afterward the bonding company insuring Winchell settled the other suits, in which Spears had sought a total of $62 million, for $2,500 "as a matter of expediency."

Spears' Denver suit was heard without a jury before Judge Robert H. McWilliams in a trial that lasted three weeks and two days. It was covered extensively in the Denver press and Byers gained a considerable measure of status over other *Post* reporters who were being sued, inevitably without success, for amounts no larger than a couple of million dollars.

Byers testified that when he was assigned to investigate Spears' claim, Palmer Hoyt had told him, "If true, it would be the most important news story of the century."

Hoyt was called to the stand and testified: "*The Denver Post* is a quasi-public institution. We would consider it of the highest import if a cure for cancer had been discovered or was about to be discovered. We also feel it would be in the public interest that false hopes not be aroused concerning the disease, or that people not be lulled into a sense of false security. We believe it would be in the public interest to assure that advertising be truthful and factual. These are things that affect the very life of our citizens."

(It is not likely that Hoyt was greatly worried about losing the case. But on the day he testified there was other troubling news. His son, Ed Hoyt, who had left *The Post* in 1951 to buy the *Free Press* in Colorado Springs, had been foreclosed by the International Typographical Union for failure to make payments on its notes.)

Judge McWilliams, who later was named to the federal bench, returned his verdict only nine days after the close of the trial. He found there was no conspiracy.

23

MILLIONS FOR A NOBLE GESTURE

In the halcyon days of newspapering the owners became powerful and wealthy, their top executives drew handsome salaries, and the men in the trenches, particularly the editorial workers, were happy to stay in the "game" for whatever they could get. It usually was very little. This was true of *The Post* where Tammen and Bonfils amassed millions. After they died their heirs paid Bill Shepherd $50,000 a year to run the paper with a $10,000 bonus being tossed in routinely. This was during the Depression, when journeymen reporters considered themselves fortunate to have jobs paying $30 or $35 a week.

The pattern held true to an extent even after Palmer Hoyt came to *The Post* in 1946. His first year's salary was $40,000, with a $5,000 increase annually during the life of his five-year contract. There was a considerable gap between his salary and those of the two top aides he inherited from Shepherd—Major Bonfils, the business manager, and Larry Martin, the managing editor. One of Hoyt's first actions, as we have learned in an earlier chapter, was to get the major's pay raised to $310 a week, or about $16,000 per year, and Martin's to $270, or about $14,000 annually. The average journeyman reporter was making $60 a week at that time although Hoyt soon increased that to $85, or $4,400 per year.

By 1964 Hoyt was being paid $105,000 per year. His next in command, Charles Buxton, was getting only one-third as much, $36,000. That year, on Campbell's motion, the directors (meaning Campbell and Helen Bonfils) increased Hoyt's salary to $125,000. Hoyt in turn got the board to raise Buxton to $45,000.

The following year, 1965, Hoyt's pay was increased to $150,000 with an additional $10,000 for expenses. Buxton was promoted from business manager to the newly created post of general manager with a pay boost to $65,000. Meanwhile, the journeyman reporter's pay under the contract with the Newspaper Guild had moved up on January 1, 1966, to a fairly respectable $162 per week, or roughly $8,500 per year.

In addition, *The Post* was providing numerous fringe benefits to employees covered by the various labor contracts. As early as 1957 the directors approved a health and welfare plan. Workers were provided without cost a $2,500 life-insurance policy, $2,500 for accidental death or dismemberment, weekly sickness and accident insurance, and comprehensive Blue Cross and Blue Shield coverage. In addition, executives were provided life insurance roughly equal to an individual's yearly salary up to $20,000. That same year the directors approved the idea of a pension plan for all employees and the business office was instructed to work up some proposals.

In addition to these improvements, Hoyt kept looking for a way to make some of the tightly held *Post* stock available to the employees. The ownership pattern was not unique among family-owned corporations. Since the Tammens were childless, the two Bonfils sisters were the only direct descendants of the founders. After May Bonfils Stanton sold her *Post* stock in 1960, Helen became the only direct descendant with an interest in the paper, and she was both elderly and without children. All the stock other than that owned by Helen and S. I. Newhouse was tied up in various trusts and foundations, which understandably were concerned less with the excellence of the paper than with its profits. Hoyt considered this an unhealthy situation. He felt it was only right that the men and women working for *The Post,* the clerks and mechanical hands as well as the executives, should have the opportunity to invest in its ownership and be given the right to share the profit of their labors. He talked about this frequently with Campbell and Helen. Campbell was sympathetic in principle but he could not in good conscience release any of the stock for which he was trustee. And Helen, too, while looking with favor on ultimate employee ownership of the paper, was reluctant to sell any of her own holdings during her lifetime. Thus it had been a major triumph for Hoyt's hopes when, in the process of thwarting Newhouse, the stock held in trust for Children's Hospital was purchased by the paper and returned to the treasury with the understanding it would become available eventually for purchase by employees. But the stock could not be sold in just any old manner. A careful, legally acceptable plan had to be drawn up.

Seeking precedents, Hoyt studied the employee-ownership plans adopted by a handful of other newspapers, among them the Milwaukee *Journal* and the Kansas City *Star* and *Times*. The situation in Milwaukee seemed to be closest to that of *The Post*. A task force of Buxton, comptroller Warren Young, and an attorney, John Moore, was assigned to draw up *The Denver Post* Employees Stock Trust Agreement patterned after the Milwaukee plan. After many months they came up with two documents, one fifty typewritten pages long and the other ten pages, spelling out all the legal ramifications.

The original proposal was to resell the Children's Hospital stock to the employees for the price that had been paid for it—$260 per share. But the longer the members of the task force looked at that figure the less they felt it could be justified as a good investment. The price had been inflated by Newhouse's determination to control *The Post*. At that price the dividends would amount to about 2.78 percent, which was only slightly more than half the interest savings banks were paying. To make the stock a reasonable investment, discounting the growth factor, some way had to be found to lower the price.

At one of its regular meetings the task force came up with an idea that would work—if Helen Bonfils would agree. It was a very large *if;* if Helen would contribute stock from her personal holdings on a share-for-share basis with that withdrawn from the treasury, employees could be offered shares at half the $260 price. At $130, dividends would amount to a more inviting 5.57 percent.

Helen took an understandably dim view of the proposal when Hoyt took it up with her. Eventually he was able to persuade her that the Employees Stock Trust could not possibly work without substantial help from her, and if it was her intention to provide for employee-ownership after her death, why not get it started now while she could enjoy the act of giving? With Seawell's blessing, Helen Bonfils on February 24, 1961, provided *The Post* with a letter agreeing to give the employee stock plan sixteen hundred shares of her personally held stock. At a price of $260 per share, the gift was worth $416,000.

"I am, of course, heartily in favor of the plan's objectives," she wrote, "and have encouraged its adoption in our consultations."

The agreement stipulated that eight hundred shares would be transferred to *The Post* during calendar year 1961 to match an equal number of shares to be withdrawn from the treasury, and that all these shares must be subscribed to before December 1. If this were accomplished, an additional eight hundred shares would be made available the following year, but if not the entire agreement would be canceled. The agreement was also contingent on a favorable tax ruling and on the understanding that labor unions would not make the employee stock plan the subject of collective bargaining and that Helen would continue to vote as a trustee all the stock she had contributed.

On March 16 the directors—Helen, Hoyt, and Campbell—met to accept her gift and now the task force hurried to nail down details of the employee-ownership plan for approval by the stockholders of *The Post*.

As finally drawn up, *The Denver Post* Employees Stock Trust was the mechanism through which employees could buy stock in the company. It would be administered by nine trustees. Six of them, from management, would be permanently named. They were Helen Bonfils, Hoyt, Buxton, Young, Henry Meier, who was Miss Bonfils' secretary and also assistant secretary and assistant treasurer of *The Post,* and Stephen H. Hart of the law firm of Holland and Hart. The other three trustees were to be elected for three-year terms from among a twenty-one-member Advisory Council elected by all the employee shareholders. The original three were Joe W. Bruce, an advertising salesman; Barry Morrison, a reporter; and I. M. Rosenblatt, a mailer. (In later years the heavy tilt toward management was corrected. Currently there are four permanent management members, four elected from the Advisory Council; and John C. Mitchell of the Boettcher Foundation as the "neutral" outside member. There are few occasions for a tie-breaking vote.)

The employees could not buy *Post* stock as such. They could purchase a "beneficial interest" in *Post* stock in the form of Trust Shares, ten of which were the equivalent of one share of *Post* stock. Trust Shares could be voted in Employees Stock Trust elections, but not in *Post* stockholder meetings. By a complex formula based on the book value of *Post* stock and earnings for the previous five years, the price of one Trust Share was pegged at thirteen dollars. This price would be calculated monthly and could fluctuate up or down. Trust Shares had to be sold back to the Employees Stock Trust when an owner retired, left the company, or died.

On November 17, 1961, the directors agreed that employee stock ownership "would result in great advantages both to the corporation and to its employees by way of increased employee interest in and attachment to the affairs of the corporation" and recommended the

plan to the stockholders. The stockholders met November 30. This
is the way the ownership lined up:

Helen G. Bonfils	17,989.2602	shares
First National Bank of Kansas City as Trustee for Helen Bonfils	1,468.9436	"
F. G. Bonfils Foundation	5,028.78	"
First National Bank of Kansas City and Denver U. S. National Bank, trustees under the will of F. G. Bonfils	17,513.6986	"
Palmer Hoyt	1.	"
E. Ray Campbell, trustee under will of Agnes Reid Tammen	17,704.6487	"
E. Ray Campbell	1.	"
May Bonfils Stanton	10.	"
The Post Standard Company (Newhouse)	14,724.0214	"
Denver Post treasury stock	19,573.6475	"
TOTAL	94,015.	"

All the stock was represented, either in person or by proxy. Before
business could begin, Donald C. McKinlay, representing Newhouse,
moved to adjourn the meeting for thirty days so that more detailed
study could be made of the employee stock ownership proposal.
The motion died for lack of a second.

McKinlay was then permitted to read a lengthy statement outlining
Newhouse's opposition to the employee-ownership proposal. He declared that under the plan employees did not become stockholders in
the full sense since they would own Trust Shares instead of *Post*
stock. "Any notion that the proposed plan will help avoid employer-
employee conflict on *The Denver Post* is naïve and unrealistic,"
McKinlay declared, citing a strike by the Mailers Union against the
Milwaukee *Journal* as evidence that workers would put union interests above that of the plan. He also contended that Helen Bonfils was
not likely to contribute to the plan after 1962, and that *The Post*
had no right to sell its treasury stock at less than fair value, that is, in
the $240 to $260 range.

McKinlay proposed that instead of the overall incentive plan represented by stock ownership, an individual incentive plan be adopted
in the form of profit sharing. He suggested that a referendum be held

to enable all employees to decide their preference. Finally, he urged *The Post* to strengthen its financial position by selling its treasury stock to Newhouse, who would be happy to pay whatever it had cost *The Post*.

The stockholders listened politely, then proceeded to vote 59,-707.3311 in favor of employee stock ownership, 14,724.0124 (Newhouse's) against, with May Bonfils Stanton's ten shares and the 19,573.6475 shares of treasury stock not voting.

Because of the delay in adopting the plan, the December 1 deadline imposed by Helen Bonfils' contribution agreement was extended to the end of the year. Even so, *The Post* had only a month to sell $208,000 worth of stock to its employees. Anticipating a heavy demand, a limit of twenty units ($260) was placed on sales to each eligible employee. But the stock proved to be somewhat less salable than hotcakes. The complicated stock trust agreement confused many and the Christmas season was not a good time to persuade people to invest. The only way to meet the goal was to lift the twenty-unit ceiling, enabling some employees to increase their commitment. In this way the first sale was completed by year's end. By mid-June of 1962 the second sixteen hundred share was sold out. Some 450 employees, about half of those eligible, were now stockholders in the company they worked for.

By April of 1964 the price of the Trust Shares had risen to $14.69 and they were paying an annual dividend of 72½ cents, equivalent to about 5 percent. Another one thousand shares from the treasury, with no contribution from Helen Bonfils this time, were put up for sale. The minutes of the board explained: "The great initial success of the plan, and the rise in the offering price for Trust Shares, have made it feasible for the sale to come solely from this source, having in mind the benefits in employee productivity, incentive and morale resulting from such a distribution."

During this period Newhouse was not much in evidence but he was biding his time. Keith Anderson kept him informed about developments in Denver. Allen Kander, who stood to make a quarter-million-dollar commission the day he delivered control of *The Post*, rarely lost an opportunity to tell Charles Goldman, Newhouse's attorney, that he was still working on the deal.

In an effort to clear the air once and for all, Seawell asked to see Kander in June of 1963 and met with Anderson a month later. A letter from Seawell to Kander after their meeting, reaffirming Helen's determination not to sell, pointed out that all the assets of the Frederick G. Bonfils Foundation and all of Helen's *Post* stock would go into the newly created Helen G. Bonfils Foundation, "a tax exempt and eleemosynary and charitable foundation," and would ultimately flow into the Employees Stock Trust.

Seawell told Anderson much the same, tossing in an offer to buy back Newhouse's *Post* stock inasmuch as he could never gain control. The gist of these conversations was duly reported to Goldman. Anderson concluded his letter with this paragraph:

> None of this is particularly surprising, since it is more or less what you and I had anticipated all along. . . . As we have pointed out before, the possibility of the Post-Standard [Newhouse] acquiring any more stock seems at the moment remote, and since present management of *The Post* will not permit Mr. Newhouse to participate in managing the newspaper, any substantial improvement of earning seems equally doubtful. Nevertheless, you and Allen Kander have told me many times that Mr. Newhouse takes a very long view of these problems, and history has usually proven him right, so I presume he will not be interested in this offer. . . .

Seawell says of these talks: "I endeavored to show them why I didn't think Newhouse could ever break the trusts and foundations and acquire control. Apparently Kander was convinced and I understood that he recommended to Newhouse that he abandon his attempts and sell his stock back to us.

"Later I heard from Kander that if we could arrange some face-saving device for Newhouse so that, in his words, Newhouse would come out of it smelling like a rose, then he would sell his stock. I asked what he meant, and Kander said if we would put Newhouse on the board of directors he would resign after three months and sell his stock. He also had to have something that was face-saving, like a statement that he had done wonders for *The Post* during his three months as director. I had to have a clear idea about what was involved so I asked what Kander would consider a fair price for the stock. The figure of four hundred fifty dollars a share was tossed out, stock Newhouse had purchased for two hundred forty dollars. Kander left me with the impression that if we couldn't work things out, Newhouse was ready to sue. I don't know whether all this was Kander's idea or whether Newhouse really told him that. Newhouse subsequently denied he'd ever said he wanted a face-saving seat on the board."

Seawell took Kander's proposals to Helen. There was some of the icy-blue Bonfils look in her eyes as she replied:

"Under no circumstance will Mr. Newhouse ever become a member of *The Denver Post* board. If he wants to fight it out, I'm ready to meet him in court."

That meeting was to come, but it was preceded by another bit of litigation in which, curiously, she was a bystander who was nicked nonetheless for more than two and a half million dollars.

This episode begins with E. Ray Campbell's failing health, which led to his departure from the scene, which in turn touched off a fast-moving series of events. Representing the Tammen interests, he had served *The Post* long and faithfully. After Shepherd's retirement in 1946 Campbell had become president of *The Post* and Hoyt's great admirer and supporter. But in the spring of 1966, at age seventy-one, Campbell submitted a one-sentence resignation to the other members of the board. It said, "I hereby resign as President and Director of *The Denver Post,* Inc. effective May 19, 1966." The same day he resigned as trustee under the will of Agnes Reid Tammen.

Some weeks earlier, when Campbell had made his intentions known, Seawell received a telephone call from Helen. She told him that Campbell was retiring and added, "You are going to get a call from Ep Hoyt asking you to become president of *The Post,* and I want you to say yes."

Seawell replied that he wanted to help her in any way he could, but he really wasn't interested in becoming president, and why didn't she assume the post?

Helen said she would prefer to remain as secretary-treasurer. "I've talked it over with Ep and we both want you to be president," she said. "I'll be in New York in a week or so and I'll have Ep come in and we'll meet in my apartment and talk about it."

Helen and Hoyt, the two remaining directors, met at her apartment at 435 East 52nd Street to formally accept Campbell's resignation and then name him honorary chairman of the board. Then they got down to the business of selecting a new president. Seawell, who was also on hand, persuaded Helen it would not look good for a virtual stranger to take over as head man at *The Post.* If Helen would take the title of president, Seawell said, he would spend half his time in Denver as secretary-treasurer of the corporation with the understanding that he would be acting for Helen as chief executive officer. And so in the plush apartment at River House Helen took the official title and a new man joined the board to guide and counsel her.

By this time Seawell was thoroughly familiar with *The Post's* legal and financial situation. One of his first recommendations was to change the articles of incorporation to eliminate cumulative voting by stockholders in the election of directors. The significance of this move is that, under cumulative voting, if a minority stockholder like Newhouse could corral enough shares he could win a seat on the board by voting all his stock for one candidate, himself. When one of Newhouse's lawyers at a special meeting of stockholders asked the purpose of the proposed change, attorney Stephen Hart replied, "It is to assist in providing a unified and harmonious firm, united management to the corporation, to avoid dissension and differences, and controversy in the board and in the affairs of the company, for the benefit of all stockholders." The only votes opposing the change were those of the Newhouse and Stanton holdings.

Even more significant than Campbell's resignation as *Post* president was the end of his tenure as trustee under the Tammen will. That put an entirely new light on the fight for control of the paper. As we have learned in Chapter 12, Campbell, Sadie Schultz, who was Tammen's secretary, and the Denver National Bank were made trustees of Mrs. Tammen's multimillion-dollar estate, the chief beneficiaries of which were her grandniece, Helen Crabbs Rippey, and her children. Sadie Schultz had died in 1965, and with Campbell's resignation the responsibility of administering the estate fell to the bank now called the Denver U. S. National. The estate was made up almost entirely of blue-chip stocks, bonds, and 17,704.6487 shares of *Post* stock. Campbell had administered the trust with a rare and dogged fidelity. His memos during this period reveal a man who resisted great pressure from three directions and clung to the course his judgment told him would best protect the value of the estate.

—On one side was Mrs. Rippey, urging him to dispose of *The Post* stock regardless of the consequences, because it wasn't making enough money for her. This notation appears in his files:

> E.R.C. and Schultz face difficult problem, if they do not sell, of going against express wishes of principal beneficiary, Mrs. Rippey, who wishes sale to take place for (1) purpose of increasing income which she says she badly needs and (2) reasons of present lack of interest in or sentiment towards *Post,* which she seems to believe has manifested no interest in last 10 years in her, her boys' future as possible employees of *Post.*

Campbell's memo went on to express the fear that the First

National Bank of Kansas City, trustee of the Bonfils Trust, might sell its holdings and help put Newhouse in a majority position. "If it is true that Newhouse does not care about dividends," Campbell's memo continued, "*Post* holdings of Tammen Trust might well decrease in value, income would be lessened, and E.R.C. would, of course no longer be officer of *Post*."

The presidency of *The Post* was never an overwhelming consideration. While he enjoyed the prestige, the twenty thousand dollars a year the job paid was only part of Campbell's income and he considered himself primarily an attorney, not a publisher.

—On a second side, Campbell was being urged by Newhouse's representative that he would be wise to sell. He had no intention of selling to Newhouse.

—Still, when pressured by his colleagues at *The Post*—the third side—to pledge not to sell the stock, he couldn't do that either. He explained the situation in a memo to himself after a conversation with Hoyt:

> I told him that as trustees we could never make any such commitment, because our sole and only duty was to do what was for the best interest of our beneficiaries, and that circumstances might arise which would dictate that we sell the *Post* stock and invest the proceeds in securities more trustworthy.
>
> I told him that presently neither of us had the slightest idea of selling; that Sadie was contemplating resigning as trustee, and that certainly I had no idea of selling the *Post* stock, but that I had to observe trust standards, one of which was that there are times when a trustee might be compelled by circumstances to sell, but that I would do no such thing without long and serious consideration with him and Helen. He seemed upset that I would not be willing to promise without qualification that I would not sell the *Post* stock.

Campbell was in the extremely difficult position of holding responsibility for both the newspaper and a trust at a time when what was good for one might not be to the advantage of the other.

It would have helped *The Post*'s position to know that the Tammen Trust's 17,704 shares were safely and permanently locked away in a friendly place, or alternatively, would be offered only to *The Post*. It would damage *The Post* extensively if, in trying to protect the trust's assets, Campbell felt obliged to make the best deal possible, which might well be with Newhouse. In the end he simply hung onto the stock, which for the time being was an acceptable alternative to Seawell if *The Post* couldn't buy it. The bank, however, would be governed by no restraints other than to look after the best interests of the heirs. And so after Campbell let it be known he would resign his trusteeship, it became imperative for *The Post* to buy the stock before Newhouse did.

On May 18, 1966, one day before Campbell's resignation as president of *The Post* was to take effect, Seawell, Hoyt, and Buxton called on officials of the Denver U. S. National Bank and offered to buy the Agnes Reid Tammen Trust's stock for $260 per share. On June 6 the offer was raised to $275 per share on the condition that the deal be closed before the annual meeting on June 8. At a meeting that afternoon the bank reported that an appraisal of the stock using *The Post*'s formula had established its value at $316 per share. Buxton pointed out the formula had been misapplied and the value mistakenly had been doubled. Later that same day the bank telephoned Seawell to say that under another formula the value had been established at $313. Seawell contended the stock wasn't worth more than $200 at the most. "In fact," Seawell said later, "I thought the bank's asking price was so outrageous that I offered to indemnify the bank for the difference between $275 and $313 to demonstrate how exorbitant their price really was. Then I decided $275 was so bloody high I didn't need any limit, and so the $313 ceiling on the indemnification was removed."

Up to this point it had not been determined who would be buying the stock on behalf of *The Post*. It might be The Denver Post, Inc., the Frederick G. Bonfils Trust, or Helen Bonfils personally. The next day, June 7, Seawell telephoned the bank to say that Miss Bonfils would be the buyer and asked if they had a deal. Here a serious breakdown in communications developed. Seawell was talking about the $275 price he had offered. The bank officer thought they were talking about the $313 evaluation and said yes, they had a deal. The error became apparent when *The Post* contingent showed up at the bank a short while later with a check for $500,000 to bind the sale. The meeting broke up in confusion. Next morning, only hours before the annual meeting was to be called to order, a bank official telephoned Seawell with a proposal to sell for $300 per share. Seawell turned it down, declaring, "We have already passed the limits of a fair price in offering $275."

The bank was negotiating the sale under broad powers written into Mrs. Tammen's will by Campbell. Article XV of the will specified that the trustees "shall have power to sell all or any part of said estate or trust estates as the case may be, at either public or private sale, with or without notice or advertisement, for cash or partly cash and partly credit, and upon such terms as to them seem advisable, without notice to or consent of and regardless of the opinion of any beneficiary under this will. . . ." Article XVII further specified that should any beneficiary "in any wise directly or indirectly contest or aid in contesting" the will and its provisions, such beneficiary "shall be absolutely barred and cut off from any share in my estate. . . ." While these provisions apparently gave the bank a completely free hand to sell the stock, it informed Mrs. Rippey that a $275 offer had been turned down, and that Helen Bonfils had in turn rejected a $300 counter offer.

The annual meeting was held on June 8 as scheduled. The only noteworthy piece of business was transfer of another five thousand shares of *Post* treasury stock to the Employees Stock Trust. Only the Newhouse-owned shares were voted against the proposal. Under the price-setting formula, each unit was now worth $16.54, which was the equivalent of $165.40 for *Post* stock.

Shortly after the meeting negotiations were resumed between the bank and *The Post*. On June 16 the bank asked Mrs. Rippey if she would accept *The Post*'s offer of $275 per share. The following day her attorney, Samuel Sherman, wrote the bank that the price was unacceptable. Sherman added that "we have information, which we believe is reliable," that in addition to *The Post* group, "Cowles, Whitney, Marshall Field, John Knight, John Mullins and Newhouse interests" would be interested in buying the Tammen Trust stock. Sherman also said Allan R. Phipps, a highly reputable Denver financier, and Homer Torrey of New York, each representing an unnamed principal, were also interested.

In view of Newhouse's continued minority position after six years of effort to escape it, and *The Post*'s lackluster profit record, it would appear that Sherman's information about the interests of these various publishers, aside from Newhouse, was more chimerical than reliable. Nonetheless, he was trying to make the point that his client's best financial interests would be served by offering the stock either at public auction or through sealed bids.

Apparently the bank was not greatly impressed by Sherman's list of potential buyers. In Helen it already had a prospect who had offered more than had ever been paid for the stock and was likely to raise her price even more. Further, Miss Bonfils had made it clear she would refuse to get into a bidding contest with another buyer.

On June 20 and 21 there were lengthy telephone consultations between Sherman in Denver and Newhouse's attorneys, Goldman and his partner, Charles Sabin, in New York. Goldman and Sabin reiterated Newhouse's interest in buying the Rippey stock and Sherman urged that "in some manner Mr. Newhouse should get on record with the Denver United States National Bank to the effect that he was willing to pay a substantial price for stock in *The Post* it offered for sale." The discussion during the call on June 21 turned to the price and Goldman said Newhouse would be willing to pay $240 per share. A memo which Sherman wrote for his files on that day contains this information:

> I explained to him that this price would do more harm than good, because *The Post* had bought the Children's Hospital Trust stock at $260 and it was quite apparent that if the bank sells the Rippey Trust stock it will expect to receive more than $260 per share. I did not tell him, however, of the outstanding offer which apparently now had been made by Miss Bonfils to buy the stock at $275 per share. I did not tell him either of the $313 figure that the trust company is considering now as being a fair price for the stock . . . my only objective in this whole transaction is to get a fair price for the stock to benefit Mrs. Rippey as the income beneficiary . . . we are not teaming up with Mr. Newhouse against the Bank except to the extent that we both are interested in having the sale of the *Post* stock conducted publicly rather than privately.

But all this conversation turned out to be an exercise in futility. Sherman did not know that on June 20 Miss Bonfils had agreed to pay the bank's asking price of $300 per share—$40 more than the previous top price. She committed herself to pay $5,311,694.61. To firm up the agreement she offered $500,000 as down payment. Since she did not have the cash immediately available, she borrowed it from *The Post.* (Two days later she repaid *The Post,* and somewhat later, interest of $147.26 for the two days.)

Meanwhile, she arranged for a loan of $2.5 million from the First National Bank of Kansas City and the balance of the purchase price from Colorado National Bank, and the stock was paid for in full on June 24.

Before the details were concluded, however, the bank insisted on holding Seawell to his offer of an indemnity agreement. Under it Helen would protect the bank against "claims, suits, liabilities, loss, damage, expenses and other items" arising from the sale. The bank's precaution poses an interesting question: Since the bank's sole responsibility was to the trust and its beneficiaries, and it was satisfied that the sale was to the trust's best interests, why did it feel it necessary to protect itself? This question has never been answered.

Helen agreed to the provision on Seawell's assurance that there seemed to be little likelihood of trouble over a reasonable commercial deal arrived at after hard arm's-length negotiations over a period of many weeks. It proved to be a costly error.

Signing of the papers was completed at 12:35 P.M. June 22. That afternoon Seawell caught a plane for California. Hoyt drove to Pueblo, Colorado, to take part in a golf tournament. Buxton went to his country club to play a few holes. Managing editor William Hornby was left to mind the shop.

Meanwhile, that same day, there was a flurry of activity in New York. Goldman got on the telephone to urge Newhouse to make an offer for the Rippey stock before it was too late, not knowing what was happening in Denver. In a memorandum to Newhouse summarizing their conversation Goldman wrote:

> I want to remind you again that according to Mr. Sherman, the Bonfils group is presently engaged in attempting to establish a reasonable price for the stock on the basis of a formula. This would seem to indicate that they may have a purchaser in mind and they may wind up facing you with a fait accompli. If I am correct in this, I think it calls for quick action on your part.

Goldman drafted a telegram for Newhouse to send and added: "It might be a good idea to leak the news to E & P [*Editor & Publisher,* the newspaper trade weekly]. Any publicity resulting from this will certainly make it impossible for the trustees at any time hereafter to claim that they did not know about the offer."

Hornby was getting ready to leave the office, well after 5 P.M. when a copyboy brought in a message that had just been received on the teletype machine. It was addressed to Helen Bonfils. Here is the text:

> I have just been advised of the stock pooling agreement dated June 7, 1966 executed by you, as one of the three stockholders of *The Denver Post, Inc.* That agreement reflects the intent of the signatories to sell in one block the stock of *The Denver Post, Inc.* covered by that agreement totalling fifty-one thousand six hundred seven point sixty (51,607.60) shares. Accordingly, I hereby offer to purchase for cash said shares at the price of five hundred dollars ($500) per share, making a total of twenty-five million, eight hundred three thousand, eight hundred dollars ($25,803,800). Mr. Howard Mc-Call, President of the Chemical Bank New York Trust Company, 20 Pine Street, New York, New York will confirm my financial ability to meet this commitment. Acceptance of this offer may be sent to

me care of my attorneys, Goldman, Evans and Goldman, Woolworth Building, New York City, and upon receipt thereof prompt arrangements will be made to transfer necessary funds against deposit of stock in a Denver bank. Also, pursuant to pooling agreement, all other stockholders of *The Denver Post, Inc.* are afforded the opportunity to sell their shares on the terms and conditions set forth above. S. I. Newhouse

The message had been dispatched from New York at 4:53 P.M. Eastern Daylight Time, which was 2:53 P.M. Denver time, nearly two and a half hours after the bank's sale to Helen Bonfils had been completed. It was received in *The Post*'s offices at 5:16 P.M. Mountain Daylight Time. These precise times became significant to later developments.

Hornby read the message. He was fully aware, of course, of Newhouse's continuing efforts to buy control of the newspaper. But he had not been made privy to the details of what had taken place in the bank offices earlier that day, and he wasn't quite sure what the telegram was all about. Hornby immediately reached Buxton at home and read him the message. The two were scheduled to attend the same social function that evening. Buxton asked Hornby to bring the telegram with him.

Newhouse's reference to the stock-pooling agreement was misleading. It did not reflect "the intent of the signatories to sell in one block the stock of *The Denver Post*." Its intent was to avoid the sale of any of the stock to an outsider unless all agreed. The three parties were the First National Bank of Kansas City and the Denver U. S. National Bank, trustees under the will of F. G. Bonfils, with 17,513 shares; The Denver U. S. National Bank, trustees under the will of Agnes Reid Tammen, with 17,705 shares; and Helen Bonfils. Her block of 16,389 shares owned personally brought the total of 51,607 shares, more than enough to control the paper.

Newhouse had sent identical telegrams to the Kansas City bank, the Denver bank, and copies to Miss Bonfils at three addresses in New York and Denver. These telegrams had been filed at 1:50 P.M., June 22, in the Western Union office in the Woolworth Building. The copy to Helen at *The Denver Post* was the only one delivered that day. The ones sent to her in New York and to the two banks were not delivered until the following day.

When Newhouse complained, Western Union explained the delays were caused in part by breakdowns in transmission equipment, by unintentional employee errors, and the fact that messages deposited at the Woolworth Building office had to be relayed to another part of New York City for transmittal. While Newhouse's attorneys suggested darkly that "the defective handling may be due to something other than mere happenstance," the fact is the delay could not have affected the bank's sale since an agreement had been reached two days earlier.

After the telegrams were dispatched Goldman mailed a copy to Sherman with a covering letter that said in part: "We do not wish to exclude entirely the possibility that our client may be able to acquire separately the shares of the Tammen Trust; in that event our client is prepared to pay $450 per share for that stock. . . ."

Now, after the deed was done and the content of Newhouse's telegram became known, the Rippey family was convinced the bank had sold their stock far too cheaply.

There were more calls between Sherman and Goldman. When Sherman reported Mrs. Rippey's intention to sue the bank, Goldman urged that besides seeking additional payment, Mrs. Rippey demanded a public sale of the stock so that Newhouse could make an offer. Sherman wrote to Goldman on July 5: "In view of the full cooperation of Mr. Newhouse and your fine firm the decision has been made by Mrs. Rippey to seek to rescind the purported sale of the Tammen Trust *Post* stock to Miss Bonfils. . . ."

On July 12 suit was filed in U. S. District Court against the bank, *The Post,* and Miss Bonfils in the names of two of Mrs. Rippey's children, Bruce, who then was living in Baltimore, and Gordon, then in Oklahoma City. They charged that the bank had failed its responsibility in not seeking other buyers before it sold the stock at $300 per share for a total of $5,311,694, that if the bank had been diligent it would have learned the stock had an actual market value of $500 per share, or $8,852,324. The sale, they complained, represented a loss to the beneficiaries of more than three and a half million dollars. They asked that the Denver U. S. National be removed as trustee of the Agnes Reid Tammen Trust, that the sale be canceled and a new trustee be directed to sell the stock at a court-supervised public sale or through sealed bids, or that the bank be required to pay the difference between the sale price and the "fair market value" of the stock.

As attorneys for the various parties maneuvered with motions, petitions, and denials, Helen proceeded with a step she had been planning all along. On August 22 she made a gift of the 17,705 shares purchased from the bank, plus the 16,389 of her previously owned stock—34,094 in all—to the Helen G. Bonfils Foundation for use in its "general, charitable purposes." During her lifetime she would collect the dividends and vote the shares. After her death the stock would be sold to *Post* employees through the Employees Stock Trust. At a value of $300 per share, the gift to the foundation was worth $10,228,200.

The trial began July 24, 1967, before U. S. District Court Judge William E. Doyle. After ten days of testimony Doyle took the case under advisement. On October 16 he returned his ruling in a fifty-three-page opinion, the main points of which were:

—The Denver U. S. National Bank did indeed breach its trust obligation when it sold the stock to Helen Bonfils for $300 per share. However, complaints against *The Post* and Miss Bonfils were dismissed since no conspiracy existed between *Post* management and the bank.

—The sale to Miss Bonfils was upheld. But a surcharge of $150 per share was imposed. This meant Judge Doyle pegged the value of the stock at $450 per share, this being the price Doyle presumed Newhouse would have paid had the breach not occurred, and the additional $150 per share would have to be paid to the Rippeys through the Agnes Reid Tammen Trust. How Judge Doyle arrived at this figure was never made clear. On June 21, Newhouse's attorney had told Sherman he was willing to pay $240, a bid which Sherman warned would do more harm than good. The next day, after Miss Bonfils had bought the stock, Goldman offered $500 per share for controlling interest and told Sherman—but not the bank—that Newhouse would pay $450 per share for the stock in the Tammen Trust.

For Helen, it was a Pyrrhic victory. The stock could not be taken away from her, or removed from the Helen G. Bonfils Foundation. But it would cost her an additional $2,655,847.30. Including legal fees, the deal had cost her more than eight million dollars.

Roger D. Knight, Jr., board chairman of the Denver U. S. National, quickly announced his decision to appeal with this statement:

> In spite of the plaintiff's charges and accusations, the court's opinion specifically exonerates the bank from any claim of self-dealing, fraud, conspiracy, undue influence or monetary gain. The court's surcharge, despite these exonerations, is surprising and appalling, after the extensive work done by the many qualified persons who participated in the decision to sell the stock . . . and to this date the bank has never received an offer of more than the selling price

of the stock. Since the court did not agree with the bank's judgment, obviously the bank must appeal this decision to a higher court.

Ultimately the bank, which would have had to carry on the appeal alone since *The Post* and Helen were dismissed from the action, decided against that course. "The bank and Miss Bonfils in no way agree with the decision of the District Court and they take particular exception to certain findings therein," a new statement read. "However, it is recognized that while an appeal might result in a more favorable conclusion for the defendants, there are grave and substantial risks including the possibility of an increase in the amount of damages awarded, the possibility of plaintiffs' damage claims against Miss Bonfils being reinstated, the possibility of a recision order, very large additional costs, adverse publicity, damage to peace of mind, loss of time and other harassment and worries as a result of continued litigation."

And so Helen paid the surcharge, the bank resigned as trustee, and each side took care of its own costs. The court approved a fee of more than $350,000 from the trust for the Rippey attorneys. The legal firm of Holland and Hart was awarded $188,000, of which *The Post* paid $96,000 and Helen $92,000.

Statements were made by the various participants. Helen Rippey, grandniece of Mrs. Tammen and principal beneficiary of the fortune founded by a man she met only a few times in early childhood, declared: "From a business standpoint, my children and I are glad to have this litigation ended. From a personal standpoint, our only regret is that our family's 72-year association with *The Post* had to be terminated so abruptly."

There was a certain nobility in Helen Bonfils' stiff-upper-lip statement: "I am gratified that my plans for continued independent and eventual employee ownership of *The Denver Post* have reached fulfillment. All of us can now concentrate on the further growth and development of *The Denver Post*."

Hoyt echoed Miss Bonfils' statement and expressed to her "the undying gratitude of the entire staff for her courageous, unselfish, and successful fight to preserve *The Post*."

But ahead was still another challenge.

AN ENDOWMENT FOR THE PERFORMING ARTS

Many scoffed when the Frederick G. Bonfils Foundation was announced late in 1927. Some considered it a sham which never would amount to much. Others were amused by the high-flown language— that the foundation would spend its income "in such specific, public, educational, charitable or benevolent project or projects as it may determine to be for the promotion of the general wellbeing of mankind."

In the five years of life that remained to him, Bonfils put only $119,269 into his foundation. But after his death in 1933 his estate, as directed by his will, poured a steady stream of funds into the foundation's coffers and Helen Bonfils as its president supervised the spending like a lady bountiful. Between 1936, when the foundation began to function under her direction, and 1973 it gave nearly eleven million dollars for a wide variety of good causes.

The gifts ranged from a half-million dollars to build the Holy Ghost Catholic Church in downtown Denver (plus many additional contributions for its upkeep) to as little as $5 for Polish War Relief. The Denver Community Chest could expect at least a $50,000 gift from the foundation each year. When Sister Mary Anne of the Servants of Mary needed a Communion outfit, the foundation wrote her a check for $15. In 1948 the foundation bought organs for fourteen churches, among them Evangelical, Methodist, and Presbyterian congregations. One year a church in Perry, Oklahoma, was given $1,000 for rubber kneelers. A *Post* carrier who needed a bicycle to make his appointed rounds was given $72.05 to pay for one. The Gideons asked for a contribution to provide Bibles for soldiers during World War II and were given $100. That same year the USO cigarette fund was given $100. The Bonfils Tumor Clinic was sent a regular contribution of $10,000 and up. Two entries in the ledgers show payments of $24 to *The Post* for a year's subscription to be sent to the Mount Carmel Convent and St. Cajetan's Convent.

Hundreds of thousands of dollars were paid out for college scholarships for deserving young men and women. One year the Little Sisters of the Poor were given $50 to buy tea for their old folks' home. In 1948 alone $20,000 went to the University of Colorado Medical School Nurses' Home, $45,000 to the Bonfils Tumor Clinic, and $27,600 to the Belle Bonfils Blood Bank. When Helen's health began to fail and she spent more and more of her time at St. Joseph Hospital, the foundation's contributions to it increased—$36,129 in 1969, $25,000 in 1971. There were scores and scores of lesser gifts —for burial of the destitute, to pay hospital and medical bills, $18.95 for elastic stockings for an elderly woman, $14.40 to buy special shoes for a boy who had trouble walking.

The foundation's gifts to the Catholic Church were lavish but one

Donald R. Seawell (left), chairman of the board of the Denver Center for the Performing Arts, and Mayor Bill McNichols examine a model of the center, which will be supported by earnings of *Post* stock. (Bill Peters)

entry shows a contribution of $325 to the rabbinical department at the University of Denver's School of Theology. In all, the foundation's gifts to churches amounted to nearly $1,430,000. More than $1,900,000 went to Community Chest and other such campaigns.

But aside from the newspaper, Helen's greatest love was music and the theater. The foundation's books show $2,181,000 was spent to support music—symphonies, the Denver Opera Foundation, the open-air *Denver Post* operettas. Another $1,920,000 went to the theater. Included in this sum was a quarter-million dollars to build the Bonfils Theatre in Denver and finance its program of community stage productions.

In compliance with her wishes, after Miss Bonfils' death in June of 1972 the Frederick G. Bonfils Foundation and Helen G. Bonfils Foundation ended their private charity status and, starting with a million-dollar cash gift, diverted their total support to the unprecedented Denver Center for the Performing Arts (DCPA).

Designed as a cultural complex covering four square blocks in downtown Denver, the Center will include a concert hall, four theaters, a large parking garage, amphitheater, and administration building, all tied together with soaring glass-roofed gallerias for shops and restaurants. The first building, now under way, is an eleven-million-dollar concert hall for the Denver Symphony. The city is providing six million dollars from a bond issue, with the balance coming from contributions.

The two Bonfils foundations are now "satellites" of the Denver Center for the Performing Arts, whose chairman is Donald Seawell. In 1972, when the change was made, the F. G. Bonfils Foundation had a portfolio valued at $9.5 million, yielding about $400,000 per year. The Helen G. Bonfils Foundation had the 34,862 shares of *Post* stock she donated to it in 1966 and 1970, plus additional income-producing properties from her estate, all of which are expected to provide about $275,000 annually. This income was earmarked for construction and support of the repertory and experimental theaters in the Center, for operating expenses of the Center, and for other Center uses. Thus the Bonfils fortune is providing in the neighborhood of $675,000 a year to support what DCPA calls "the only performing arts center in the country to have an initial substantial endowment."

24

PIPELINE TO THE WHITE HOUSE

One Friday afternoon in October of 1960, while they were playing golf, Ep Hoyt told Chuck Buxton he had decided *The Post* would endorse John F. Kennedy in the upcoming Presidential election. Although Hoyt was a registered Republican, Buxton had expected that he would opt for Kennedy. What surprised Buxton was that Hoyt had made up his mind.

"What about that meeting tomorrow?" Buxton asked.

Hoyt had scheduled a rare Saturday meeting of his top news executives and editorial writers to discuss endorsement of a Presidential candidate. Presumably a choice was to be made at the meeting.

"We'll hold it anyway," Hoyt replied.

Hoyt always regarded the newspaper's endorsement of political candidates as a solemn obligation based on earnest appraisal of all the available facts. An endorsement was not a popularity contest or an attempt to predict the winner. Even though it might be apparent from public-opinion polls conducted for *The Post* that a candidate would be soundly thrashed on election day, Hoyt would not hesitate to endorse him if he was the better man.

While Hoyt took all elections seriously, he was particularly concerned about the 1960 Presidential race. A gut feeling—something he relied on as often as pure cerebration—told him the primary issue was national survival. (Hoyt spoke of survival so often in conferences with the editorial writers that Paul Conrad, who delighted in the outrageous, penciled a cartoon for the staff's amusement. It showed Hoyt as Groucho Marx who then had a popular television program in which contestants were rewarded for saying a "magic word" unknown to them but revealed to the audience. Conrad's contestants were Kennedy and Nixon. A rubber duck holding in its bill a piece of paper with the word "survival" written on it descended from the ceiling, and Hoyt was shown exclaiming, "You've said the magic word!")

President Eisenhower, Hoyt contended, had let the nation drift for eight years while the Soviet Union was racing ahead as a military power, developing the hydrogen bomb and, as demonstrated by Sputnik, the rockets capable of delivering them on U. S. cities. He had been furious when a member of Eisenhower's cabinet dismissed Sputnik as a beeping basketball in the sky. Hoyt was convinced the country must elect a President who could lift the people out of their lethargy and lead them back to greatness and he probed the psyches of Kennedy and Richard Nixon for signs of that leadership. He was not really comfortable with either man at first. If he had a choice, it would have been Nelson Rockefeller. In fact, in April of 1959, when many Presidential hopefuls were jockeying for attention, *The Post* editorially had urged a draft of Rockefeller. They had first met in 1943, when Hoyt was in Washington as director of the domestic division of the Office of War Information and Rockefeller was President Roosevelt's Coordinator of Inter-American Relations. Hoyt had been struck then by Rockefeller's grasp of issues and administrative ability. But after the party conventions had settled on Kennedy and Nixon, Hoyt set out to learn more about them.

When Nixon entered Bethesda Naval Hospital briefly, Hoyt went to see him. They had a far-ranging talk and Hoyt came away feeling that Nixon, in trying too hard to satisfy the conservatives within the Republican party, stood for nothing. Later, Rockefeller invited Hoyt to meet with Nixon and some of his advisers in New York. Among others at the meeting were Fred A. Seaton, the Nebraska publisher who was Eisenhower's secretary of the interior, and Senator Jacob K. Javits of New York. They were members of a liberal bloc and they hoped Hoyt might be able to persuade Nixon to take a more positive stance. Hoyt came away from the meeting with a sense of hopelessness. "If Nixon would come out for something, almost anything, we could support him," he told Rockefeller. "But I don't think he can or will."

He got a different impression of Kennedy. When Kennedy visited Denver that summer Hoyt and Mort Stern, by then editor of the editorial page, were invited to meet with him privately. Stern recalls that Kennedy listened attentively and Hoyt did most of the talking for more than an hour while Democratic leaders waited impatiently in the ballroom downstairs for their chief to appear. Afterward Hoyt said he thought Kennedy was a very astute young man.

Meanwhile Hoyt continued his probing. Two members of the editorial-page staff were assigned to prepare position papers, one on

When Henry Cabot Lodge (left) telephoned, Hoyt had a negative answer for him. (Jack Riddle)

the side of endorsing Kennedy, the other on Nixon. Only after he had studied these reports did Hoyt finally decide to back Kennedy. After talking to Buxton on the golf course Hoyt that night told his wife, Helen May, of his decision. She was a staunch Nixon supporter. The news upset her so much that she said she would telephone Henry Cabot Lodge, Nixon's running mate and another old Hoyt friend, to see if he couldn't change her husband's mind.

There were twelve or fifteen men in Hoyt's office the next day for the editorial meeting. Without revealing that he had made his decision, Hoyt said he wanted a free and open discussion on the merits of the two Presidential candidates after which a poll would be taken to help him decide which man to back. Hoyt listened carefully to the give-and-take and it soon became apparent that most of the editors favored Kennedy. Hoyt then began his poll and had progressed perhaps halfway around the room when his secretary opened the door and told him there was an important long-distance telephone call. Hoyt excused himself and stepped out into the secretary's anteroom to take the call. He did not close the door nor did he try to keep his conversation secret. Those sitting closest to the door could hear his deep, rumbling voice clearly. "Yes, Cabot," they heard him answer, "I know what you're going to say. Yes, well, as a matter of fact we're just having a meeting of our top executives. Now, Cabot, if you were the candidate there would be no question of our stand, but we just can't go for Nixon. Our editors are unanimous for Kennedy. I'm afraid that's the way it's going to be."

There were some pleasantries after which Hoyt returned to his desk. Without a word of explanation he continued polling the editors. No one now remembers whether the vote really turned out unanimously for Kennedy. Probably it did not because Nixon had his supporters and Hoyt's aides never hesitated to disagree with him. But there was no question in anyone's mind that *The Post* would endorse whomever Hoyt chose. Nor is there much doubt that Hoyt knew how his editors would vote before he called the meeting as a step in establishing a consensus. But it wouldn't have embarrassed him if he had guessed wrong and had to override the majority. He knew, and his aides knew, that he was the boss and had the ultimate responsibility. A week after the meeting *The Post* published the following editorial:

For Survival and a Greater America
The *Denver Post* Endorses Kennedy

Like many another American faced this year with the hard choice between two able, experienced young candidates for the presidency, we have put long hours of investigation, discussion and soul-searching into our decision.

We conclude that Sen. John F. Kennedy would be the more appropriate leader at the start of a decade in which nothing less than the survival of the nation is at stake.

After all is said and all the records are examined, two central facts stand out:

First, that of the two men, only Senator Kennedy has recognized the critical position in which the United States now stands in the race for supremacy with the Soviet Union.

Second, that of the two men, only Senator Kennedy has summoned the nation to make the total commitment to victory without which the victory over our single-minded adversary cannot be had.

Vice President Nixon, despite the many things about him that appeal to us, has tried to convey to the nation the impression that everything is going well for us in the race and that only if some unforeseen development comes along might we need to do more.

In this sense, we believe, he has repudiated his alliance with Gov. Nelson Rockefeller of New York, which alliance seemed at the time of the Republican convention to imply that Nixon would turn his back on the complacency of the Eisenhower administration.

Richard Nixon has been saying in this campaign that those of us who are not satisfied with things as they are, are "downgrading" America.

But that is just exactly opposite from the truth. We and Governor Rockefeller and Senator Kennedy have been calling for a greater America—more powerful, more dedicated and more influential in the world.

Vice President Nixon has accused his opponent of casting a cloak of second-rateness over America. What Senator Kennedy has actually said is that he will not settle for the nation being less than first in anything.

That's the kind of thinking that will rally America to new and greater deeds. . . .

In the last analysis, it boils down to this: America can drift, or it can take a positive approach to the future.

For the past few years we have been told that drift, doing the least that could be done in any circumstances, was the "safe" way.

We should know by now, it was not. History shows conclusively that those peoples who tried to play it safe, to hold on to what they had and dare nothing more, were only setting themselves up to lose everything.

In this campaign Senator Kennedy has taken the positive side. That's why we're for him.

The editorial attracted an enormous amount of interest. It was the first time *The Post* had endorsed a Democratic Presidential candidate since it backed Woodrow Wilson in 1916. Locally the conservative Republicans, mostly influential and socially prominent members of the business community, were outraged and said so. They were joined by conservative Catholics who feared that young Kennedy would be unduly influenced by the Vatican. *The Post* was the first large Western newspaper to declare for Kennedy—only the Bee papers of Sacramento, Modesto, and Fresno, California, had endorsed him up to then—and the news was reported by the wire services. Robert W. Lucas once observed the Democrats would be on the phone immediately to say thanks for a favorable editorial while the Republicans as a rule wouldn't bother to respond. Hoyt recalled what Lucas had said when Bobby Kennedy telephoned the next day to express his appreciation for the editorial. A few hours later Ted Kennedy called. And the following day the candidate himself phoned.

Jack Kennedy said he was sure the editorial would help him a great deal. Then he said he had heard the editors of the New York *Times* were about evenly divided between the two candidates and asked what Hoyt thought could be done to swing the balance in his favor. Hoyt replied that the *Times* was a highly independent power unto itself, that its editors never permitted outsiders to interfere with their judgment, but he knew Arthur Hays Sulzberger and would be glad to get in touch with him. Sulzberger was polite but noncommittal and asked Hoyt to send a copy of *The Post*'s editorial. It is not likely *The Post* editorial influenced the editors of the *Times* one way or the other but on October 27 they came out in favor of Kennedy. Kennedy telephoned again, this time to ask Hoyt about the situation at the Toledo (Ohio) *Blade*. "Oh, that's Paul Block," Hoyt said. "His word is law at the *Blade,* but I'll see what I can do." The *Blade* endorsed Kennedy October 30. (Kennedy captured New York but Nixon won in both Colorado and Ohio.)

There is little doubt that during much of this period Hoyt was regarded as a more prestigious figure in Washington than in Denver. In Denver, even after many years, he still was looked upon as something of a carpetbagger from Oregon who had set himself up as the "emperor" of the Rocky Mountain Empire. In Washington, he was seen as the articulate, independent editor of a large and influential newspaper circulated across a huge part of the West, a man who had distinguished himself in service to the nation and who had many friends in high places.

Hoyt's first real contact with Washington began in 1943, when, almost out of desperation, Elmer Davis summoned him to straighten out the mess in the domestic division of the Office of War Information. Hoyt's straight talk—and performance to back it up—attracted the notice of many influential persons including President Roosevelt. Through William O. Douglas, whose star was in the ascendant, Hoyt met an energetic young Congressman from Texas, Lyndon B. Johnson. The two were cast in the same forthright mold and soon became good friends.

A few months after Hoyt moved to Denver, President Harry Truman tapped him for membership on the Air Policy Commission, a hardworking blue-ribbon group charged with charting the course of civil aviation in the rapidly expanding air age. In this assignment he became well acquainted with men like James V. Forrestal, the first secretary of defense, and future Air Force secretaries like Stuart Symington, Thomas K. Finletter, and Harold E. Talbot. Hoyt and Dwight Eisenhower were occasional golfing partners during Ike's trips to Colorado, but of all the Presidents Hoyt was closest to Johnson.

Hoyt was in Washington on business not long after Johnson succeeded to the Presidency when he got a summons to the White House. Johnson talked at some length about the problems he faced and the two men made a good-natured agreement: Hoyt would not ask the President for anything; Johnson would not ask Hoyt to serve in any official capacity; Johnson would feel free to ask Hoyt for advice and Hoyt would not give Johnson any advice he didn't believe in.

Johnson broke the understanding only once. He reached Hoyt by telephone about two o'clock one morning and asked him to go on the U. S. Advisory Commission on Information as a personal favor. Hoyt suspected, correctly as it turned out, that Johnson was worried about the way news was emanating from Saigon and wanted him to investigate and come up with some recommendations. Hoyt discovered that Barry Zorthian, head of the U. S. Information Service in Vietnam, also was having to function as censor. Hoyt reported that these incompatible responsibilities damaged the very able Zorthian's credibility, and they should be separated.

During the Johnson years *The Post*'s telephone operators became familiar with the women on the White House switchboard and Hoyt became accustomed to calls from the President at all hours. Apparently Hoyt had more than a little influence on a notably headstrong President, as witness what occurred in the middle of October, 1964.

Johnson had scheduled a killing series of speeches as his election campaign approached a climax. After hopscotching around the country he was to host a barbecue at his Texas ranch for several hundred Democratic county chairmen at week's end. But there were other things going on around the world that same week. Britain was in the throes of another of its periodic cabinet crises. Khrushchev was ousted as premier and Soviet Communist party chief and replaced by Kosygin and Brezhnev. And Red China joined the nuclear club by exploding its first atomic bomb. The world was wobbling on its axis and Johnson was busy playing the consummate American politician. As Hoyt contemplated all these developments he kept seeing a picture of Johnson taken by a *Post* photographer some days earlier on a Denver street—the President standing in the back of a sedan, arms upraised, silhouetted against the sky, enjoying the crowd's adulation and a perfect target for any psychopath with a gun. So the call that came from Presidential adviser Abe Fortas was not altogether unexpected.

Fortas explained he thought Hoyt was the only one who could talk turkey to the President and persuade him to cancel his appearances. What Hoyt told Johnson when his call got through was that the world was ablaze and he, as the people's regent for peace, ought to be talking from the top of that world and not from the back seat of a car at a shopping-center political rally.

"But the schedule has been made," Johnson protested lamely.

"It can be unmade," Hoyt urged. "Look, Boss, you've got to get some rest."

President
Lyndon B. Johnson
and friend.

"I'll call you back," Johnson said. Next day an aide telephoned to assure Hoyt that all but two key speeches had been canceled.

It was also during the 1964 campaign that Johnson was gently set down by his Denver adviser with a typically Hoytesque story. Some fifty Johnson-for-President committees had been set up around the country by various business and professional organizations and he suggested to Hoyt that it might be a good idea to form a committee of editors to support him.

"Mr. President," said Hoyt, a longtime devotee of parimutuel wagering at greyhound races, "I'm sure you know about dog racing. Do you know why they use greyhounds instead of other breeds?"

The President admitted ignorance.

"Because," Hoyt went on, "all the other breeds—German shepherds, fox terriers, cocker spaniels—naturally pick a leader and follow him. But greyhounds are different. Every greyhound thinks he's the best damned dog in the world and he's out to prove it. You never see them agreeing on anything. Mr. President, good editors are like greyhounds. The only way Barry Goldwater could beat you would be for you to organize an Editors-for-Johnson committee."

Hanging in Hoyt's office is a photograph of the editor and the President walking together under a White House arbor. There are others in the background but their faces are obscured and it is obvious the group is en route somewhere, perhaps to a meeting. It may or may not be significant that Hoyt is shown a step or two ahead of the President. Lyndon Johnson's inscription on the photo reads: "To Palmer Hoyt, my devoted friend and trusted counsellor."

When Johnson declined to run in 1968 Hoyt was, if anything, relieved. The Boss, as Hoyt liked to call him, was a weary man close to exhaustion from carrying the millstone of Vietnam. *The Post* had no difficulty endorsing Hubert Humphrey over Nixon.

By the 1972 campaign Hoyt was retired. Buxton, who had been with Hoyt since *Oregonian* days, his closest confidant and right-hand man for more than two decades at *The Post,* was now editor and publisher. If it can be said that Hoyt shared some of Fred Bonfils' flair and showmanship, then it can be said similarly that Buxton displayed the business acumen, solidity, and conservatism that made Bill Shepherd such a welcome leader after the flamboyant years. Under Buxton it was not difficult for *The Post,* like a vast majority of newspapers, to endorse Nixon over George McGovern. This is what *The Post* said on November 5, 1972:

> As we look at the record, and review the campaign that is drawing to a close, we are persuaded that Mr. Nixon, and not Sen. George McGovern, has demonstrated the ability to guide the nation for the next four years.
>
> Mr. Nixon has acted responsibly and with imagination on the international scene. He has responded to the long-standing economic problems with courage and determination. He has moved steadily toward a resolution of the Vietnam problem.
>
> He has demonstrated the capacity to lead and grow, whereas Mr. McGovern has not shown comparable qualities as the nominee of a great political party.
>
> The time has come to return Mr. Nixon to office and get on with the business of the nation.

Then came the Watergate revelations. *The Post* studied the spreading stain first with misgivings, then with horror. Buxton was attending a conference at Sea Island, Georgia, the weekend of the "Saturday Night Massacre" when Attorney General Elliot Richardson resigned rather than carry out Nixon's orders to fire Watergate prosecutor Archibald Cox. The publishers at the meeting were abuzz over the news, but none of them seemed ready to do anything about it. On the long flight home Buxton made up his mind that it was time to take an editorial stand. Back in Denver William H. Hornby, the executive editor, independently had reached a similar conclusion. They were talking about it the next day when Seawell dropped in to see Buxton. After only a brief discussion the three agreed that Hornby would draft an editorial calling for Nixon's resignation or impeachment. On Sunday, November 4, 1973, *The Post* published the following editorial:

Resignation or Impeachment Only Way Out

The office of the presidency, as Richard Nixon realized in the concept of his campaign when he sought to "bring us together," is much more than just an office at the head of one branch of our government. The presidency must be the national focus of our ultimate loyalty and confidence. Ironically, it was just a year ago this Sunday that *The Post* wrote its final editorial supporting Mr. Nixon for the presidency because among other reasons we believed he was the better man to produce effective national unity.

The American people must have an instinctive trust in their President, strong enough to override in time of crisis the inevitable partisan feelings of difference on lesser issues. One can disagree with a president on issues such as impoundment of funds, on the structure of a welfare program, of a move in world politics. But in a time of national crisis, such as the recent alerting of our military forces in the Middle Eastern situation, the people must be able to trust automatically the President's integrity. And on simpler matters, it is intolerable that on a question of whether or not the tapes were really lost, a great number of people simply don't take the word of their President. . . .

What is not arguable is that, right or wrong, the situation has now degenerated to where the trust of the people in the President's integrity is shattered. Halfway measures cannot restore that confidence, whether among our people or among our allies overseas.

How then can this intolerable situation be resolved? First, the office of the vice presidency must be promptly filled by congressional action. . . . When the vice presidency is filled, the Republican party . . . should try to persuade the President to resign.

Stepping aside from the office of the presidency when trust has been lost is not a new idea. Lyndon Johnson, although elected by a mandate nearly as large as that of Richard Nixon, realized that Vietnam had broken his relationship of trust with the people. He stepped aside by not running again, and history thinks well of him for it. Similarly history would think well of a Nixon decision to step down, not as admission of guilt, but as a recognition that the needed trust essential to the conduct of his office has been lost. Richard Nixon would gain stature by such a selfless move.

If, however, resignation is not in the cards, then this newspaper has come to the reluctant conclusion that only an impeachment proceeding will heal our hemorrhaging of national confidence in the presidency. . . . An impeachment process before the elected representatives of the people is the only method, short of resignation, that can now finally resolve the erosion of trust in the presidency.

It would be a national decision in which all the evidence is brought out and a vote taken. . . .

If the matter goes to trial and the Senate decides the evidence does not justify the President's removal, well and good! The people will have spoken by the best Constitutional means available to them, and by the rules. That would put an end to it, and the President could go about his business vindicated by a reliable tribunal.

If the Senate should vote to remove the President, so be it! It should be the end of a regrettable chapter, not of the country. . . .

By coincidence the New York *Times* and the Detroit *News* chose the same weekend to urge Nixon's ouster and this stirred up some unexpected national attention. Word of *The Post*'s editorial was broadcast by television and radio stations Saturday night and telephone calls, overwhelmingly in favor, began to flow in. But, to borrow a pair of expressions much in vogue during this period, substantial numbers of Americans at that point in time were not ready to bite the bullet of impeachment or resignation. By midweek letters to the editor were running about 3 to 1 against the editorial. Most of them were well reasoned, expressing disappointment rather than anger at *The Post*'s position. As many as possible of the letters were published in the "Open Forum" opposite the editorial page. On two days a solid page was devoted to nothing but Nixon letters. Normally the flow of letters on any single editorial subsides after two or three days; those on the resignation and impeachment issue continued for nearly two weeks. Isabelle Truscott Holmes, who has handled the "Open Forum" for some twenty years, cannot remember any issue that provoked a greater public response. The next largest followed the assassination of President Kennedy, and that was an outflow of grief rather than comment on a national issue.

When President Nixon finally did resign the letter response was not exceptional. The public was not surprised and its emotions had been spent.

Vignette

"LONELINESS IS A TERRIBLE THING"

A few minutes before the second-edition deadline on May 1, 1959, managing editor Bob Lucas hurried out of Hoyt's office and tossed two sheets of paper on his assistant's desk. On one was a brief news story. Penciled on the second sheet was a headline.

"Get this in the paper on page one," Lucas ordered. "Below the fold will be okay." By that he meant the story should be placed on the lower half of the page where it would not be too conspicuous. "Run them exactly as is. Don't change a word."

The assistant glanced at the headline before reading the story and remarked, "The middle line is short. It won't fit very good."

"Never mind," Lucas replied. "The boss wrote it."

This is the way the story appeared:

MISS BONFILS
MARRIED
TO OIL MAN

Announcement was made Friday of the marriage of Miss Helen G. Bonfils, prominent in theater circles in New York and Denver, and Edward Michael Davis, Denver oil man. They were married April 2.

The marriage ceremony was performed at the Frank Gould estate at Irvington-on-Hudson. Attending were Robert L. Reed, general counsel for the Sun Oil company, and Mrs. Reed. The party was entertained at dinner later by Mr. and Mrs. Reed at the Ardsley country club.

Mr. Davis is the owner of the Tiger Oil Company with offices in the First National Bank building and is associated with Miss Bonfils and Haila Stoddard in the production of "Come Play With Me" which opened at the York Theater in New York City Thursday night.

Knowledgeable readers noticed several things odd about the story. The bride was identified only as "prominent in theater circles" whereas in almost every previous mention it was noted that she was secretary-treasurer of *The Denver Post.* Nothing was said of her first marriage, to George Somnes, who had died three years earlier. And the wedding had taken place a month before the announcement was published.

As a matter of fact, the first Hoyt heard of the marriage was when Helen telephoned him from New York on May 1. She said she wanted him to know, but nothing should appear in the paper. Hoyt argued vehemently—something he rarely did with her—that her marriage was news and should be reported in *The Post,* and eventually he got her reluctant approval.

In Denver social circles the news was read with some bewilderment. Who was Edward Michael Davis? An oil man? Wasn't Helen's chauffeur named Mike Davis? Could she have married *him?*

At Shugie's Lounge, a friendly neighborhood tavern run by Sam Sugarman in East Denver, the regulars also read the news with great interest. Mike Davis had been Sugarman's janitor, later promoted to bartender's assistant. He could scarcely read or write, but he was an ingratiating sort when he wanted to be. After he quit his job he came back one day to show off a Cadillac. "I've found me a gold mine," he boasted. "I chauffeur for an old lady and she likes me so much she gave me this car." When his friends rudely expressed disbelief, he displayed registration papers showing the Cadillac was his. As they discussed the marriage, one of the customers observed, "I guess for once Mike wasn't bullshitting us."

Edward Michael Davis had indeed gone to work as a driver for Helen and George Somnes. After Somnes died in 1956 friends noticed that Helen seemed to be depending more and more on her chauffeur. Presently he quit driving for her and became an oil wildcatter doing business as Tiger Oil Company. Tiger Mike, he liked to be called.

Helen was sixty-nine years old when she married Davis. He was perhaps half her age. Elmer Strain, the veteran of *The Post*'s advertising department, recalls congratulating Helen one day when she came to the office soon after her marriage. "Elmer," she said sadly, "I just got so lonesome."

Gretchen Weber, *The Post*'s fashion artist, who had known Helen since girlhood, was sitting with her at a party when an elderly gentleman came up. "Oh, Miss Helen," he said, "I'm so glad you married and have someone to look after you."

Davis was standing behind her chair as she replied, "My dear, I don't need anyone to look after me. You know no one will ever take the place of George." Later, when Gretchen asked Helen point-blank why she had married Davis, she replied, "Dear, loneliness is a terrible thing." She offered no other explanation and Gretchen didn't feel it was necessary.

The honeymoon was brief. Helen's health began to deteriorate and she was in and out of hospitals. They quarreled often and Davis became demanding and abusive. His forays into oil were interspersed with lengthy visits to Las Vegas. Miss Bonfils' tax records list gifts totaling $574,873 to Davis, but this probably is only the tip of the iceberg of her fortune that went into his ventures.

Davis began to talk about what he would do when he owned *The Post*. Helen realized nothing would be gained if she succeeded in keeping control of *The Post* away from Newhouse, only to have it fall into Tiger Mike's hands. With Seawell's guidance she rewrote her will to provide that if she died first, the half of her estate her husband would be entitled to under Colorado law would come from assets other than her *Post* stock. Then to make doubly sure he would not get the paper she gave all her *Post* stock to the Helen G. Bonfils Foundation, which could dispose of it only to the Employees Stock Trust.

Finally, overcoming religious scruples, Helen filed for divorce on charges of cruelty in July of 1971. By then she was bedridden much of the time. Davis hired a battery of expensive legal talent to contest the suit. Among his attorneys were Stephen L. R. McNichols, former governor of Colorado, and the famed Melvin M. Belli of San Francisco. The decree was granted that December. A private agreement, sealed by court order, was reached on division of property. Miss Bonfils was then eighty-two years old, still sharp of mind but quite enfeebled. Only a few more months of life remained.

25

HELEN'S TRIUMPH THAT
CAME TOO LATE

Federal Judge William E. Doyle's decision in the Rippey family's suit against the Denver U. S. National Bank delighted the Rippeys to the tune of $2.6 million. It shocked Helen Bonfils, who had to pay that sum in order to keep the 17,705 shares of *Denver Post* stock for which she already had paid $5.3 million. And it frustrated Samuel Newhouse, who had hoped the court would cancel the sale and make the stock available to the highest bidder. If Newhouse could have bought the stock he would have control of *The Post* within reaching distance. But by paying the surcharge as the court directed, Miss Bonfils had balked him once again.

Now, with the stock locked away and control apparently beyond his grasp, Newhouse was faced with the need to come up with a new strategy or the unfamiliar and unpleasant alternative of admitting defeat.

On February 14, 1968—Valentine's, a peculiarly inappropriate day in view of what was to transpire—attorney Charles Sabin of New York met with Seawell at his office at *The Post*. Less than three months had passed since Judge Doyle's decision. Charles Goldman was dead and Sabin had taken over as Newhouse's chief legal counsel. Sabin was accompanied to the meeting by Fred E. Neef and Robert Swanson, Newhouse's Denver attorneys. Also present was Warren Young, *The Post*'s comptroller.

Stripped of its varnish, what Sabin came to say was this: Mr. Newhouse would be happy to sell his *Post* stock to Seawell's group, but at his price. If he didn't get his price he would bring a lawsuit of some kind against *The Post* and/or its management.

The meeting had started in a proper, perhaps even cordial atmosphere but all present could sense the chill as Seawell bristled and replied he could not discuss purchase of the stock under threat of a lawsuit.

Sabin quickly backed off, declaring no threat had been intended. Then he said he understood Seawell had offered $450 a share for Newhouse's block of 14,724 shares.

Ridiculous, Seawell retorted. Seawell said that in a discussion with Neef he had suggested that Newhouse donate his stock to the Helen G. Bonfils Foundation, and if the $450-a-share value could be sustained on the basis of the Rippey litigation, Newhouse would net a great deal more out of the tax-deductible charity contribution than he could ever expect to get by selling the stock.

Seawell went on to observe that there were only three possible buyers for Newhouse's shares—*The Post,* Helen Bonfils personally, and the Frederick G. Bonfils Trust. Miss Bonfils' resources were so depleted, Seawell continued, that she was not in position to buy the block. He had no authority to speak for the Frederick G. Bonfils Trust, but he could say *The Post* would purchase it for a fair price. He then offered to find out whether the trustees of the Frederick G. Bonfils Trust would be interested in buying the stock, and at what price.

The meeting ended on this note, which must have been small consolation to Sabin and his employer. Subsequently Seawell met with representatives of the First National Bank of Kansas City and the Denver U. S. National, cotrustees of the F. G. Bonfils Trust. Both groups said that earlier studies had shown *Post* stock to be worth no more than $212 per share. Since then three things had happened to drop the value: The question of control seemed to have been settled; *Post* earnings had declined; issuance of treasury stock to the Employees Stock Trust had watered down the value of outstanding shares. They guessed the stock was worth perhaps $165 per share, but agreed to recommend an offer of $240 per share—which was the price Newhouse had paid in 1960—if they could get rid of him. (At $240, the 17,704 shares would be worth $4,248,960. At $450, they would be priced at $7,966,800.)

Two weeks after their first meeting, Seawell and Sabin had lunch at The Players club in New York. Seawell reported that the F. G. Bonfils Trust would be willing to pay $240, and this was also *The Post's* top price. Sabin said he would relay the information to Newhouse, who was in Mexico. Despite the high stakes the two attorneys were playing for, it was a congenial lunch lasting more than two hours. Sabin expressed interest in The Players club and Seawell took him on a tour of the building. Some weeks later Seawell was notified that Newhouse had turned down the $240 offer.

Late in April Sabin flew to Denver for another meeting with Seawell. Neef and Swanson were with him again and this time Buxton sat in. Sabin said that after studying the testimony in the Rippey case, Newhouse had become convinced there was a conspiracy among the directors of *The Post* to entrench their control of the property, and that Newhouse had decided to sue the officers and directors unless they were willing to pay his price for the stock. Sabin added that Neef had been building up a case and would now explain the legal theories under which he intended to proceed.

Seawell broke in, declaring he would be glad to listen to what Neef had to say provided it was understood all negotiations for the stock were ended. "As an officer and director of *The Post,*" he said, "I cannot be in the position of offering to buy stock from Mr. Newhouse in order to avoid a suit against the newspaper or its management."

Seawell and Buxton then left the room while Sabin conferred with his colleagues. When the meeting was resumed Neef said he would drop the matter of a suit for the time being, and Sabin said he would like to explain a plan under which *The Post* could pay $450 for the stock. Seawell cut him off again, saying it would be a waste of time since there wasn't the remotest possibility *The Post* would pay that kind of price for stock which would have to be resold to employees for about one-third of the cost. The meeting ended with Seawell inviting Sabin and his colleagues to play golf that afternoon. The invitation was declined.

As they discussed the situation later Seawell, Hoyt, and Buxton wondered whether pride might not be involved in Newhouse's insistence on the $450 price. They decided to offer $450 for one thousand of the shares, and $240 per share on the balance. At another meeting in New York in mid-May Seawell told Sabin of the two-price offer. Sabin said he didn't think pride was a factor but promised to relay word to Newhouse. Most of the rest of the luncheon was spent in a discussion of wines, with Sabin digressing long enough to assure Seawell that he, Miss Bonfils, and Hoyt would have lifetime jobs at *The Post* if Newhouse gained control.

A couple of weeks later, when Seawell was still in New York Sabin telephoned to report the two-price offer had been turned down. Sabin asked for one last meeting to try to work out a sale. They met at Sabin's office in the Woolworth Building. Sabin stayed with the $450 price but suggested that payment could be made over ten years from dividends the stock earned, with the balance payable in a lump sum at the end of that time. Seawell rejected the plan, contending the $450 price was still as ridiculous as it had been at the beginning of the bargaining.

It was now apparent that negotiations were at an end and Neef soon would file the lawsuit he had worked up for Newhouse. On June 11 Neef visited Seawell's offices in Denver and reviewed orally the demands Newhouse intended to make in court. The written demands were delivered at the annual meeting of *Post* directors the following day. The demands were flatly rejected and suit was filed in U. S. District Court in Denver on July 29, 1968. The plaintiff was the Herald Company of New York, owned by Newhouse. The defendants were Miss Bonfils, Hoyt, Campbell, *The Denver Post, Inc.,* and eight trustees of the Employees Stock Trust. The suit charged mismanagement by *Post* officials through improper use of company funds to perpetuate their control, and asked the court to take eight actions to correct injustices to minority stockholder interests. The main points were these:

—Purchase in 1960 with company funds of the Children's Hospital stock, which was returned to the treasury, was "without corporate purpose," in other words, a bad deal. The court was asked to order the sale of the 15,321 remaining shares to the highest bidder at a public auction.

—Some of the treasury stock had been turned over to the Employees Stock Trust for sale to *Post* employees. The court was asked to order public sale of 5,850 shares from the Stock Trust and dissolution of the Trust.

—Miss Bonfils, Hoyt, and Campbell as directors had authorized payment of $376,171 from *Post* funds as interest on money borrowed to pay for the Children's Hospital stock. The court was asked to require them to reimburse *The Post*.

—*The Post* had loaned Miss Bonfils $500,000 for two days, to be used as a down payment on the Rippey stock until other financing could be arranged. Newhouse contended this was illegal and further evidence of mismanagement.

—Increases from $50,000 to $75,000 in salary for Miss Bonfils and Seawell in December of 1967, retroactive to January, were alleged to be exorbitant. The court was asked to determine proper salaries.

—*The Post* paid $89,004 in legal fees in connection with the

Rippey suit. The court was asked to require Miss Bonfils and Hoyt to reimburse *The Post* for this amount.

—The court was asked to restore cumulative voting to *The Post*'s bylaws.

Now *The Post* rolled out a battery of attorneys to answer the charges. Named to defend the corporation and its officers were Jay H. Topkis, Mark H. Alcott, and Arthur J. Goldberg, then of the New York firm of Paul, Weiss, Goldberg, Rifkind, Wharton and Garrison; William C. McClearn and Edwin S. Kahn of the Denver firm of Holland and Hart, which had helped set up the Employees Stock Trust; William H. Erickson, later to become a justice of the Colorado Supreme Court; the law firm of Akolt, Shepherd & Dick to represent Campbell, who later was dropped from the suit; and Walter J. Predovich and Lester A. Ward of the law firm of Predovich and Ward of Pueblo, Colorado.

Goldberg, the former secretary of labor, U. S. Supreme Court Justice, and ambassador to the United Nations, flew to Denver to consult with his clients. One of the younger attorneys, as a matter of protocol, asked Goldberg how he preferred to be addressed. He said he would like to be called Mr. Justice Goldberg. But Hoyt, with characteristic bluntness, ended that so far as he was concerned. Clapping an arm around Goldberg's shoulder, he rumbled, "Aw, c'mon, Art, let's forget that Mister Justice baloney and get down to the business of winning this suit."

After the usual preliminary legal skirmishes *The Post* two days before Christmas filed a reply and a vigorous counterattack. In essence the reply to Newhouse's charges was simple:

The Post denied mismanagement had taken place. The defendants admitted they had attempted to keep Newhouse from acquiring control of the newspaper and contended the purpose, which was to assure continued prosperity and well-being of *The Post,* was proper. *The Post* also pointed out that while a Newhouse representative had objected to setting up the Employees Stock Trust in 1961, no objections were made at any time between 1960 and 1968 to *The Post* purchasing its own stock to implement the plan. *The Post* also denied that specific expenditures were improper, or that the salaries paid its officers were exorbitant.

In its counterclaim, *The Post* charged Newhouse with attempting to stifle competition in the news dissemination, newspaper advertising, and rotogravure printing businesses by absorbing his competitors. *The Post* pointed out that Newhouse directly or indirectly owned or had a substantial interest in twenty-two newspapers, held through fifteen corporations; seven television stations; seven radio stations; twenty cable-television operations; twenty nationally distributed magazines; and a news service; and that he gained his interests by acquiring formerly independent enterprises. In brief he was accused of violating antitrust provisions of the Sherman and Clayton acts.

The Post followed up with a federal court suit in New York. It charged that since Newhouse already owned Art Gravure Corporation of Cleveland, the nation's fourth leading printer of rotogravure newspaper magazines, his efforts to control *The Post,* the sixth largest roto-magazine printer, would result in violation of antitrust laws.

Lengthy pretrial depositions confirmed something that had been discovered in depositions preceding the Rippey trial—that S. I. Newhouse had a most unusual way of running his vast communications empire. He had no office he called his own, but moved about from one of his operations to another and used whatever desk was handy. He depended on his managers, accountants, and attorneys—first Goldman, then Sabin—to keep track of details. They funneled a stream of memos to their employer. Newhouse read and promptly discarded them. He kept no files. Under questioning he couldn't remember the circumstances of a two-million-dollar loan from the Chemical Bank. Time and again he professed no recollection of specific events. When shown memos from Goldman's files he could not remember having read them, but he admitted readily that if a memo was addressed to him then in all probability he had seen it.

Erickson asked Newhouse during one deposition session: "You talked to Charles Goldman and told him to contact Keith Anderson and suggest that Mr. Sherman institute suit against *The Denver Post* to question the purchase of the Children's Hospital stock?"

Newhouse, referring to a Goldman memorandum entered as an exhibit, replied, "That indicates that I did. I have no recollection of it. But that indicates I did."

Erickson in his questioning pursued Newhouse's charge that Hoyt, Seawell, Campbell, and Miss Bonfils had conspired against him even though he had offered them lifetime jobs. "What did any of them stand to gain personally from this so-called conspiracy to entrench themselves in the paper?" he asked.

Newhouse's reply was confusing: "They could have gotten so much more out of the property, I assume, than what they were presently receiving at the time in 1963 or 1964 or 1965, that I was going to maintain their present status."

Under further questioning Newhouse said he had not known what these people were being paid when he made the offer. Earlier, he had admitted he rarely saw the newspaper he wanted to control, didn't subscribe to it, wasn't familiar with its operation, and hadn't visited Denver since buying May Bonfils Stanton's stock in 1960.

Trial of the Denver suit began February 26, 1970, a Thursday, before U. S. District Judge A. Sherman Christensen on temporary assignment from the Utah district. Four days of testimony were heard, followed by a day of closing arguments. Neither Miss Bonfils nor Newhouse testified.

On Thursday, March 5, in four hours of rambling monologue, Judge Christensen delivered an oral opinion that succeeded primarily in confusing everyone and leaving each side with the impression it had won on the major issues of the case. One point that both sides understood was that the "judgment"—in other words, what would really happen as the result of the court's "opinion"—would not be determined until after Judge Christensen had studied "remedies" which he asked the litigants to suggest. *The Post* was so unsure about the meaning of Judge Christensen's verdict that it published its report under a thoroughly noncommittal headline: *"Post* Stock Case Findings Issued in 4-Hour Ruling." Over the main headline was a kicker which said: "Hearing on Final Remedy Scheduled in April." Reporter Fred Gillies, who covered the trial, wrote:

> U. S. District Judge A. Sherman Christensen Thursday did not grant the request of a minority stockholder in *The Denver Post, Inc.* for a forced, public sale of the stock held in its treasury and employee stock trust.
>
> But Christensen, in a four-hour ruling, ordered *The Post* director-defendants to make restitution to its treasury for any financial loss from past transfers of more than 5,000 shares of *Post* stock from the corporation's treasury to the employees trust fund at a price half that paid by the corporation for the stock in July 1960.
>
> A hearing will be held in April, when details of the restitution will be proposed by both sides to the litigation for final ruling by the judge. . . .

The *Rocky Mountain News* was equally unspecific in its headline —"Judge Renders Opinion in Newhouse Suit Against *Post*"—but reporter Peter Blake's somewhat irreverent story was easier to follow:

> After listening to a rambling, 4½ hour opinion Thursday in

Samuel I. Newhouse's stockholder suit against *The Denver Post*, lawyers for both sides could concede no greater loss than lunch.

Judge A. Sherman Christensen, on loan for the trial from the Utah U. S. District Court, talked from 10:45 A.M. to almost 3:30 P.M., taking only two ten-minute breaks. He did not render a judgment with his opinion.

Newhouse apparently won the major legal victory: a ruling that *Post* management had unlawfully conspired to use corporate assets for the purpose of perpetuating its own control.

But *Post* lawyers contended this was of little significance since, they said, the judge didn't allow Newhouse the remedy he really wanted: The forced public sale of the stock in the *Post* treasury and employee trust.

Newhouse forces denied the judge barred a public sale. They maintained that the remedy options are "wide open."

There will be no way to resolve this argument until the transcript is prepared. . . .

For the record, here are Judge Christensen's rulings on the other points: The Stock Trust, payment of interest, the $500,000 loan to Miss Bonfils, and the payment of legal fees were all upheld. The retroactive pay raises were ruled "improper." Seawell's raise after December, 1967, was approved but Miss Bonfils' was disallowed in view of her illness that "put her out of the range of *Post* corporate powers." And finally, *The Post*'s ban on cumulative voting was upheld.

Fred Gillies had written accurately that Judge Christensen did not grant Newhouse's request for a forced public sale of certain *Post* stock, mainly the stock bought from Children's Hospital. What the judge ruled was that *Post* management had been wrong when, ten years earlier, it had used company funds to buy this stock, and something ought to be done to correct that wrong. Then he asked both sides to suggest a remedy.

Newhouse's attorneys promptly proposed a public auction of the disputed stock and, to the enormous consternation of *The Post*'s lawyers, Judge Christensen accepted the suggestion. He agreed it was the only way to correct what he termed the illegal use of corporate funds in 1960 "to purchase a block of *Post* stock with the primary aim of freezing control of the corporation in the incumbent group."

Judge Christensen's order specified that 15,552 shares of *Post* stock must be sold at public auction at a minimum price of $413 per share—more than $5.4 million. If the auction did not bring in this sum, Helen Bonfils and Hoyt as the two top officials of *The Post* would be required to make up the difference up to a limit of $3,124,818.

This block represented about 16.5 percent of *Post* stock. If Newhouse purchased it, his holdings would total slightly more than 31 percent and give him a firm springboard from which to negotiate for additional *Post* stock with the bank trustees of the Frederick G. Bonfils estate and Foundation.

Among his other judgments, Christensen ordered Miss Bonfils and Hoyt to pay $188,193—80 percent of *The Post*'s legal fees in the Newhouse suit—and further ordered *The Post* to assume $300,000 in legal fees for Newhouse's attorneys.

This was a decision *The Post* could not live with. An appeal was made to the Tenth U. S. Circuit Court of Appeals in Denver and another hearing was opened on January 24, 1972. Nearly a dozen years had passed since the stock purchase that led to the legal action. More than three and a half years had sped by since Newhouse filed his suit. And once more the attorneys rose to go over the evidence and make their pleas. Three judges heard the appeal—Delmas C. Hill of Wichita, Kansas; Oliver Seth of Santa Fe, New Mexico; and James E. Barrett of Cheyenne, Wyoming. When the hearing ended, court insiders predicted that a judgment would be returned by midsummer. But summer turned to fall, Christmas came, and still there was no word.

Shortly after 8 A.M. on Friday, December 29, 1972, reporter Fred Gillies picked up his telephone in the crowded, clamorous *Post* city room and called Howard Phillips, clerk of the Circuit Court of Appeals. For several months Gillies had made it part of his routine to call Phillips early each morning with a single question. And each time the reply had been the same: "Nope, nothing yet, but it ought to be here any day now." This day Gillies got the same reply.

Concealing his disappointment, Gillies said cheerfully, "Okay, but don't forget you're going to let me know the minute it shows up. I have a hunch this is the day."

Phillips laughed. "That's what you said yesterday, and last week, and last month."

"It" was the Circuit Court's decision that was of far more than passing reportorial interest to Gillies and his colleagues in the city room. "It" would have a profound effect on the newspaper for which they worked, on all *The Post*'s eighteen hundred employees. Less directly, it would touch the lives of several hundred thousand *Post* readers in a half-dozen states.

That day Gillies' telephone rang just before 11 A.M. The moment he recognized Phillips' voice the reporter knew what the message would be.

"It's here," Phillips said. Gillies rattled off a brief memo on his Underwood to alert city editor Bob Carrington, grabbed his coat, and hurried the five blocks to the Federal Courthouse.

Phillips handed Gillies a fifty-one-page typewritten manuscript. Familiarity with legal documents led Gillies directly to the last few pages, where he found the passage he was looking for:

"The judgment of the trial court is REVERSED, as indicated here, and the case is REMANDED with directions to DISMISS the action."

The Post had won its appeal! Gillies telephoned the news to Carrington, then rushed back to the office, where he hammered out a brief story for that day's home edition. In *The Post*'s executive offices there was nothing but joy. The appeals court had overruled Judge Christensen on every count unfavorable to *The Post*. In canceling the forced sale of the stock the appellate judges found no evidence "that a conspiracy or any wrongful plan, scheme, or design between the directors existed." The decision was written by Judge Hill and concurred in by the other two.

They declared that even if it were conceded for the sake of argument that the directors bought the stock to prevent it from falling into Newhouse's hands, "we find nothing bad or sinister in the directors having such a motive. In fact, we find that motive no more sinister than the desire of Newhouse to gain control of the *Post* corporation." The penalties against Miss Bonfils and Hoyt were dropped as was the assessment of legal fees, and the pay increases for Miss Bonfils and Seawell were allowed to stand.

In short, it was a complete and total victory for *The Post*. One observer remarked that the decision could not have been more favorable if *The Post*'s attorneys had written it. Aside from the satisfaction of being vindicated by a high federal tribunal, *The Post*'s management was particularly pleased by some philosophical observations in the Appellate Court's ruling. One passage of pertinence to all connected with the newspaper industry deserves repeating here:

A corporation publishing a newspaper such as *The Denver Post* certainly has other obligations besides the making of a profit. It has an obligation to the public, that is, the thousands of people who buy the paper, read it, and rely upon its contents. Such a newspaper is endowed with an important public interest. It must adhere to the ethics of the great profession of journalism. The readers are entitled

Idealized oil portraits of the Bonfils sisters: Helen on left, May at right.

to a high quality of accurate news coverage of local, state, national and international events. The newspaper management has an obligation to assume leadership, when needed, for the betterment of the area served by the newspaper. Because of these relations with the public, a corporation publishing a great newspaper such as *The Denver Post* is, in effect, a quasi-public institution.

Such a newspaper corporation, not unlike some other corporations, also has an obligation to those people who make its daily publication possible. A great number of the employees are either members of a profession or highly skilled and specialized in their crafts. Many of them have dedicated their lives to this one endeavor. The appellants' sincere interest in their employees also refuted the allegation of illegal design. *The Post's* concern for their employees is exemplified in all the employee benefits provided. For instance, the employees are given inter alia, hospitalization insurance, medical insurance, and retirement pensions. Indeed, approximately 11 per cent of *The Post's* total expenses go for these employee benefits. With the implementation of the Employees Stock Trust, employees also will be allowed eventually to own *The Post*. . . .

More than thirteen years had passed since Newhouse first sought to gain control of *The Post*. In that time most of the principals had passed from the scene. May Bonfils Stanton, who had started the chain of events when she sold her stock, died in 1962. Her sister,

Helen, died in 1972. Palmer Hoyt, implacable foe of chain newspaper ownership, who had been hired by Helen as *The Post*'s editor and publisher in 1946, retired in 1970. E. Ray Campbell, trustee for another large block of stock and president of *The Post* until forced to retire in 1966 because of ill health, died in 1971.

It remained for the survivors to assess the value of the victory against the cost. Legal fees alone had drained more than a million dollars from *Post* coffers. More damaging was the psychological burden of the seemingly endless series of lawsuits. Preoccupied with these problems, the newspaper's leadership lagged in a period when rapidly changing conditions demanded vigor. Time and again the second layer of *Post* executives had proposals turned down with comments like: "We just can't move now while that damned lawsuit is hanging over our heads," or "We'll have to take care of that as soon as we get that Newhouse case settled."

Still, the Appellate Court's decision had been strong vindication of the concept of local newspaper ownership in Denver, carrying with it the opportunity to serve the community with greater sensitivity to its needs and deeper concern for its welfare than if the ownership lay elsewhere.

As the Appellate Court had directed, Newhouse's suit was dismissed on January 23, 1973. He had the option of appealing the decision to the U. S. Supreme Court, but for once in his amazing career he acknowledged defeat. Seven months later, on August 28, 1973, he sold his *Post* stock to the Frederick G. Bonfils Foundation, which, along with the Helen G. Bonfils Foundation, by then had become a satellite of the Denver Center for the Performing Arts. The price was $4,785,306.96, the equivalent of $325 per share for stock bought at $240 a share. After holding the stock for thirteen years his "profit" was $1,251,541.83, but only his accountants know how much he netted from this great experience after paying his tax and his attorneys.

As a result of the sale *The Post*'s stock-ownership picture looked like this:

F. G. Bonfils Foundation	46.9012%
Helen G. Bonfils Foundation	44.7570
Post Employees Stock Trust	8.3240
TOTAL	99.9822%

Thus more than 91 percent of the stock is held for the benefit of the Performing Arts Center. And Donald R. Seawell is the center of power as president and chairman of the board of *The Denver Post,* and also chairman of the board of the Denver Center for the Performing Arts. The employees at this point own only about 8 1/3 percent through the Employees Stock Trust, and the tiny fractional balance is held by the Helen G. Bonfils estate, Charles E. Stanton, and by Seawell, Buxton, and Earl R. Moore to qualify as directors.

It is a shame that Helen did not live to savor her ultimate victory. Indeed, during the five years of the Newhouse litigation time wrought many corporate changes within *The Post,* but always without altering her objectives. It is not difficult to imagine that Frederick G. Bonfils, his blue eyes flashing, would have applauded the ferocity and single-minded determination with which his younger daughter had maintained the independence of the newspaper he and Harry Tammen founded.

THE NEW CHIEFS

An era ended for *The Denver Post* when Palmer Hoyt retired on December 31, 1970. But in another sense there was no change. Even though he no longer occupied the office on the second floor, the imprint he left on the newspaper was indelible. What went on in the plant was uninterrupted continuation of the work Hoyt had started, for the men he left in charge were his men. He had given them responsibilities and the freedom to exercise them as, more by osmosis than direction, they learned to practice his kind of journalism.

Hoyt's departure was not without pain. A man of such dynamic restlessness who had spent so many exciting years in the catbird seat cannot ever prepare adequately for graceful retirement. If he had given thought to the day he would cease to be the editor of a great newspaper, when he was no longer at the vortex of the daily maelstrom of activity, he brushed it aside. Thus it was with some shock, and no little resentment (which he carefully masked), that he learned in the spring of 1970 that his ten-year contract, which was to expire at the end of December, would not be renewed. He was by then seventy-three years old. He had been editor and publisher of *The Post* for twenty-four years, three times longer than he had been top man at the *Oregonian*. The years had sapped some of his once boundless energy but had done nothing to blunt his mind. He felt he was capable of directing *The Post* for many more years.

What he was not fully aware of was the way the pressures of the difficult years had abraded his relationship with Helen Bonfils. For a long time he had made it a point to talk with her by telephone almost daily about matters both important and inconsequential. One day he got the word that she had said she was tired of hearing from him so regularly. He quit calling her.

It is probable that, despite the outwardly warm relationship that existed between Miss Bonfils and Hoyt, she never quite gave him the unquestioning confidence and affection she had reposed in Shepherd, and which she later was to give to Seawell. Perhaps the friction found its tiny origins the day she heard that he had said he could sweet-talk her into anything he wanted. Whether he had actually made such a boast, she believed he had and it irritated her proud spirit. Certainly there were many old friends around her who had resented Hoyt's sudden importance in her affairs and would have been pleased to see him get his comeuppance. There were other irritants. Miss Bonfils had not approved of Hoyt's second marriage and her relations with Helen May Hoyt were, to say the least, not cordial. For a period soon after his arrival in Denver Hoyt drank more than he should have, and Miss Bonfils didn't like it. Hoyt quit drinking altogether, but it is understandable that she should compare the new editor of her father's paper with the abstemious Frederick G. Bonfils himself. Perhaps without intending to, she felt that in taking over control of and improving *The Post*—as he had been hired to do— Hoyt at the same time was usurping an inviolable status reserved for F. G. While there is no evidence that she expressed such thoughts to anyone, close associates remember her complaining that Ep seemed to think he was more important than *The Post* and this she could not accept.

There was a painful meeting with Hoyt in her hospital room, Suite 1026 of St. Joseph Hospital, where a number of *Post* board meetings had been held as an accommodation to her. Miss Bonfils, who abhorred confrontation, tried to tell him the time had come to name a new editor and publisher and didn't entirely succeed. He left his office for the last time one day in the fall of 1970, several months before his contract expired, to give his successor an opportunity to get settled. But in retirement Hoyt was generously treated. He was given an office in a downtown building, a secretary, and a lifetime job as consultant to *The Post* at fifty thousand dollars per year plus his normal pension.

The community paid its tribute at a glittering testimonial dinner that filled the ballroom of the Brown Palace Hotel. Gov. John A. Love of Colorado was toastmaster and Hubert H. Humphrey flew in from Washington to be the main speaker. Among the tributes was a plaque signed by five governors—Love of Colorado, Calvin L. Rampton of Utah, David Cargo of New Mexico, Jack Williams of Arizona, and Stan Hathaway of Wyoming—expressing gratitude for Hoyt's "quarter century of service and dedication to the progress of our Rocky Mountain Empire."

Most meaningful was a book made up of hundreds of letters written to Hoyt for the occasion. Such letters are often excessively generous, but excerpts from four of them provide an insight into the scope of Hoyt's influence. The first is from Seawell, by then president of *The Post*. The second is from Stewart L. Udall, former secretary of the interior, and the other two are from newspapermen:

Seawell wrote: "In St. Paul's Cathedral there is a simple plaque which says of Sir Christopher Wren, 'If you seek his monument, look around you.' Equally, it can be said of Palmer Hoyt, 'If you seek his monument, read *The Denver Post*.' Some tangible evidence of our love and admiration may be seen in the establishment by *The Denver Post* of the Palmer Hoyt Scholarship at the University of Denver's Department of Communications. Our most extravagant hope is that some day a recipient of the scholarship may turn out to be another Palmer Hoyt."

Udall's comment: "I think of you as one of the nation's rich men. Few have contributed more to rational discourse—few have raised the banner of sanity so high in times of emotional turmoil. I sometimes think the country would have 'jumped the track' long ago if it weren't for the few Ep Hoyts of the world."

J. Montgomery Curtis, vice-president of Knight Newspapers, Inc., who as director of the American Press Institute at Columbia University spent many years helping professionals to become better newspapermen, had this to say: "You took a newspaper famous for its excesses, tamed it gradually with a sure hand, adjusted it to the highest standards. You not only lost no circulation. You gained it, and you increased the advertising. How many times has there been such a conversion in American journalism? I know of none. Blessings be upon you, my friend. You are a symbol of what all newspapermen ought to be."

And finally, there was Jack Foster, who as editor of the *Rocky Mountain News* had watched *The Post*'s metamorphosis into a dynamic, responsible journal: "I take a great deal of satisfaction in knowing that, with all our sturdy competition, we have given to this community two newspapers with its best interests always at heart. I would not want a better competitor than you and *The Denver Post* have been. I salute you tonight, Ep, as one of the giants of the profession which to both of us is our whole life. In the days of your retirement you can look back and say: 'I have made a great newspaper. I have helped make a great community. I have made great young newspapermen to carry on.' "

Let us look for a moment at that community of which Foster writes. Since 1946, when Hoyt arrived, Colorado's population has nearly doubled to two and a half million. Denver's growth in that period is even more spectacular. It was an isolated, easygoing community of some 350,000 in 1946. Today Metropolitan Denver sprawls over five counties and the population is approaching 1,400,-000—as many as lived in all of Colorado in 1946. Few could foresee such explosive growth at the end of World War II, but Hoyt knew change would come and Colorado and Denver must be ready for it. He nudged the community awake through *The Post*.

Bob Lucas offers an apt comment on Hoyt's concerns: "Ep's instincts for the public interest and his unwavering support of that instinct remains his noblest quality. The world of journalism has seen fewer better examples of ennobling performance than that of Ep Hoyt."

Even before the campaign to elect progressive young Quigg Newton as Denver's mayor, Hoyt was demanding better highways to stitch the sprawling state together. That effort led inevitably to persuading the legislature to adopt a ton-mile tax to force the trucking industry to pay a larger share of the cost of building and maintaining highways.

There were many other *Post* campaigns. Hoyt and *The Post* never underestimated the importance of water in Colorado. They fought to keep a greater share of the bounty that flows out of the state as well as to develop new supplies to slake Denver's growing thirst. When new technology led to uncontrolled and potentially disastrous exploitation of underground reservoirs, reporter Robert Hansen engineered a masterful campaign that led to the rewriting of Colorado's inadequate groundwater laws. (E. Ray Campbell liked to dramatize the importance of water to the arid West by declaring, "It's a dark day whenever the sun shines on Colorado," which according to the National Weather Service is 70 percent of all daylight hours.)

In Denver itself, former mayor Thomas G. Currigan credits Hoyt with making possible the Skyline Urban Renewal Project, which is transforming the eyesore lower downtown area into a showplace of handsome new buildings. Currigan says, "The Skyline project, one of the nation's largest, would never have become reality if it were not for Ep Hoyt."

The Post's attacks on McCarthyism were of national historical significance, but they also had a profound effect on the regional scene. Tom L. Popejoy, former president of the University of New

Mexico, was moved to write: "The University of New Mexico, and other institutions of learning in the Mountain West, suffered a great deal during the McCarthy years. They would have suffered much more—and perhaps not survived as free market places for ideas—had it not been for the wise voice of *The Post* reminding the people of the democratic traditions and the dangers of abandoning them."

In the latter years of Hoyt's administration *The Post* was devoting more space to news and editorial matter than any other afternoon newspaper in the United States. In total editorial space in 1969, *The Post* was third behind two morning giants, the Los Angeles *Times* and the Miami *Herald,* with the New York *Times* in fourth position. In some years *The Post* received job applications from more than a thousand reporters, editors, and photographers—seasoned veterans as well as those fresh out of college—and although only about one applicant in a hundred could be hired, Hoyt was proud that so many newspapermen would want to work on his paper.

The Post's circulation did not keep pace with the soaring population for a good reason. Rising production and delivery costs made it prudent to cut back on subscriptions going to the far reaches of the Rocky Mountain Empire and distribution was limited to approximately 260,000 daily and 350,000 Sunday, give or take ten to fifteen thousand. The quality of the paper did not go unnoticed. Along with the usual complaints every newspaper receives, there were frequent letters like this from Russell V. Williams, a Denver businessman:

> To be blunt about it: You run a damned good paper. As a matter of fact, last fall, after a few weeks in Chicago, I returned thinking that I should tell you that. Either the Chicago papers have slipped or *The Post* has advanced. In either case, for one who wants to keep posted on the economy and on world affairs, *The Post* is truly the paper to read.

In view of Miss Bonfils' advanced age, and in anticipation of Hoyt's retirement, several corporate changes were made in August of 1970. Seawell, who was under pressure to return full-time to his New York law firm, made up his mind to leave private practice and devote his energies to *The Post*. Miss Bonfils resigned as president, then was elected to the new office of chairman of the board, and also as secretary. This opened the way for Seawell to become president and treasurer, in other words, the top man. No one had any doubt who Hoyt's successor would be, and he made it official by recommending to the board that Buxton be named editor and

Charles R. Buxton,
Hoyt's strong right arm
and successor.

publisher and a director. Hoyt also recommended that William H. Hornby, the managing editor, be promoted to the to-be-created position of executive editor. Buxton then picked the business manager, Robert H. Shanahan, to succeed him as general manager, and Robert Zeis moved into Shanahan's old slot. Thus, while a new team was running the show, the men in the key posts were veterans of *The Post* staff who had worked up through the ranks. Buxton had been so close to Hoyt's side for so long that there was no sense of a changing of the guard.

Still, there were striking differences between Hoyt and Buxton. Hoyt enjoyed hopping around the country making speeches. Buxton was more effective in committee rooms. Hoyt liked direct attacks on a broad front, leaving the detailed supportive staff work to an aide, which was usually Buxton. Hoyt was mercurial, his mind flitting restlessly from one interest to another. Buxton was unflappable; he could spend days punching keys on his calculator to build a case for a million-dollar expenditure to improve the profit picture three years in the future. Buxton made no effort to emulate Hoyt's methods or Hoyt's personality; he was his own man and there was no reason for him not to be himself.

Hornby, Montana-born and with a master's degree in journalism from Stanford University, had come to *The Post* in 1957 with excellent credentials but limited newspaper experience. He had been a reporter and copyreader on the San Francisco *News* in 1947 and 1948, and a reporter in the San Francisco Associated Press bureau in 1949. For the next two years he was a research assistant at the Hoover Library at Stanford, then spent another two years in Paris and at The Hague as information officer for a Marshall Plan agency. In 1953 he returned home to Kalispell, Montana, to help run a family lumber business, which oddly enough Buxton also had done. Hornby worked briefly for the Great Falls (Montana) *Tribune* before joining *The Post* as a copyreader, then copydesk chief. He was an editorial writer when, in August of 1960, he was summoned into Hoyt's office.

Hoyt asked Hornby how much reportorial experience he had. Hornby replied that he had done a little reporting, but most of his experience was in the editing side.

Hoyt then asked about his managerial experience. Hornby said he had run a lumber business for about a year and a half.

That seemed to satisfy Hoyt. He said he wanted to give Hornby, then thirty-seven years of age, a tryout as acting managing editor to fill the vacancy left by the departure of Lucas.

Hornby replied that if he took the assignment he did not want it on an acting basis. "Give me the job," he said, "and if I don't make it, you can throw me out. The only other condition is that I want to pick my own assistants."

Hornby took over at a time when Hoyt was no longer charging around the country. His personal life had settled down and his concerns were dominated by Newhouse's attacks. No one could tell how much of the newspaper's resources would have to be spent in the courts. No one knew who would end up owning the paper, and these worries gnawed at Hoyt. *The Post* was in a period when no spectacular changes were wanted or required, and Hornby found his job was to keep it on a steady course. Hoyt was still "the old man," and no major move was taken without letting him know about it. But Buxton was making many of the key decisions and Hornby learned it was wise to sound him out first before broaching an important problem with Hoyt. As the years went by Hornby found that more and more often Hoyt would say, "Clear it with Chuck," or, as evidence of his confidence in Hornby, "Do what you think best." Of Hoyt's last years as boss, Hornby says: "His managing editor just had to know what he wanted, and then go ahead and do it. Even so, he never neglected the paper. Ep always read it and he could bring you up sharply if you missed something. He was not an easy man to work for. But he was a great editor and a wise man."

(Mort Stern, one of Hornby's predecessors, tells another story about Hoyt, the boss. One day he asked Stern to get a little news item involving an advertiser into the paper. Stern passed the assignment down the line, then went on to other matters. Several days later Hoyt asked what had been done about the item. Stern said he didn't know, but would check.

("When I returned to the boss's office," says Stern, "he was steamed up. In the first place, he said he didn't like his orders being ignored. And in the second place, we had to get over the notion that just because a man was an advertiser we should treat him worse than a nonadvertiser. As soon as I got the chance, I explained the item had been in the paper the very day he ordered it. 'All right,' Hoyt said in a no-nonsense tone. 'But the point's the same. And don't let it happen again.' ")

Hornby's counterpart on *The Post*'s business side is Robert H. Shanahan, a happily gregarious native Denverite who after Navy service in World War II attended the University of Denver's School of Business. He was graduated in 1948 and went to work at the lowest rung of *The Post*'s advertising hierarchy, classified salesman. Within nine months he was promoted to the retail sales staff, served for a time as personnel director, then retail advertising manager. By 1957 he was director of the entire advertising department. When Buxton moved up to general manager in 1965, Shanahan became business manager.

Helen Bonfils died June 6, 1972. She was eighty-three years old, and the last link with *The Post*'s founders. The Mass of the Resurrections was sung for her at the Church of the Holy Ghost, which she had built as a memorial to her father, by Archbishop James V. Casey. He described her as "a great and lovely woman whose death comes at the end of a long and fruitful life, and filled far beyond the measure of most. Miss Bonfils," the archbishop continued, "seemed to seek out the unloved, those who had no one to help them, those living on the brink of despair. In Helen Bonfils, they found a warm, compassionate, responsive heart," and there were thousands who agreed.

The casket was placed in the Bonfils family mausoleum, where her father and mother and her first husband, George Somnes, are also interred.

The Post's editorial in memoriam stressed her dedication to the newspaper and the people who supported it:

> Some newspaper owners are remote and indistinct figures to the people who work for them and to the communities in which their businesses flourish. This could never have been said of Helen G. Bonfils. She was passionately involved with her community and with

The new team: Seated, Donald R. Seawell, president and chairman of the board, and around him, from left, Robert Zeis, assistant secretary-treasurer and business manager; John Rogers, managing editor; Earl R. Moore, secretary-treasurer; Charles R. Buxton, executive vice-president, editor, and publisher; William H. Hornby, vice-president and executive editor; Robert H. Shanahan, vice-president and general manager; Robert Pattridge, editor of the editorial page. (David Cupp)

The Denver Post—and in neither case was it an involvement with an abstraction. In plain terms, she loved the people of Denver and the people who produced *The Post,* and in both cases the people returned that affection openly and enthusiastically. . . . Her total commitment to the public good shall continue to be our model and our guide.

With Miss Bonfils' death, corporate changes she had approved were put into effect. Seawell became chairman of *The Post*'s board in addition to president. Buxton, who was vice-president as well as editor and publisher, took the new title of executive vice-president. Hornby and Shanahan were named vice-presidents. Earl R. Moore, Miss Bonfils' longtime business consultant, became secretary-treasurer. Robert Zeis, *Post* business manager, became assistant secretary.

Despite all these changes there was no "new" *Post,* just as there had been no "new" *Post* when Frederick G. Bonfils died in 1933. There were other changes, too, of course. Barney Nover followed Hoyt into retirement and the Washington bureau was closed briefly until it could be reestablished with Leonard Larsen in charge. A seasoned and sometimes acerbic observer of the political scene, he

Page 1 of *The Post* on December 31, 1970, Hoyt's last day as editor and publisher, although he had turned over the reins several months earlier.

provides *The Post* with excellent regionally oriented coverage that the wire services cannot. Larsen now has two assistants at his outpost on the Potomac. James Idema left as editor of the editorial page and Mort Stern returned to that seat briefly before departing for academia, first as dean of the communications school at the University of Alabama, then journalism dean at the University of Colorado, which was the job he wanted in the first place. Under the steady hand of Robert Pattridge, who answers directly to Hornby,

Page 1 of *The Post* on April 29, 1975.

the editorials have taken a more middle-of-the-road stance. The women's section is long gone; it's called "Living" now and the features frequently are about current subjects like liberation, abortion, inflation, and rape as well as the standbys like food, fashions, and interior decorating.

In 1974 *Time* magazine characterized *The Post* as flabby. The whizbang, muscle-flexing days are gone, but there are many who would consider *Time*'s adjective inaccurate. Today's *Post* is more staid, perhaps even stodgy on occasion. But it is also more responsible, more thoughtful.

The environment in which the press must function today has changed the nature of all newspapers, some more than others. Two-alarm fires and two-bit scandals are no longer their lifeblood. The electronic media can fill the air with bulletins about an assassination or an election before the newspapers can crank up their presses. Although many may yearn for the old days, the print media have a new role today and those members who do not adapt to it are, like the dinosaur, doomed by the changing environment.

The economics of publishing have changed drastically, as Hoyt realized when he declared *The Post*'s first objective was to remain solvent. As the following table reveals, *The Post*'s gross revenues have risen steadily but because of increasing costs the net profit after taxes has remained fairly constant except for a few bad years. That means that more and more dollars are being taken in while a dwindling percentage of the gross remains behind as net profit. (For comparison with earlier days, see table in Chapter 11.)

Early in 1975 it was projected that if *The Post* published as many pages as it did the previous year, the cost of newsprint alone would be three and a quarter million dollars higher. New labor contracts, to help employees keep pace with the soaring cost of living, boosted *The Post*'s payroll from $34 million in 1974 to $37.5 million in 1975—25 percent of this sum in fringe benefits. A reporter with a minimum of six years experience is now paid $341 per week—$17,732 a year. While television has comparable labor costs, TV doesn't require newsprint. It is impossible to pass on these costs automatically to advertisers and subscribers. So there must be tighter management if *The Post*—or any other newspaper—is to return a reasonable profit or even to survive.

Does this mean, then, that *The Post,* which paid such a dear price over so many years in its fight for independence, must sell its soul for a mess of pottage?

Hardly.

Fred Bonfils and Harry Tammen, for all their faults and weaknesses, published a forceful newspaper that someone said could no more be ignored than a punch in the nose. Ep Hoyt restored that vigor and gave the paper respectability. The road to respectability and responsibility has been too long, the heritage too rich, for *The Denver Post* to become just another newspaper living out a fat and flaccid existence.

Year	Circulation Daily	Sunday	Gross Revenue	Net Profit After Taxes	Percentage of Profit	Dividend Payments	
1946	193,833	316,613	$ 6,845,000	$1,781,000	26.02	$1,200,000	
1947	199,406	330,660	8,461,000	1,636,000	19.34	1,200,000	
1948	212,782	347,353	9,859,000	1,358,000	13.77	1,050,000	
1949	224,220	355,160	11,063,000	1,598,000	14.44	200,000	
1950	229,308	360,974	11,634,000	877,000	7.54	535,000	
1951	228,481	358,478	12,809,000	980,000	7.65	560,000	
1952	220,077	355,940	14,526,000	1,059,000	7.29	560,000	
1953	224,220	351,430	15,020,000	810,000	5.39	553,000	
1954	239,630	351,721	15,556,000	685,000	4.40	552,000	
1955	245,896	350,254	17,513,000	1,040,000	5.94	600,000	HOYT ERA
1956	257,533	351,532	19,175,000	1,007,000	5.25	598,000	
1957	252,133	342,870	19,356,000	745,000	3.85	598,000	
1958	252,441	336,008	19,374,000	772,000	3.98	598,000	
1959	254,421	338,718	21,063,000	1,114,000	5.29	598,000	
1960	259,233	338,798	21,051,000	677,000	3.22	598,000	
1961	268,507	350,469	21,599,000	806,000	3.73	447,000	
1962	248,926	347,139	23,377,000	1,001,000	4.28	550,000	
1963	252,111	351,981	23,584,000	837,000	3.55	551,000	
1964	255,423	352,108	24,476,000	876,000	3.58	573,000	
1965	252,005	339,711	25,646,000	1,108,000	4.32	620,000	
1966	252,502	339,440	28,675,000	1,004,000	3.50	625,000	
1967	251,990	340,188	28,931,000	698,000	2.41	628,000	
1968	248,520	340,507	32,682,000	833,000	2.55	631,000	
1969	247,368	343,185	36,528,000	586,000	1.60	635,000	
1970	250,712	350,403	39,507,000	198,000	.50	636,000	
1971	249,642	356,534	44,210,000	1,149,000	2.60	636,000	
1972	255,215	364,228	50,258,000	1,287,000	2.56	636,000	BUXTON ERA
1973	255,543	361,089	56,196,000	1,268,000	2.26	693,000	
1974	245,175	349,265	60,143,000	523,000	.87	725,000	

REFERENCES AND ACKNOWLEDGMENTS

CHAPTER 1—Newspapers, which survive by recording daily history, seldom seem to get around to keeping a full account for their own activities. This became all too evident in probing into the sparse and musty documents pertaining to the origins of *The Denver Post*. Aside from the microfilm files of *The Post,* perhaps most useful in researching this area was material—including the text of the original bill of sale—assembled in 1943 by Louis McMahon, then *The Post's* comptroller. The following books also were useful:

The First Hundred Years, an authoritative history of the *Rocky Mountain News* by Robert L. Perkin.

Timber Line by Gene Fowler, a highly entertaining mix of fact and fiction, published in 1933 in the anticipation Hollywood would buy it for a movie. Metro-Goldwyn-Mayer did indeed buy movie rights, but the film was never made. *Post* files produced a copy of a letter from William C. Shepherd, then editor and publisher, to Will H. Hays, president of the Motion Picture Producers & Distributors of America, declaring Fowler's book "was written from a very antagonistic viewpoint." Shepherd went on to complain: "If the picture were handled from Mr. Fowler's point of view, it would be nothing but a personal attack on Mr. Bonfils, and the general public, not knowing him, would be misled. . . ."

So The People May Know, a booklet written by Lawrence Martin, former managing editor, and distributed by *The Post* in 1950 in conjunction with the opening of its new plant. Martin treated *The Post's* early history gingerly, but his references to names, dates, and other details were valuable.

To Hell in a Handbasket, H. Allen Smith's hilarious account of life at *The Post* in the late Twenties.

CHAPTER 2—Because he died earlier, and was somewhat less

belligerent, Harry Tammen is not so well-remembered as F. G. Bonfils. But individuals who knew him personally—Frank Ricketson, Jr., and Jim Hale among others—contributed warm recollections. Hale worked at *The Post* for more than thirty years, beginning in 1920. He was interviewed at his son's home in Burbank, California. Jim's sight was gone, but his memory was sharp. Mr. and Mrs. Arthur G. Rippey were most gracious about making Tammen memorabilia available.

VIGNETTE—The whole story of the burial of Buffalo Bill is in *The Post's* bound files. Fred Garlow, Buffalo Bill's grandson, was tracked down in Cody, Wyoming, between duck-hunting expeditions to confirm some points.

CHAPTER 3—Anne O'Neill Sullivan, Bonfils' secretary; Robert Stouffer, his chauffeur; Elmer Strain, an employee who kept careful notes about his work at *The Post;* Leverett A. Chapin, Caroline Bancroft, Joy Swift, and Gretchen Weber were among those who submitted to long interviews for material used in this chapter. Published sources included files of the Kansas City *Times* and *Star, Rocky Mountain News,* Fremont County (Colorado) *Record, So The People May Know,* and *The Post.* There was also correspondence with the U. S. Military Academy; Mrs. Forest Evans, who is librarian in Troy, Missouri; Nelson Heath Meriweather, a historian of Hannibal, Missouri; and Dr. Marian M. Ohman of the University of Missouri. Michael Balfe Howard, now editor of the *Rocky Mountain News,* kindly made available reports and papers pertaining to the Bonfils suit prepared by their attorney, the late Col. Philip S. Van Cise.

VIGNETTE—H. Ray Baker was so proud of his big-fish caper that he wrote about it several times in *Empire Magazine.*

CHAPTER 4—In addition to the bound files of *The Post,* many individuals contributed anecdotes for this chapter—Stouffer, Hale, Chapin, Frank Johnson, Gene Lindberg, H. Allen Smith, Ricketson, etc., etc., etc.

VIGNETTE—Nate Gart is a man of leisure these days, but he came up the hard way, as he relates in this vignette.

CHAPTER 5—The world's greatest authority on Lord Ogilvy is his son, Jack, who has written numerous articles about his colorful sire, and really ought to do a book. Jack, and two of Lord Ogilvy's coworkers, Jim Hale and Joy Swift, provided most of the material in this chapter.

VIGNETTE—Everyone knew the Levands. Some of them offered the details used here.

CHAPTER 6—We went straight to the printed record—the voluminous coverage, column after column in *The Post, Rocky Mountain News,* and Denver *Times*—for this chapter on the story of quick-tempered, fist-throwing editors. So slanted was some of the coverage that it was difficult to believe the papers were reporting the same incident.

VIGNETTE—Details of the mob's invasion of *The Post* were fully reported in the newspapers. Several old-time employees confirmed the anecdotes about Mr. Ethell and the doors in the men's room.

CHAPTER 7—Poring over old copies of *The Post* and *News* made this one of the more enjoyable chapters to write. Also consulted were the Kansas City *Journal,* Kansas City *Star,* Kansas City *Post,* Perkin's book, bylaws of the Associated Press, corporate records of *The Post,* and archives of the Jackson County (Missouri) Historical Society.

VIGNETTE—There it was, the telegram to President Coolidge, right there on page 1 of *The Post* for February 20, 1929.

CHAPTER 8—It was widely rumored that reporter Diedrich Stackelbeck had written the secret story of his role in *The Post's* connection with the Teapot Dome scandal, but no one had seen the manuscript since he died in 1936. Stackelbeck's obituary said he had a seventeen-year-old son, Emil, then a student at St. John's Military Academy in Salina, Kansas. Perhaps Emil would know about the manuscript. But the academy reported it had lost track of Emil after 1949. So we had to go to other sources, notably the verbatim report of hearings before the U. S. Senate Committee on Public Lands and Surveys in February of 1924. When *The Post's* Washington bureau didn't seem to be making much headway in locating a copy, we tried the Denver Public Library. They had one, and they allowed it to be checked out only after we promised to defend it with our lives. Nine months later the Library of Congress did provide a photocopy. Gene Giancarlo and Alice Pitts of the American Society of Newspaper Editors dug deep into their archives for details about the way the editors decided to deal with Bonfils.

VIGNETTE—Much of the material in this section is, of necessity, hearsay. The known sources are mentioned in the text.

CHAPTER 9—Wally and Peggy Reef, who were assigned by

the *News* to investigate Bonfils' background, spent a long afternoon with me in their pleasant Denver home recalling their experiences. Judge Edwin P. Van Cise added details to flesh out information in Denver newspapers, and the records in the files of his late father, Colonel Van Cise.

VIGNETTE—Caroline Bancroft, Jim Hale, Emmet Wilt, Louis O'Brien all contributed anecdotes.

CHAPTER 10—We looked up the last wills of F. G. Bonfils and Belle Bonfils, read a deposition by Helen Bonfils in a suit filed by her sister, May, interviewed Robert Stouffer and May's husband, Charles Edward Stanton. The files of *The Post, News,* and corporate minutes of *The Post* also provided details.

VIGNETTE—Charles Edward Stanton declined to give his age but talked freely about many other matters in this vignette, as did Pat Collins and others.

CHAPTER 11—Numerous *Post* employees who lived through the Shepherd years contributed to this chapter. Among them were Jim Hale, Frank Haraway, Alexis McKinney, Bill White, George Eichler. Published sources include *The Post, Saturday Evening Post,* Heart Mountain *Sentinel, Colorado Magazine.* Barron B. Beshoar also provided material for this chapter as well as the vignette that follows.

VIGNETTE—Dick Wanek, executive secretary of the Denver Newspaper Guild, made his records available to supplement recollections of Beshoar and others.

CHAPTER 12—Among those interviewed for this chapter were Mrs. Bertha Campbell, Arthur and Helen Rippey, Jack and Frankie Foster, Palmer Hoyt. Documentary sources included the last will of Agnes Tammen, correspondence files of E. Ray Campbell, *The Post*'s corporate minutes, and an unpublished doctoral thesis titled *Palmer Hoyt and The Denver Post* by Mort Stern. Stern's study proved particularly useful in writing this and subsequent chapters.

VIGNETTE—Gene Cervi was a gadfly with vision. Hoyt ignored his rantings, but he and other *Post* executives read Cervi's *Journal*.

CHAPTER 13—Several long interviews with Palmer Hoyt were backstopped by Stern's thesis. Also consulted were *The Post*'s corporate minutes, and various sources mentioned in the text.

VIGNETTE—Charles R. Buxton now carries the imposing title of executive vice-president, editor, and publisher. Dooley was managing editor when he left *The Post* in 1956 to launch a short-lived business weekly in San Francisco. When that venture died of malnutrition he joined Hearst's *Examiner* and eventually became its competent and popular editor before being forced out in an internal power struggle.

CHAPTER 14—In addition to various individuals and sources named earlier, Lorena Jones of San Diego contributed to this chapter. Mrs. Jones labored long for *The Post,* first in the advertising department, and later as head librarian.

VIGNETTE—Bob Stapp is now information director at Denver's Stapleton International Airport. He recalls that his story on Randolph Churchill was picked up by the wire services and circulated around the world.

CHAPTER 15—Establishment of an editorial page which became widely respected within a short time was certainly one of Hoyt's major accomplishments. Fred Colvig founded the page and a succession of able editors carried on. The author knew all of them personally. Ed Hoyt supplied recollections from Nantucket, Massachusetts, and Bob Lucas from Black Butte Ranch, Oregon, where he lives in busy retirement.

VIGNETTE—Paul Conrad related his story over lunch in the Los Angeles *Time*'s luxurious executive dining room. Pat Oliphant was interviewed in his somewhat more Spartan quarters at *The Post.*

CHAPTER 16—George Kelly's book, *The Old Gray Mayors,* and the files of *The Post* lend documentary support to recollections of Hoyt and many others regarding the Quigg Newton mayoralty campaign. *The Post*'s coverage of the Joe Sam Walker case was so thorough the problem was to condense the mass of information.

VIGNETTE—Odd bits of information filed away in a reporter's memory come in handy. John Randolph told me about his part in the cow story in Tokyo during the Korean War.

CHAPTER 17—Buxton spent the major part of his time in the late Forties putting together the new *Post* plant. His recollections supplemented those of Hoyt and the sparse factual information in *Post* records. Fenwick still grows a little pale when talking about his assignment.

VIGNETTE—Alexis McKinney isn't positive that he was responsible for the silver dollar caper but admitted it sounded like one of his ideas and agreed to take the credit. George Kelly provided a detailed written account of his part in the manuscript that vanished.

CHAPTER 18—E. Ray Campbell meticulously kept copies of his correspondence, which backs up much of the material in this chapter. Hoyt, Mrs. Campbell, Buxton, records of National Labor Relations Board hearings, Stern's thesis, McKinney, and others were interviewed.

VIGNETTE—Ed Hoyt's editorial provided Buxton with one of his most unforgettable moments—being escorted off the *Queen Elizabeth.*

CHAPTER 19—Palmer Hoyt admits he thought Senator McCarthy had a legitimate target when he charged the State Department was overrun with Communists. But his suspicions were soon aroused, and the story of *The Post's* courageous campaign to force McCarthy to come up with proof or shut up can be read in the pages of the newspaper.

VIGNETTE—Jim Kelley, Bob Pattridge, Don Davis, and John Buchanan all confirm Leonard Larsen's version.

CHAPTER 20—The story of how May Bonfils Stanton came to sell her *Post* stock unfolds like a drama. Charles Edward Stanton, Donald Seawell, Buxton, E. Ray Campbell's papers, a deposition by S. I. Newhouse and Newhouse correspondence subpoenaed by *The Post,* May Bonfils' will—all contributed to the relating of the full story for the first time.

VIGNETTE—The author researched the Elijah story for an article for *Reader's Digest* in 1956. Both Fenwick and Bernard Kelly knew Harry Galbraith well.

CHAPTER 21—Interviews with George Brown, John Rogers, and Mort Stern, plus the author's long friendship with Larry Tajiri, contributed to this chapter. This might be a good place to tell another "racial" story. During the Paris Summit Conference in May of 1960 the author and Eddy Gilmore of the Associated Press were outside the Soviet embassy waiting for Nikita Khrushchev to appear. Alexsei Adzhubei, editor of *Izvestia* and Khrushchev's son-in-law, drove up and exchanged greetings with Gilmore, who spoke Russian fluently. Then he saw the author, frowned, and asked belligerently, "What nationality are you?" Since I didn't understand, Gilmore replied for me, "He's an American of Japanese ancestry." Adzhubei broke into a smile and shook my hand. "I thought you were a colleague of Chiang Kai-shek," he said. "American, ah, that's good."

VIGNETTE—Gene Lindberg did so many remarkable things that his colleagues were inclined to take him for granted. Lynn Lilliston, now of the Los Angeles *Times,* suggested he had a part in this book.

CHAPTER 22—The author was editor of *Empire* starting with

its sixth issue in November of 1950 until 1956, and from 1963 until January, 1974.

VIGNETTE—Bob Byers now is information director at Massachusetts Institute of Technology. His recollections provided important insights into the eleven-million-dollar libel suit.

CHAPTER 23—It was necessary to read a tall stack of legal material to get into this episode. Interviews with Hoyt, Buxton, Hornby, Seawell, attorney William Erickson, depositions by S. I. Newhouse, subpoenaed Newhouse correspondence, minutes of *Post* corporate meetings, E. Ray Campbell's correspondence, and files of *The Post* all provided pertinent details.

VIGNETTE—Earl R. Moore, secretary-treasurer of *The Post* and Helen Bonfils' financial adviser for many years, provided tax records and other details of the Bonfils philanthropies.

CHAPTER 24—Buxton, Hoyt, Stern, Paul Conrad, Larry Weiss, Hornby, Isabelle Truscott Holmes, and others supplemented material from the pages of *The Post.*

VIGNETTE—The author was the assistant to whom Lucas gave the wedding story.

CHAPTER 25—Attorneys William Erickson and William Mc-Clearn interviewed Seawell, Buxton, and Warren Young on October 9, 1968, not long after S. I. Newhouse sued *The Post,* regarding the chronology of contacts between Newhouse representatives and *Post* representatives. These incidents were still fresh in the minds of *Post* officials and a detailed account was taken down. This memorandum, which helped *Post* attorneys prepare their defense, was made available to the author. Other records, court transcripts as well as newspaper accounts, were used as sources for this chapter. Judge Delmas Hill was asked to comment on the thinking behind his decision but he declined, saying: "I have always been of the opinion it is undesirable and in many instances improper for a judge to comment on cases he has heard, and for that reason I am not inclined to comply with your request."

CHAPTER 26—Various *Post* executives submitted to interviews for this chapter.

There were many others, unnamed, who contributed details that helped bring *The Post* story to life. But in addition, the author would be remiss if he did not acknowledge the assistance of the girls in the *Post* library; Bernard Kelly, who copyread the manuscript; Margaret Schmidt, who patiently dug out circulation figures; Mary

Masunaga, who transcribed tapes; Elsie Gentry, who made many trips deep into *The Post*'s basement storage area in search of old documents; comptroller Don Haynie, who provided financial data; and not least, Wanda Romeo, who carefully typed two drafts of the manuscript in between taking care of her secretarial duties.

INDEX